DERRIDA AND JOYCE

SUNY series in Contemporary French Thought

David Pettigrew and François Raffoul, editors

DERRIDA AND JOYCE
Texts and Contexts

EDITED BY

Andrew J. Mitchell

and

Sam Slote

STATE UNIVERSITY OF NEW YORK PRESS

Published by
STATE UNIVERSITY OF NEW YORK PRESS, ALBANY

© 2013 State University of New York

All rights reserved

Printed in the United States of America

No part of this book may be used or reproduced in any manner whatsoever without written permission. No part of this book may be stored in a retrieval system or transmitted in any form or by any means including electronic, electrostatic, magnetic tape, mechanical, photocopying, recording, or otherwise without the prior permission in writing of the publisher.

For information, contact
State University of New York Press, Albany, NY
www.sunypress.edu

Production, Laurie Searl
Marketing, Michael Campochiaro

Library of Congress Cataloging-in-Publication Data

Derrida and Joyce : texts and contexts / Andrew J. Mitchell and Sam Slote, eds.
   p. cm. — (SUNY series in contemporary French thought)
"Texts by Jacques Derrida": P.
Includes bibliographical references and index.
   ISBN 978-1-4384-4639-4 (hc : alk. paper)—ISBN 978-1-4384-4638-7 (pb : alk. paper)
   1. Joyce, James, 1882–1941—Criticism, textual.   2. Derrida, Jacques—Criticism and interpretation.   3. Literature—Philosophy.   4. Modernism (Literature)   5. Postmodernism (Literature)   I. Mitchell, Andrew J., 1970–   II. Slote, Sam.   III. Derrida, Jacques. Selections. English. 2013.

PR6019.O9Z5295 2013
823'.912—dc23
                                                                          2012018268

10 9 8 7 6 5 4 3 2 1

Contents

List of Photographs — ix
Acknowledgments — xi
Key to Abbreviations — xiii
Note on the Translations — xvii

INTRODUCTION
DERRIDA AND JOYCE: ON TOTALITY AND EQUIVOCATION — 1
   Andrew J. Mitchell and Sam Slote

I. TEXTS BY JACQUES DERRIDA

Ulysses Gramophone: Two Words for Joyce — 19

   YES, LAUGHTER — 19
      translated by François Raffoul

   CIRCUMSTANCES — 20
      translated by François Raffoul

   TWO WORDS FOR JOYCE — 22
      translated by Geoffrey Bennington

   ULYSSES GRAMOPHONE: HEAR SAY YES IN JOYCE — 41
      translated by François Raffoul

The Night Watch — 87
   translated by Pascale-Anne Brault and Michael Naas

II. Returns

1. Joyce—Event—Derrida—Event—Joyce 111
   Jed Deppman

2. Joyce's Resonance in *Glas* 133
   Sam Slote

3. Meaning Postponed: *The Post Card* and *Finnegans Wake* 145
   Andrew J. Mitchell

4. The Mother, of All the Phantasms . . . 163
   Michael Naas

5. Matricidal Writing: Philosophy's Endgame 183
   Christine van Boheemen-Saaf

III. Departures

6. Sero-Positives: Belatedness and Affirmation in Joyce, Cixous, and Derrida 201
   Laurent Milesi

7. JJ, JD, TV 213
   Louis Armand

8. "mememormee": Notes on Derrida's Re-Markings of Desire and Memory in Joyce 227
   Alan Roughley

9. Of Chrematology: Joyce and Money 245
   Simon Critchley and Tom McCarthy

IV. Recollections

10. Signature/Countersignature: Derrida's Response to *Ulysses* 265
    Derek Attridge

11. TWO JOYCES FOR DERRIDA   281
    Jean-Michel Rabaté

Selection of Photographs   299
Contributors   303
Index   307

Photographs

Figure 1. Jacques Derrida, 1982 Pompidou Center.
Paris, France. *Photo courtesy of Fritz Senn.*　　　　　　　299

Figure 2. Jacques Derrida, 1984 James Joyce Symposium.
Frankfurt-am-Main, Germany. *Photo courtesy of Morris Beja.*　　300

Figure 3. Jacques Derrida, 1984 James Joyce Symposium.
Frankfurt-am-Main, Germany. *Photo courtesy of Fritz Senn.*　　301

Figure 4. Jacques Derrida, 1984 James Joyce Symposium.
Frankfurt-am-Main, Germany. *Photo courtesy of Fritz Senn.*　　302

Acknowledgments

We would like to thank Sean Latham and Carol Kealiher, the editors of *James Joyce Quarterly*, for permission to reprint Andrew J. Mitchell's "Meaning Postponed: *The Post Card* and *Finnegans Wake*" (*James Joyce Quarterly* 44, 1 [Fall 2006], 59–76]) and Louis Armand, then editor of *Hypermedia Joyce Studies*, for permission to reprint Simon Critchley and Tom McCarthy's "Of Chrematology: Joyce and Money" (*Hypermedia Joyce Studies* 4, 1 [2003], http://www.geocities.com/hypermedia_joyce/). We would like to thank the Trinity College Arts and Social Science Benefactions Fund for providing assistance with the publication of this volume. We are grateful to our two series editors, David Pettigrew and François Raffoul for their support and encouragement throughout the process of preparing this volume. Geoffrey Bennington was an early supporter of this project and kind enough to provide us with a new translation of "Two Words for Joyce." His assistance in dealing with the estate, archive, and thought of Jacques Derrida has been invaluable. François Raffoul provided us with translations of "Ulysses Gramophone," as well as "Yes, laughter" and "Circumstances," and was an ardent supporter of the project throughout. We would also like to thank Pascale-Anne Brault and Michael Naas for all their work in both securing the rights and rendering the translation of Derrida's "La Veilleuse." We thank Fritz Senn, Murray Beja, and Derek Attridge for providing us with the photographs that accompany this text; we extend our thanks likewise to the estate of Jacques Derrida, and to Marguerite Derrida in particular, for allowing their reproduction here. Our volume is much the better thanks to the efforts of all these people. Andrew J. Mitchell would like to thank Amy Alexander for her indefatigable encouragement. Sam Slote would like to thank Ivana Milivojevic for saying "yes."

Key to Abbreviations

All of the following works are cited parenthetically in the text by the abbreviation indicated. References to the works of Derrida supply English/French pagination for the editions listed. Modification to translations are noted by "tm," notes of the translators and editors by "TN."

Works by James Joyce

CW	*The Critical Writings of James Joyce*, ed. Ellsworth Mason and Richard Ellmann (New York: Viking Press, 1959).
D	*Dubliners*, ed. Robert Scholes and A. Walton Litz (New York: Viking Press, 1969).
FW	*Finnegans Wake* (London: Faber and Faber, 1975).
LI, LII, LIII	*Letters of James Joyce*, vol. I, ed. Stuart Gilbert (New York: Viking Press, 1957, reissued with corrections 1966); vols. II & III, ed. Richard Ellmann (New York: Viking Press, 1966).
P	*A Portrait of the Artist as a Young Man*, ed. Chester G. Anderson (New York: Viking Press, 1968).
SL	*Selected Letters of James Joyce*, ed. Richard Ellmann (New York: Viking Press, 1975).
U	*Ulysses: The Corrected Text* ed. Hans Walter Gabler et al. (London: The Bodley Head, 1993).

Works by Jacques Derrida

AF	*Archive Fever*, trans. Eric Prenowitz (Chicago: University of Chicago Press, 1996), translation of *Mal d'archive* (Paris: Galilée, 1995).

KEY TO ABBREVIATIONS

DI *Dissemination*, trans. Barbara Johnson (Chicago: University of Chicago Press, 1981), translation of *La Dissémination* (Paris: Seuil, 1972).

EH *Edmund Husserl's "Origin of Geometry": An Introduction*, trans. John P. Leavy Jr. (Lincoln: University of Nebraska Press, 1978), translation of *L'Origine de la géométrie de Husserl: Introduction et traduction* (Paris: Presses Universitaires de France, 1962).

EO *The Ear of the Other*, ed. Christie McDonald, trans. Peggy Kamuf (Lincoln: University of Nebraska Press, 1988), translation of *L'Oreille de l'autre*, ed. Claude Lévesque and Christie McDonald (Montréal: V1b, 1982).

G *Glas*, trans. John P. Leavey Jr. and Richard Rand (Lincoln: University of Nebraska Press, 1986), translation of *Glas* (Paris: Galilée, 1974).

HC *H. C. for Life, That Is to Say . . .* , trans. Laurent Milesi and Stefan Herbrechter (Stanford: Stanford University Press, 2006), translation of *H.C. pour la vie, c'est à dire . . .* (Paris: Galilée, 2002).

MP *Margins of Philosophy*, trans. Alan Bass (Chicago: University of Chicago Press, 1982), translation of *Marges de la philosophie* (Paris: Minuit, 1972).

NW "The Night Watch," trans. Pascale-Anne Brault and Michael Naas, in this volume 87–108, translation of "La Veilleuse," in Jacques Trilling, *James Joyce ou l'écriture matricide* (Belfort, France: Editions Circé, 2001), 7–32.

OG *Of Grammatology*, trans. Gayatri Spivak (Baltimore: The Johns Hopkins University Press, 1976), translation of *De la grammatologie* (Paris: Minuit, 1967).

PC *The Post Card*, trans. Alan Bass (Chicago: University of Chicago Press, 1987), translation of *La Carte postale* (Paris: Flammarion, 1980).

PI *Points . . . Interviews, 1974–1994*, ed. Elisabeth Weber, trans. Peggy Kamuf et al. (Stanford: Stanford University Press, 1995), translation of *Points de suspension* (Paris: Galilée, 1992). The translators of the interviews cited in our volume are as follows: "Between Brackets I" (PI 5–29/13–36), "Ja, or the *faux-bond*

II" (PI 30–77/37–81), "Unsealing ('the old new language')" (PI 115–31/132–40), "Heidegger, the Philosophers' Hell" (PI 181–90/193–202), "'There Is No One Narcissism' (Autobiophotographies)" (PI 196–215/209–28), "Istrice 2: Ich bünn all hier" (PI 300–26/309–36), "A 'Madness' Must Watch Over Thinking" (PI 339–64/349–75), all translated by Peggy Kamuf; "Comment donner raison? 'How to Concede, with Reasons?'" (PI 191–95/203–7), trans. John P. Leavey Jr.

PSI, PSII *Psyche: Inventions of the Other*, ed. Peggy Kamuf and Elizabeth Rottenberg, trans. various, vol. I (Stanford: Stanford University Press, 2007), vol. II (Stanford: Stanford University Press, 2008), translations of *Psyché: Inventions de l'autre*, second edition, vol. I (Paris: Galilée, 1998), vol. II (Paris: Galilée, 2003). The translators of the essays cited in our volume are as follows: "Psyche: Invention of the Other" (PSI 1–47/11–61), trans. Catherine Porter; "Des Tours de Babel" (PSI 191–225/203–35), trans. Joseph F. Graham; "Telepathy" (PSI 226–61/237–70) and "Aphorism Countertime" (PSII 127–42/131–44), trans. Nicholas Royle; "How to Avoid Speaking: Denials" (PSII 143–95/145–200), trans. Ken Frieden and Elizabeth Rottenberg; "A Number of Yes" (PSII 231–40/239–48), trans. Brian Holmes.

RP *Resistances of Psychoanalysis*, trans. Peggy Kamuf, Pascale-Anne Brault, Michael Naas (Stanford: Stanford University Press, 1998), translation of *Résistances de la psychanalyse* (Paris: Galilée, 1996).

SP *Speech and Phenomena*, trans. David B. Allison (Evanston: Northwestern University Press, 1979), translation of *La Voix et le phénomène* (Paris: Presses Universitaires de France, 1967).

TW "Two Words for Joyce," trans. Geoffrey Bennington, in this volume 22–40, translation of "Deux mots pour Joyce," *Ulysse gramophone* (Paris: Galilée, 1987), 15–53.

UG "Ulysses Gramophone: Hear Say Yes in Joyce," trans. François Raffoul, in this volume 41–86, translation of "Ulysse gramophone: Ouï-dire de Joyce," *Ulysse gramophone: Deux mots pour Joyce* (Paris: Galilée, 1987), 57–143.

WD *Writing and Difference*, trans. Alan Bass (Chicago: University of Chicago Press, 1978), translation of *L'Écriture et la différence* (Paris: Seuil, 1967).

Note on the Translations

The translations of the essays offered here have been editorially adjusted to bring Derrida's references to *Ulysses* into accordance with the Gabler edition of the text: James Joyce, *Ulysses: The Corrected Text*, ed. Hans Walter Gabler with Wolfhard Steppe and Claus Melchior (London: The Bodley Head, 1993). In "Ulysses Gramophone: Hear Say Yes in Joyce," Derrida cites from: James Joyce, *Ulysses* (Harmondsworth: Penguin, 1968). In "Night Watch," Derrida cites from: James Joyce, *Ulysses* (New York: Random House, 1961). In cases where an alteration introduced by the Gabler edition bears on the discussion at hand it has been duly noted in the text, otherwise the changes from Gabler have been silently adopted.

Derrida's own interpolations within the quotations he cites are set within chevrons. All editorial interpolations are set within square brackets.

Ulysses Gramophone: Two Words for Joyce

The translation here of Derrida's *Ulysse gramophone: Deux mots pour Joyce* (Paris: Galilée, 1987) provides the English reader with the complete and definitive versions of these essays for the first time. The versions contained in that book and translated here are revised by Derrida from earlier lecture versions ("Two Words for Joyce") or first publications ("Ulysses Gramophone").

"Yes, laughter"

This text comprises the back jacket copy to *Ulysse gramophone*. It appears here in its first English translation by François Raffoul.

"Circumstances"

This text serves as an introduction to the volume *Ulysse gramophone* as a whole. It appears here in its first English translation by François Raffoul.

"Two Words for Joyce"

This new translation of "Two Words for Joyce" is by Geoffrey Bennington. An earlier translation of the lecture version of that text, likewise by Professor Bennington, based on the transcript of a talk given by Derrida at the Centre Georges Pompidou, Paris, in November, 1982, first appeared in *Post-Structuralist Joyce: Essays from the French*, ed. Derek Attridge and Daniel Ferrer (Cambridge: Cambridge University Press, 1984). This earlier version was published in French in *L'Herne James Joyce*, ed. Jacques Aubert and Fritz Senn (Paris: L'Herne, 1985), 203–16. Professor Bennington's new translation is of Derrida's revised text in *Ulysse gramophone*.

"Ulysses Gramophone: Hear Say Yes in Joyce"

This first full translation of "Ulysses Gramophone: Hear Say Yes in Joyce" is by François Raffoul. The essay is based on Derrida's opening address to the Ninth International James Joyce Symposium, held in Frankfurt am Main, June 12, 1984 (although the text is dated from May 11, 1984, the day Derrida was looking for postcards in a Tokyo hotel). A previous translation of the lecture version of Derrida's text, by Tina Kendall and revised by Shari Benstock, appeared as "Ulysses Gramophone: Hear Say Yes in Joyce," in the proceedings of that Symposium, *James Joyce: The Augmented Ninth*, edited by Bernard Benstock (Syracuse, NY: Syracuse University Press, 1988). That translation was revised by Derek Attridge in light of the expanded 1985 first French publication of the text in *Genèse de Babel: Joyce et la création*, ed. Claude Jacques (Paris: CNRS, 1985) and appeared in *Acts of Literature*, ed. Derek Attridge (New York: Routledge, 1992). The final version of the text presented here is newly translated from *Ulysse gramophone* and includes an important footnote on Rosenzweig missing from earlier versions.

"The Night Watch"

This essay is Derrida's preface to Jacques Trilling's *James Joyce ou l'écriture matricide* (Belfort: Circé, 2001) and his last published writing on Joyce. It makes its first appearance in English here in a translation by Pascale-Anne Brault and Michael Naas. Trilling's essay first appeared in *Etudes freudiennes* 7–8 (April 1973): 7–70. All translations of Trilling are by the translators.

INTRODUCTION

Derrida and Joyce:
On Totality and Equivocation

Andrew J. Mitchell and Sam Slote

> Joyce is a great landmark in the history of deconstruction.
> —Jacques Derrida, "The Villanova Roundtable:
> A Conversation with Jacques Derrida"[1]

> once in the dairy days of buy and buy
> —James Joyce, *Finnegans Wake* (161.13–14)

The conjunction of James Joyce and Jacques Derrida brings together what many would consider to be the arch representative of high modernism with the signal figure of postmodernism, a writer who authored some of the boldest experiments with the English language with a thinker who reinvented theory as deconstruction and ineradicably changed the way texts are read, studied, and written. Even within the singular history of encounters between philosophy and literature—Heidegger and Hölderlin, Benjamin and Baudelaire, Sartre and Genet, to name only a few—the Derrida and Joyce relation would still hold a special place. Derrida does not comment upon Joyce (even when engaged in seemingly straightforward exegesis), but thinks with him, through him, and allows Joyce a shaping hand in his own set of philosophical concerns. While Derrida has perhaps devoted more pages in his oeuvre to other literary figures (Mallarmé and Celan immediately come to mind), there is no one to whom he has returned more often and across such a great variety of works in the course of an almost forty year engagement.

Derrida and Joyce: Texts and Contexts brings together all of Derrida's published writings on Joyce, in fresh, new translations, along with essays in interpretation of this engagement. In regard to Derrida's texts, our volume features the first complete translation of Derrida's book *Ulysses Gramophone*, containing the essays "Two Words for Joyce" (translated by Geoffrey Bennington) and "Ulysses Gramophone: Hear Say Yes in Joyce" (translated by François Raffoul, who likewise translated the introduction and jacket text to the volume). The versions contained in that book and translated here are revised by Derrida from earlier lecture versions ("Two Words for Joyce") or first publications ("Ulysses Gramophone"). While these earlier versions have previously appeared in English, the final, expanded versions have not and appear here for the first time. The translation of *Ulysses Gramophone* is complemented here by the first English translation of Derrida's essay "The Night Watch" (translated by Pascale-Anne Brault and Michael Naas). Full details on these translations can be found in the preceding note on the translations. Across these texts, Derrida's commitment to interrogating the bounds of philosophy and literature, of reason and its other, of the "outside" of the text, is on full display in all the flamboyance and provocation of his concerns.

Derrida and Joyce: Texts and Contexts examines the importance of the Derrida/Joyce relation on a number of fronts, from explicit treatments of Derrida's readings of Joyce (part 2, Returns), to elaborations of the consequences of this encounter (part 3, Departures), and concludes with ruminations on Derrida's participation at the two Joyce events he famously attended (part 4, Recollections). In so doing, the editors hope to demonstrate that the Derrida/Joyce relationship does not concern the appropriation of a literary exemplar, nor the establishing of a disciplinary privilege between philosophy and literature, nor even a comprehension of the thought of another, but instead a relentless pursuit for the limits of any and all such efforts at totalization (appropriation, establishment, comprehension), a concern endemic to both philosophy and literature and any possible relationship between them. Joyce's towering literary efforts provide Derrida occasion to observe the staggering failure of any totality, even the most encyclopedic and multilingual, to ever truly complete itself. But Derrida does not simply observe the failure, he provokes the fall, finds himself claimed by the same ambiguities, the same equivocations, and through this participation, finds himself falling at the same time under the mastery of Joyce. Totalization remains ineradicably equivocal. The Derrida/Joyce relation stages this deconstructive play of totality and equivocation, situating itself at the fecund limit between them.

In his lecture "Two Words for Joyce"—which was first delivered at the Centre national d'Art et de Culture Georges Pompidou at a symposium honoring the centennial of Joyce's birth in 1982—Derrida claims that "yes, every time I write, and even in academic things, Joyce's ghost is always coming on board" (TW 27/27). Certainly, Derrida had referred to Joyce on a number of previous occasions, sometimes cryptically, but here he affirms

Joyce's presence, albeit spectral, throughout the entire range of his philosophical writings with a "yes" that echoes Molly's ambiguous, polymorphous "yes" (itself the subject of Derrida's next major contribution to Joyce studies). Derrida's affirmation of Joyce is equivocal, not least because in the same piece he also admits "I'm not sure of loving Joyce, of loving him all the time" (TW 24/20). So, apparently, Joyce's ghost is *always* coming on board even though Derrida is unsure of loving Joyce *all the time*. Joyce is the visitor who is not always welcome.

Given that the visitor is not a resident of one's home, but comes from somewhere beyond its bounds, comes aboard from outside the domain of one's own, the idea of a visitor brings with it a thinking of the outside. Derrida's repeated engagements with Joyce, from the passing mentions to the three fuller engagements later in his career, concern the question of an "outside" to Joyce's work. Joyce stands as a paradoxical figure of totality for Derrida. Joyce's work, or rather the "event" of Joyce—*Ulysses* and *Finnegans Wake* most of all (it is only with some difficulty that one could see the claim holding for *Chamber Music*)—leads Derrida to ruminations on a vast Joyce "computer" (UG 59/97) or Joyce "software" (TW 25/22–23) that would encompass and appropriate the entirety of culture and ourselves along with it. This Joyce is infinitely appropriative, an authority and master beyond reckoning.

But Joyce is also a figure of ambiguity and the equivocal for Derrida. The event of Joyce is an event of division and confusion of languages (Derrida's frequent recourse to the story of the Tower of Babel in conjunction with Joyce emphasizes just this point). Yet the confusion of Joyce is the confusion of literature. Joyce stands as the event of literature's confusion, its distancing from itself in writing itself, its division within itself, the equivocal play of the spoken and the written (the "gramophonic"). Joyce's work would seem to embody the deconstruction of meaning theorized by Derrida to an unprecedented degree.

Derrida is not sure of "loving" Joyce and he notes that this "affect" controls the "scene of our relationship with whoever writes" (TW 23/19). Derrida is not sure that Joyce is loved, "Except when he laughs—and you'll tell me that he's always laughing. That's true, I'll come back to it, but then everything is played out between the different tonalities of his laughter" (TW 23/20). The ambiguous affect of loving and not loving Joyce is tied precisely to the ambiguous laughter of Joyce's text. For Joyce's laughter is the sneering laughter of total mastery and dominance and/or the welcoming laughter of release, a laughter that laughs beyond the project of totalization, at the naïveté of it. The difference is a difference of tone. Derrida's relation to Joyce is always an equivocal one, as a brief survey of his works will show.

Derrida's equivocal response to Joyce is not without significance since in his first major work, a lengthy introduction to his translation of Edmund

Husserl's brief essay "Origin of Geometry" (1962), he grandly proposed Joyce as an alternative to Husserl's project to render philosophical thinking univocal, dependent as it was upon a vision of language as self-identical, transparent, and ahistorical (EH 101–3/102–5). For Derrida in that work, Joyce stands as an exemplar of the equivocal, Joyce's writing seeking "to repeat and take responsibility for all equivocation itself, utilizing a language that could equalize the greatest possible synchrony with the greatest potential for buried, accumulated, and interwoven intentions within each linguistic atom, each vocable, each word, each simple proposition, in all wordly cultures and their most ingenious forms (mythology, religion, sciences, arts, literature, politics, philosophy, and so forth)" (EH 102/104). And so, for Derrida, Joyce, the Joycean text, stands as an alternative to the philosophical project exemplified by Husserl, though by no means in simple opposition to it. There is a strange agreement between the two, we detect a Joycean "project" as well, equally expansive: "this writing resolutely settles itself within the labyrinthian field of culture 'bound' by its own equivocations, in order to travel through and explore the vastest possible historical distance that is now at all possible" (EH 102/104–5). For Derrida, both Husserl's and Joyce's approaches to language share the wish to "assume and interiorize the memory of a culture in a kind of recollection (*Erinnerung*) in the Hegelian sense" (EH 102/104). The questions raised here regarding the relationship between Joyce's writing and the systematizing projects of philosophy remain central for Derrida's readings of Joyce throughout his career.

In this way, Joyce, or rather Derrida's reading of Joyce, would be another moment in the long quarrel between philosophy and literature. Philosophy—so the argument goes—tends to view literature as inessential and more than a few theorists of literature have taken this definition as their own. Philosophy, it is said, deals with ideas and the fundamental concepts and structures that govern our knowledge and understanding of the world, whereas literature is basically mere rhetoric, stories about dragons, everyday people, everyman, and so on. In other words, literature is little more than a distracting entertainment, but one that threatens to lead us away from the truth that philosophy proudly proclaims.

Of course, such a binaristic opposition between philosophy and literature is rarely, if ever, pure. Even Plato's apparent denunciation of literature in *The Republic*—the archetype of philosophy's denigration of literature—is not without some irony. As Jed Deppman cogently argues in his contribution to this volume, Derrida does not simply hold Joyce as the antithesis to Husserl, rather, he brings up Joyce within his essay to suggest that the Husserlian project of transparency is already tinged by Joycean polyvalence. In his essay in this volume Jean-Michel Rabaté continues in this direction and argues how the name "Joyce" within Derrida's work is not (just) simply an author, but rather an exemplary model of the act of equivocation embodied by literature. For Derrida, Joyce is literature par excellence.

While Derrida signals a certain Joycean strain within Husserl, the situation is once again nothing one-sided or unambiguous. For Derrida likewise signals a Husserlian side of Joyce. Joyce's project of taking responsibility "for all equivocation itself" (EH 102/104) depends upon univocity and "could only succeed by allotting its share to univocity, whether it might draw from a given univocity or try to produce another. Otherwise, the very text of its repetition would have been unintelligible; at least it would have remained so forever and for everyone" (EH 103/105). From the start, then, Derrida reads Joyce in a tensed relation to philosophy, at once proposing an equivocal alternative to univocal transparency and likewise casting an equally expansive and controlling project of appropriative "recollection" of his own. And so, if Derrida can be called a literary philosopher (that is, a philosopher thinking through literature), then Joyce is, perhaps, a philosophical litterateur. On the one hand, Joyce, as perhaps the embodiment of literature par excellence (and Derrida remains equivocal on this point), embodies that which disturbs univocal metaphysics, but, on the other hand, as the embodiment par excellence of this disruption, Joyce, the logodaedalus, has domesticated said disruption. In this way, Derrida signals that Joyce, the Joycean oeuvre, marks a problem for both philosophy and literature as rigorously defined or "totalized" disciplines, a problem that serves as the *entrée* to this volume.

While Derrida does not engage Joyce's texts in a sustained manner until the 1980s, Joyce nonetheless gets aboard a number of Derrida's most pivotal works before then. After the Husserl essay, the name "Joyce" appears through the sixties and seventies as though a sigil of both the greatest accomplishment of totalization since Hegel and simultaneously the foremost exemplar of literary resistance to totalization. Passing references in two 1964 essays collected in *Writing and Difference* set the stage. On the one hand, the lengthy reading of Lévinas, "Violence and Metaphysics," closes with a quote from Joyce that would seem to ally him with the agenda of philosophy: "this proposition from perhaps the most Hegelian of modern novelists: 'Jewgreek is greekjew. Extremes meet'" (WD 153/228; quoting U 15.2098–99).[2] Joyce here stands as a thinker invested in the reconciliation of opposition, a la Hegel. On the other hand, one of the opening epigraphs to "Cogito and the History of Madness" quotes Joyce in conversation with Jacques Mercanton regarding *Ulysses*, "In any event this book was terribly daring. A transparent sheet separates it from madness" (WD 31/51).[3] Here Joyce would seem positioned as a writer aware of the limits of order and the dangerous proximity of its other (precisely the concerns at stake in this critical engagement with Foucault). The sheet of separation is transparent, the isolation imperfect, the boundary permissive.

This permissive reading of Joyce surfaces again in 1968, in Derrida's genre-breaking treatment of Plato's *Phaedrus*, "Plato's Pharmacy" (first published in *Tel Quel*), where consideration is again on the limits of the *logos* and its relation to its other, as well as on another Joycean theme, paternity. Derrida has the following footnote to a discussion of the role of the egg in ancient Egyptian mythology: "The paragraph that is about to end here will have marked the fact that this pharmacy of Plato's also brings into play Bataille's text, inscribing within the story of the egg the sun of the accursed part; the whole of that essay, as will quickly become apparent, being itself nothing but a reading of *Finnegans Wake*" (DI 88 fn. 20/99 fn. 17). In the 1982 address, Derrida called his Plato essay "a sort of indirect, perhaps distracted, reading of *Finnegans Wake*" (TW 28/29). The allusion, more provocative than substantive, would appear to be to the role of the "hen" (Greek "one"), the hen whose scratching makes up "The letter! The litter!" (FW 93.24) and the scrambling of whose egg, its mixing and dispersal, is proclaimed necessary for there to be any human "home": "you wish to ave some homelette, yes, lady! Good, mein leber! Your hegg he must break himself. See, I crack, so, he sit in the poele, umbedimbt!" (FW 59.30–32). Joyce here figures as a thinker of dissemination against hegemonic unity.

This Joyce climbs aboard the eclectic works of the seventies as well. In form and style Derrida's *Glas* has elicited numerous comparisons to *Finnegans Wake* even though it contains precious few references or allusions to Joyce. *Glas* is an extended meditation upon the possibility of Hegelian *Aufhebung* that works by pairing Hegel with an "other," in this case Jean Genet. The two columns of the text both engage in and undermine the processes of dialectic and, in so doing, suggest the terms of Derrida's reading of Joyce as that which equivocates between interiority and alterity. The rapport between *Glas* and Joyce is the subject of Sam Slote's essay in this volume.

In the first part of *The Post Card*, "Envois," which consists of a series of postcards by Derrida apparently addressed to his lover, Joyce and the *Wake* make a number of appearances, with mention of "Another fraternal couple in pp making war on itself, *the penman and the postman*" (PC 142/154). Joyce's thinking of the postman's relation to the penman mirrors much of Derrida's concerns for "postality" in the text, and this relation is at the center of Andrew J. Mitchell's contribution to the volume. *The Post Card* also makes mention of a trip to Joyce's grave at the Fluntern cemetery in Zürich by Derrida and J. Hillis Miller (PC 148/160–61) and takes up the issue of Babel and Babelization in regard to *Finnegans Wake* (PC 240–41/257–58).[4] In fact, Derrida's next major communication on Joyce, the 1982 "Two Words for Joyce," is an expansion of the two words from the *Wake* that he singles out for consideration in "Envois," "he war" (FW 258.12): "'he war' . . . YHWH declaring war by decreeing *la dichemination*, by deconstructing the tower, by saying to those who wished both to make a name for themselves, the Chemites, and to impose their particular language as the universal language, by saying 'Babel' to them" (PC 142/154–55). Again, as in "Plato's Pharmacy," Joyce figures as the thinker/writer of dissemination/dishemination.

"Two Words for Joyce," Derrida's 1982 address and first explicit treatment of Joyce, could be seen as an extension of this comment on Babel in *The Post Card*.[5] Clearly, this had occupied him for some time since he (briefly) mentioned the *Wake* and Babel in a roundtable discussion on translation at a 1979 symposium in Montreal (see EO 98–110/132–46 and 133–35/176–78) and in the essay "Des Tours de Babel" (PSI 191–225/203–35), which directly feeds into the 1982 address. In "Des Tours de Babel," Derrida elaborates the idea that the myth of Babel is fundamental to equivocation. The problem is laid out in the word Babel that in Hebrew means "God, the father" (*Ba'bel*) and "confusion" (*Bavel*), relating thus to both the one and the many, unity and difference. According to the biblical myth, at the destruction of the tower of Babel, God created the plurality of languages that exists today. Therefore the tower bears both His name (*Ba'bel*) and the confusion (or confounding of languages) that ensued (PSI 192–93/204–5). The two words that Derrida chooses from the *Wake* in his 1982 essay, "he war," exemplify this Babelian confusion in that they command the confusion of the Shemites (the builders of Babel) in the wake of the tower's destruction:

> "He war" calls for translation, both orders and forbids transposition into the other language. Change me—into yourself—and above all do not touch me, read and do not read, say and do not say otherwise what I have said and which will have been: in two words *which was*. Alliance and double-bind. For the "he war" also tells of the unreplaceability of the event that it is. It is what it is, which is also unchangeable because it has already been, a past without appeal which, before being and being present, was. So that's war declared. Before being, that is being a present, it was: was *he*, *fuit*, the late god of fire the jealous god. (TW 33–34/40)

But it is with his two addresses in the eighties—"Two Words for Joyce," the 1982 Pompidou Center address and "Ulysses Gramophone: Hear Say Yes in Joyce," a 1984 address to the Joyce Symposium in Frankfurt am Main—that the question of Joycean totality comes to the fore in all its equivocity and ambiguity. As Derrida puts it in "Two Words," Joyce's greatness lies in bringing about an event of such magnitude that "henceforth you have only one way out: *being in memory of him*" (TW 24/21). This is not a matter of you remembering him, no, but of you being remembered by him, inhabiting his memory. The Joycean obligation is then "to be in his memory, to inhabit a memory henceforth greater than all your finite recall can gather up, in a single instant or a single vocable, of cultures, languages, mythologies, religions, philosophies, sciences, histories of spirit or of literatures. I don't know if you can love that, without resentment and without jealousy" (TW 24/21–22). The totalizing drive of Joyce's absorption and disaggregation of culture and history makes us part of his programming, where "in advance and forever it inscribes you in the book you are reading" (TW 24/22). We become part of the programming "on this 1000th generation computer, *Ulysses*, *Finnegans Wake*, compared with which the current technology of our computers and our micro-computerized archives and our translating machines remains a *bricolage*, a prehistoric child's toy" (TW 25/22). We become part of the Joyce "software," the "joyceware" that places us in his memory. This condition of Joycean "hypermnesia" is the subject of both Alan Roughley and Louis Armand's essays in this volume. Armand examines the technicity of hypermnesia in the *Wake* as transformative of communication, agency, signification, and ultimately even identity. Roughley, on the other hand, looks at how Joyce has inhabited Derrida's work in a perpetual hypermnesic dialogue not unlike the relation between Plato and Socrates that Derrida described in *The Post Card*.

Part of the inescapable nature of Joyce is attributable to the "Joycean institution" (UG 58/94) or Joyce industry, in the parlance of the times, that presides over the "signature" of Joyce. The Joyce scholar has "mastery over the *computer* of all memory, plays with the entire archive of culture" (UG 59/97). The computer programs everything that will come after it, "We are caught in this net. We find all the gestures to take the initiative of a movement announced in a superpotentialized text that will remind you, at a given time, that you are caught in a network of language, writing, knowledge and *even of narration*" (UG 60/97). The signature of Joyce is the affirmation of this mastery and presides over this program.

"Ulysses Gramophone" is consequently an exploration of the way in which this affirmation must remember itself in order to sustain itself. The affirmation must be archived, in other words, written somewhere and maintained. This is the gist of the term "gramophone," the utterance (*phonê*) must be archived and recorded (*grammê*) for the utterance to remain true to itself, for it to abide there must be a recording and archiving. The two are dependent upon one another and the point holds for any utterance. Insofar as every utterance is an *assertion*, a pronouncement of itself, it is likewise an affirmation ("a *yes* is co-extensive with every statement" [UG 72/124]). As a result, we are faced with the "ineluctable gramophony of the 'yes'" (UG

67/114), for all affirmation is divided within itself, it must on the one hand record itself to support its later memory of itself (remembering as necessary to an affirmative self-identity, the keeping of a promise, of one's word) and it must affirm itself to someone or something outside of itself (though even in affirming itself to itself this division is operative).[6] This makes "saying yes" (*l'oui-dire*) dependent upon an other who hears it and acknowledges receipt, a matter of "hearsay" (*l'ouï-dire*). As such, the simple "yes" that occupies Derrida in his lecture, Molly's yes and also Joyce's signature (which functions as an affirmation like the yes), is something divided within itself, split by both its relation to everything outside of it on which it depends for its self-assertion, and also by its relation to itself as evidenced by its need to be remembered and restored from somewhere that it is not.

The signature operates at a distance from itself, dependent on something or someone other than itself to relay itself back to itself (all the problems of the penman and the postman return here): "*Yes*, condition of every signature and performative, addresses itself to some other, which it does not constitute, and it can only begin by *asking*, as a response to an always prior demand, to *ask* him or her to say *yes*" (UG 74/127).[7] In posing the question of response, "Ulysses Gramophone" deals with matters of responsibility and is thus a key text for signaling the ethical dimensions of Derrida's work. In having an undecidable referent, Molly's "yes" is irresponsible and so the question is how does one respond to the irresponsible, which is, in effect, also to ask, how does one respond to the undecidable ambiguity of the magnum opus that is Joyce. "Reciprocally, two responses or two responsibilities refer to each other without having any relation between them. The two sign yet prevent the signature from gathering itself. All they can do is call for another *yes*, another signature. And furthermore, one cannot differentiate between two *yeses* that *must* gather together like twins, to the point of simulacrum, the one being the gramophony of the other" (UG 80/141). Laurent Milesi's essay in this volume explores this issue of responsibility in Derrida's reading of Joyce in relation to the various textual dialogues he participated in with Hélène Cixous: he construes these dialogues as responses apropos responsibility.

But even this computer and software that seeks to encompass all of history and culture within its program cannot so simply succeed. Joyce's texts have all the strategies and subversions of writing at their disposal. Joyce as literature is at odds with Joyce as cultural archive. In "Two Words," this plays out in a drama of citation. Joyce's text is always quotable, detachable, and thus insertable within other projects and contexts. In quoting Joyce, his text is given an authoritative position, but that authority is also simultaneously subverted, in that he is now at an unknown author's disposal and made to serve another's ends:

Paradoxical logic of this relationship between two unequal texts, two programs or two literary "softwares." Whatever the difference between them, to the point of incommensurability, the "second" text, the one which, fatally, refers to the other, quotes it, exploits it, parasites it and deciphers it, is no doubt the minute parcel *detached* from the other, the offspring, the metonymic dwarf, the jester of the great anterior text which would have declared war on it in tongues. And yet (one can see this precisely with Joyce's books which play both roles, the ancestor and the descendant), it is also another set, quite other, bigger and more powerful than the all-powerful which it drags off and reinscribes elsewhere, in another sequence, in order to defy, with its ascendancy, genealogy itself. (TW 26/25)

The text for all its authority is still subject to the crudest appropriation, citation, and misuse, and this inherently qua written work and despite any and all the best and worst efforts of the caretakers of that signature. For Derrida, there is a freedom to be found in this, the freedom of an opening: "In this war of languages, everything we could say after it looks in advance like a minute self-commentary with which this work accompanies itself. And yet the new marks carry off, enlarge and project elsewhere—one never knows where in advance—a program that appeared to constrain them, or at least watch over them. This is our only chance, minuscule but completely open" (TW 27/26). The repurposing of Joyce expands the range of the computer program, to be sure, but in order for the program to grow, it must reach beyond itself, and in that extension, in that surface of contact with the outside, that moment of alterity, there is chance.

"Ulysses Gramophone" takes up this issue of an outside to totality in terms of the signature, and Derek Attridge's contribution to this volume focuses on the relation between signature and countersignature in Derrida's readings. For Derrida, the confirmation of our affirmation is the countersignature of the other:

> Now with the event signed Joyce, a *double-bind* has at least become explicit (for it already has had a hold on us ever since Babel or Homer, and all that followed): on the one hand, one must write, one must sign, one must make new events with untranslatable marks happen—and this is the desperate call, the distress of a signature that demands a *yes* from the other; but on the other hand, the singular novelty of any other *yes*, of any other signature, already finds itself programophoned in the Joycean corpus. (UG 61/99–100)

Here Derrida shows that even what comes from the outside may not be the singular event so hoped for and desired, but instead something already preprogramed. Put in terms drawn from *Ulysses*, we can never be sure when we "introduce the necessary breach for the coming of the other, an other that one could always call Elijah, if Elijah is the name of the unpredictable other for whom a place must be kept" whether the Elijah as other who shows up, if he shows up, will in fact be Elijah the other, or "Elijah, the head of the megaprogramotelephonic network" and thus pre-envisioned by the computer all along (UG 70/120). For this reason, Derrida claims in regard to the repeated yes that "this essential repetition is haunted by an intrinsic threat, by the interior telephone that parasites it as its mimetic-mechanical double, as its unceasing parody" (UG 56/89). The singularity and novelty of the yes is challenged from the outset, contaminated, by the recording of it necessary for it to be itself.

When Derrida wonders whether he loves Joyce or not, he emphasizes that this is a question of affect and feeling, of a certain tonality. Joyce is loved when he is laughing, but he is laughing all the time, we are told. Laughter, the hallmark of affirmation from a Nietzschean perspective, becomes the fundamental mood of Joyce:

> the totalizing hermeneutic that constitutes the task of a global and eternal foundation of Joycean studies will find itself before what I hesitate to call a dominant affect, a *Stimmung* or a *pathos*, a tonality that re-traverses all the others, but which nonetheless does not belong to the series of the others since it just re-marked them all, adding itself to them without letting itself be added up or totalized, like a remainder that is both quasi-transcendental and supplementary. (UG 68/116)

Derrida would be free to go ahead and love Joyce all the time, were it not for the fact that even this laughter suffers division. Laughter arises as the transpartition between the totality and its other, where we encounter "a writing about which it is no longer possible to decide if it still calculates, calculates better and more, or if it transcends the very order of calculable economy, or even of an incalculable or an undecidable which would still be homogeneous with the world of calculation" (TW 38/51). The contribution to this volume from Simon Critchley and Tom McCarthy takes up the economic side of Derrida's reading with particular attention on the role of money in both authors' work and thought. For Derrida at this point, "A certain quality of laughter would accord something like affect to this beyond of calculation, and of all calculable literature" (TW 38/51). But the transpartitioning quality of this laughter means that on the one hand, it is the laughter of the system, the sneering laughter of the conquering master, "I can hear a reactive, even negative yes-laughter resonate. It exults in a hypermnesic mastery, and by spinning a spider web that defies any other possible mastery" (UG 68/117). On the other hand, it means that there is also a laughter that laughs at the very project of mastery, "there is a James Joyce who can be heard laughing at this omnipotence" (UG 69/117). This laughter aims in a different direction, toward the outside, a calling out to what lies beyond, a calling out or a calling back, a welcoming laughter that begins "to introduce the necessary breach for the coming of the other" (UG 70/120). To not be sure of loving Joyce is to remain faithful to this equivocal situation—*equivocation as the pathos of responsibility*.

This divided laughter threatens to vibrate and resound through the institutional edifice of literary and philosophical scholarship and bring down its walls, soliciting the crumbling of its foundations. It is uncapturable, they are no longer capable of capturing. An implication of this equivocality is that the Joycean text is not necessarily reducible to a singular determinant of meaning; the Joycean text equivocates, and it does so by incorporating all sorts of meanings from many different languages across the widest number of possible fields. The implication here is that the task of reading Joyce will not be fulfilled by simply parsing away the references, by an *explication du texte*, since that would reduce Joyce to a simple plurivocity, that is, to the realm of a singular determinant of meaning. In this way, Derrida has here proposed a mode of reading Joyce that is largely at odds with the methods and practices of traditional literary scholarship. For Derrida is not simply noting an ambiguous quality to Joyce's texts, where Joyce would simply provide us with an undecidable choice among equally qualified meanings. Rather, Derrida reads Joyce at the limits of meaning itself, where there are no longer any discrete meanings nicely arrayed for us to choose from (indeed Derrida goes so far as to question what even counts as a single word, the very countability of words), but instead we are faced with the linguistic friction of meaning's emergence, the "sending" of meaning. We might also add that the type of reading Derrida proposes is likewise at odds with many of the interpretations of Joyce that are done under the rubric of the "Derridean."

Both the 1982 and 1984 addresses, which were collected together in the 1987 French volume *Ulysse gramophone*, seem to mark the culmination of Derrida's engagement with Joyce. The totality of the hypermnesic cultural computer of Joyce is shown to undo itself on its own. The very extension that increases its domain undoes its self-presence. The very other that it seeks to appropriate it needs for its self-confirmation. The other that it contacts in confirmation of itself simultaneously undoes its self-identity in a showing of dependency. All the major themes of Derrida's thinking of meaning—citation, grafting, postality, mediation, technology, and the signature—play predominant roles in his reading of Joyce. As do the philosophers who most preoccupy Derrida's investigations in his other works and lectures. In crafting his interpretation, Derrida enlists the assistance of Hegel (Joyce is a system builder and his work comparable to the *Encyclopaedia*), Nietzsche (Nietzschean affirmation is subject to the same doubling logic as Joyce's yes), Husserl (pure univocity and equivocity are equally impossible), and Heidegger (existence is a call, but this fact disrupts its purported self-presence[8]). While Derrida had previously deployed the name Joyce selectively, and briefly, throughout a number of key works, by the late 1980s he seems to have largely abandoned Joyce, apart from a few passing references and comments during interviews.[9] It is as if he had managed to overcome his "admiring resentment" (TW 26/24) and had out-Joyced Joyce, no longer needing him "on board." And yet, in a move that shows how a presumed mastery over equivocation is never final, whether Joyce's or his own, Derrida did essay one further contribution to Joyce studies.

In 2001, Derrida wrote an introduction for the republication of a monograph by his friend the psychoanalyst Jacques Trilling, *James Joyce ou l'écriture matricide*.[10] Entitled "The Night Watch," this essay adds an essential and (seemingly) final piece to Derrida's concern with Joyce. In 1994, at the conclusion of "The Villanova Roundtable: A Conversation with Jacques Derrida," Derrida is asked about his relationship to Joyce.[11] In the lengthy answer that follows, he lays out three main areas of this relation. He refers first to the "impossible task of precisely gathering in a totality, in a potential totality, the potentially infinite memory of humanity," which, as he explains, "is made possible only by loading every sentence, every word, with a maximum of equivocalities, virtual associations, by making this organic linguistic totality as rich as possible."[12] We have seen this ground covered in "Two Words for Joyce." The third point raised is likewise one with which we are familiar, this time through "Ulysses Gramophone," that of the doubling of the yes, "when you say 'yes,' you imply that in the next moment you will have to confirm the 'yes' by a second 'yes.' When I say 'yes,' I immediately say 'yes, yes.' I commit myself to confirm my commitment in the next second, and then tomorrow, and then the day after tomorrow."[13] But what Derrida raises as the second point of his relationship to Joyce had hitherto received no sustained treatment by him, though it is a theme that preoccupies so many of his other works, the question of filiation and paternity. Here he remarks on the supposed asymmetry between paternity and maternity, the "legal fiction" of fatherhood, in Joyce's famed expression, versus the natural fact of motherhood. Derrida quickly sketches the lines of an argument against this purportedly self-evident maternity, "today the mother is also a legal fiction [. . .]. Motherhood is something which is interpreted, the theme of a reconstruction from experience. What one calls today surrogate mothers, for instance, and all the enormous problems that you are familiar with, attest to the fact that we do not know who the mother is. [. . .] if we had time, I would try to show what the equivocal consequences would be of this fact that the situation of the mother is the same as that of the father."[14] The opportunity for drawing out these consequences is provided by "The Night Watch," and we are pleased to publish Derrida's essay in this volume, in its first English translation by Pascale-Anne Brault and Michael Naas.[15]

The tension between writing and totalization that ran throughout the previous engagements with Joyce returns in this strange essay in striking form. "The Night Watch" is again very much concerned with totality, but this time on the part of the subject. The subject who appears in the world has always been born into the world, but this birth remains inappropriable or, to use Trilling's term, "uncircumventable" (NW 91/12) in that one cannot get behind it. As it has been a staple of Derrida's thinking that to write is to accept a certain death, the writer consequently could be seen as someone acting against their birth, contradicting it. Insofar as birth is understood as stable, as "a being or an origin" (NW 92/15), then to write is to wish to never have been born, to have no origin. Through the logic of Trilling and Derrida, writing becomes a form of matricide, a deconstruction of a purportedly pure origin and inception. Regarding this impure and non-inceptual origin, Derrida writes that "Matricide puts us on the path of a birth irreducible to all ontology, to all ontological or phenomenological thinking about originarity" (NW 92/15). The act of matricide would thus contain a strange ambiguity. On the one hand, it would be the recourse of a subject who wished to eradicate all marks of dependence in an impossible quest for self-sufficiency and self-identity. It would be driven by a desire for totality and completion. On the other, matricide would be the writing that makes way for birth of a different sort, a birth without the purity of origin, where *"being born,"* as Derrida emphasizes, comes to me "from the other" (NW 92/15). This tension is played out in the ambiguity between the mother and maternity in the essay and it returns once again to Derrida's Joycean tension between totality and its other, an innovative return, to be sure, and one with consequences for our understanding of Derrida's thinking of the phantasm, the feminine, authorship, natality, and alterity, to name just a few of the concerns addressed. We are fortunate to include here two exceptional essays commenting on "The Night Watch," one by its co-translator, Michael Naas, detailing the logic of the phantasm operative in the essay, and one by Christine van Boheemen-Saaf taking up the problematic erasure of woman in the text.

If, in "The Night Watch," the moment of birth is the uncircumventable exteriority that occasions interiority, then, for Derrida, the event "Joyce" is the uncircumventable exteriority of philosophy, the unwelcome visitor who marks and re-marks philosophy as incomplete. Confronted by an ineradicable, uncircumnavigable, ineluctable equivocation and always from the outset being forced to respond, having already said yes to this condition, being so tied to the other for even the simplest self-affirmation that we can no longer be said to be ourselves, to be marked by the other through and through, to never be whole while seeking to be whole, to be written ourselves while at the same time writing, such is the equivocal situation of this existence. Perhaps no one will have helped us to understand our situation more than Joyce and Derrida.

Notes

1. "The Villanova Roundtable: A Conversation with Jacques Derrida," in *Deconstruction in a Nutshell: A Conversation with Jacques Derrida*, ed. John D. Caputo (New York: Fordham University Press, 1997), 3–28; 26.

2. In a footnote to this line, Derrida writes of Joyce's familiarity with Victor Bérard's work on the Semitic roots of Odysseus (WD 320–21 fn. 92/228 fn.1), suggesting that he is *au courant* enough with Joyce criticism to know of this influence.

3. Jacques Mercanton, "The Hours of James Joyce," trans. Lloyd C. Parks, *Portraits of the Artist in Exile*, ed. Willard Potts (San Diego: Harcourt Brace Jovanovich, 1986), 206–52; 226, translation of *Les Heures de James Joyce* (Paris: Actes sud et l'aire, 1988), 55.

4. J. Hillis Miller recalls the trip in his *The Medium Is the Maker: Browning, Freud, Derrida, and the New Telepathic Ecotechnologies* (Eastbourne, UK: Sussex Academic Press, 2009), 50: "Derrida and I did go together . . . to visit Joyce's tomb in the Zürich cemetery near the zoo. The animal cries from that zoo appear in *Finnegans Wake*. We did stand laughing before the tomb of Egon Zoller, '*Erfinder des Telephonographen*,' with its engraved ticker tape machine and its carved Alpha and Omega. Derrida, as we stood looking at the tomb, did connect it to his then current writing about telecommunication networks, that is, the 'Envois.' He asked me to take a photograph later and send it to him, which I did have a friend do. It may be among his remains. It is the case that we searched for Peter Szondi's tomb, but failed to find it, though I found it easily enough on another visit to that cemetery. I do not remember, however, having a car in Zürich, so I do not see how I could have driven him up to the cemetery, as he asserts. Maybe I have forgotten, or maybe I rented a car for the occasion" (see PC 148/160–1).

5. Already in the 1962 *Husserl's Origin of Geometry: An Introduction* the Tower of Babel was at stake. Derrida cites Leibniz's *New Essays on Human Understanding* as a progenitor of the Husserlian project of univocity: "For we have the option of fixing significations, at least in some learned language, and of agreeing on them, so as to pull down this Tower of Babel" (G. W. Leibniz, *New Essays on Human Understanding*, ed. and trans. Peter Remnant and Jonathan Bennett [Cambridge: Cambridge University Press, 1996], 337). The Derrida citation occurs at EH 100–1 fn. 108/102 fn. 3), but the reference given is incorrect (Theophil's statement is at Book III, Chap. IX, §10).

6. Derrida returns to the issue a few years later in a 1987 text on the work of Michel de Certeau entitled "A Number of Yes" (PSII 231–40/239–48).

7. See also Rodolphe Gasché, *Inventions of Difference* (Cambridge: Harvard University Press, 1994), 236–50.

8. For another Heideggerian resonance around the term *war* in "Two Words for Joyce" (and all of Derrida's concerns with the Tower of Babel), directed at the dispersal of being as Babelian detour, see Sam Slote, "No Symbols Where None Intended: Derrida's War at *Finnegans Wake*," in *James Joyce and the Difference of Language*, ed. Laurent Milesi (Cambridge: Cambridge University Press, 2003), 195–207.

9. See for example, "Shibboleth: For Paul Celan" (1986) where Joyce is briefly contrasted with Celan ("Shibboleth: For Paul Celan," trans. Joshua Wilner and Thomas Dutoit, in Jacques Derrida, *Sovereignties in Question: The Poetics of Paul Celan*, ed. Thomas Dutoit and Outi Pasanen [New York: Fordham University Press, 2005], 1–64; 27, translation of *Schibboleth pour Paul Celan* [Paris: Galilée, 1986], 51); the 1987 interview "Heidegger, the Philosophers' Hell," where Derrida remarks that his writings on Joyce are formally affected by the event of Joyce (PI: 188/200); *Monolingualism of the Other; or, The Prosthesis of Origin* (delivered 1992), where Joyce names the legal fictions of paternity and maternity in a lengthy discussion of European Jewish intellectuals (*Monolingualism of the Other; or, The Prosthesis of Origin*, trans. Patrick Mensah [Stanford: Stanford University Press, 1998], 92, translation of *Le Monolinguisme de l'autre* [Paris: Galilée, 1996], 112); and "The Villanova Roundtable: A Conversation with Jacques Derrida" of 1994, where Derrida gives a lengthy summary of his concerns with Joyce ("Villanova Roundtable," 25–28).

10. Jacques Trilling, *James Joyce ou l'écriture matricide* (Belfort: Circé, 2001).

11. Jacques Derrida, "Villanova Roundtable," 25–28.

12. Ibid., 25.

13. Ibid., 27.

14. Ibid. 26–27.

15. Derrida discusses the transformations of the family with Elizabeth Roudinesco in their *For What Tomorrow . . . : A Dialogue*, trans. Jeff Fort (Stanford: Stanford University Press, 2004), chap. 3 "Disordered Families," 33–46, translation of *De quoi demain . . . : Dialogue* (Paris: Fayard/Galilée, 2001), 63–82. Even in this discussion, though, a reference is made back to the "Night Watch" essay as providing the philosophical basis for the topic at hand: "No doubt it would be necessary to sharpen the distinction between mother and maternity, the desire of the mother and the desire for maternity. I have tried to do this elsewhere," where a footnote refers the reader to "The Night Watch" (Derrida and Roudinesco, *For What Tomorrow . . .* , 42/76).

I

Texts by Jacques Derrida

Ulysses Gramophone: Two Words for Joyce

and

The Night Watch

Ulysses Gramophone:
Two Words for Joyce

Yes, laughter

translated by François Raffoul

Yes, laughter.

Throughout Joyce's oeuvre, the yes and laughter are intertwined. They form one and the same condition of possibility, a kind of transcendental that for once provokes laughter while making one think. It indeed accompanies all significations, the history and languages of the encyclopedia. It thus exceeds them also, in an unfolding whose anamnestic power resembles the last challenge of literature—literature and philosophy. Joyce has more than one laughter, but how can one distinguish between them? And can one, without laughing, inquire about the *yes*, its origin or its essence? Yes, this is always a response. Now the responsibility of affirmation must be repeated: *yes, yes*. Hence the circle. For it then divides itself in order to safeguard memory or institute the promise: repetition, citation, simulacrum, comedy, parasitism, technology of communication, bank archives, telephone, typewriter or gramophone, a loan for a datum.

Confessions or short travel reports, these lectures navigate around certain privileged places: for example a gramophone or Molly's inexhaustible *yes* in *Ulysses*, the war of idioms declared by God (*and he war*) in *Finnegans Wake*.

Babel, the struggle for power of languages: who has the rights of translation, knowledge, and authority? These questions were once addressed to the improbable institution of Joycean studies at the University of Modern Times that Joyce simultaneously prescribed and prohibited.

Circumstances

translated by François Raffoul

How could a discourse, in two words, encircle itself without turning in circles? How could it speak about something (other) without ceasing to speak about itself, and indeed returning to itself [*y revenant*], two words in one?

If we followed the gaps of these ageless metaphors or this incredible typology, we would have to accept that a discourse must speak about itself in order to interrupt narcissism, in any case to bring it to view or to thought. To speak about itself, about what happens and arrives [*arrive*] to it or with it in order to address itself to the other and at last tell him or her something else. We would have to accept that a voice still resonates with its inscription in the circle, when it says *around*.

Around: to turn around, to keep oneself around. In the circumstance, Ulysses the *revenant*.

These two essays not only retain the mark, as one sometimes says, of their circumstance. When they still had, in the present tense, the form of a speech, they were first given with the intent of exhibiting the said circumstance. Such circumstance was not *around* but rather occupied the center of a journey, quite close to a kernel of reflection. What was then said seemed to concern it, to turn around it, to speak about it, whether it was a symposium or what renders possible—or completely impossible, one and the other, one like the other—such a symposium, the constitution of the Joycean critique, an institution of "Joyce studies."

As for keeping oneself or turning *around*, let us note in passing, the circular *motions* of the conference or the circumference, of the circumnavigation or the circumcision, the turns and returns of all kinds adumbrate here the most recurrent motifs.

Is reference possible as circumference? What does it bring back? What is the scope [*portée*] or bearing [*port*] of this question in return?

It is thus, by circumstance, a situation of speech, *Revue Parlée* in one case, *Symposium* in the other, which becomes here the privileged theme, an object of analysis, the title of questions; a situation of speech along with the singular events that cannot be separated from it. I therefore neither could, nor wanted to, neutralize its effects after the fact. To suspend the reference to these singular events, to attempt to mitigate their circumstance, or even to erase what is left of it, would this not amount to destroying these texts, annihilating them a second time? But this time in order to better safeguard them, to safeguard them from what in them was destined for an immediate consumption? Would this not amount to returning them to their conditions as self-destructive artifacts, bound by their formation, or their very destination, to expend themselves on the spot, as *self-destroying* or *self-consuming* objects?[1] Perhaps they are in fact that. Perhaps they have remained so. Perhaps it is appropriate only now to confirm it.

But why? Why confirm it? Under what conditions can or *should* these marks be repeated? What can it mean for them to *remain*? One never knows whether such an operation can be repeated, and whether the apparatus named *gramophone* or tape recorder [*magnétophone*] is essential to it. One never knows whether such an operation has ever been undertaken. Let us say that through this publication I have wanted, after the fact, to share this concern, to submit a hypothesis, to multiply questions.

"Two Words for Joyce" corresponds to the transcription of a short discourse, improvised on the basis of a few notes, and delivered on November 15, 1982, at a conference entitled *Pour James Joyce*, which was organized by the Centre Georges-Pompidou "in *La Revue Parlée*," the Irish Embassy in Paris and the British Council. The conference was coordinated by Jacques Aubert and Jean-Michel Rabaté, who presided over the session, and who himself presented a lecture before mine and that of Hélène Cixous. The transcription of the taped lecture was first published in English (*Post-Structuralist Joyce: Essays from the French*, ed. Derek Attridge and Daniel Ferrer [Cambridge: Cambridge University Press, 1984], then in French in *L'Herne* 50 [1985]).

Ulysses Gramophone was given on June 12, 1984, in Frankfurt, at the opening of the James Joyce International Symposium, and first published in *Genèse de Babel: Joyce et la création*, ed. Claude Jacques (Paris: CNRS, 1985).

Notes

1. TN: These last two expressions in English in the original.

Two Words for Joyce

translated by Geoffrey Bennington

I

It is very late, it is always too late with Joyce, I shall say only two words.

I do not yet know in what language, I do not know in how many languages.

How many languages can be lodged in two words by Joyce, inserted or inscribed, kept or burned, celebrated or violated?

I shall say two words, supposing that words in *Finnegans Wake* can be counted. One of Joyce's great bursts of laughter resounds through this challenge: just try to count the words and the languages I consume! Put your principle of identification and numeration! What is *a* word?

I shall no doubt return to Joyce's laughter. As for the languages, Jean-Michel Rabaté tells me that the experts have counted at least forty.

Two words then, simply to put back into play what Hélène Cixous has just been saying: the primal scene, the complete father, the law, *jouissance* through the ear, *by the ear*, more literally, by the word ear, in the ear mode,[1] in English, for example, and supposing that enjoyment [*jouir*] via the ear is, for the most part, feminine.

What are these two English words?

They are only half English, if you will, if you will hear them, that is, do a little more than hear them: read them.

I take them from *Finnegans Wake* (258.12):

HE WAR

I spell them out: H-E-W-A-R, and sketch a first translation: HE WARS—he wages war, he declares war, he makes war, which can also be pronounced by babelizing a bit (for it is in a particularly Babelian scene of the book that these words rise up), by Germanizing, then, in Anglo-Saxon, HE WAR: he was. He was he who was. I am he who is, who am,

I am that I am, says Yahweh, supposedly. Where it was, he was, declaring war. And it was true. Pushing things a bit, taking the time to draw on the vowel and to lend an ear, it will have been true, *wahr*. That's what can be guarded (*wahren, bewahren*) in truth. God guards. He guards himself thus, by declaring war.

He, is "He," the "him," the one who says "I" in the masculine, "He," war declared, he who was war declared, in declaring war he was he who was and he who was true, the truth as being a war, he who has declared war verified the truth of his truth by war declared, by the act of declaring the war that was in the beginning. Declaring is an act of war, he declared war in tongues [*langues*] and on language and by language, which gave languages, that's the truth of Babel when Yahweh pronounced its vocable, Babel, difficult to say if it was a name, a proper name or a common noun sowing confusion.

I'll stop here, provisionally, through lack of time. Other transformations remain possible, a very great number about which I'll say another two words later.

II

Coming here, I said to myself that there are basically perhaps only two great manners, or rather two greatnesses, in this madness of writing by which whoever writes effaces himself, leaving, only to abandon it, the archive of his own effacement. These last two words bespeak madness itself.

Perhaps that's an overly extreme simplification. There are certainly other greatnesses, but I take the risk of saying it so as to say something of my feeling about Joyce.

I do indeed say "my feeling": that major affect which, beyond all our analyses, evaluations, interpretations, controls the scene of our relationship with whoever writes. One can admire the power of a work and have, as they say, a "bad relationship" with its signatory, at least the signatory as one projects his or her image, reconstructs, or dreams, or offers him or her the hospitality of a haunting. Our admiration for Joyce ought to have no limit, no more than should the debt owed to the singular *event* of his work. It is no doubt preferable to talk here of an event rather than a work or a subject or an author. And yet, I'm not sure I love Joyce. Or more exactly: I'm not sure he is loved. Except when he laughs—and you'll tell me that he's always laughing. That's true, I'll come back to it, but then everything is played out between the different tonalities of his laughter, in the subtle difference that separates several qualities of laughter. Knowing whether one loves Joyce, is that the right question? In any case, one can attempt to account for these affects, and I do not believe that the task is a secondary one.

I'm not sure of loving Joyce, of loving him all the time. It's to explain this possibility that I talked of two greatnesses. Two measures for that act of writing by which whoever writes pretends to efface himself, leaving us caught in his archive as though in a spider's web.

Let's simplify outrageously. There is first of all the greatness of whoever writes in order to give, in giving, and therefore in order to give to forget the gift and the given, what is given and the act of giving. Beyond any return, any circulation, any circumference. This is the only way of giving, the only possible—and impossible—way. The only possible way—as impossible. Before any restitution, symbolic or real, before any gratitude, the simple memory, in truth the mere awareness of the gift, by giver or receiver, annuls the very essence of the gift. The gift must open or break the circle, remain without return, without a sketch, even a symbolic one, of gratitude. Beyond any consciousness, of course, but also beyond any symbolic structure of the unconscious. Once the gift is received, the work having worked to the extent of changing you through and through, the scene is other and you have forgotten the gift and the giver. Then the work is "loveable," and if the "author" is not forgotten, we have for him or her a paradoxical gratitude, which is however the only gratitude worth its name if it is possible, a simple gratitude without ambivalence. That is what's called love, I'm not saying that it happens, perhaps it never *presents itself*, and the gift I'm describing can doubtless never make a present. At least one can dream of this possibility, and it is the idea of a writing that gives.

As for the other greatness, I shall say, with some injustice perhaps, that for me it's like Joyce's greatness, or rather that of Joyce's writing. Here the event deploys such plot and scope that henceforth you have only one way out: *being in memory of him*. Not only overwhelmed by him, whether you know it or not, but obliged by him, constrained to measure yourself against this overwhelming.

Being in memory of him: not necessarily to remember him, no, but to be in his memory, to inhabit a memory henceforth greater than all your finite recall can gather up, in a single instant or a single vocable, of cultures, languages, mythologies, religions, philosophies, sciences, histories of spirit or of literatures. I don't know if you can love that, without resentment and without jealousy. Can one pardon this hypermnesia which indebts you in advance? In advance and forever it inscribes you in the book you are reading. One can pardon this, this Babelian act of war only if it happens always, from all time, with each event of writing, thus suspending each one's responsibility. One can pardon it only if one remembers too that Joyce himself must have endured this situation. We remember it because he first wanted to remind us of it. He was the patient of this situation, it's his theme, or, I prefer to say, his scheme. He talks about it often enough for there to be no simple confusion between him and some sadistic demiurge, setting up a hypermnesiac machine, there in advance, decades in advance, to compute you, control you, forbid you the slightest inaugural syllable. For you can say nothing that is not programed on this 1000th-generation computer, *Ulysses*, *Finnegans Wake*, compared with which the current technology of our computers and our micro-computerized archives and our translating machines remains a *bricolage*, a prehistoric child's toy. A toy whose mechanisms, especially, drag their feet. Their slowness is incommensurable with the quasi-infinite speed of the movements on Joyce's cabling. And how could one simulate a work of this type? If these questions are so formidable, this is because they do not primarily concern the speed of the mental *operations* of a subject (author or reader). What is the speed in question here, then? How could one calculate the speed with which a mark, an indexed piece of information, is placed in relation with another in the "same" word or from one end of the book to the other? For example, at what speed is the Babelian theme or the word "Babel," in each of their components (but how could you count them?), coordinated with *all* the phonemes, semes, mythemes, etc., of *Finnegans Wake*? The criterion of speed is perhaps not pertinent: it comes under a kinetic objectivity with no common measure with the essence of what is taking place here. Here and everywhere else, but Joyce's work has for us the privilege of having made these questions a *practical* challenge, right on the work, a work whose structure and theme make this provocation explicit. Counting the connections, calculating the speed of the communications or the length they travel, would at least be impossible, *de facto*, so long as we have not constructed the machine capable of integrating all the variables, all the quantitative or qualitative factors. This won't be happening any time soon. In any case this machine would only be the weighty double of the "Joyce" event, the simulation of what this name signs or signifies, the signed work, the Joyce software today, *joyceware*. No doubt it is being built, the worldwide institution of Joyce studies, James Joyce Inc. is working on it, unless it already is it.

It is with this sentiment, or one should say this resentment, that I must have been reading Joyce for a long time. Am I the only one? Ellmann has recently quoted the avowals of so many writers, critics, artists, all admirers or friends of Joyce, who expressed something of this malaise. But I'm not sure that one can say "reading Joyce" as I just have. Of course, one can do nothing but read Joyce, whether one knows it or not. But the utterances of the type: "I am reading Joyce," "read Joyce," "have you read Joyce?" have always seemed to me to be comical, irresistibly. Joyce is the one who wanted to make us laugh, burst out laughing when faced with such phrases. What exactly do you mean by "read Joyce"? Who can pride himself on having "read" Joyce?

Imprisoned in this admiring resentment, one remains on the edge of reading; for me this has been going on for more than twenty-five years, and the endless diving in throws me back onto the bank, on the brink of another possible dip, *ad infinitum*. Is this true to the same extent of all works? In any case, I have the feeling that I haven't yet begun to read Joyce, and this "not having begun to read" defines the odd—I would even say active and invasive—relationship I have with this work. For there are so many other oeuvres, as you know, of which we can say no such thing. We have begun to read them, we have even finished reading them after the first page: a well-known program.

That is why I've never dared to *write on* Joyce. At most I've tried to mark in what I write (you were kind enough to recall this, dear Jean-Michel Rabaté, so as to incite me to talk about it) Joyce's scores [portées], Joyce's reaches [portées].[2] Beyond the musical measure that can be recognized in this word, which speaks too of the generous proliferation of the animal, I shall also hear this in it: such and such a text *bears* [porte] in truth the signature of Joyce, it *bears* Joyce and lets itself be borne by him, or even borne off [*deporter*] in advance. Paradoxical logic of this relationship between two unequal texts, two programs or two literary "softwares." Whatever the difference between them, to the point of incommensurability, the "second" text, the one which, fatally, refers to the other, quotes it, exploits it, parasites it and deciphers it, is no doubt the minute parcel *detached* from the other, the offspring, the metonymic dwarf, the jester of the great anterior text which would have declared war on it in tongues. And yet (one can see this precisely with Joyce's books which play both roles, the ancestor and the descendant), it is also another set, quite other, bigger and more powerful than the all-powerful which it drags off and reinscribes elsewhere, in another sequence, in order to defy, with its ascendancy, genealogy itself. Each writing resembles not the grandson as grandfather, but, beyond Oedipus, *both* a detached fragment of a program and a more powerful program than the other, a part derived from but already bigger than the whole of which it is *a part*, from which it is *apart* [*dont elle est* partie].

Finnegans Wake already represents this parting, this departure, and this partition with respect to all the culture, all the history and all the languages it condenses, puts in fusion and fission by each of its forgings, at the heart of each lexical or syntactic unit, with each phrase that it forges, stamping invention on it. In the simulacrum of this forgery, in the ruse of the invented word, the greatest possible memory is stamped and smelted.

Finnegans Wake is a little, a little what?, a little son, a very little grandson of Western culture in its circular, encyclopedic, Ulyssean and more than Ulyssean totality. And then it is, simultaneously, much bigger than even this odyssey. *Finnegans Wake* comprehends it, and this prevents it, dragging it outside itself in an entirely singular adventure, from closing in on itself and on this event. What is called writing is the paradox of such a topology.

Given this, the future holds itself in reserve. The "situation" of *Finnegans Wake* thus also prefigures our "situation" with respect to this immense text. In this war of languages, everything we could say after it looks in advance like a minute self-commentary with which this work accompanies itself. And yet the new marks carry off, enlarge, and project elsewhere—one never knows where in advance—a program that appeared to constrain them, or at least watch over them.

This is our only chance, minuscule but completely open.

III

I'm replying to your suggestion, then. Yes, every time I write, and even in academic things, Joyce's ghost is always coming on board. Twenty years ago, in *Husserl's Origin of Geometry: An Introduction*,[3] at the very center of the book, I compared the strategies of Husserl and of Joyce: two great models, two paradigms with respect to thought, but also with respect to a certain "operation" of the relationship between language and history. Both try to grasp a pure historicity. To do this, Husserl proposes to render language as transparent as possible, univocal, limited to that which, by being transmittable or locatable in a tradition, thereby constitutes the only condition of a possible historicity. Some minimal readability, an element of univocity or an analyzable equivocality, must resist the Joycean overload and condensation for a reading *to begin to take place*, and for the work's legacy, even if it is always in the mode of "I would never have started reading." For example, something of the meaning of *He war* must cross the threshold of intelligibility, through the thousand and one meanings of the expression, for a history to take place, if at least it is to take place, and at least the history of the work. The other great paradigm would be the Joyce of *Finnegans Wake*. He repeats and mobilizes and babelizes the asymptotic totality of the equivocal. He makes this his theme and his operation. He tries to bring to the surface, with the greatest possible synchrony, at top speed, the greatest power of the meanings buried in each syllabic fragment, subjecting each atom of writing to fission in order to overload its unconscious with the whole memory of man: mythologies, religions, philosophies, sciences, psychoanalysis, literatures. And the operation deconstructs the hierarchy which, in one sense or another, subordinates these latter categories to one or another of them. This generalized equivocality does not translate one language into another on the basis of common nuclei of meaning. It talks several languages at once, it parasites them as in the example of *He war* to which I shall return in a moment. For there will remain the question of knowing what one should think of the possibility: writing several languages at once.

A few years later, I had the feeling that without too much difficulty one could have presented "Plato's Pharmacy" as a sort of indirect, perhaps distracted, reading of *Finnegans Wake*, which mimes, between Shem and Shaun, between the penman and the postman, down to the finest, most finely ironized detail, the whole scene of the *pharmakos*, the *pharmakon*, the various functions of Thoth, th'other, etc. I cannot here reconstitute, even remotely, the extreme complexity of this network. I had to be content with playing, in a single note, at recalling that, of course, "as will quickly have been understood," the whole of "Plato's Pharmacy" was only "a reading of *Finnegans Wake*."[4] This double genitive implied that this modest essay was read in advance by *Finnegans Wake*, in its wake or its lineage, at the very moment that "Plato's Pharmacy" was itself presenting itself as a reading-head or principle of decipherment (in short another piece of software) for a possible understanding of *Finnegans Wake*. There again, there is a paradoxical metonymy: the most modest, the most miserable descendant of a corpus, its sample in another language, can appear to be more capacious than what it allows to be read.

I pass quickly over "Scribble,"[5] the title of that introduction to the *Essai sur les hiéroglyphes*, a partial translation of Warburton's essay, in which, beyond even the title and the quotations, I constantly refer to *Scribbledehobble: The Ur-Workbook for Finnegans Wake* (1961).

And I pass quickly over *Glas*, which is also a sort of *Wake*, from one end to the other, the long procession in two columns of a joyful theory, a theory of mourning.

Above all, a few years later, *The Post Card* is haunted by Joyce, whose funerary stele stands at the center of the "Envois" (the visit to the cemetery in Zurich). The specter invades the book, a shadow on every page, whence the resentment, sincere and feigned, always mimed, of the signatory. He sometimes confides his impatience in his addressee, whom, in the first words of the book, two years earlier, he had conceded was right ("Yes, you were right . . ."):

> You are also right about Joyce, one time is enough. It's so strong that in the end nothing resists it, whence the feeling of facility, however deceptive it might be. One asks oneself what he wound up doing, that one, and what made him run. After him, no more starting over, draw the veil and let everything come to pass behind the curtains of language at the end of its rope. A coincidence nonetheless, for that seminar on translation I followed all the Babelian indications in *Finnegans Wake* and yesterday I wanted to take the plane to Zurich and read out loud sitting on his knees, starting with the

beginning (Babel, the fall, and the Finno-Phoenician motif, *"the fall (bababadalgh) [. . .]. The great fall of the offwall entailed at such short notice the pftjschute of Finnegan [. . .] Phall if you but will, rise you must: and none so soon either shall the pharce for the nunce come to a setdown secular phoenish . . ."*) up to the passage on Gigglotte's Hill and Babbyl Market toward the end, passing through *"The babbelers with their thangas vain have been (confusium hold them!) [. . .] Who ails tongue coddeau, aspace of dumbillsilly? And they fell upong one another: and themselves they have fallen . . ."* and through *"This battering babel allower the door and sidenposts . . ."* and the entire page up to *"Filons, filoosh! Cherchons la flamme! Fammfamm! Fammfamm!"* through this passage which you know better than anyone (p. 164) and in which I suddenly find *"the babbling pumpt of platinism,"* through that other one around *"the turrace of Babbel,"* the entire passage about Anna Livia Plurabelle, translated in part, in which you will find things that are absolutely unheard of; and that everything that comes around *"A and aa ab ad abu abiad. A babbel men dub gulch of tears"* or around *"And shall not Babel be with Lebab? And he war. And he shall open his mouth and answer: I hear, O Ismael . . . And he deed . . . ,"* up to *"O Loud . . . Loud . . . Ha he hi ho hu. Mummum."* I draw out the text, as one says of actors, at least up to *"Usque! Usque! Usque! Lignum in . . . Is the strays world moving mound of what static babel is this, tell us?"* (PC 240–41/257–58)

Elsewhere, in front of Joyce's funerary monument: "He has read all of us—and plundered us, that one. I imagined him looking at himself posed there—by his zealous descendants I suppose" (PC 148/161).

Read and pillaged in advance, then. The whole scriptural and postal scenography of *Finnegans Wake* is put back into play, starting with the couple Shem/Shaun, the penman/the postman, up to the war over the invention of the postage stamp and the penny post which is to be found written in Joyce's book (PC 138–39, 142/151, 155). With a whole family of James, Jacques, Giacomo, *Giacomo Joyce* runs rhythmically through the *Envois* which are sealed, near the end, by the *Envoy* of Giacomo Joyce: "Envoy: love me love my umbrella."

> 11 *August* 1979 ⟨. . .⟩ James (the two, the three), Jacques, Giacomo Joyce—your *counterfacture* is a marvel, the counterpart to the *invoice*: "Envoy: love me love my umbrella."
>
> ⟨. . .⟩ I forgot, Giacomo also has seven letters. Love my *ombre, elle*—not me. "Do you love me?" And you, tell me (PC 238–39/255).

But I repeat, it is above all the Babelian motif which obsesses the "Envois." Here we get back to the *he war* to which I should like to return in conclusion. If you will permit, I shall read first a fragment of the card which quotes the "he war":

> *no my love that's my wake*. The other day, while speaking to you about all these pp (private *picture postcard* and *penny post*), I was first of all struck by this: prepayment institutes a general equivalent which regulates the tax according to the size and weight of the *support* and not the number, tenor or quality of the "marks," even less on what they call the meaning. This is unjust and stupid, barbarous, even, but of an immense import [*d'une immense portée*]. Whether you put one word or one hundred in a letter, a word of one hundred letters or one hundred words of seven letters, the price is the same, this is incomprehensible, but this principle has the capacity to account for everything. Let's drop it. In writing *penny post* I had also foretold in my memory that *Jean le facteur* (Shaun, John *the postman*) was not very far off. Another fraternal couple in pp making war on itself, *the penman and the postman*. The writer, Shem, is the heir of H.C.E., *Here Comes Everybody*, which I translate in my idiom as "Here comes whoever will have in body loved me" ["*Ici vient quiconque m'aura en corps animé*"]. So I looked for the *penny post* for two hours, and here it is, at least here is one that one day you might bind to an all-powerful "*he war*" (YHWH declaring war by decreeing *la dichemination*, by deconstructing the tower, by saying to those who wished both to make a name for themselves, the Chemites, and to impose their particular language as the universal language, by saying "Babel" to them, I call myself and I impose my name as father, a name that you confusedly understand as "Confusion," try, I beg you, to translate but indeed I hope that you will not be able to, this is my *double-bind*) while passing through "*his penisolate war*" and the "*sosie sesthers*" of the first page. Here then, from page 307 of *Finnegans Wake*: "Visit to Guinness' Brewery, Clubs, Advantages of the Penny Post, When is a Pun not a Pun?" Facing this, in the margin in italics, the names, you know. Here: "Noah. Plato. Horace. Isaac. Tiresias." On the preceding page, I'm sampling only this, for later: "A Place for Everything and Everything in its Place, Is the Pen mightier than the Sword?" which pulls the following string for example (p. 211): "a sunless map of the month, including the sword and stamps, for Shemus O'Shaun the Post . . ." Reread what follows in the vicinities of "Elle-trouve-tout" and "Where-is-he?; whatever you like . . . ," etc. Look at them, Sword/Pen.

I just called you, it was impossible, you understood clearly, one has to be naked on the telephone. But at the same time it suffices that you undress for me to see myself naked. Our story is also a twin progeniture, a procession of Sosie/sosie, Atreus/Thyestes, Shem/Shaun, S/p, p/p, (*penman/postman*) and more and more I metempsychose myself from you, I am with the others as you are with me (for the better, but also, I see clearly, for the worse, I do the same things to them). Never have I imitated anyone so irresistibly. I am trying to shake myself for if I love you infinitely I do not love everything about you I mean those inhabitants of you with their little hats

the uniquely each time that I love: beyond everything that is, you are the one—and therefore the other. (PC 141–43/154–55)

IV

"He war," then. Then, *he war*. I speak, I read: he *was*, then in several languages.

But how to read these two words? Are there two of them? More or less? How to hear them? How to pronounce them? How to pronounce on their subject?

The question "how to hear them?" multiplies itself, moreover. It echoes in the passage from which I extract these two words with the unjustifiable violence that the situation imposes on us, the little time at our disposal. How to hear them? Everything around speaks of the ear and to the ear: what speaking means but first what *listening* means: lending one's ear (*e ar, he, ar, ear, hear*) and obeying the father who raises his voice, the lord who talks loud (*Lord, loud*). What rises so high is praise (*laud*). This audio-phonic dimension of the divine law and its sublime height is announced in the English syllabification of *he(w)ar*, is doubled in the *w* and disseminates, for both seme and form, on the whole page.[6] The rhythm of biblical writing is mimed by the "And . . ." of "And he war . . ." I read very loudly:

> And let Nek Nekulon extol Mak Makal and let him say unto him: Immi ammi Semmi. And shall not Babel be with Lebab? And he war. And he shall open his mouth and answer: I hear, O Ismael, how they laud is only as my loud is one. If Nekulon shall be havonfalled surely Makal haven hevens. Go to, let us extell Makal, yea, let us exceedingly extell. Though you have lien amung your posspots my excellency is over Ismael. Great is him whom is over Ismael and he shall mekanek of Mak Nakulon. And he deed. Uplouderamainagain!

For the Clearer of the Air from on high has spoken in tumbuldum tambaldam to his tembledim tombaldoom worrild and, moguphonoised by that phonemanon the unhappitents of the earth have terrerumbled from fimament unto fundament and from tweedledeedumms down to twiddledeedees.

Loud, hear us!

Loud, graciously hear us!

Now have thy children entered into their habitations. And nationglad, camp meeting over, to shin it, Gov be thanked! Thou hast closed the portals of the habitations of thy children and thou hast set thy guards thereby, even Garda Didymus and Garda Domas, that thy children may read in the book of the opening of the mind to light and err not in the darkness which is the afterthought of thy nomatter by the guardiance of those guards which are thy bodemen, the cheeryboyum chirryboth with the kerrybommers in their krubeems, Pray-your-Prayers Timothy and Back-to-Bunk Tom.

Till tree from tree, tree among trees, tree over tree become stone to stone, stone between stones, stone under stone for ever.

O Loud, hear the wee beseech of thees of each of these they unlitten ones! Grant sleep in hour's time, O Loud! That they take no chill. That they do ming no merder. That they shall not gomeet madhowiatrees. Loud, heap miseries upon us yet entwine our arts with laughters low!

Ha he hi ho hu.

Mummum. (258.11–259.10)

Let us leave to one side, given the lack of time, numerous intersecting motifs, accumulated or condensed in the immediate context of "he war" (fall "Byfall," the curtain drops, applause—"Upploud!" "Uplouderamainagain!"—after the *Gotterdämmerung*-"gttrdmrnrng"; the double: Garda Didymus and Garda Domas, the two policemen; Vico's ghost everywhere, the children's prayer, etc. (257–58), and let us limit ourselves, so to speak, to all that passes through the voice and the phenomenon, the phenomenon as phoneme: at the center of the sequence, hear the "phonemanon."

It reflects, in a state of extreme concentration, the whole Babelian adventure of the book, or rather its Babelian underside: "And shall not Babel be with Lebab?" The palindrome overturns the tower of Babel. It also speaks of the book.[7]

A few examples among others:

"The babbelers with their thangas vain have been (confusium hold them!) they were and went; thigging thugs were and houhnhymn songtoms were and comely norgels were and pollyfool fiansees. ⟨. . .⟩ And they fell upong one another: and themselves they have fallen" (15.12–19); or again: "and we list, as she bibs us, by the waters of babalong" (103.10–11), "the babbling pumpt of platinism" (164.11), "the turrace of Babel" (199.31), "Is the strays world moving mound or what static babel is this, tell us?" (499.33–34), "to my reputation on Babbyl Malket for daughters-in-trade being lightly clad." (532.24–26), etc. . . .

In the landscape immediately surrounding the *he war*, we are, if such a present and such a place are possible, at Babel. It's the moment when Yahweh declares war, *he war* (exchange of the final R and the central H in the anagram's throat), he punishes the Shem, those who, according to Genesis, declare their intention of building the tower *to make a name for themselves*. They bear the name "name" (Shem). And the Lord, the Most High, be he blessed (*Lord, loud, laud*), declares war on them by interrupting the construction of the tower. He deconstructs by speaking the vocable of his choice, the name of confusion (*bavel*) which by confusion, in the hearing, could be confused with a word indeed signifying "confusion." Once this war is declared, he was it (*war*) by being himself this act of war which consisted in declaring, as he did, that He was the one He was (*war*). The God of fire assigns to the Shem the necessary, fatal, and impossible translation of his name, of the vocable with which he signs his act of war, of himself. The palindrome ("And shall not Babel be with Lebab?") overthrows the tower but plays too with the meaning and the letter, the meaning of being and the letters of being, of "being,"[8] (*be, eb, baBEl/lEBab*), as it does with the meaning and the letter of the name of God, EL, LE. The names of the father (*Dad, Bab*) are moreover dispersed on the same page, along with those of the Lord and of an Anglo-Saxon god (*Go to, Gov*) which can spread out elsewhere into governor and *scapegoat*.

This act of war is not necessarily anything other than an election, an act of love, the very alliance. We would have to reread here the prodigious pages around this "paleoparisien schola of tinkers and spanglers who say I'm wrong *parcequeue* . . ." (151.9–10). We would find the following: ". . . for aught I care for the contrary, the all is *where* in love as war and the plane where . . ." (151.36–152.1). And as in Ponge's *Le Soleil placé en abîme*, the redheaded whore is not far from the father, in his very bed she becomes one with him: "*In my Lord's Bed by One Whore* . . ." (105.34). This is in the great series introduced by "Thus we hear of . . ." (104.5). But I break off this reconstruction here.

So what happens when one tries to translate this "he war"? It is impossible not to want, to want violently, to do so. Reading even consists, from its very first movement, in sketching out translation. "He war" calls for translation, both orders and forbids transposition into the other language. Change me—into yourself—and above all do not touch me, read and do not read, say and do not say otherwise what I have said and which will have been: in two words *which was*. Alliance and double-bind. For the "he war" also tells of the unreplaceability of the event that it is. It is what it is, which is also unchangeable because it has already been, a past without appeal which, before being and being present, was. So that's war declared. Before being, that is being a present, it was: was *he, fuit*, the late god of fire the jealous god.⁹ And the call to translate rejects you: thou shalt not translate me. Which will also perhaps be translated in the banning of translation (as "representation," "image," "statue," "imitation," so many inadequate translations of "temunah").¹⁰ It immediately follows the moment at which YHWH names himself ("Me, YHWH, your Elohim . . ."). The law enounced in the performative dimension is thus also the ban on the very principle of translation, the ban in the very principle of translation, as one and the same experience of language, of the one language as one God. And, just as impossible, transgression consists, among other things, in translating *just that*. And in perverting into a description or a constatation (*he war*) in the third person, what was a first-person performative, the performative of the first person or rather of the first word.

V

What happens when one attempts to translate *he war*?

Nothing, everything.

Beyond immense difficulties, an essential limit remains. The difficulties: is it possible to make heard, to hear, all the semantic, phonic, graphic virtualities that communicate with the *he war* in the totality of the book and elsewhere? The essential limit repeats Babel, the act of war declared, but not declared, that Joyce is reprinting here. It pertains to the graft, without any possible rejection, of one language onto the body of another.

In two words, of which each figures the head, the capital or, if you prefer, the principal member of the phrase: the subject, the verb.

Imagine the most powerful and refined translation machines, the most competent translation teams. Their very success cannot but take the form of a failure. Even if, in an improbable hypothesis, they had translated everything, they would by that very fact fail to translate the multiplicity of languages. They would erase the following simple fact: a multiplicity of idioms, not only of meanings but of idioms, must have structured this event of writing which now stands as law. It will have laid down the law *about itself*. It *was* written *simultaneously* in both English and German. Two words in one, *war*, and thus a double noun, a double verb, a noun and a verb which were in the beginning. *War* is an English noun, a German verb, it resembles an adjective (*wahr*) in that same language, and the truth of this multiplicity returns, from the attributes—the verb is also an attribute: who is he? The one who was—back toward the subject, *he*, and is divided from the origin.

In the beginning, difference, that's what happens, that's what has already taken place, *there*, that's what was when language [*le langage*] was act, and the tongue [*la langue*] writing. Where it was, *He* was.[11]

The German *war* will only have been true (*wahr*) in declaring war on English. Making war on it in English. A war that is no less essential—of the essence—for being fratricidal. *The fact* of the multiplicity of languages, what was *done* as confusion of languages can no longer let itself be led back, by translation, into *one* language, nor even (I'll come to this in a moment) into *language* [la *langue*].

To translate "he war" into the system of a single language[12] is to erase the event of the mark, not only of *what* is said in it but its saying and writing, which also form, in this case, the essential content of what is said. It is to erase the mark of its law and the law of the mark. The current concept of translation is still regulated according to the *twice one*, the operation of passing from one language into another, each of them forming an organism or a system the rigorous integrity of which remains presupposed, like that of a body proper. The translation of the Babelism involving at least two languages would demand an equivalent that would restore not only all the semantic and formal potentialities of the hapax *he war*, but also the multiplicity of languages in it, the *coition* of that event, in truth its very number, its numerous and rhythmic essence, the one different in itself, and from itself, in the *différance* of itself, as Heraclitus would have said in French.

You can always try. Translation is necessary. Is that not what I am doing here? Yes, but you need more than two words. So I am not translating, or am translating without translating. It is not only *Finnegans Wake* which here resembles a too-powerful, oversized calculator incommensurable with any translating machine conceivable today. It is already the event that the book translates, mimes, *repeats*, it is the act of war before which it, *Finnegans Wake*, will have presented itself. This event *was*, it remains impossible to erase but one can only erase it. And what was in the beginning is just that, this drama, this "action" that can only be erased because it is impossible to erase. Not an event with a double character: erasable/unerasable. This very duplicity, this war internal to the "action" that is an act of language, or rather, as we are going to *see*, of writing, that is the very event, as it was in truth: war, the essence of war. Not the God of war, but war in God, war for God, war *in* the name of God as one says fire *in* the forest, war taking hold in the name of God. There is no war without a name of God and no

God without war. That is, see above, without love. You can translate war as love, it is in the text.

For a little while now, I've been speaking out loud.

In proffering *he war*, I entrust myself to this truth, so often recalled: in this book, in this event worked on by the confusion of languages, multiplicity remains controlled by a dominant language, English. Now despite the need to "phonetize," despite this book's appeal for reading out loud, for song and for timbre, something essential in it passes the understanding as well as the hearing,[13] hear in that a graphic or literal dimension, literally literal, a muteness that one should never pass over in silence. You can't do without it. This book could not be read without it.

For the Babelian confusion between the English *war* and the German *war* cannot fail to disappear, in becoming determined, when listened to. One must choose, and it is always a drama. Confusion, in difference, is erased; and with confusion the difference is also erased when it is pronounced. One is constrained to *say* it *either* in English *or else* in German. It cannot therefore be received as such by the ear. Nor by the eye alone. Confusion in difference requires a space *between* eye and ear, a phonetic writing inducing the pronunciation of the visible sign but resisting its pure erasure in the voice. Here the homography (*war* as an English *and* a German word) retains the effect of confusion. It shelters the Babelism which plays, then, between speech and writing. An Anglo-Saxon commerce, an exchange of a piece of merchandise (*ware*) under the standard of truth, in time of war, in the name of God. This has to pass through acts of writing. The event is linked to the spacing of its archive. It would not take place without it. You need it to be put into letters and onto the page. Erase the typeface, mute the graphic percussion, subordinate the spacing, that is, the divisibility of the letter—and here I emphasize what is inaudible, its di-*visibility*—and you would again reappropriate *Finnegans Wake* into a monolingualism, subjugate it to the hegemony of a single language. Of course this hegemony remains indisputable, but its law henceforth appears *as such*. It shows up in the course of a *war* through which English tries to erase the other, the other domesticated idioms, neo-colonized, to present them for reading from only one angle. Which was never so true. Today.

But one must also read the resistance to this commonwealth. It is pronounced but primarily written against it. Against Him. And this is indeed what happens. Between islands of language, across each island. Ireland and England would merely be emblems of this. What matters is the contamination of the language of the master by the language he claims to subjugate, on which he has declared war. In doing so he locks himself in a double-bind from which YHWH himself will not have escaped. If it is impossible to sing in German and English at one and the same time, the written form retains polyglossia by placing the tongue at risk.

He war—God's signature. In giving the law, and language, that is, languages, he declared war. The inauguration of the law, the institution of languages supposes no right, even if this originary violence claims to put an end to war, to transform it into conflict, Kant would say, that is, subject it to possible arbitration. The originary assignation of the law is neither the supposed brutality of nature or the animal, nor the manifestation of right. It is not yet that, and never again will be.

He war: the quotation of this signature replays the whole of the world's memory, in *Finnegans Wake*; one can only quote, "mention," as the speech act theorists would say, rather than "use," the "I" which thenceforth becomes "he," Him, or the "he," a pronoun cited rather than a "real" subject, aimed at by some direct reference. "He" and not "she," he who was *he* in declaring war, by the fact of the war that he made. He resounds, he gives himself to be heard, he articulates himself and makes himself heard right up to the end: in opposition to the *Mummum*, to the last murmur which closes the sequence, a maternal inarticulated syllabification which falls as close as can be to the "hush" [*chut*] or the fall [*chute*] after the last vocalization, the series of expiring vowels, voices out of breath:

Ha he hi ho hu
Mummum.

These are the last words, and they are no longer words, this is the last word of the sequence. In the series of vowels, echoing a certain IOU (I owe you) in *Ulysses*, a reading of which should happen here but cannot be fulfilled, the *he* reappears, a simple second place in the sequence of a general hubbub. And if the page is turned, after a broad blank there is the beginning of book II, chapter 2.

I content myself here with letting read and resound:

As we there are where are we are we there UNDE ET UBI from tomtittot to teetootomtotalitarian. Tea tea too OO. (260.1–3)

The final "Mummum," maternal syllable or infant's apostrophe of the mother could, if one so wished, be made to resound with the final *yes* [*oui*] of *Ulysses*, said to be feminine, the "yes" of Mrs Bloom, of ALP, or of any "wee" girl, as has been noted, Eve, Mary, Isis, etc. The Great Mother on the side of the river, of time, of vowel and of life, but the Father on the side of the law, creation, consonant and fall. In William York Tindall's book on *Finnegans Wake*, I came across the following sentence where the word *hill* plays more or less innocently with the personal pronoun, the third-person masculine in our language, *il*. Not to speak of the *île*, the island, and of *whore*: "As he ⟨HCE⟩ is the hill in Joyce's familial geography, so she is the river ⟨. . .⟩. This 'wee' (or *oui*) girl is Eve, Mary, Isis, any woman you can think of, and *a poule*—at once a riverpool, a whore, and a little hen."[14]

What was I saying? Yes: "I'm not sure I love Joyce . . . I'm not sure he is loved . . . except when he laughs . . . he's always laughing . . . everything is played out in the difference between several tonalities of laughter."

That is what I had suggested as I started. The question would then be this: why does laughter here traverse the whole of the experience which relates us to *Finnegans Wake*? Why does it not let itself be reduced to any of the other modalities, apprehensions, affections, whatever their richness, their heterogeneity, their overdetermination? And what does this writing teach us of the essence of laughter when it sometimes laughs at the essence, at the limits of the calculable and the incalculable? When the totality of the calculable is outplayed by a writing about which it is no longer possible to decide if it still calculates, calculates better and more, or if it transcends the very order of calculable economy, or even of an incalculable or an undecidable which would still be homogeneous with the world of calculation? A certain quality of laughter would accord something like affect to this beyond of calculation, and of all calculable literature. The word *affect* would then be indeterminate, an X still, save by what in it would expose any supposed mastering and manipulative activity of the subject to what is given beyond calculation, even before any project, any significance.

Perhaps, perhaps, this quality of laughter, and none other, resounds, very loud or very soft, I don't know, through the tears of the prayer that immediately precedes the "Ha he hi ho hu" at the end: "Loud, heap miseries upon us yet entwine our arts with laughters low."[15]

Laugh down low of the signature, sign the signature with a laugh, calm the crazy laughter and the anguish of the proper name in the murmured prayer, forgive God by asking him to let us perform the gesture of giving according to art, and the art of laughter.

At the beginning, that resentment I was talking about. Always possible with respect to Joyce. But it was a way of considering, on a small scale, Joyce's revenge with respect to the God of Babel. That vindictive God Spinoza cannot get over in the *Tractatus Theologico-Politicus*: he gave laws to avenge himself! But this God, *already*, tortured his own signature. He was this torment: *a priori* resentment with respect to any possible translator.

I order you and forbid you to translate me, to interfere with my name, to give a body of writing to its vocalization.

And through this double commandment he signs. The signature does not come after the law, it is the divided act of the law: revenge, resentment, reprisal; revindication *as* signature. But also as gift and gift of languages. And God lets himself be prayed to, he condescends and leans over (Loud/low). Prayer and laughter absolve perhaps the pain of signature, the act of war with which everything will have begun. This is art, Joyce's art, the space given for his signature made into the work.

He war: it's a countersignature, it confirms and contradicts, effaces by subscribing. It says "we" and "yes" in the end to the Father or to the Lord who speaks loud—there is scarcely anyone but Him—but here leaves the last word to the woman who in her turn will have said "we" and "yes."

Countersigned God, God who signeth thyself in us, let us laugh, *amen, sic, si, oc, oïl.*[16]

Notes

1. TN: The French text plays here on the homophony of "le mode oreille" and "le mot d'oreille."

2. TN: Derrida plays here and in the following sentence on three senses of the word "portée": (1) range, reach, or scope; (2) musical staff or stave; (3) litter in the veterinary sense.

3. TN: EH 102–5/104–8.

4. TN: DI 88 n.20/99 n.17.

5. TN: "Scribble (*pouvoir/écrire*)," in William Warburton, *Essai sur les hiéroglyphes* (Paris: Aubier, 1977); translated by Cary Plotkin as "Scribble (writing-power)," *Yale French Studies* 58 (1979), 116–47.

6. Along with the sense of "war," the signaling of the recourse to German, etc., this audiophonic dimension of *he war* is one of the very numerous things which must be passed over in silence in the very commendable translation of *Finnegans Wake* by Philippe Lavergne (Paris: Gallimard, 1982), which I did not know when I gave this lecture. "And he war" is rendered by "Et il en fut ainsi" (p. 278)! But let us never speak ill of translations, especially this one.

7. Philippe Lavergne recalls the two Irish words *leaba*, bed, and *leabhar*, book.

8. TN: "Joue aussi avec le sens et la lettre, le sens de l'etre et les lettres de l'etre, de 'être' ": playing on the homophony between "lettre(s)" and "*l'être.*"

9. The most serious game would consist here in consuming at this point the whole *Theological-Political Treatise*, in recognizing in it a text both larger and smaller than *Finnegans Wake*, urn and cell. The demonstration could begin at any point in either text, for example here: "But we should depart as little as possible from the literal sense, and therefore we must first ask whether this unique expression, 'God is a fire,' ⟨*Deus est ignis*⟩ admits any but a literal sense [. . .]. Now the

word "fire" also stands for anger and jealousy (see Job 31:12), and therefore Moses's statements ['God is a fire,' 'God is jealous ⟨zelotypus⟩'] are readily reconciled, and we are justified in concluding that they are one and the same. ⟨. . .⟩ Hence, we must evidently deduce that this is what Moses believed, or at least what he wanted to teach, however much we may think this statement conflicts with reason." Spinoza, *Theological-Political Treatise*, translated by Michael Silverthorne and Jonathan Israel (Cambridge: Cambridge University Press, 2007), 101. TN: I have inserted the passage in brackets on the basis of the French translation of Spinoza quoted by Derrida, it does not appear in the English. See Spinoza, *Traité des autorités théologique et politique*, trans. Madeleine Francès, chap. 7, in *Spinoza, Oeuvres Complètes*, ed. Roland Caillois, Madeleine Francès, and Robert Misrahi (Paris: Gallimard, 1954), 711–34, 715–16. In the body of the text, Derrida also plays on the sense of "feu" meaning late or deceased.

10. Michal Govrin, "The Jewish Ritual as a Genre of Sacred Theatre," *Conservative Judaism* 36:3 (1983), 15–34.

11. TN: "La où c'etait, Il fut": refers to Freud's famous closing to lecture 31 of the *New Introductory Lectures on Psychoanalysis*: "Wo es war, soll Ich warden," translated by James Strachey as "Where id was, there ego shall be" in Sigmund Freud, *The Standard Edition of the Complete Psychological Works of Sigmund Freud*, 24 volumes (London: The Hogarth Press, 1974), volume 22, 3–182; 80.

12. As has just been tried in French: "Et il en fut ainsi"! [and thus it came to pass]. No more war.

13. TN: "Quelque chose d'essentiel y passe l'entendement aussi bien que l'ecoute": the connotation of hearing (*entendre*) in "entendement" (understanding) is carried over in the translation to cover "écoute" (listening) too.

14. William York Tindall, *A Reader's Guide to "Finnegans Wake"* (London: Thames and Hudson, 1969), 4.

15. I do not know if "laughters low" can be translated, as Lavergne does, by "sourire discret." But how to translate—for example, the opposition of the first and last word of the prayer, Loud/low? And must one translate? On what criteria will one rely to decide that here one must translate, or at least try, and there not? Another example: should one, or should one not, translate "Ha he hi ho hu," where the "he" is also the homophone of a "real" word in the language? Which thus exists: *he war*. But does not the question "must one translate" arrive always too late? It cannot be the object of a deliberate decision. Translation has begun with the first reading, and even—this is the thesis of these two words—before reading. There is scarcely anything but writing in translation, as Genesis tells us. And Babel is also the difference of pitch [*hauteur*: height] in the voice (*loud/low*) as well as in space. The elevation of the tower is interrupted by the *he war*: "Let's go! Let's get down! Let's confuse their lips there, man will no longer hear his neighbor's lip" (Genesis 11: 7–8 [translated from André Chouraqui's French translation as used by Derrida]).

16. TN: One finds in Latin two distinct terms for signifying assent (*yes*): *hoc*, "this," and *hoc ille*, "this (is) it," which became *oc* and *oïl*, respectively.

Ulysses Gramophone: Hear Say Yes in Joyce

translated by François Raffoul

I

Oui, oui, you are hearing me well, these are French words.

To be sure, and I do not need to confirm it with another sentence, it suffices that you have heard this first word, *oui*, to know, at least if you know enough French, that thanks to the authorization generously granted to me by the organizers of this James Joyce Symposium, I would address you, more or less, in the language supposed to be mine [*ma langue supposée*], this last expression nevertheless remaining a quasi-Anglicism.

However, can *oui* be cited and translated? This is one of the questions that I intend to raise in this talk. How will one translate the sentences that I just sent your way? The one I began with, just as Molly begins and ends what one calls a bit lightly her monologue, namely with the repetition of a *oui*, does not merely *mention*, it *uses* in its own way the two *ouis*, those that I now cite: *oui, oui*. In my *incipit*, you could not decide, and you still cannot, whether I was telling you *oui* or whether I was citing, or, more generally speaking, whether I mentioned the word *oui* twice to recall, I am citing, that these are indeed French words.

In the first instance, I affirm or acquiesce, I subscribe, I approve, I respond or I promise, I commit myself in any case and I sign: To take up the old *speech act theory* distinction, still useful up to a point, between *use* and *mention*, the use of the *oui* is always at least implicated in the moment of a signing.

In the second instance, I would have mentioned or cited, rather, the *oui, oui*. Now, if the act of citing or mentioning no doubt also supposes some signing and confirmation of the mentioning act, it still remains implicit and the implicit *oui* is not to be confused with the cited or mentioned *oui*.

Thus, you still do not know what I meant to *say* or *do* by beginning with this sentence: "*Oui, oui*, you are hearing me well, these are French words." In truth, you do not hear me or understand me well at all.

I repeat the question: how will one translate the sentences that I just sent your way? To the extent that they mention, or cite the *oui*, it is the French word that they repeat and the translation is in principle absurd or illegitimate: *yes, yes*, these are not French words. When at the end of the *Discours de la Méthode*, Descartes explains why he decided to write in the language of his country, the Latin translation of the *Discours* simply omits this paragraph. What would be the sense of writing in Latin a sentence that essentially states: here are the good reasons why I am presently writing in French? It is true that the Latin translation was the only one to have violently erased this affirmation of the French language. For it was not indeed one translation among others, since it claimed to return the *Discours de la Méthode*, according to the prevailing law of philosophical society of the time, to what should have been the true original in its true language. Let's leave this for another occasion.[1]

I simply wanted to emphasize that the affirmation of a language by itself is untranslatable. The act that, in a language, *remarks* the language itself thus affirms it twice, once by speaking it, and once by saying that it is thus spoken; it opens the space of a *re-marking* that at once and in the same double-stroke, defies and calls for a translation. Following a distinction that I ventured elsewhere with respect to the history and name of Babel, what remains *untranslatable* is in the end the only thing to *translate*, the only thing *translatable*.[2] What is to be translated in the translatable can only be the untranslatable.

You have already understood that I was preparing the way to speak to you about the *oui*, or at least about some of its modalities, and as a first sketch in certain passages from *Ulysses*.

To put an end without delay to the interminable circulation or circumnavigation, to avoid the aporia while seeking the best beginning, I threw myself in the water, as one says in French, and I decided to surrender myself along with you to a chance encounter. With Joyce, chance is always recaptured by law, sense, and the program, in accordance with the overdetermination of figures and ruses. And yet the chance character of encounters and the random nature of coincidences are themselves affirmed, accepted, yes, even approved in all occurrences [*échéances*]. In all occurrences, that is to say, in all the genealogical chances that divert a legitimate filiation, in *Ulysses* and probably elsewhere. This is all too clear in the encounter between Bloom and Stephen, to which I will return shortly.

To throw oneself in the water, I was saying. I was thinking of the water of a lake, to be precise. But you might have thought: a bottle in the sea, you know Joyce's word. Lakes were not that foreign to him, I will clarify this further.

The chance to which I said *oui*, thereby deciding to surrender *you* to it, I shall give it the proper name of Tokyo.

Tokyo: would this city find itself in the Western circle that leads back to Dublin or Ithaca?

An errancy without calculation, the path [*randonnée*] of a *randomness*[3] led me one day to this passage ("Eumaeus," *The shelter*, 1 a.m.) where Bloom names "the coincidence of meeting, discussion, dance, row, old salt of the here today and gone tomorrow type, night loafers, the whole galaxy of events, all went to make up a miniature cameo of the world we live in" (U 16.1222–25).

"The galaxy of events" was translated in French by a "gerbe des événements"[4] that loses all the milk and thus also the milky tea that constantly irrigate *Ulysses* to precisely make of it a milky way or "galaxy." Allow me here another parenthetical. We were wondering what happens to the *oui* when it is repeated, whether in a "mention" or in a citation. What happens when it becomes a trademark, the nontransferable title of a kind of commercial license? And since we are here spinning in milk, what happens when *yes* becomes, yes, a brand or a brand name of yogurt? I will often refer to Ohio, this marked place in *Ulysses*. Now there is in Ohio a brand of Dannon yogurt which is simply called YES. And under the big YES that is on the lid, the ad slogan says: "Bet You Can't Say No to Yes."

"Coincidence of meeting," states the passage I was in the process of citing. A bit further the name *Tokyo* appears: suddenly, like a telegram or the heading of a newspaper page, *The Telegraph*, which is below Bloom's elbow, "as luck would have it" (U 16.1233), it is said at the beginning of the paragraph.

The name *Tokyo* is associated with a battle, "Great battle, Tokio" (U 16.1240). It is not Troy but Tokyo in 1904: the war with Russia.

Now I happened to be in Tokyo more than a month ago, and it is there that I began to write this lecture, or rather to dictate its main points to a small pocket tape recorder.

I decided to date it in this way—now dating is signing—that morning of May 11 when I was looking for postcards in a sort of newsstand in the "basement" of the Okura hotel. I was specifically looking for postcards portraying Japanese lakes, shall we say precisely inland seas. I had the idea of following the edges of the lake in *Ulysses*, of venturing in a great tour of the lakes, between the lake of life that is the Mediterranean Sea and the *Lacus Mortis* mentioned in the hospital scene, precisely dominated by the maternal symbol: "⟨. . .⟩ they come trooping to the sunken sea, *Lacus Mortis* [. . .]. Onward to the dead sea they tramp to drink ⟨. . .⟩" (U 14.1091–96).

In truth, I had first thought, for this lecture on *Ulysses*, to *address*, as you say in English, the scene of the postcard, in a sense the inverse of what I had done in *The Post Card*, where I had tried to restage the Babelization of the postal system in *Finnegans Wake*. You probably know this better than I, an entire set of postcards perhaps suggests the hypothesis that the geography of Ulysses' trips around the Mediterranean lake could well have the structure of a postcard or cartography of postal sendings. This will be verified progressively, but for now I am singling out a phrase from J. J. that speaks of the equivalence between a postcard and a publication. Any public writing, any open text is also offered as the displayed, not private, surface of an open letter, and thus of a postcard, with its address included in the message, hence suspect, with its language both coded and stereotypical. Trivialized by the very code and number. Reciprocally, any postcard is a public document, deprived of any *privacy*,[5] and which furthermore, by this very fact, falls under the scope of the law. This is precisely what J. J. says: "And moreover, says J. J. ⟨these are not just any initials⟩, a postcard is publication. It was held to be sufficient evidence of malice in the testcase Sadgrove v. Hole. In my opinion an action might lie" (U 12.1071–73). Translate: there would be cause for pursuing this before the law, to *sue*,[6] but also: the action could lie. At the beginning there is the *speech act* . . .[7]

One will find the trace or relay of this postcard to follow, then, in Mr. Reggy's postcard, "his silly postcard" that Gerty could tear "into a dozen pieces" (U 13.596). There is also, among others, the "postcard to Flynn" on which, in addition, Bloom remembers having forgotten to write the address, which underlines the character of anonymous publicity: a postcard does not have a proper addressee, apart from whoever acknowledges receipt through some inimitable signature. *Ulysses*, an immense postcard. "Mrs. Marion. Did I forget to write address on that letter like the postcard I sent to Flynn?" (U 13.843–44). I single out these postcards in the course of a discursive, or, more precisely, narrative path that I cannot reconstitute each time. There is here an ineluctable problem of method to which I will return later on. The postcard without address that cannot be forgotten comes back to Bloom at the very moment when he searches for a lost letter. "Where did I put the letter? Yes, all right" (U 13.779). We can assume that the reassured "yes" accompanies and confirms the return of memory: the location of the letter has been found again. A bit further, after Reggy's "silly postcard," we come across the "silly letter": "Damned glad I didn't do it in the bath this morning over her silly I will punish you letter" (U 13.786–87). Let us allow the perfume of this bath and the vengeance of the letter the time to arrive to us. This increase in derision includes Molly's sarcasms against the one who "now hes going about in his slippers to look for £10000 for a postcard U p up O sweetheart May ⟨. . .⟩" (U 18.228–29).

I was thus buying postcards in Tokyo, in an underground passage of the Okura hotel. Now the sequence that mentions, in a telegraphic style, "Great battle, Tokio," after having recalled the "coincidence of meeting," the misleading genealogy and the erratic seed that links Stephen to Bloom, the "galaxy of events," etc., is a passage from another postcard. Not, this time, from a postcard without address, but from a postcard without a message. One would therefore say from a postcard without text and which would be reduced to the mere association of an image and an address. Now it so happens that here the address is also fictitious. The addressee of this card without message is a kind of fictitious reader. Before returning to it, let us form a circle with the "Tokyo" sequence, which I must cite: It follows closely the extraordinary exchange between Bloom and Stephen on the motif of *belonging*:

> "You suspect, Stephen retorted with a sort of half laugh, that I may be important because I belong to the *faubourg Saint Patrice* called Ireland for short" (U 16.1160–62).
>
> —I would go a step farther, Mr. Bloom insinuated ⟨by rendering: "a step farther" as "*un peu plus loin*,"⁸ the French translation, notwithstanding the co-signer J. J., misses, among so many other things, the "step father" which superimposes, at the heart of all these genealogical fantasies, with their genetic crossovers and hazardous disseminations, a dream of legitimation through adoption and return of the son or through marriage with the daughter⟩.
>
> ⟨Now, one never knows who belongs to whom, what to whom, what to what, who to what. There is no subject of the belonging, no more than there is an owner of the postcard: it remains without an assigned addressee⟩.
>
> —But I suspect, Stephen interrupted, that Ireland must be important because it belongs to me.
>
> —What belongs? queried Mr. Bloom, bending, fancying he was perhaps under some misapprehension. Excuse me. Unfortunately I didn't catch the latter portion. What was it you? ⟨. . .⟩
>
> ⟨Stephen then hastens matters:⟩—We can't change the country. Let us change the subject. (U 16.1160–71)

It is not enough to go to Tokyo to change the country, or even the language.

A bit farther, then, the return of the messageless postcard addressed to a fictitious addressee. Bloom thinks of the chance nature of encounters, the galaxy of events; he dreams of writing, writing about what happens to him, as I do here, his story, "my experiences," as he says, and as it were keeping a chronicle of it, a diary [*journal*] in a newspaper [*journal*], a personal *diary* or *newspaper*, by freely associating.

Here is, we are getting to it, the postcard close to Tokyo: "the coincidence of meeting ⟨. . .⟩ the whole galaxy of events ⟨. . .⟩. To improve the shining hour he wondered whether he might meet with anything approaching the same *luck* ⟨my italics⟩ as Mr. Philip Beaufoy if taken down in writing suppose he were to pen something out of the common groove (as he fully intended doing) at the rate of one guinea per column, *My Experiences*, let us say, *in a Cabman's Shelter*" (U 16.1222–31).

My experiences, that is, both my "phenomenology of spirit," in the Hegelian sense of a "science of the experience of consciousness," and the great circular return, Ulysses' auto-biographico-encyclopedic circumnavigation: one has often spoken of the Odyssey of the phenomenology of spirit. Here, the phenomenology of spirit would have the form of a diary of consciousness and of the unconscious in the chance form of letters, telegrams, newspapers called, for instance, the *Telegraph*, long-distance writing, and finally, taken out of a sailor's pocket, postcards whose text at times only displays a phantom address.

Bloom has just spoken of *My Experiences*: "The pink edition extra sporting of the *Telegraph* tell a graphic lie lay, as luck would have it, beside his elbow and as he was just puzzling again, far from satisfied, over a country belonging ⟨still⟩ to him and the preceding rebus the vessel came from Bridgwater and the postcard was addressed A. Boudin find the captain's age, *his eyes* ⟨I emphasize the word *eyes*, I will return to this⟩ went aimlessly over the respective captions which came under his special province the allembracing give us this day our daily press. First he got a bit of a start but it turned out to be only something about somebody named H. du Boyes, agent for typewriters or something like that. Great battle, Tokio. Lovemaking in Irish, £200 damages" (U 16.1232–41).

I will not analyze here the stratigraphy of this "Tokio battle" field, experts could do that without end; the constraints of a conference only allow me to narrate to you, like a postcard cast to sea, *my experiences in Tokyo*, and then raise in passing the question of the *yes*, of chance, and of the Joycean experience as expertise: what is an expert, a PhD in things Joycean? What of the Joycean institution, and what am I to think of the hospitality that it honors me with today in Frankfurt?

Bloom associates the allusion to the postcard with what itself already presents a pure associative juxtaposition, an apparently insignificant contiguity, while underlying its insignificance: it is the question of the captain's age, which one must guess rather than calculate, after the presentation of a series of facts, the figures of a "rebus" without any obvious relation to the question at hand. Nonetheless, what this joke makes clear is that the captain is the captain of a ship.

Now the postcard is precisely the one that a sailor was talking about, a sea-traveler, a captain who, like Ulysses, returns one day from a long circular journey around a Mediterranean lake. A few pages above, same place, same time: "—Why, the sailor answered upon reflection upon it, I've circumnavigated a bit since I first joined on. I was in the Red Sea. I was in China and North America and South America. ⟨. . .⟩ I seen icebergs plenty, growlers. I was in Stockholm and the Black Sea, the Dardanelles under Captain Dalton, the best bloody man that ever scuttled a ship. I seen Russia ⟨. . .⟩ I seen maneaters in Peru ⟨. . .⟩" (U 16.458–70).

He went everywhere except to Japan, I said to myself, and yet here he is getting a messageless postcard out of his pocket. As for the address, it is fictitious, as fictitious as *Ulysses*, and this is the only thing that Ulysses has in his pockets: "He fumbled out a picture postcard from his inside pocket which seemed to be in its way a species of repository and pushed it along the table. The printed matter on it stated: *Choza de Indios. Beni, Bolivia*.

> All focussed their attention on the scene exhibited, at a group of savage women in striped loincloths ⟨. . .⟩.
>
> His postcard proved a centre of attraction for Messrs the greenhorns for several minutes, if not more. ⟨. . .⟩
>
> Mr. Bloom, without evincing surprise, unostentatiously turned over the card to peruse the partially obliterated address and postmark. It ran as follows: *Tarjeta Postal, Señor A Boudin, Galeria Becche, Santiago, Chile*. There was no message evidently, as he took particular notice.
>
> Though not an implicit believer in the lurid story narrated ⟨. . .⟩, having detected a discrepancy between his name (assuming he was the person he represented himself to be and not sailing under false colours after having boxed the compass on the strict q.t. somewhere) and the fictitious addressee of the missive which made him nourish some suspicions of our friend's *bona fides*, nevertheless ⟨. . .⟩. (U 16.473–99)

I am thus in the process of buying postcards in Tokyo, pictures of lakes, and I am apprehensive about giving an intimidated presentation before "Joyce scholars" on the *yes* in *Ulysses* and on the institution of Joyce studies, when, in the store where I find myself by chance, in the basement of the Okura hotel, "coincidence of meeting," I fall upon a book entitled *16 Ways to Avoid Saying No*, by Maasaki Imai. It was, I thought, a book of commercial diplomacy. It is said that out of courtesy Japanese avoid, as much as possible, to say *no* even if they mean to say *no*. How does one makes a *no* heard when one means to say *no* without saying it? How one translates *no* by *yes*, and what does translation mean when confronted with the singular couple of the yes/no, this is a question that awaits us in return.[9] Next to this book, on the same shelf and by the same author, another book, still in an English translation: *Never Take Yes for an Answer*.

Now, if it is very difficult to say anything with any certainty, and certainly metalinguistic, on this singular word *yes*, which names nothing, which describes nothing, and whose grammatical and semantic status is most enigmatic, I believe that one can at least affirm this about it: *it must be taken for an answer*.[10] It always has the form of an answer. It occurs after the other, to answer the claim or the question, at least implicit, of the other, even if of the other in me, of the representation in me of another speech. The *yes* implies, Bloom would say, an "implicit believer" to some call by the other. The *yes* always has the sense, the function or the mission of an *answer*, even if this answer, we will see this too, at times has the scope of an unconditional and originary commitment. Now our Japanese author advises us to never take "yes for an answer." This could mean two things: *yes* can mean *no*, or *yes* is not an answer. Outside of the diplomatic-commercial context in which it seems to be located, this cautiousness could take us further.

But I continue the chronicle of "my experiences." At the very moment when I was writing down these titles, an American tourist of the most typical type leaned over my shoulder and sighed: "So many books! What is the definitive one? Is there any?" It was a very small bookstore, a newsstand, really. I almost replied to him, "yes there are two of them, *Ulysses* and *Finnegans Wake*,"[11] but I kept this *yes* to myself and smiled dumbly like someone who does not understand the language.

II

Up to this point I have talked to you about letters in *Ulysses*, about postcards, typewriters, and telegrams: there is still missing the telephone and I must tell you about a telephonic experience.

For a long time, and still today, I thought that I would never be ready to give a lecture on Joyce before an audience of experts. What is an expert, when it comes to Joyce, this is my question. Still intimidated, and behind schedule, I found myself quite embarrassed in March when my friend Jean-Michel Rabaté called me on the phone asking me for a title. I did not have one. All I knew was that I wanted to treat the *yes* in *Ulysses*. I had even tried, casually, to count them: more than 222 occurrences of the word *yes* in the so-called original version (and we know better than ever with what caution we must use this expression).[12] I only reached that number, no doubt imprecise, after a first count that only took into account the explicit *yeses*.[13] I indeed mean the word *yes*, for there can be a *oui*, a *yes*, without the word *yes* and especially since, immense problem, the count is no longer the same in the translation. The French translation adds a lot of them. More than a quarter of these *yeses* are gathered in what is ingeniously called Molly's monologue: as soon as there is a *yes*, a break will have occurred in the monologue, and the other is connected to some telephone.

When Jean-Michel Rabaté called me, I had thus decided to question, if I can put it this way, the *yeses* of *Ulysses* as well as the institution of Joyce experts; and also what happens when a *yes* is written, cited, repeated, archived, recorded, gramophoned, and made a subject of translation and transference.

Still, I did not have a title, only a statistic and a few notes on a single page. I asked Rabaté to wait a minute, I went back up to my room, took a quick look at the page of notes, and a title came to mind with a sort of irresistible brevity, the authority of a telegraphic order: the saying yes in Joyce [*l'oui dire de Joyce*]. You are hearing me well, the saying *yes* in Joyce but also the saying or the *yes* that is heard, the *saying yes* that travels like a citation or like a circulating rumor, circumnavigating through the labyrinth of the ear, what one only knows through *ouï-dire*, hearsay.[14]

This can only play out in French, in the confused and Babelian homonymy between the *oui*, with only one dotted "i" [*un point sur l'i c'est tout*[15]] and the *ouï* with an umlaut or two points. The untranslatable homonymy can be heard (by hearsay, then) more than it can be read *with the eyes*,[16] this last word, *eyes*, I should note in passing, itself giving the grapheme *yes* to be read more than heard. *Yes* in *Ulysses* can thus only be a mark that is both spoken and written, vocalized as grapheme and written as phoneme, yes, *in a word gramophoned*.

The *ouï dire* thus seemed to me a good title, sufficiently untranslatable and potentially capable of encapsulating what I wanted to say about the *yes* of Joyce. Rabaté said "yes" to me over the phone, agreeing with that title. A few days later, less than a week, I received his wonderful book, *Joyce, portrait de l'auteur en autre lecteur*, whose fourth chapter is entitled "Molly: ouï-dire" (with an umlaut).[17] "Curious coincidence, Mr. Bloom confided to Stephen unobtrusively" (U 16.414), at the moment when the sailor declares that he already knew Simon Dedalus; "coincidence of meeting" (U 16.1222–23), Bloom says a bit later about his encounter with Stephen. I therefore decided to keep this title as a subtitle to commemorate the coincidence, certain as I was that we were not telling the same story under that same title.

Now, and Jean-Michel Rabaté can attest to this, it was during a similar chance encounter (I was driving my mother and jumped out of my car onto a Paris street when I saw Jean-Michel Rabaté) that we later told each other, after my return from Japan, that this coincidence had to have been "telegraphed," as it were, through a rigorous program whose pre-recorded necessity—as on an answering machine, and even if it went through a great number of wires—must have gathered in some central site and acted upon us, one and the other, one with or on the other, one before the other without any possibility of assigning any legitimate belonging. But this story of correspondences and telephones does not end here. Rabaté must have shared with someone by telephone my title, which did not fail to produce certain deformations, specifically Joycean and programmed at the expert center, since one day I received a letter on letterhead from the Ninth International James Joyce Symposium from Klaus Reichert with this paragraph: "I am very curious to know about your Lui/Oui's which could be spelt Louis as well I suppose. And the Louis' have not yet been detected in Joyce as far as I know. Thus it sounds promising from every angle."

There is at least one fundamental difference between Rabaté, Reichert, and myself, as there is between all of you and myself, namely competence. All of you are experts, and belong to the most singular of institutions. That institution bears the name of the one who has done everything, and said so, to make it indispensable and to make it function for centuries, like a new tower of Babel to "make a name" again, like a powerful reading, signing, and countersigning machine in the service of his name, of his "patent." But this is an institution that, as in the case of God with the tower of Babel, he did everything to render impossible and improbable in its principle, to deconstruct in advance, to the point of undermining the very concept of a competence on which an institutional legitimacy could be based, whether it is a competence in knowledge or know-how.

Before returning to this question, that is, the question of what you and I are doing here, with competence and incompetence, I remain a few moments more connected on the phone, before interrupting a more or less telepathic communication with Jean-Michel Rabaté.

We have up to this point accumulated letters, postcards, telegrams, typing machines, etc. One must recall that if *Finnegans Wake* is the sublime Babelization of a *penman* and a *postman*,[18] the motif of postal *différance*, of remote control [*télécommande*] and telecommunication, is already powerfully at work in *Ulysses*. And this is even *remarked*, as always, *en abyme*. For instance, in "THE WEARER OF THE CROWN": "Under the porch of the general post office shoeblacks called and polished. Parked in North Prince's street His Majesty's vermilion mailcars, bearing on their sides the royal initials, E. R., received loudly flung sacks of letters, postcards, lettercards, parcels, insured and paid, for local, provincial, British and overseas delivery" (U 7.15–19). This "remote control" technology of television is not an external contextual element, as it affects from within the most elemental meaning, including the inscription or statement of the quasi smallest word, the gramophony of the *yes*. This is why the circumnavigating errancy of a postcard, letter, or telegram displaces destinations only in the continuous buzzing sound of a telephonic obsession, or, if you take into account a gramophone or an answering machine, a telegramophonic obsession.

If I am not mistaken, the first phone call rang with these words from Bloom: "Better phone him up first" (U. 7.219) in the sequence entitled "AND IT WAS THE FEAST OF THE PASSOVER" (U 7.203). A little earlier, he had repeated, a bit mechanically, like a record, this prayer, the most serious for a Jew, the one that should never be allowed to become mechanical or be gramophoned, "*Shema Israel. Adonai Elohenu*" (U 7.209).

If, more or less legitimately (for everything is legitimate and nothing is when one borrows some segment in the name of a narrative metonymy), one singles out this element in the most manifest thread of the story, one can then speak of a telephonic *Shema Israel* between God, who is at an infinite distance (*a long distance call, a collect call from or to the "collector of prepuces"* [U 1.394; 9.609]),[19] and Israel. *Shema Israel* means, as you know, call to Israel, listen Israel, hello Israel, address to the name of Israel, *a person-to-person call*.[20] The scene of the "better phone him up first" takes place in the offices of the newspaper *The Telegraph* [*Le télégramme*] (and not *The Tetragram*) and Bloom had just stopped to watch a type of typewriter, or rather, a typesetting machine, a typographic matrix ("He stayed in his walk to watch a typesetter neatly distributing type" [U 7.204]). And since he "Reads it backwards first" (U7.205), composing the name Patrick Dignam, the name of the father, Patrick, from right to left, he recalls his own father reading the Haggadah in the same way. In this paragraph, around Patrick, one could follow the whole series of fathers, of the twelve sons of Jacob, etc., and the word "practice" appears twice to chant this patristic and *perfectly* paternal litany. ("Quickly he does it. Must require some practice." And twelve lines lower, "How quickly he does that job. Practice makes perfect.") Almost immediately thereafter, we read: "better phone him up first": "plutôt un coup de téléphone pour commencer," says the French translation.[21] Let us say: a phone call [*un coup de téléphone*], rather, to begin. In the beginning, there must have been some phone call.

Before the act, or the word, was the telephone. In the beginning was the telephone. We can hear this *coup de téléphone*, which plays on apparently random numbers and on which there would be much to say, ring all the time. And it opens within itself this *yes* toward which we slowly return, circling around it. There are several modalities or tonalities of the telephonic *yes*, but one of them amounts to simply registering that we are *there*, present, listening, on the end of the line, ready to answer but without answering anything else for the moment than the readiness to answer (hello, yes: I am listening, I hear that you are there, ready to talk at the moment when I am ready to talk with you). In the beginning was the telephone, yes, at the beginning of the phone call.

A few pages after the "Shema Israel" and the first phone call, right after the unforgettable Ohio scene under the title of *Memorable Battles Recalled* (you are hearing well that from Ohio to the Tokyo battle a voice moves very quickly), a certain telephonic *yes* resonates with a "bingbang" that recalls the origin of the universe. A competent professor just passed by. "—A Perfect cretic! the professor said. Long, short and long," after the cry "Ohio!," "My Ohio!" (U 7.367–69). Then, at the beginning of "O, HARP EOLIAN!" (U 7.370), there is the sound of trembling teeth as one applies "dental floss" (and if I tell you that that very year, before going to Tokyo, I had passed through Oxford, Ohio, and even bought "dental floss"—that is, an Eolian harp—in a drugstore in Ithaca, you would not believe me. You would be wrong, it is true and can be verified). When the "resonant unwashed teeth" vibrate in the mouth to the "dental floss," one hears: "Bingbang, bangbang" (U 7.374); Bloom then asks to make a call. "I just want to phone about an ad" (U 7.376). Then "the telephone whirred inside" (U 7.384). This time the Eolian harp is no longer the "dental floss" but the telephone, the cables of which are elsewhere the "navel cords" that connect to Eden. "—Twenty eight. No. Twenty. Double four, yes" (U 7.385). One does not know whether this *Yes* is in a monologue, approving the other within (yes, this is the right number) or whether he is already speaking to the other at the end of the line. And one cannot know. The context is cut, it is the end of the sequence.

Yet at the end of the following sequence ("SPOT THE WINNER"), the telephonic "yes" rings again in the very same offices of *The Telegraph*: "—Yes, *Evening Telegraph* here, Mr. Bloom phoned from the inner office. Is the boss . . .? Yes, *Telegraph*. . . . To where? Aha! Which auction rooms? . . . Aha! I see. Right. I'll catch him" (U 7.411–13).

It is said several times that the phone call is *interior*. "Mr. Bloom ⟨. . .⟩ made for the *inner* door" (U 7.375; emphasis added) when he wants to make a call; then "The telephone whirred *inside*" (U 7.384; emphasis added); and finally "Mr. Bloom phoned from the *inner* office" (U 7.411; emphasis added). A telephonic interiority, then: for before any apparatus bearing that name in modernity, the telephonic *technē is* at work within the voice, multiplying the writing of the voices without instruments, as Mallarmé would say, a mental telephony which, inscribing the far, distance, *différance*, and spacing in the *phōnē, at the same time* institutes, prohibits, *and* disrupts the so-called monologue. At the same time, in the same way, from the first phone call and the simplest vocalization, from the monosyllabic quasi-interjection of the "oui," "yes," "ay." And *a fortiori* for the "yes, yes" that the theoreticians of the *speech act* propose as examples of the performative and that Molly repeats at the end of the so-called monologue, the "Yes, Yes, I do" consenting to marriage. When I speak of mental telephony, even masturbation, I implicitly cite "THE SINS OF THE PAST: (*in a medley of voices*) He went through a form of clandestine marriage with at least one woman in the shadow of the Black church. Unspeakable messages he telephoned mentally to Miss Dunn at an address in D'Olier street while he presented himself indecently to the instrument in the callbox" (U 15.3027–31).

The telephonic spacing is in particular superimprinted on the scene called "A DISTANT VOICE." The latter crosses all the lines of the network, the paradoxes of competence and of the institution, here represented by the figure of the professor, and, in all senses of the word, the *repetition* of the "yes," between *eyes and ears*. One can draw all these telephonic lines from a single paragraph:

A DISTANT VOICE
—I'll answer it, the professor said going. ⟨. . .⟩
—Hello? *Evening Telegraph* here. Hello? . . . Who's there? . . .
Yes . . . Yes. . . . Yes. ⟨. . .⟩
The professor came to the inner door. ⟨"inner" again⟩
—Bloom is at the telephone, he said. (U 7.657–71)

Bloom is-at-the-telephone. The professor thus defines a particular situation at a given moment of the narration, to be sure, but as always in the stereophony of a text which gives several layers to each statement and always allows metonymical borrowings to which I am not the only reader of Joyce to give in to, in a way both legitimate and abusive, authorized and improper, he also names the permanent essence of Bloom. One can read it through this particular paradigm: *he is at the telephone*, he is always there, he belongs to the telephone, and he is both attached and destined to it. His being is a being-at-the-telephone. He is connected to a multiplicity of voices or answering machines. His being-there is a being-at-the-telephone, a being toward the telephone, in the way in which Heidegger speaks of the being toward death of Dasein. I am not playing when I say this: The Heideggerian Dasein is also a being-called, it is always, it is said in *Being and Time*, and as my friend Sam Weber reminded me, a Dasein who only has access to itself from the Call (*der Ruf*), a call from afar that is not necessarily heard through words, and which in a certain way says nothing. One could apply to this analysis, to the last detail, the entire section 57 of *Sein und Zeit* on *der Ruf*, for example, around sentences like this one: "Der Angerufene ist eben dieses Dasein; aufgerufen zu seinem eigensten Seinkönnen (Sich-vorweg . . .). Und aufgerufen ist das Dasein durch den Anruf aus den Verfallen in das Man . . .": "The called one is precisely *this* Dasein; summoned, provoked, called toward its ownmost possibility of being (ahead of itself). And Dasein is thus summoned by this call from or out of the fall in the 'they.'"²² . . . I unfortunately do not have the time to conduct this analysis, within or beyond a jargon of *Eigentlichkeit* that still resonates in this university.

> —Bloom is at the telephone, he said.
> —Tell him go to hell, the editor said promptly. X is Davy's publichouse, see? (U 7.671–73)

Bloom is at the telephone, connected to a powerful network to which I will return shortly. In his essence he belongs to a polytelephonic structure. But he is at the telephone in the sense in which one *waits* at the telephone. When he says "Bloom is at the telephone," as I will later say, "Joyce is at the telephone," the professor is saying: he waits for someone to answer him, something the editor, who decides about the future of the text as well as about its safekeeping and truth, does not want to do—and who at this point sends him down to hell, into the *Verfallen*, in the hell of censured books. Bloom waits for someone to answer him, for someone to say to him "hello, yes." He asks for someone to say *yes*, *yes*, to him, beginning with the telephonic *yes* indicating that there is indeed another voice, if not an answering machine, at the end of the line. When, at the end of the book, Molly says "yes, yes," she responds to a request, but a request that she requests. She is at the telephone even in bed, requesting, waiting for someone to ask her, on the telephone (since she is alone), to say "yes, yes." And the fact that she asks that "with my eyes" does not prevent her from being at the telephone, on the contrary: "⟨. . .⟩ well as well him as another and then I asked him with my eyes to ask again yes and then he asked me would I yes to say yes my mountain flower and first I put my arms around him yes and drew him down to me so he could feel my breasts all perfume yes and his heart was going like mad and yes I said yes I will Yes" (U 18.1604–9).

The last *Yes*, the last word, the eschatology of the book only gives itself to be *read* since it is distinguished from others by an inaudible capital letter, just as the literal incorporation of the yes in the eye (*oeil*) of language, the *yes* in the *eyes*, remains also inaudible and only visible. *Langue d'oeil*.²³

We still do not know what *yes* means and how this little word, if it is indeed a word, functions in language and in what one imperturbably calls speech acts. We do not know if it shares anything with any other word from any language, even with a "no" that is certainly not symmetrical to it. We do not know if there is a grammatical, semantic, linguistic, rhetorical, philosophical concept capable of that event marked *yes*. Let us leave that aside for the moment. Let us act *as if*, and this is not a mere fiction, it did not prevent us, on the contrary, from hearing what a *yes* commands. We will ask the difficult questions later, if we have the time.

The *yes* on the telephone can be traversed in one and the same occurrence by several intonations whose differentiating qualities are possibilized on stereophonic long waves. They may seem to be limited to interjection, to the mechanical quasi-signal indicating either the sheer presence of the interlocutor Dasein at the end of the line (hello, yes?) or the passive docility of the secretary or of the subordinate ready to register orders like an archiving machine: "yes, sir," or limiting oneself to give merely informative answers; "yes, sir," "no, sir."

An example among many others. I deliberately choose it in those places where a typewriter and the name H.E.L.Y'S lead us to the last piece of furniture of this vestibule or of this techno-telecommunicational preamble, a certain gramophone, at the same time that they connect it on the network of the prophet Elijah. Here it is, but of course I section and select, filter the noise:

> Miss Dunne hid the Capel street library copy of *The Woman in White* far back in her drawer and rolled a sheet of gaudy notepaper into her typewriter.
>
> Too much mystery business in it. Is he in love with that one, Marion? Change it and get another by Mary Cecil Haye."
>
> The disk shot down the groove, wobbled a while, ceased and ogled them: six.
>
> Miss Dunne clicked at the keyboard:
>
> —16 June 1904. ⟨Almost eighty years.⟩
>
> Five tallwhitehhatted sandwichmen between Monypeny's corner and the slab where Wolfe Tone's statue was not, eeled themselves turning H.E.L.Y'S and plodded back as they had come. ⟨. . .⟩
>
> The telephone rang rudely by her ear.
>
> —Hello. Yes, sir. No, sir. Yes, sir. I'll ring them up after five. Only those two, sir, for Belfast and Liverpool. All right, sir. Then I can go after six if you're not back. A quarter after. Yes, sir. Twentyseven and six. I'll tell him. Yes: one, seven, six.
>
> She scribbled three figures on an envelope.
>
> —Mr. Boylan! Hello! That gentleman from *Sport* was in looking for you. Mr. Lenehan, yes. He said he'll be in the Ormond at four. No, sir. Yes, sir. I'll ring them up after five. (U 10.368–96)

III

The repetition of the *yes* can take mechanical, servile forms, bending the woman to her master; but this is not by accident, even if any response to the other as a singular other must, it would seem, escape it. The *yes* of affirmation, of assent or consent, of alliance, engagement, signature, or gift, must carry this repetition within itself if it is to be of any value. It must immediately and *a priori* confirm its promise and promise its confirmation. This essential repetition is haunted by an intrinsic threat, by the interior telephone that parasites it as its mimetic-mechanical double, as its unceasing parody.

We shall return to this fatality. But we can already hear the gramophony that records writing within the liveliest voice. It reproduces it *a priori*, in the absence of any intentional presence of the affirmer. Such a gramophony certainly responds to the dream of a reproduction that *preserves*, as its truth, the living *yes*, archived in its liveliest voice. But by this very fact, it allows the possibility of a parody, a technology of the yes that persecutes the most spontaneous and the most giving desire of the *yes*. To respond or correspond [*répondre à*] to its destination, this *yes* must reaffirm itself immediately. Such is the condition of a signed commitment. The *yes* can say *itself* only if it promises to itself the memory of itself. The affirmation of the *yes* is an affirmation of memory. *Yes* must preserve itself, and thus repeat itself, archive its voice to give it once again to be heard.

This is what I call the gramophone effect. *Yes* gramophones itself and telegramophones itself *a priori*.

The desire for memory and the mourning of the yes set into motion the anamnesic machine. As well as its hypermnesic unleashing. The machine reproduces the living, and duplicates it with its automaton. The example I choose for it has the benefit of a twofold contiguity: from the word "yes" to the word "voice" and the word "gramophone" in a section that speaks of the desire for memory, desire as memory of desire, and desire for memory. It takes place in Hades, in the cemetery, around 11 a.m., the moment of the *heart* (as Heidegger would still say, the place of preserving memory and truth), and here of the Sacred Heart [*Sacré-Coeur*]:

> The Sacred Heart that is: showing it. Heart on his sleeve. ⟨. . .⟩
> How many! All these here once walked round Dublin. Faithful departed. As you are now so once were we.
> Besides how could you remember everybody? Eyes, walk, voice. Well, the voice, yes: gramophone. Have a gramophone in every grave or keep it in the house. After dinner on a Sunday. Put on poor old greatgrandfather Kraahraark! Hellohellohello amawfullyglad kraark awfullygladaseeragain hellohello amawf krpthsth. Remind you of the voice like the photograph reminds you of the face. Otherwise you couldn't remember the face after fifteen years, say. For instance who? For instance some fellow that died when I was in Wisdom Hely's. (U 6.954–69)[24]

With what right do we borrow or interrupt a quotation from *Ulysses*? It is always legitimate and illegitimate, to be made legitimate like an illegitimate child. I could follow the sons of Hely, Bloom's old boss, in all kinds of genealogies. Rightly or wrongly, I judge it more economical here to rely on the associations with the name of the prophet Elijah [*Élie*], to whom many passages are devoted, or rather whose arrival is regularly promised. I pronounce *Élie* in the French style, but in the English Elijah you can hear Molly's *Ja* resonate, if Molly gives voice to the flesh (remember that word) which always says "yes" (*stets bejaht*, Joyce recalls, reversing Goethe's words).[25] I will not seek further on the side of a "voice out of heaven, calling: *Elijah! Elijah!* And He answered with a main cry: *Abba! Adonai!* And they beheld Him even Him, ben Bloom Elijah, amid clouds of angels ⟨. . .⟩" (U 12.1914–16).

No, I go without transition toward repetition, toward what is called the "*second coming of Elijah*" in the brothel (U 15.2175–76). The gramophone, the character and the voice, if I may put it this way, of the gramophone just cried out: "Jerusalem! / Open your gates and sing / Hosanna . . ." (U 15.2171–73). Second coming of Elijah, near "the end of the world." Elijah's voice gives itself as a telephonic center or as a triage station. All the networks of communication, transportation, transfers, and translations go through him. Polytelephony goes through Elijah's programophony. Do not forget, whatever you can do with it, that—Molly recalls it—ben Bloom Elijah had lost his position at his boss Hely's. He had thought of prostituting Molly, of making her pose nude for a very rich man.

Elijah is just a voice, a skein of voices. That voice says: "c'est moi qui opère tous les téléphones de ce réseau-là."[26] French translation, sanctioned by Joyce, for "Say, I am operating all this trunk line. Boys, do it now. God's time is 12.25. Tell mother you'll be there. Rush your order and you play a slick ace. Join on right here. Book through to eternity junction, the non-stop run" (U 15.2190–93). I would insist in French on the fact that one must *louer* (book, booking), reserve one's seats with Elijah, one must praise [*louer*] Elijah, sing his praises [*en faire la louange*]. And the location/booking of such praise is none other than the *livre* (book) which holds the place of an "eternity junction" as transferential and teleprogramophonic central. "Just one word more," Elijah continues, who then evokes a second coming of the Christ and asks whether we are all ready, Florry Christ, Stephen Christ, Zoe Christ, Bloom Christ, etc. "Are you all in this vibration? I say you are" (U 15.2199–2200), translated into French by "Moi je dis que oui,"[27] a problematic translation—although not illegitimate—to which we will need to return. And the voice of the one who says "*que* oui," "yes," Elijah, says to those who are in the *vibration* (a word that is essential in my eyes) that they can call him at any time, immediately, instantaneously, without even going through technology or a postal system but by way of the sun, through cables and solar rays, through the voice of the sun, one would say through photophone or heliophone. He says "by sunphone": "Got me? That's it. You call me up by sunphone any old time. Bumboosers, save your stamps" (U 15.2206–7). Thus do not write me letters, save your stamps, you may collect them as Molly's father does.

We have reached this point because I told you about my trip experiences, *roundtrip*, and a few phone calls. If I tell stories, it is in order to delay the moment when I would speak about serious things and because I am too intimidated. Nothing intimidates me more than a community of experts in Joyce studies. Why? I first wanted to speak to you about it, speak to you about authority and intimidation.

I wrote the page that I am about to read in the plane that was taking me to Oxford, Ohio, a few days before the trip to Tokyo. I decided then to raise before you the question of competence, of legitimacy, and of the Joycean institution. Who has the recognized right to speak about Joyce, to write on Joyce, and who does it well? What do competence and performance consist of here?

When I accepted to speak before you, before the most intimidating assembly in the world, before the greatest concentration of knowledge on such a polymathic body of work, I was first appreciative of the honor that was done to me. And I wondered how I had made anyone believe that I deserved it in the slightest way. I do not intend to answer this question here. But I do know, like you do, that I do not belong to your large and impressive family. I prefer the word "family" to that of "foundation" or "institute." Someone answering, yes, in Joyce's name, succeeded in linking the future of an institution to the singular adventure of a *signed* proper name, for writing one's proper name does not amount yet to signing. If in a plane you write your name on a custom form that you give out upon arriving in Tokyo, you have not signed yet. You sign when the gesture with which, in a certain place, preferably at the end of the card or the book, you inscribe your name again, takes then the sense of a *yes*, this is my name, I certify it and, yes, yes, I could certify it again, I will remember later, I promise it, that it is indeed I who did sign. A signature is always a "yes, yes," the *synthetic* performative of a promise and of a memory that makes any commitment possible. We shall return to this obligatory point of departure for any discourse, according to a circle that is also that of the *yes*, of the "so be it," of the amen and of the hymen.

I did not feel worthy of the honor that had been bestowed upon me, far from it, but I must have harbored the secret desire to belong to this powerful family that tends to encompass all others, including their hidden stories of bastardy, legitimation, and illegitimacy. If I accepted, it was mostly because I suspected the existence of some perverse challenge in a legitimation so generously offered.

You know this better than I, the worry about family legitimation is what makes both *Ulysses* and *Finnegans Wake* vibrate. I was thinking in the plane of the challenge and the trap, because these experts, I said to myself, with the lucidity and experience that a long acquaintance with Joyce gave them, must know better than others how much, behind the simulacrum of a few signs of complicity, references, or citations in each of my books, Joyce remains foreign to me, as if I did not know him. They know that incompetence is the basic truth of my relation to a work that in the end I only know indirectly, by hearsay, rumors, gossip [*on-dit*], secondhand exegeses, and always partial readings. For these experts, I said to myself, it is time that this deception is exposed; and how could it be better exposed or denounced than at the opening of a large symposium?

Thus, to defend myself against this hypothesis, almost a certainty, I asked myself: in the end, what would competence mean, in the case of Joyce? And what can a Joycean institution or family, a Joycean international, be? I do not know to what extent one can speak of Joyce's modernity, but if there is one, aside from the apparatus of postal and programophonic technologies, it lies in the fact that the declared project to mobilize generations of academics during centuries of Babelian edification must itself have been adjusted to a model of the technology and division of academic labor that could not be that of past centuries. The design to bend vast communities of readers and writers to this law, to retain them through an interminable transferential chain of translation and tradition can be traced back to Plato as well as to Shakespeare, to Dante and to Vico, not to mention Hegel or other finite divinities. But none of them was able to calculate his effect as well as Joyce was, by adjusting it to certain types of world research institutions ready to utilize not only means of transportation, communication, organizational programming that facilitate an accelerated capitalization, an unhinged accumulation of knowledge interests blocked in the name of Joyce, even though he lets all of you sign with his name, as Molly would say ("I could often have written out a fine cheque for myself and write his name on it" [U 18.1525–26]), but also modes of archiving and the consultation of data unheard of by all the grandfathers that I just named, omitting Homer.

This is where the intimidation lies: the Joycean experts are the representatives as well as the effects of the most powerful project to program over centuries the totality of research in the onto-logico-encyclopedic field—while commemorating his own signature. A *Joyce scholar*[28] by right disposes of the totality of competences in the encyclopedic field of the *universitas*. He or she has the mastery over the *computer*[29] of all memory, plays with the entire archive of culture—at least the so-called Western culture and of what within it returns to itself according to the Ulyssean circle of the encyclopedia; and this is why one can always dream at least of writing *on* Joyce and not *in* Joyce, from the phantasm of some Far-East capital, without in my case harboring much illusion on this subject.

You know the effects of this pre-programming better than I, they are both admirable and terrifying, at times of an intolerable violence. One of them has the following form: nothing can be invented *on the subject* of Joyce. All that can be said of *Ulysses*, for example, is already anticipated, including, as we saw, the scene of the academic competence and the ingenuity of meta-discourse. We are caught in this net. We find all the gestures to take the initiative of a movement announced in a superpotentialized text that will remind you, at a given time, that you are caught in a network of language, writing, knowledge, and *even of narration*. This is one of the things that I wanted to demonstrate earlier, when telling you all these stories, all true, I might add, of postcards, trips to Ohio, or phone calls with Rabaté. We have been able to verify it, all this had its narrative paradigm, was *already* narrated in *Ulysses*. Everything that happened to me, including the narration that I would attempt to make of it, was said in advance, narrated in advance in its dated singularity, prescribed in a sequence of knowledge and narration: within *Ulysses*, to say nothing of *Finnegans Wake*, by this hypermnesic machine capable of storing in a giant epic work, with the memory of the West and virtually all the languages of the world, *the very traces of the future*. Yes, everything has already happened to us with *Ulysses*, and in advance signed by Joyce.

It remains to be seen what happens to this signature in these conditions, this is one of my questions.

This situation reverses everything and this is due to the paradox of the *yes*. The question of the *yes*, moreover, always refers to that of the *doxa*, of that which is opined in opinion. This is the paradox: at the moment when the work of such a signature sets to work the most competent and efficient machine of production and reproduction—others would say when it submits to this, or in any case relaunches it *for itself* so that it can come back to itself—it also simultaneously ruins its model. At least it threatens to ruin it. Joyce relied on the modern university but he challenges it to reconstitute itself after him. He outlines its essential limits. In the end, there cannot be a Joycean competence, in the strong and rigorous sense of the concept of competence, with the criteria of evaluation and legitimation that are attached to it. There cannot be a Joycean foundation or family. There cannot be a Joycean legitimacy. What relation does this situation have with the paradox of the *yes* or the structure of a signature?

The classical concept of competence supposes that one can rigorously dissociate knowledge (in its act or position) from the event in question, and especially from the equivocation of written or oral marks, let us say gramophonies. Competence supposes that a meta-discourse is possible, neutral and univocal with respect to a field of objectivity, whether or not it has the structure of a text. In principle, the performances regulated by this competence must be able to lend themselves to a remainderless translation with respect to a corpus that is itself translatable. They must especially not be, for the most part, of a narrative style. One does not tell stories in the university, in principle. One does history, one narrates in order to know and explain, one speaks about narrations or epic poems, but events and stories must not appear there as institutionalized knowledge. Now with the event signed Joyce, a *double-bind* has at least become explicit (for it already has had a hold on us ever since Babel or Homer, and all that followed): on the one hand, one must write, one must sign, one must make new events with untranslatable marks happen—and this is the desperate call, the distress of a signature that demands a *yes* from the other; but on the other hand, the singular novelty of any other *yes*, of any other signature, already finds itself programophoned in the Joycean corpus.

I do not only perceive the effects of this challenge of this *double-bind* on myself, in the terrified desire that I might have of belonging to a family of the representatives of Joyce of which I could only be a bastard. I also perceive them in you.

On the one hand, you have the legitimate assurance of possessing or of being on the way to constituting a super-competence, on a par with a corpus that virtually includes all others treated in the university (the sciences, technologies, religions, philosophies, literatures, and, coextensive with all that, languages). Nothing transcends this hyperbolic competence. Everything is *internal*, mental telephony; everything can be integrated into the domesticity of this programotelephonic encyclopedia.

On the other hand, one must know at the same time, and *you know it*, that the signature and the *yes* that occupy you are capable—it is their destination—of destroying the very root of this competence, of this legitimacy, of its domestic interiority, capable of deconstructing the academic institution, its internal or interdepartmental borders as well as its contract with the extra-academic world.

Hence this mixture of assurance and distress that one can sense in the "Joyce scholars." On the one hand, as crafty as Ulysses, they know, like Joyce, that they know more, that they always have one more trick up their sleeves; whether when it is a question of a totalizing synthesis, or of a subatomistic micrology (what I call "divisibility of the letter"), no one does it better, everything can be integrated in the "this is my body" of the corpus. On the other hand, this hypermnesic interiorization can never close itself on itself. For reasons pertaining to the structure of the corpus, of the project and signature, one cannot secure any principle of truth or legitimacy. Therefore you also have the feeling that, since nothing can surprise you from within, something finally might happen to you from an unpredictable outside.

And you have guests.

IV

You wait for the arrival or the second coming of Elijah. And, as a good Jewish family, you always keep a seat at the table for him. While waiting for Elijah, even if his coming is already gramophoned in *Ulysses*, you are all ready to recognize, without too many illusions I think, the external competence of writers, philosophers, psychoanalysts, linguists. You even ask them to open your conferences. And for instance to ask a question like: what is happening today in Frankfurt, in the city where the Joycean international, the cosmopolitan yet very American James Joyce Foundation, established Bloomsday 1967—the president of which, representing a very large American majority, is in Ohio (still Ohio!)—pursues its edification in a modern Babel that is also the capital of the book fair and of a famous philosophical school of modernity? When you call on incompetent people, such as myself, or on allegedly external competences, even though you know that there aren't any, isn't it in order to both humiliate them and because you are expecting from these guests not only some news, some good news that would come to finally free you from the hypermnesic interiority in which you run in circles like madmen in a nightmare but also, paradoxically, a legitimacy? For you are both very sure and very unsure of your rights, and even of your community, of the homogeneity of your practices, methods, and styles. You can count on no consensus, no axiomatic agreement among yourselves. In the end, you do not exist, you are not authorized [*fondés*] to exist as a foundation, and this is what Joyce's signature gives you to be read. You call on strangers so that they come to tell you, which is what I do by responding to your invitation: you do exist, you intimidate me, I recognize you, I recognize your paternal and grandpaternal authority, recognize me, give me a diploma in Joycean studies.

Naturally, you don't believe a word of what I am telling you right now. And even if it was true and even if, yes, it is true, you would not believe me if I told you that my name is also Elijah: That name is not inscribed, no, on my birth certificate but it was given to me on my seventh day. Elijah, moreover, is the name of the prophet who is present at *all* circumcisions. He is the patron, as it were, of circumcision. The chair on which the newborn baby boy is held during the circumcision is called "Elijah's chair." We should give this name to all the "chairs" of Joycean studies, to the "panels" and the "workshops" organized by your foundation. In fact, rather than "Postcard from Tokyo," I had thought of calling this lecture "Circumnavigation and Circumcision."

A Midrash tells the story that Elijah had complained about how Israel had forgotten the alliance, that is to say, forgotten circumcision. God would have then given him the order to be present at all circumcisions, perhaps as a form of punishment. One could have made this scene of signature bloody by connecting all the announced arrivals of the prophet Elijah to the event of circumcision, moment of entry into the community, the alliance, and legitimacy. At least twice in *Ulysses*, one finds the expression "collector of prepuces": "The islanders, Mulligan said to Haines casually, speak frequently of the collector of prepuces" (U 1.393–94), or "Jehovah, collector of prepuces":

> —What's his name? Ikey Moses? Bloom.
> He rattled on:
> —Jehovah, collector of prepuces, is no more. I found him over in the museum where I went to hail the foamborn Aphrodite. (U 9.607–10)

Each time, and often near an arrival of milk or foam, circumcision is associated to the name of Moses, as in this passage where, before "the name of Moses Herzog," "—Circumcised? Says Joe.—Ay, says I. A bit off the top" (U 12.19–20). "Ay, says I": yes, says I, or also: I says I, or I (says) I, yes (says) yes: I: I, yes: yes, yes, yes, I, I, etc. Tautology, monology, but judgment synthetic *a priori*. You could also have played on the fact that in Hebrew the word for "stepfather" (stepfather: recall Bloom when he claims to be ready before Stephen to go "a step farther") also names the circumciser. And if Bloom has a dream, it is to have Stephen become part of the family and thus, by way of marriage and adoption, to circumcise the Greek.

Where are we thus going with the alliance of this Joycean community? What will become of it at this rate of accumulation and commemoration in one or two centuries, taking into account the new technologies of archiving and storing of information? In the end, Elijah is not me, nor some stranger who would come to say this thing to you, the news from outside, maybe the apocalypse of Joycean studies, namely the truth, the final revelation (and you know that Elijah was always associated with the apocalyptic discourse). No, Elijah, it's you, you are *Ulysses'* Elijah, who appears as the great telephonic center ("HELLO THERE, CENTRAL!" [U 7.1042]), the triage station, the network through which all information must transit.

One can imagine the existence soon of a giant computer of Joycean studies ("operating all this trunk line . . . Book through to eternity junction . . ."). It would capitalize all the publications, would coordinate and teleprogram the lectures, conferences, theses, the *papers*,[30] would construct indexes in all languages. One could consult it at any moment via satellite or heliophone ("sunphone"), day and night, relying on the "reliability" of an answering machine: hello, yes, yes, what are you asking for? Oh! For all the occurrences of the word "yes" in *Ulysses*? Yes. It would remain to be seen whether the basic language of such a computer would be English and whether its certificate (its "patent") would be American, due to the overwhelming and significant majority of Americans in the trust of the Joyce foundation. It would also remain to be seen whether one can consult this computer with respect to the yes in all languages, if one can be content with the word *yes* and whether the yes, in particular the one involved in the operations of consultation, can be counted, calculated, numbered. A circle will lead me later to this question.

In any case, the figure of Elijah, whether it is that of the prophet, of the circumciser, of the polymathic competence and telematic mastery, is only a synecdoche of the Ulyssean narration, at once smaller and greater than the whole.

We should therefore abandon a twofold illusion and intimidation. 1. No truth can come from the outside of the Joycean community and without the experience, the cunning, and the knowledge accumulated by expert readers. 2. But inversely or symmetrically, there is no model for "Joycean" competence, no possible interiority and closure for the concept of such a competence. There is no absolute criterion to measure the pertinence of a discourse on a text signed "Joyce." The very concept of competence finds itself shaken up by this event. For one must write, write in one language, respond to the *yes* and countersign in another language. The very discourse of competence (that of neutral and metalinguistic knowledge, safe from all untranslatable writing, etc.) is also incompetent, the least competent one with respect to Joyce; who, incidentally, also finds himself in the same situation whenever he speaks of his "work."

Instead of pursuing these generalities, and given the time passing fast, I return to the *yes* in *Ulysses*. For a very long time, the question of the *yes* has mobilized or permeated everything that I attempt to think, write, teach, or read. To only speak of readings, I had devoted seminars and texts to the *yes*, to the double *yes* in Nietzsche's *Zarathustra* ("Thus spake Zarathustra," Mulligan says in fact [U 1.727–28]), the *yes, yes* of the hymen which is always the best example for it, the *yes* of the great midday affirmation, and then the ambiguity of the double *yes*: One of them comes down to the Christian assumption of one's burden, the "*Ja, Ja*" of the donkey overburdened, as the Christ was with memory and responsibility; the other *yes* is a *yes* that is light, airy, dancing, solar, also a yes of reaffirmation, promise, and oath, a *yes* to the eternal return. The difference between the two *yeses*, or rather between the two repetitions of the *yes*, remains unstable, subtle, and sublime. One repetition haunts the other. The *yes* always finds its chance with a certain woman for Nietzsche, who also, like Joyce, predicted that one day there would be professorships created to study his *Zarathustra*. Similarly, in Blanchot's *The Madness of the Day*, the quasi-narrator attributes the power to say *yes* to women, to the beauty of women, beautiful insofar as they say *yes*: "Yet I have met people who have never said to life, 'Quiet!', who have never said to death, 'Go away!' Almost always women, beautiful creatures."[31]

The *yes* would then be of the woman—and not only of the mother, the flesh, the earth, as one says so often about Molly's *yes* in most of the interpretations that are devoted to it: *Penelope, bed, flesh, earthy, monologue,* says Gilbert,[32] and so many after him, or even before him, and here Joyce is not more competent than any other. This is not false, and is even the truth of a certain truth, but this is not all and it is not so simple. The law of genre seems to me largely overdetermined and infinitely more complicated whether it is the sexual or grammatical gender [*genre*], or rhetorical technique. To call this a monologue is nothing but somnambulistic carelessness.

I have thus wanted to hear again Molly's *yeses*. But could this be done without making them resonate with all the *yeses* that announce them, correspond to them and keep them at the end of the line throughout the whole book? Last summer, in Nice, I thus reread *Ulysses*, first in French, then in English with a pencil in hand, counting the *oui*, then the *yeses*, and sketching a typology. As you can imagine, I was dreaming of connecting myself on the computer of the Joyce foundation, and the result of the count was not the same from one language to the other.

Molly is not Elijah, is not Moelie (and you know that the Mohel is the circumciser) and Molly is not Joyce, but nonetheless: her *yes* circumnavigates and circumcises, it encircles *Ulysses*' last chapter, since it is both her first and last word, her opening and closing fall: "Yes because he never did ⟨. . .⟩" (U 18.1) and at the end: "⟨. . .⟩ and yes I said yes I will Yes" (U 18.1608–9). The last *Yes*, the eschatological yes, occupies the place of the signature, at the bottom right of the text. Even if we distinguish, as we should, Molly's *yes* from that of *Ulysses*, of which it is only a figure and a moment, even if we distinguish, as we also should, these two signatures (Molly's and that of *Ulysses*) from that of Joyce, they read and call each other. They call each other precisely through a *yes* that always sets up a scene of call and demand: it confirms and countersigns. Affirmation demands *a priori* confirmation, repetition, the safekeeping and memory of the *yes*. A certain narrativity is to be found at the simple core of the simplest "yes": "I asked him with my eyes to ask again yes and then he asked me would I yes to say yes ⟨. . .⟩" (U 18.1605–6).

A *yes* never comes alone, and one is never alone in saying *yes*. Nor does one laugh alone, as Freud said, I will return to this. Freud also emphasizes that the unconscious knows nothing of the *no*. In what way does the question of Joycean signature implicate what I will call here, curiously, the question of the *yes*? There is a question of the *yes*, a demand for the *yes*, and perhaps, for this is never certain, an unconditional and inaugural affirmation of the *yes* that cannot necessarily be distinguished from the question or the demand. Joyce's signature, at least that which interests me here and whose phenomenon I will never claim to exhaust, cannot be reduced to the appending of his seal in the form of the patronymical name and the play of signifiers, as one says, in which to reinscribe the name "Joyce." The inductions that have taken place for a long time through these plays of association and society pastimes are facile, tedious, and naïvely jubilatory. Even if they are not always without pertinence, they begin by confusing a signature with the simple mention, apposition or manipulation of one's official name. Now, neither in its juridical scope, as I suggested above, nor in the essential complexity of its structure, does a signature amount to the sole mention of the proper name. Nor can the proper name itself, which a signature does not merely spell out or mention, be reduced to the legal surname. This one runs the risk of creating a smoke screen toward which the psychoanalysts would hasten, in their rush to conclude. I tried to show this in the case of Genet, Ponge, or Blanchot.[33] As for the scene of the surname, the first pages of *Ulysses* should suffice to help educate a reader.

V

Who signs? Who signs what in the name of Joyce? The answer should not take the form of a key or of a clinical category that one pulls out of a hat at the occasion of a conference. Nonetheless, as a humble preamble, one that perhaps interests me alone, I thought it possible to raise that question of the signature through the question of the *yes* that it always implicates, and insofar as it weds here or *marries* (*se marie*: I insist on this French word) the question of knowing who laughs and how it laughs *with* Joyce, *in* Joyce, singularly so since *Ulysses*.

Who is the man who laughs? Is it a man? And that which laughs, how does it laugh? Does it laugh? For there is more than one modality, more than one tonality of laughter, as there is an entire gamut [*gamme*] (a polygamy) in the "game" or "gamble"[34] of the *yes*. Why this—gamut, "game," and "gamble"? Because before the gramophone, just before, and Elijah's speech as operator of the grand telephone central, the gnome, the "hobgoblin" speaks *in French* the croupier's language. "*Il vient!* 〈Elijah, I assume, or the

Christ⟩ *C'est moi! L'homme qui rit! L'homme primigène!* (*he whirls round and round with dervish howls*) *Sieurs et dames, faites vos jeux!* (*He crouches juggling. Tiny roulette planets fly from his hands.*) *Les jeux sont faits!* (*the planets rush together, uttering crepitant cracks*) *Rien va plus!*" (U 15.2159–63).[35] "Il vient," "rien va plus," in French in the original. The French translation does not make a mention of it; the French thus erases the French, at the risk of cancelling a connotation or an essential reference in this self-presentation of the man who laughs.

Since we speak of translation, tradition, and transfer of *yes*, let us note that the same problem arises for the French version of the *oui* when it is found, as one says, "*en français dans le texte*," "in French in the original," and even in italics. The erasure of these marks is all the more serious since the "Mon père, oui," then takes on the sense of a citation that displays all the problems of the cited *yes*. In episode 3 ("Proteus"), shortly after the evocation of the "Ineluctable modality of the visible" and of the "ineluctable modality of the audible" (U 3.1, 13), in other words, the ineluctable gramophony of the "yes," "sounds solid" names the same passage through the "navel cord" that puts into question the consubstantiality of father and son, and this quite close to a scripturo-telephonic and Judeo-Hellenic scene. "Hello! Kinch here. Put me on to Edenville. Aleph, alpha: nought, nought, one. ⟨. . .⟩ Yes, sir. No, sir. Jesus wept: and no wonder by Christ" (U 3.39–40, 68–69). On this same page 44 (and we must, for essential reasons, treat things here by contiguity), what the French translation, cosigned by Joyce, renders by *oui*, is not yes but first "I am" and second "I will." We will return to this in a circular way. Here is thus the passage, followed closely by the mother's postal order that Stephen cannot cash in a French post office (counter "closed") and by the allusion to the "blue French telegram, curiosity to show:—Nother dying come home father" (U 3.197–99)[36]:

—C'est tordant, vous savez. Moi, je suis socialiste. Je ne crois pas en l'existence de Dieu. Faut pas le dire à mon père.
—Il croit?
—Mon père, oui. (U 3.169–72)[37] (In French in the original.)

Since the question of signature remains entirely open before us, the modest but indispensible preliminary dimension of its elaboration should be situated, I believe, at the intersection of the *yes*—the visible *yes* and the audible *yes*, the *oui ouï*, the *heard yes*, without any etymological filiation between the two words "*oui*" and "*ouï*," of the "*yes for the eyes*" and the "*yes for the ears*," and of laughter, at the intersection of the *yes* and *laughter*. In sum, through the telephonic lapsus that made me say or hear *ouï dire*, "hear say," it was the *oui rire*, "yes laughter," which was making its way, as well as the consonantal difference from the d [of *dire*] to the r [of *rire*]. These, moreover, are the only consonants of my name.

Why laugh? Everything has probably been said already on laughter in Joyce, as well as on parody, satire, derision, humor, irony, and mockery. And also on his Homeric and Rabelaisian laughter. It perhaps remains to think, precisely, laughter as remainder. What does laughter mean? [*Qu'est-ce que ça veut dire, le rire?*] What does laughter want? [*Qu'est-ce que ça veut rire?*]

Once we recognize in principle that in *Ulysses* the virtual totality of experience, of sense, of history, of the symbolic, of languages and writings, the great cycle and the great encyclopedia of cultures, of scenes and affects, the sum total of sum totals in sum, tends to unfold and recompose itself by playing out all its combinatory possibilities, with a writing that seeks to occupy there virtually all places, well, the totalizing hermeneutic that constitutes the task of a global and eternal foundation of Joycean studies will find itself before what I hesitate to call a dominant affect, a *Stimmung* or a *pathos*, a tonality that re-traverses all the others, but which nonetheless does not belong to the series of the others since it just re-marked them all, adding itself to them without letting itself be added up or totalized, like a remainder that is both quasi-transcendental and supplementary. And it is the yes-laughter [*oui-rire*] that over-marks not only the totality of writing but all the qualities, modalities, genres of laughter whose differences could be classified in some typology.

Why, then, the yes-laughter *before and after all*, for all that a signature accounts for? Or leaves out [*laisse pour compte*]? Why this remainder?

I do not have the time to begin this work and typology. Cutting through fields, I will simply say two words on the double relation, thus the unstable relation that informs with its double tonality my reading or rewriting of Joyce, this time beyond even *Ulysses*, my double relation to this yes-laughter. My presumption is that I am not alone in projecting this double relation. It would be instituted and requested, required by the Joycean signature itself.

With one ear, with a certain hearing [*ouïe*], I can hear a reactive, even negative yes-laughter resonate. It exults in a hypermnesic mastery, and by spinning a spider web that defies any other possible mastery, as impregnable as an alpha and omegaprogramophone in which all histories, stories, discourses, types of knowledge, all the signatures to come that Joycean institutions as well as a few others might address would be prescribed and computed in advance beyond any actual computer, pre-understood, captive, predicted, partialized, metonymized, exhausted, just like the subjects, whether they know it or not. And science or consciousness cannot help in any way, to the contrary. It merely allows putting its supplemental calculation at the service of the master signature. It can laugh at Joyce but in this way is indebted to him. As it is said in *Ulysses* (197), "*Was du verlachst wirst Du noch dienen.* / Brood of mockers" (U 9.491–92).[38]

There is a James Joyce who can be heard laughing at this omnipotence—and at this great trick [*tour*] played. I speak about Ulysses' tricks and turns, Ulysses the cunning one, the great tour he concluded when on his return he returned from everything.[39] This is certainly a triumphant and jubilatory laughter, but a jubilation always betrays some mourning, and laughter can also be with a resigned lucidity. Indeed, omnipotence remains a phantasm, as it opens and defines the dimension of phantasm. Joyce cannot *not know this*. He cannot not know this—for instance that the book of all books, *Ulysses* or *Finnegans Wake*, remains but one volume among millions of titles in the Library of Congress, forever absent, no doubt, in the little newsstand of a Japanese hotel, lost also in a non-book archive whose accumulation has no longer anything in common with the library. Billions of tourists, whether Americans or not, will have less and less opportunities to run into this thing in some "curious meeting." And this crafty little book, some would consider it still too clever, industrious, manipulative, overloaded with a knowledge impatient to show itself by hiding itself, by *supposing* itself under everything: *in sum*, bad literature, vulgar in that it never leaves its chance to the incalculable simplicity of the poem, grimacing with an overcultivated and hyperscholastic technology, literature of a subtle doctor, a little too subtle, in other words, the literature of a Doctor Pangloss with his eyes newly opened (wasn't this somewhat Nora's opinion?) who would have had the calculated chance of being censored, and thus launched, by the U.S. postal authorities.

Even in its resignation to the phantasm, this yes-laughter reaffirms the mastery of a subjectivity that gathers all by gathering itself, or by delegating itself to the name, in what is nothing but a great general rehearsal [*répétition*], during the course of the sun, for one day from the Orient to the Occident. It condemns and condemns itself, at times sadistically, sardonically: cynicism of a grimace, of sarcasm and sneer, *brood of mockers*. It condemns itself and accuses itself, it takes upon itself the whole of memory, and it takes on the resumption, the exhaustion, and the second coming. There is no contradiction in saying so: this yes-laughter is that of Nietzsche's Christian donkey, the one that cries out *Ja ja*, perhaps even that of the Judeo-Christian animal that wants to make the Greek laugh once circumcised from his own laughter: an absolute knowledge as truth of religion, assumed memory, guilt, literature of burden [*somme*] as one speaks of a "beast of burden," literature of summons [*sommation*], moment of the debt: A, E, I, O, U (U 9.213), *I owe you*, this "I" constitutes itself from the debt itself; where it was, it comes to itself only on the basis of the debt.[40]

This relation between the debt and vowels, between the "I owe you" (I.O.U.) and vocalization, should have led me, but I do not have the time for it, to connect what I attempted to say elsewhere, in *The Post Card* or in "Two Words for Joyce," about the "and he war" and *Finnegans Wake*'s "Ha, he, hi, ho, hu" (FW 259.9), with *Ulysses*' I.O.U., a strange anagram of the French *oui*, translated horribly and didactically by "Je Vous Dois"[41] in the version authorized by Joyce, the one to which he said yes and thus consented to. Did he say it in French, all in vowels, or in English? Laughter laughs about having generations of heirs, readers, guardians, Joyce scholars,[42] and writers forever in its debt.

This yes-laughter of encircling reappropriation, of omnipotent Odyssean recapitulation, accompanies the setting up of an apparatus virtually capable of impregnating in advance its own certified signature, including perhaps also Molly's, all the countersignatures to come, even after a death of the artist as an old man, who then only carries off an empty shell, the accident of a substance. The filiation machine—legitimate or illegitimate—is functioning well, is ready for anything, to domesticate, to circumscribe or circumvent everything; it lends itself to the encyclopedic reappropriation of absolute knowledge that gathers itself as the Life of Logos, that is to say, also in the truth of natural death. We are here in Frankfurt to bear witness to this, in commemoration.

Yet, the eschatological tone of this yes-laughter seems to me to be inhabited or traversed, I prefer to say *haunted*, joyfully ventriloquized by an entirely different music, by the vowels of a completely different song. I can hear it too, quite close to the other one, like the yes-laughter of a gift without debt, light affirmation, practically amnesic, of a gift or an abandoned event, which is called in classical language "the work," a signature lost and without proper name that names and reveals the cycle of reappropriation and domestication of every paraph only to limit its phantasm; and in so doing, in order to introduce the necessary breach for the coming of the other, an other that one could always call Elijah, if Elijah is the name of the unpredictable other for whom a place must be kept, and no longer Elijah the grand operator of the central, Elijah the head of the megaprogramotelephonic network, but the other Elijah, Elijah the other. But this is a homonym, Elijah can always be either one at the same time, one cannot call on one without risking getting the other. And one must always run this risk. I thus return, in this last movement, to the risk or the chance of this contamination of one yes-laughter by the other, to the parasiting of an Elijah, that is, an ego, by the other.

Why did I associate the question of laughter, of a laughter that *remains*, as fundamental and quasi-transcendental tonality, to that of the "yes"?

In order to wonder what happens/arrives [*ce qui arrive*] with *Ulysses*, or with the happening/arrival [*arrivée*] of whatever or whomever, that of Elijah for instance, and we must attempt to think the singularity of the event: and thus the uniqueness of a signature, or rather an irreplaceable mark that cannot necessarily be reduced to a phenomenon of copyright readable through a proper name, after circumcision. We must attempt to think circumcision, if you will, on the basis of a possibility of the mark, that of a feature preceding and providing its figure. Now if laughter is a fundamental or abyssal tonality in *Ulysses*, if the analysis of it is exhausted by none of the available knowledge precisely because it laughs from knowing and at knowledge, then laughter bursts out at the very event of signature. Now there is no signature without *yes*. If signature does not amount to manipulating or mentioning a name, it supposes the irreversible commitment of the one who confirms, by *saying* or by *doing yes*, the contract of a mark left behind.

Before wondering about who signs, whether Joyce is or is not Molly, and about the difference between the author's signature and that of a figure or fiction signed by the author, before debating on sexual difference as duality and stating one's conviction with respect to the "one-sidedly womanly woman" character (I cite Frank Budgen and a few others after him) of Molly the beautiful plant, the herb or the *pharmakon*, or the "one-sidedly masculine" character of James Joyce,[43] before taking into account what he said of the "nonstop monologue" as "the indispensable countersign to Bloom's passport to eternity"[44] (the competence of the Joyce of letters and conversations does not seem to me to enjoy any privilege), before manipulating clinical categories and a psychoanalytic knowledge that are derivative of the possibilities of which we speak here, we will wonder what a signature is: it requires a *yes* "older" than the question "what is?" since this question already supposes it, "older" than Knowledge. We will wonder why the *yes* always arrives/happens as a "*yes, yes.*" I say the *yes* and not the word "yes" for there can be some *yes* without a word.

PS: (January 2, 1987.) A *yes* without word thus could not be a "word-origin," an archi-word (*Urwort*). It resembles it, nonetheless, and there lies the whole enigma, as one can resemble God. And it is true that the *yes* of which Rosenzweig spoke has the original character of an *Urwort* only to the extent that it is a silent word, mute, a sort of transcendental of language, before and beyond any affirmative statement. It is the *yes* of God, the *yes* in God: "This is the power of the Yes, that it adheres to everything, that unlimited possibilities of reality lie hidden in it. It is the original word of language (*Urwort*), one of those which make possible—not sentences but, to begin with, simply words that go into sentences, words as elements of the sentence. *Yes* is not an element of the sentence, nor even the shorthand sign of a sentence, although it can be used as such: in reality it is the silent companion of all the elements of a sentence, the confirmation, the 'sic,' the 'amen' behind every word. It gives to every word in the sentence its right to existence, it offers it the chair where it may sit, it 'sets.' The first Yes in God establishes the divine essence in all infinity. And the first Yes is 'in the beginning.' "[45]

VI

It would thus be necessary, it would have been necessary, to preface all these discourses by a long meditation, learned and thoughtful, on the meaning, the function, and especially the presupposition of the *yes*: before language, in language but also in an experience of the plurality of languages that perhaps no longer pertains to a linguistics in the strict sense. Broadening the scope toward a pragmatics, although necessary in my view, remains insufficient so long as it does not open onto a thinking of the trace or of writing, in the sense that I attempted to articulate elsewhere and that I do not want to reconstitute here.

What is being said, written, and what happens/arrives with *yes*?

Yes can be implied without the word being said or written. This allows, for instance, the multiplication of *oui* in the French translation everywhere where one supposes that a *oui* is marked by English sentences in which the word "yes" is absent. However, since a *yes* is coextensive with every statement, it is very tempting, in French but first in English, to duplicate everything by a sort of continuous *yes*, to double even the articulated *yeses* by the simple mark of a rhythm, intakes of breath in the form of pauses or murmured interjections, as it happens sometimes in *Ulysses*: the *yes* comes, from me to me, from me to the other in me, from the other to me, to confirm the basic telephonic "hello": yes, that's right, that's what I am saying, I am speaking, yes, there I am, I am speaking, yes, yes, you are hearing me, I can hear you, yes, we are here speaking, there is language, you are hearing me well, this is the case, it is taking place, it happens/arrives, it writes itself, it marks itself, yes, yes.

We start again from the *phenomenon yes*, the *yes* that is manifest and manifestly marked as a *word*, whether spoken, written, or phonogramed. Such a word says, but says nothing by itself, if by saying we mean to designate, sow, or describe something that would be outside language or outside marking. Its only references are other marks, which are also marks of the other. Since the yes says, shows, names nothing outside marking, some might be tempted to conclude from this that *yes* says nothing: an empty word, *barely* an adverb, since any adverb, following the grammatical category according to which one situates the *yes* in our languages, has a richer, more determined semantic charge than the *yes*, even if it always supposes it. In sum, the *yes* would be transcendental adverbiality, the ineffaceable supplement of all verbs: in the beginning was the adverb, yes, but as an interjection, still very close to a preconceptual vocalization, the perfume of a discourse.

Can one sign with a perfume? In the same way that one cannot replace *yes* by a thing that it would supposedly describe (in fact it describes nothing, states nothing even if it is a sort of performative implied in any statement: yes I am stating, it is stated that, etc.) nor even by the thing it is supposed to approve or affirm, likewise one cannot replace the *yes* by the names of concepts supposed to describe this act or this operation, if it is even an act or an operation. The concept of activity or actuality does not seem to me apt to account for a *yes*. And one cannot replace this quasi-act by "approval," "affirmation," "confirmation," acquiescence," "consent." The word "affirmative" used in the military in order to avoid all kinds of technical risks does not replace the yes, but still presupposes it: yes, I do say "affirmative."

What does this *yes*, which names, describes, designates nothing, and which has no reference outside marking, gives us to think? Outside marking and not outside language for the *yes* can occur without words, in any case without the word *yes*. Because of its radically non-constative or non-descriptive scope, even if it says *yes* to a description or to a narration, *yes* is through and through, and par excellence, a performative. But this characterization seems to me insufficient. First because a performative must be a sentence, and a sentence sufficiently endowed with meaning by itself, in a given conventional context, to produce a particular event. Now I do believe, yes, that—to state this in a classical philosophical code—*yes* is the transcendental condition of every performative dimension. A promise, an oath, an order, a commitment, always imply a *yes, I sign*. The *I* in the *I sign* says *yes* and says *yes* to itself even if it signs a simulacrum. Any event brought about by a performative mark, any writing in the broad sense, engages a *yes*, whether or not phenomenalized, that is, verbalized or adverbalized as such. Molly says *yes*, she recalls *yes*, the *yes* she says with her eyes to ask for *yes* with her eyes, etc.

We are here in a place that is *not yet* the space where the great questions of the origin of negation, of affirmation and denegation can and must be deployed. And not even the space where Joyce was able to reverse the "*Ich bin der Geist der stets verneint*" by saying that Molly is the flesh that always says *yes*. The yes we are referring to now is "prior" to all these reversible alternatives, to all these dialectics. They presuppose and include it. Before the *Ich* in *Ich bin* affirms or denies, it posits itself or pre-poses itself: not as an ego, a conscious or unconscious ego, masculine or feminine subject, spirit or flesh, but as the pre-performative force that, in the form of an "I" for instance, marks that the *I* addresses itself to some other, however indeterminate he or she may be: "Yes-I," "yes-I-say-to-the-other," even if *I* says "no" and even if *I* addresses itself without speaking. The minimal and basic *yes*, telephonic *hello* or tap through a prison wall, marks, before meaning [*vouloir dire*] or signifying: "I-there," listen, answer, there is some mark, there is some other. Negativities may ensue, but even if they engulfed everything, such a "yes" can no longer be erased.

I had to yield to the rhetorical necessity of translating this minimal and undetermined, almost virginal, address into words, and words such as "I," "I am," "language," etc., at the place where the position of the *I*, of being and of language are still derivative with respect to this *yes*. This is the whole difficulty for those who want to say something about the *yes*. A metalanguage will always be impossible on this subject to the extent that it will itself suppose an event of the *yes* that it will not be able to understand. This will be the same for any accounting or computation, for any calculation aiming to adjust a series of *yeses* to the principle of reason and its machines. *Yes* marks that there is an address to the other.

This address is not necessarily a dialogue or an interlocution, since it supposes neither voice nor symmetry, but in advance the haste of a response that is already asking. For there is some other, thus if there is some *yes*, the other is no longer produced by the same or the ego. *Yes*, condition of every signature and performative, addresses itself to some other, which it does not constitute, and it can only begin by *asking*, as a response to an always prior demand, to *ask* him or her to say *yes*. Time only appears from this singular anachrony. These commitments may remain fictitious, fallacious, always reversible, and the address may remain divisible or undetermined; this changes nothing in the necessity of the structure. It breaks *a priori* any possible monologue. Nothing is less a monologue than Molly's "monologue" even if, within certain conventional limits, one is justified in considering it as belonging to the genre or kind "monologue." But a discourse situated between two qualitatively different "Yeses," two "Yeses" in capital letters, thus two gramophoned "Yeses," could not be a monologue, at most a soliloquy.

But we understand why the appearance of a monologue can impose itself here, precisely because of the *yes, yes*. The *yes* says nothing and asks nothing but another *yes*, the *yes* of an other which we will see is analytically—or by an *a priori synthesis*—implied in the first *yes*. The latter only poses itself, proposes itself, marks itself in the call for its confirmation, in the *yes, yes*. It begins with the *yes, yes*, by the second *yes*, by the other *yes*, but since it is still only a *yes* that *recalls* (and Molly *remembers* and *recalls* herself from the other *yes*), one is always tempted to call this anamnesis a monologue. And a tautology. The *yes* says nothing but the *yes*, another *yes* that resembles the first *yes* even if it says *yes* to the coming of a wholly other *yes*. It seems monotautological or specular, or imaginary, because it opens the position of the *I*, itself the condition of any performativity. Austin recalls that the grammar of the performative par excellence is that of a sentence in the first person of the present indicative: yes, I promise, I accept, I refuse, I command, *I do, I will,* etc. . . . . "He promises" is not an explicit performative and it cannot be so except if an "I" is implied, as for instance, in: "I swear that he promises, etc."

Recall Bloom at the chemist's. He speaks to himself, among other things, about perfumes. And also recall that Molly's *yeses,* the herb, also belong to the element of perfume. I could have, and I thought about doing it for a moment, transformed this paper into a treaty of perfumes, that is, of the *pharmakon*, and titled it "Of the Perfumative in Ulysses." Recall that Molly remembers all these *yeses,* and remembers herself through all these *yeses* as so many consents to that which smells good, namely perfume: "he asked me would I yes to say yes my mountain flower ⟨Bloom's name, Flower, pseudonymized on the postcard as *poste restante*, evaporates here⟩ and first I put my arms around him yes and drew him down to me so he could feel my breasts all perfume yes ⟨. . .⟩" (U 18.1605–8). At the very beginning of the book, the bed, flesh, and the yes are also calls of perfume: "To smell the gentle smoke of tea, fume of the pan, sizzling butter. Be near her ample bedwarmed flesh. Yes, yes" (U 4.237–39).

The "yes, I will" seems tautological, it unfolds the repetition called and presupposed by the so-called primary yes, which in sum only says "I will" and "I" as "I will." Well, do recall, I was saying, Bloom at the chemist's. He speaks to himself about perfumes: "⟨. . .⟩ had only one skin. Leopold, yes. Three we have" (U 5.498–99). A line further: "But you want a perfume too. What perfume does your? *Peau d'Espagne*. That orangeflower" (U 5.499–501). From there, he goes to the bath, then to a massage: "Hammam. Turkish. Massage. Dirt gets rolled up in your navel. Nicer if a nice girl did it. Also I think I. Yes I. Do it in the bath" (U 5.502–4). If one isolates this passage ("Also I think I. Yes I"), as one always has the right, and not, one has the minimal *proposition*, moreover equivalent to the *I will*, which manifests the hetero-tautology of the *yes* that is implied in every cogito as thinking, positing of self and will to position of self. But despite the umbilical, narcissistic or navel-gazing [*nombrilique*] scene, *navel cord again,* despite the archi-narcissistic and auto-affective appearance of this "Yes-I" that dreams of massaging itself, of washing itself, of appropriating itself, of making itself clean by itself in the caress, the *yes* addresses itself to some other and can only appeal to the *yes* of the other, and begins by responding. We are running out of time, I hurry up and use an even more telegraphic style. The French translation for "I think I. Yes I" is quite insufficient, since it proposes "Je pense aussi à. Oui, je," instead of "Je pense je," I think the I or the *I* thinks *I*, etc. As for the "Curious longing I" that follows immediately, becomes in French "Drôle d'envie que j'ai là, moi."[46] The response, the *yes* of the other, comes from elsewhere to bring him out of his dream, in the somewhat automatic form of the *yes* of a chemist. "Yes, sir, the chemist said" (U 5.507), who twice tells him how much he owes: "Yes, sir, the chemist said. You can pay altogether, sir, when you come back" (U 5.514–15). The dream of a perfumed bath, a clean body, and a smooth massage goes on as far as the Christly repetition of a "this is my body," a repetition thanks to which one crosses oneself in ecstasy like the anointing of the Lord: "Enjoy a bath now: clean trough of water, cool enamel, the gentle tepid stream. This is my body" (U 5.565–66). The following paragraph refers to the anointing of Christ ("oiled by scented melting soap" [U 5.568]), the navel, the flesh ("his navel, bud of flesh," the remainder of the umbilical cord as remainder of the mother), and it's the end of the chapter with, again, the word "flower," Bloom's other signature: "a languid floating flower" (U 5.571–72).

The great dream of perfumes unfolds in "Nausicaa"; it is a movement of fidelity to Molly that begins with a "Yes. That's her perfume" and articulates itself as a grammar of perfumes.

This self-position of the self in the *yes* returns unceasingly, each time in a different form, all through the journey. One of those places, among others (I cite it because it is quite close to one of the A. E. I. O. U.) is the one that calls the "I" an "entelechy of forms." But "I" is there both *mentioned* and *used*:

> But I, entelechy, form of forms, am I by memory because under everchanging forms.
> I that sinned and prayed and fasted.
> A child Conmee saved from pandies.
> I, I and I. I.
> A.E.I.O.U. (U 9.208–13)

A bit further: "Her ghost at least has been laid for ever. She died, for literature at least, before she was born" (U 9.215–16). This is the section about the ghost and the French Hamlet *"lisant au livre de lui-même"* (U 9.114).⁴⁷ John Eglinton says there, concerning the French, that "Yes ⟨. . .⟩. Excellent people, no doubt, but distressingly shortsighted in some matters" (U 9.127–28).

Elsewhere, at the end of "Nausicaa," Bloom writes then erases something in the sand:

> Write a message for her. Might remain. What?
> I. ⟨. . .⟩
> AM. A. (U 13.1256–64)

The self-position in the *yes*, or the Ay, is nonetheless neither tautological nor narcissistic, nor is it egological even if it initiates the movement of circular reappropriation, the odyssey that can give rise to all these determined modalities. It keeps open the circle it begins. Similarly, it is not yet performative, not yet transcendental although it remains presupposed by all performativity, *a priori* for any constative theoricity, for all knowledge and transcendentality. For that very reason, it is pre-ontological, if ontology says what is or the being of what is. The discourse about being presupposes the responsibility of the *yes*: yes, what is said is said, I respond—or it is responded—to the call of being, etc. . . . Still in a telegraphic style, I would then situate the possibility of the yes and of the yes-laughter in the place where transcendental egology, the onto-encyclopedia, the great speculative logic, fundamental ontology, and the thought of being open onto a thinking of the gift and of sendings that they presuppose but cannot incorporate. I cannot develop this argument as I would need to and as I have attempted to do elsewhere. I will content myself with connecting these remarks to those, at the beginning of this journey, which concerned the network of postal sendings in *Ulysses*: postcard, letter, check, telegramophone, telegram, etc.

The self-affirmation of the *yes* can only address itself to the other by recalling itself to itself, by saying to itself *yes, yes*. The circle of this universal presupposition, quite comical in itself, is like a sending to oneself, a sending-back from oneself to oneself that *at the same time never leaves itself and yet never arrives at itself*. Molly says to herself (apparently speaking to herself alone), she recalls that she says *yes* by asking the other to ask her to say *yes*, and she begins or ends up by saying *yes* by responding to the other in her, but in order to tell that other that she will say *yes* if the other asks her, *yes*, to say *yes*. These sendings and sendings back always mimic the situation of the questions/answers of the Scholastics. And we see the scene of "sending oneself to oneself" replayed many times in *Ulysses* in its literally postal form. As well as always marked with derision, like phantasm and failure themselves. The circle does not close. For lack of time, I will but mention three examples. First, Milly, who at the age of four or five was sending herself love notes comparing herself to a "looking glass" ("*O Milly Bloom* ⟨. . .⟩ / *You are my lookingglass*" [U 4.287–88]). She left to that end "pieces of folded brown paper in the letterbox" (U 4.285–86). This is, at least, what the French translation says ("Elle s'envoyait";[48] the English text is less clear, but never mind). As for Molly, the philatelist's daughter, she sends herself everything, like Bloom and Joyce, but this is remarked *en abyme* in the literality of the sequence that narrates how she also sends herself to herself through the post of bits of paper: "like years not a letter from a living soul except the odd few I posted to myself with bits of paper in them ⟨. . .⟩" (U 18.698–99). Four lines above, she is sent or *sent back* by him: "but he never forgot himself when I was there sending me out of the room on some blind excuse [. . .]" (U 18.694–95).

VII

It is thus a question of sending oneself. And in the end, of sending someone to oneself who says *yes*, without needing, in order to say it, what the idiom or slang babelizes in the name of "getting off" ["*s'envoyer*," "*s'envoyer soi-même en l'air*"] or "getting off with somebody" ["*s'envoyer quelqu'un*"].⁴⁹ The "sending oneself" barely allows itself a detour via the virgin mother when the father imagines that he sends himself the seed of a consubstantial son: "a mystical estate, an apostolic succession, from only begetter to only begotten ⟨. . .⟩" (U 9.838–39). This is one of the passages on "*Amor matris*, subjective and objective genitive, may be the only true thing in life. Paternity may be a legal fiction" (U 9.842–44). My third example precedes it slightly and comes immediately after the *Was Du verlachst wirst Du noch dienen*: "He Who Himself begot middler the Holy Ghost and Himself sent Himself, Agenbuyer, between Himself and others, Who ⟨. . .⟩" (U 9.493–94). Two pages further:

> —Telegram! he said. Wonderful inspiration! Telegram! A papal bull!
> He sat on a corner of the unlit desk, reading aloud joyfully:
> —*The sentimentalist is he who would enjoy without incurring the immense debtorship for a thing done.* Signed: Dedalus. (U 9.548–51)

To be more and more aphoristic and telegraphic, I would say to conclude that the Ulyssean circle of *sending oneself* governs a reactive yes-laughter, the manipulative operation of hypermnesic reappropriation, when the phantasm of a signature wins out, and a signature gathering the sending in order to gather itself by itself. But when, and this is only a question of rhythm, the circle opens, reappropriation is renounced, the specular gathering of the sending can be joyfully dispersed in the multiplicity of unique yet countless sendings, then the other *yes* laughs, the other, yes, laughs.

Now, the relation of a *yes* to the Other, of a *yes* to the other and a *yes* to the other *yes*, must be such that the contamination of the two *yeses* remains fatal. And not only as a threat: but also as a chance. With or without words, heard in its minimal event, a *yes* demands *a priori* its own repetition, its own memorizing, and that a *yes* to the *yes* inhabits the arrival of the "first" *yes*, which is therefore never simply originary. One cannot say *yes* without promising to confirm it and to remember it, to harbor it, countersigned in another says *yes*, without promise and memory, without the promise of memory. Molly remembers, recalls herself [*se rappelle*].

This memory of a promise initiates the circle of reappropriation, with all the risks of technical repetition, automated archives, gramophony, simulacrum, of errancy without an address and destination. A yes must entrust itself to memory. Having come already from the other, in the dissymmetry of the demand, and from the other to whom it is asked to ask for a *yes*, the *yes* entrusts itself to the memory of the other, of the *yes* of the other and of the other *yes*. All the risks are already crowding around, as early as the first breath of the other. And the first breath is suspended in the breath of the other, already, always a second breath. It remains so out of sound and out of sight, in advance connected to some "gramophone in the grave."

We cannot separate the twin *yeses*, and yet they remain wholly other. Like Shem and Shaun, like writing and the post. Such a coupling seems to me to secure, not so much the signature of *Ulysses*, but the *vibration* of an event that *only happens by asking, only succeeds in asking* [qui n'arrive qu'à demander]. A differential vibration of several tonalities, of several qualities of yes-laughters that cannot be stabilized in the indivisible simplicity of one single sending, from oneself to oneself, or from a single co-signing, but which call for the countersigning of the other, for a yes that would resonate in an entirely different writing, another language, another idiosyncrasy, with another timbre.

I return to you, to the community of Joycean studies. Suppose that a department of Joycean studies, under the authority of an Elijah Professor, Chairman, or Chairperson, decided to put my reading to the test by instituting a "program," the first phase of which would consist in sketching a great typology of all the *yeses* in *Ulysses*, before moving on to the yes in *Finnegans Wake*. The chairperson agrees (the chair, the flesh [*la chair*], always says yes) to buy an nth-generation computer that would be up to the task. The proposed operation could go quite far, I could keep you for hours describing what I have myself computed with a pencil: the mechanical counting of the *yeses* legible in the original, more than 222 in all, of which more than a quarter, at least 79, are to be found in Molly's so-called monologue (!), an even greater number in French, if we include the types of words, phrases, or rhythmic pauses that are effectively translated by "*oui*" ("ay," "well," "he nodded," etc.),[50] even at times in the absence of the word "yes." Another count would be necessary in each language, with a special treatment reserved for those used in *Ulysses*. What should we do, for example, with "*mon père, oui*," which is in French in the original, or with that "*O si certo*" whose "yes" stands as near as possible to Satanic temptation, that of the spirit saying "no" ("You prayed to the devil ⟨. . .⟩ *O si, certo!* Sell your soul for that ⟨. . .⟩" [U 3.130–32]). Beyond this very perilous counting of the explicit *yeses*, the chairperson would decide or promise two tasks which would be impossible for the computer of which we have today the concept and mastery. These are two impossible tasks for the reasons I have given and which I reduce to two main types.

1. By hypothesis, we would have to organize the different categories of *yeses* according to a large number of criteria. I have found at least ten categories of modalities.[51] This list cannot be closed, since each category can be divided into two, depending on whether *yes* appears in a manifest *monologue* as a response to the other *within oneself*[52] or in a manifest *dialogue*. We would have to take into account the different tonalities of these alleged modalities of the *yes*, in English and in all languages. Now, even if we suppose that we could give the computer the relevant instructions to discern these subtle changes in tone, which is already quite doubtful, the over-marking of every *yes* with the remainder of a quasi-transcendental *yes-laughter* can no longer give rise to a diacritical analysis ruled by binary logic. The two qualitatively different *yes-laughters* call out to each other and imply each other irresistibly as soon as they both demand and risk the signed pledge. One doubles the other: not as a countable presence, but as a specter. The *yes* of memory, the recapitulating mastery, the reactive repetition immediately duplicates the light, dancing *yes* of affirmation, the open affirmation of the gift. Reciprocally, two responses or two responsibilities refer to each other without having any relation between them. The two sign yet prevent the signature from gathering itself. All they can do is call for another *yes*, another signature. And furthermore, one cannot differentiate between two *yeses* that *must* gather together like twins, to the point of simulacrum, the one being the gramophony of the other.

I hear this vibration as the very music of *Ulysses*. The computer today cannot enumerate these interlacings, despite all the many ways it is already able to help us. Only a computer which has not yet been invented could answer that music in *Ulysses*, by attempting to integrate its other language and writing, and therefore by adding its own score. What I say or write here only advances one proposition, a small piece in comparison with that other text that the unheard-of computer would be.

2. Hence the second form of the argument. The operation assigned to the computer or the institute by the "chairperson,"[53] its very program, in fact, presupposes a *yes*—some would call it a speech act—which, in responding as it were to the event of the *yeses* in *Ulysses* and to their call, to that which in their structure is or proffers the call, both *belongs and does not belong* to the analyzed corpus. The chairperson's *yes*, like that of the program of whoever writes on *Ulysses*, responding and countersigning in some way, can neither be counted nor discounted, anymore than the *yeses* that it calls for in turn. It is not just binarity, but also and for the same reason totalization, which proves impossible, as well as the closing of the circle, and *Ulysses*' return, and Ulysses himself, and the sending to oneself of some indivisible signature.

Yes, yes, this is what provokes laughter, and one never laughs alone, as Freud said correctly, never without sharing something of the same repression.[54]

Or, rather, this is what provokes laughter [*donne à rire*] as it(d) makes one think [*donne à penser*]. And as it(d) gives [*ça donne*], quite simply, beyond laughter and beyond the *yes*, beyond the *yes/no/yes*, beyond the *ego/not-ego*, which can always turn into a dialectic.

But, is it possible to sign with a perfume?

Only another event can sign, or countersign to bring it about that an event has already happened. This event, which one naïvely calls the first event, can only affirm itself through the confirmation of the other: a wholly other [*tout autre*] event.

The other signs. And the yes relaunches itself infinitely, much more than, and quite differently from, "yes, yes, yes, yes, yes, yes, yes," Mrs. Breen's week of seven *yeses* when she listens to Bloom tell her the story of Marcus Tertius Moses and Dancer Moses: "Mrs. Breen (*eagerly*) Yes, yes, yes, yes, yes, yes, yes" (U 15.575–76).

I decided to stop here because I almost had an accident as I was jotting down this last sentence, when, on leaving the airport, I was driving home returning from Tokyo.

Notes

1. TN: Derrida takes up the issue in a four-part series of lectures under the general title "Transfer Ex Cathedra: Language and Institutions of Philosophy," held at the University of Toronto from May 31–June 25, 1984, that is, concurrent with the composition and delivery of "Ulysses Gramophone" (internally dated May 11, 1984, presented at the International James Joyce Symposium on June 12, 1984). The first two lectures—"If There Is Cause to Translate I: Philosophy in Its National Language (Toward a 'licterature en françois')" and "If There Is Cause to Translate II: Descartes' Romances, or The Economy of Words"—address the linguistic problem of Descartes' *Discours de la Méthode* mentioned in the text above. See Jacques Derrida, "Transfert Ex Cathedra: Le Langage et les Institutions Philosophiques" in *Du droit à la philosophie* (Paris: Galilée, 1990), 281–394, 281–341. English translation: "Transfer Ex Cathedra: Language and Institutions of Philosophy," trans. Jan Plug et al., in *Eyes of the University: Right to Philosophy 2*, ed. Jan Plug (Stanford: Stanford University Press, 2004), 1–80, 1–42.

2. TN: See Jacques Derrida, "Des Tours de Babel," English translation: "Des Tours de Babel," trans. Joseph F. Graham (PSI 191–225/203–35).

3. TN: In English in the original.

4. TN: James Joyce, *Ulysse*, ed. Jacques Aubert, trans. Auguste Morel, Stuart Gilbert, Valery Larbaud, *Œuvres complètes*, vol. 2 (Paris: Gallimard, 1995), 697.

The credit line for the translation reads: "Traduction intégrale d'*Ulysse* par Auguste Morel, assisté de Stuart Gilbert, entièrement revue par Valery Larbaud et l'auteur [Complete translation of *Ulysses* by Auguste Morel, assisted by Stuart Gilbert, entirely reviewed by Valery Larbaud and the author]." Derrida's citations from this edition will be rendered into English within the notes when not included in the main text; here, "sheaf of events."

    5. TN: In English in the original.

    6. TN: In English in the original.

    7. TN: In English in the original.

    8. TN: Joyce, *Ulysse*, 694.

    9. The treatment of this question would be heavily overdetermined by the Irish idiom, which weighs silently and obliquely on the entire text. In its own way, Irish also avoids *yes* and *no* in their direct form. To the question, "Are you sick?," it replies neither by *yes* nor *no*, but by "I am" or "I am not." "Was he sick?" "He was" or "he was not," etc. The way in which the *hoc* could have taken on the meaning of "yes" is no doubt not foreign to this process. *Oïl* (*hoc illud*) and *oc* have thus served to designate languages by the way in which people were saying *yes* in them. Italian was sometimes called the *si* language. Yes, the name of the language. TN: One finds in Latin two distinct terms for signifying assent (*yes*): *hoc ille*, "this (is) it," and *hoc*, "this," which became *oïl* and *oc*, respectively. See TW 39/53.

    10. TN: In English in the original.

    11. TN: In English in the original.

    12. TN: Gabler's edition of *Ulysses* was launched at the same symposium at which Derrida delivered this talk.

    13. Since then, the week after this lecture, a student and friend whom I met in Toronto called my attention to another calculation. This one resulted in a much higher number, probably because it included all the *ay*—I note in passing that since it is pronounced like the word I, it raises a problem to which I will return. Here is this other calculation, from Noel Riley Fitch in *Sylvia Beach and the Lost Generation: A History of Literary Paris in the Twenties and Thirties* (New York: Norton, 1983). If I cite the entire paragraph, it is because of its importance beyond the arithmetic of the yes: "One consultation with Joyce concerned Benoist-Méchin's translation of the final words of *Ulysses*: 'and his heart was going like mad and yes I said Yes I Will.' The young man wanted the novel to conclude with a final 'yes' following the 'I will.' Earlier Joyce had considered using 'yes' (which appears 354 times in the novel) as his final word, but had written 'I will' in the draft that Benoist-Méchin was translating. There followed a day of discussion in which they dragged in all the world's greatest philosophers. Benoist-Méchin, who argued that in French the '*oui*' is stronger and smoother, was more persuasive in the philosophical discussion. 'I will' sounds authoritative and Luciferian. 'Yes,' he argued, is optimistic, an affirmation to the world beyond oneself. Joyce, who may have changed his mind earlier in the discussion, conceded hours later, 'yes,' the young man was right, the book would end with 'the most positive word in the language'" (109–10).

    14. TN: Derrida plays here on the homonymy in French between *oui* (yes) and *ouïe* (hearing), between *oui dire* (saying yes) and *ouï-dire* (hearsay).

15. TN: Derrida plays here on two idiomatic expressions in French: "Un point c'est tout," literally "one point, that is all," which means "period!" as a way to end a discussion, and "mettre les points sur les i," which means to spell things out.

16. TN: In English in the original.

17. TN: Petit-Rœulx, Belgium: Cistre, 1984. Rabaté revised this book for its English translation (which was dedicated to Derrida), *James Joyce, Authorized Reader* (Baltimore: The Johns Hopkins University Press, 1991). In the English version, the chapter Derrida refers to is now the fifth chapter and is titled "Spinning Molly's Yarn."

18. TN: In English in the original.

19. TN: In English in the original.

20. Elsewhere, in the brothel, it is still the circumcised who say the "Shema Israel," and there is also the *Lacus Mortis*, the Dead Sea: "THE CIRCUMCISED: (*in dark guttural chant as they cast dead sea fruit upon him, no flowers*) *Shema Israel Adonai Elohenu Adanai Echad*" (U 15.3227–28). And while we are speaking of *Ulysses*, of the Dead Sea, and of the gramophone, and soon of laughter, here is, from *Remembrance of Things Past*: "He stopped laughing; I should have liked to recognize my friend, but, like Ulysses in the *Odyssey* when he rushes forward to embrace his dead mother, like the spiritualist who tries in vain to elicit from a ghost an answer which will reveal its identity, like the visitor at an exhibition of electricity who cannot believe that the voice which the gramophone restores unaltered to life is not a voice spontaneously emitted by a human being, I was obliged to give up the attempt." A little higher up: "The familiar voice seemed to be emitted by a gramophone more perfect than any I had ever heard." *The Past Recaptured*, trans. Andreas Mayor (New York: Vintage, 1971), 188–89. Biographies: "Those of the earlier generation—Paul Valéry, Paul Claudel, Marcel Proust, André Gide (all born around 1870)—were either indifferent to or hostile toward his work. Valéry and Proust were indifferent. ⟨. . .⟩ Joyce had only one brief meeting with Proust, who died within months after the publication of *Ulysses*" (Fitch, *Sylvia Beach and the Lost Generation*, 95). ". . . coincidence of meeting . . . galaxy of events . . ." TN: "a person-to-person call" in English in the original.

21. TN: James Joyce, *Ulysses*, 138.

22. TN: Martin Heidegger, *Sein und Zeit* (Tübingen: Max Niemeyer Verlag, 1993), 277; the English is translated from Derrida's translation of this passage.

23. TN: Play on *Langue d'oïl*, which was the ancient northern Gallo-Romance language, the word *oïl* signifying *yes*.

24. I am told that James Joyce's grandson is here, now, in this room. This citation is obviously dedicated to him.

25. TN: In a letter to Frank Budgen dated August 16, 1921 Joyce writes: "Though probably more obscene than any preceding episode it seems to me to be perfectly sane full amoral fertilisable untrustworthy engaging shrewd limited prudent indifferent *Weib. Ich bin der* [sic] *Fleisch der stets bejaht*" (SL 285). The German phrase translates as "Woman. I am the flesh that constantly affirms" and is an inversion of Mephistopheles' characterization of himself in Goethe's *Faust*: "Ich bin der Geist der stets verneint [I am the spirit that constantly negates]." See J.W. von Goethe, *Faust I & II*, trans. Stuart Atkins, *Goethe: The Collected Works*, vol. 2 (Princeton: Princeton University Press, 1994), 36, l. 1338, translation modified.

26. TN: Joyce, *Ulysse*, 560: "It's me who operates all the telephones in this network here."

27. TN: Joyce, *Ulysse*, 560: literally, "Me, I say but yes," figuratively, "I say yes."

28. TN: In English in the original.

29. TN: In English in the original.

30. TN: In English in the original.

31. TN: Maurice Blanchot, *The Madness of the Day*, trans. Lydia Davis (Barrytown, N.: Station Hill Press, 1981), 7.

32. TN: Stuart Gilbert, *James Joyce's "Ulysses"* (New York: Vintage, 1955), 385.

33. TN: See Jacques Derrida, *Glas* (Paris: Galilée, 1974), English translation: *Glas*, trans. John P. Leavey Jr. and Richard Rand (Lincoln: University of Nebraska Press, 1986); *Signéspongel/Signsponge*, bilingual edition, trans. Richard Rand (New York: Columbia University Press, 1984); *Parages* (Paris: Galilée, 1985), English translation: *Parages*, ed. John P. Leavey, trans. various (Stanford: Stanford University Press, 2011).

34. TN: Both words in English in the original.

35. TN: the interspersed French here reads, "He comes! It's me! The laughing man! The primal man! . . . Ladies and gentlemen, make your bets! . . . The bets are finished! . . . No more bets! [literally, nothing goes anymore]."

36. TN: In editions prior to Gabler's, the text of the telegram was "Mother dying come home father."

37. TN: The French reads: "It's screamingly funny, you know. Myself, I'm a socialist. I don't believe in the existence of God. Don't tell this to my father." "He's a believer?" "My father, yes."

38. TN: The German reads: "what you ridicule, you will yet serve."

39. TN: In French, the expression "revenir de tout" also has the colloquial sense of having done it all, with the connotation of having lost, as a consequence, all of one's illusions.

40. TN: "La où c'etait, Il fut," a veiled reference to Freud's famous closing to lecture 31 of the *New Introductory Lectures on Psychoanalysis*: "Wo es war, soll Ich warden," translated by James Strachey as "Where id was, there ego shall be" (in Sigmund Freud, *The Standard Edition of the Complete Psychological Works of Sigmund Freud*, 24 volumes [London: The Hogarth Press, 1974], volume 22, 3–182, 80).

41. TN: Joyce, *Ulysse*, 216: "I Owe You."

42. TN: In English in the original.

43. TN: "Molly Bloom is the creation of a man; and James Joyce is, perhaps, as one-sidedly masculine as D. H. Lawrence was one-sidedly feminine" (Frank Budgen, *James Joyce and the Making of "Ulysses"* [Oxford: Oxford University Press, 1989], 269).

44. TN: Budgen, *James Joyce*, 270.

45. TN: Franz Rosenzweig. *The Star of Redemption*, trans. Barbara E. Galli (Madison: The University of Wisconsin Press, 2005), 35.

46. TN: Joyce, *Ulysse*, 94: "Strange desire that I have here."

47. TN: "reading from the book of himself," from Mallarmé's "Hamlet et Fortinbras" (*Œuvres complètes*, vol. 2, ed. Bertrand Marchal [Paris: Gallimard, 2003], 275).

48. TN: Joyce, *Ulysse*, 68: "She sent herself."

49. TN: Derrida plays here on the sexual connotation of the expression "s'envoyer en l'air" or "s'envoyer quelqu'un," literally "to send oneself up in the air"

or "to send oneself someone," and which in slang is equivalent to "getting off," and "getting off with someone."

50. Here are a few examples [TN: Pagination for the 1995 French edition follows the reference to the Gabler edition]: 1.252/10: *oui* purely and simply added; 3.11/41: *oui* for "I am"; 3.25/42: *oui* for "I will"; 3.144/46: *oui* for "ay"; 6.177–78/102–3 *Oui mais* for "Well but"; 6.289/106: *Oh mais oui* for "O, he did"; 6.536/114: *Je crois que oui* for "I believe so"; 6.695/119: *Oh mais oui* for "O, to be sure"; 7.123/135: *fit oui de la tête* for "nodded"; 7.185/137: *oui* for "Ay"; 7.364/143: *Pardi, oui* for "So it was"; 8.584–85/188: *Je crois que oui* for "I believe there is"; 8.781/194: *Oui, merci* for "Thank you"; 8.786/195: *Oui* for "Ay"; 8.842/196: *Hé oui* for "Ay"; 9.193/215: *Oui-da, il me la fallait* for "Marry, I wanted it"; 9.387/221: *Oui. Un oui juvénile de M. Bon* for "Yes, Mr. Best said youngly" [TN: In compiling his original list, Derrida used the 1948 Gallimard edition. As one of the emendations to the translation that Morel made in the 1950s, this line was changed to *Oui, fit juvénilement M. Bon*]; 9.540/226: *Oui-da* for "Yea"; 9.679/230: *Oh si* for "O, yes"; 9.1084/243: *Oui da* for "Ay"; 10.25–26/247: *Oh oui* for "Very well, indeed" [TN: A mistake in Derrida's collation: "Oh oui" translates "Oh yes"; "Very well, indeed" is several lines earlier]; 10.219/254: *Dame oui* for "Ay"; 10.870/274: *Elle fit oui* for "She nodded"; 10.906/275: *Oui, essayez voir* for "Hold him now"; 11.56/289: *Oui, Oui* for "Ay, ay"; 11.451/301: *oui, essayez voir* for "hold him now"; 11.496/303: *Mais oui, mais oui, appuyait M. Dedalus* for "Ay, ay, Mr. Dedalus nodded"; 11.627/307: *Oui, mais* for "But ⟨. . .⟩"; 11.824/313: *Oui, certainement* for "It certainly is"; 11.992/319: *Oui, chantez-nous ça* for "Ay do"; 11.1277/328: *Oui, oui* for "Ay, ay"; 12.322/339: *Oui* for "Ay" [TN: Another mistake in collation: The *Oui* translates as "Yes" a few lines earlier and this "Ay" is translated as "Pardi"]; 12.335/339: *Que oui* for "Ay"; 12.698–99/350: *Ben oui pour sûr* for "So I would" (complicated syntax); 12.843/355: *Ah, oui* for "Ay"; 12.1371/371: *Oui* for "Ay"; 12.1379/371: *Oui* for "Ay"; 12.1625/379: *Oui* for "That's so"; 12.1644/380: *Oui* for "Well"; 13.262/397: *oui* for "so I would"; 13.297/398: *Oui* for "Nay"; 13.842/416: *Ah oui!* for "What?"; 13.929/419: *Sapristi oui* for "Devil you are"; 13.936/419: *Oui!* for "See!"; 13.1206–7/429: *Elle regardait la mer le jour où elle m'a dit oui* for "Looking out over the sea she told me"; 14.609/453: *Oui da* for "Ay"; 15.264/494: *Je crois que oui* for "I suppose so"; 15.2200/560: *Moi je dis que oui* for "I say you are"; 15.4297/633: *Oui, je sais* for "O, I know"; 16.465/671: *Ben oui* for "Why"; 16.609/676: *Oui* for "Ay"; 16.690/679: *Si, si* for "Ay, ay"; 16.697/679: *Si, si* for "Ay, ay"; 18.266/811: *oui* for "well" [TN: "well" is a mistake made in the first edition; Gabler corrects to "west"]; 18.268/811: *oui bien sûr* for "but of course"; 18.882/832: *oui* for "ay"; 18.1260/846: *bien oui* for "of course"; 18.1502/854: *le disait oui* for "say they are." In total, more than fifty displacements of various kinds. A systematic typology could be attempted.

51. For instance: 1. The "yes" as a question: *oui? Allô?*: "Yes? Buck Mulligan said. What did I say?" (U 1.197); 2. The "yes" of rhythmic breathing in the form of a monologic self-approval: "Two in the back bench whispered. Yes. They knew ⟨. . .⟩" (2.34–35), or "Yes, I must" (3.60); 3. The "yes" of obedience: "Yes, sir" (3.85); 4. The "yes" marking an agreement on some fact: "O yes, but I prefer Q. Yes, but W is wonderful" (3.140); 5. The "yes" of passionate, desiring, breathing: "Be near her ample bedwarmed flesh. Yes, yes" (4.238–39); 6. The "yes" of calculating, precise,

determined breathing: "Yes, exactly" (5.310); 7. The "yes" of distracted politeness, as in "Yes, yes" (6.7); 8. The "yes" of emphatic confirmation: "Indeed yes, Mr. Bloom agreed" (6.542); 9. The "yes" of patent approval: "Yes, Red Murray agreed" (7.55); 10. The "yes" of insistent confidence: "Yes, yes. They went under" (7.568). This list is by definition open and the difference between monologue or manifest dialogue can also lend itself to all those parasitings and grafts that are most difficult to take entirely into account.

52. Closure is thus impossible. It poses new and destabilizing questions to the institution of Joycean studies. This is due to a variety of reasons. First, to those I just mentioned about the structure of a *yes*. Second, those pertaining to the new relation that Joyce deliberately and mischievously instituted—from a certain date—between the "prior-to-text" and the so-called completed or published work. He watched over [*veillé sur*] his archive. We know now that at a given point, aware of how the archive of the "work in progress" would be treated, he made it a part of the work itself and began to save rough drafts, sketches, approximations, corrections, variations, and studio works (I am thinking here of Ponge's *La Fabrique du Pré* [Geneva: Skira, 1971], or the manuscripts of *La Table* [Montreal: Éditions du Silence, 1982]). He thus deferred his signature at the very moment of the "ready for press." He has thus given to generations of academics, guardians of his "open work," a new, and in principle infinite, task. Rather than surrender accidently and posthumously to the "genetic criticism" industry, he instead, one might say, constructed the concept for it and programmed its routes and dead ends. The diachronic dimension, the incorporation or rather the addition of variants, the manuscript form of the work, the "page proofs," the typographical errors themselves, indicate essential moments in the work and not the accident of a "this is my corpus."

"I am exhausted, abandoned, no more young. I stand, so to speak, with an unposted letter bearing the extra regulation fee before the too late box of the general postoffice of human life" (U 15.2777–80).

53. TN: In English in the original.

54. TN: See Sigmund Freud, *Jokes and Their Relation to the Unconscious*, trans. James Strachey, in *The Standard Edition of the Complete Psychological Works of Sigmund Freud*, 24 volumes (London: The Hogarth Press, 1953–74), volume 8, 143.

The Night Watch[1]
(over "the book of himself")

translated by Pascale-Anne Brault and Michael Naas

"Aha! I know you, Grammer!"[2]

—James Joyce, *Ulysses*

Mallarmé . . . about Hamlet. He says: il se promène, lisant au livre de lui-même, don't you know, reading the book of himself.

—James Joyce, *Ulysses*, cited by Jacques Trilling[3]

Chapter 11, which takes place in the dwelling of the Sirens, reproduces a fugue *per canonem*, complete with trills, semibreve, staccato, presto, glissando, martellato, fortamento, pizzicati.

—Jean Paris, *James Joyce par lui-même*, cited by Jacques Trilling

. . . to read the effects of the text in a sort of polyphony, in multiple registers . . .

—Jacques Trilling, *James Joyce ou l'écriture matricide*

In a word, in brief, as befits a preface, I will speculate about a working hypothesis, one that will remain for me, to be sure, the object of a risky choice. It is a deliberate selection that I intend to sign, a boldly assumed sorting out, a *tri*, I might even say an essay, a trial run, an experimental attempt, a *try*[4] (a word that apparently has the same etymology as *tri*).

To what hypothesis am I referring? The author of this book, so well known and so well-versed in literature, psychoanalysis, music, and a few other arts, here proposes, he too, he first of all, to sort things out, to *trier*. My own *tri* would thus raise the stakes or speculate upon his own. For

Jacques Trilling would have proposed a *tri* or sorting out between the *mother* and *maternity*.

To distinguish between the mother and maternity, to sort them out [*trier*], to draw an infinitely fine but indivisible line between them, even when the thing seems undecidable—that, I would say, is Trilling's decisive gesture, his critical operation, his *krinein*. And this operation takes place at the very moment he reminds us of the inevitability or fatality for the one who writes, and par excellence for Joyce, of a certain matricide.

But here is the aporia that never fails to appear—and far from paralyzing the matricidal desire this aporia actually exacerbates it, begins by motivating it, and opens the way for it: if one distinguishes between [*trier*] the mother and maternity, it follows that one can dream of doing away with the mother, some particular mother, though one will never be done with the maternity of the mother. "One can always murder the mother," says Trilling, "but one will not for all that have done away with maternity. . . ."[5] One can always attempt (or *try*[6]) to kill the mother, but the best one can do is succeed in murdering some particular mother or figure of the mother, while maternity itself, maternity in its phantasm, survives. And it—or she—watches [*elle veille*], the night watcher or night vigil, the nightlight or vigil light [*veilleuse*]. She—or it—survives [*survit*] and surveys [*surveille*]. Funeral vigil [*veillée funèbre*]. Wake.[7] Maternity goes on, and will always go on, defying the matricide. One can kill the mother, yes, but one will never be done trying to be done with maternity, which, as a result, is never over and done with (an interminable analysis, therefore, since "one is never done killing off mourning"[8]). Maternity or the hounding of matricide. By chasing after matricide, by giving chase with such perseverance, one chases it away, deferring it and attempting to exclude it. Maternity is that which will never be done calling for *and* escaping impossible matricide. And thus impossible mourning. And it will never be done provoking writing. Watching over it and surveying it, like a specter that never sleeps.

The key witnesses here: Ulysses, Joyce, and a few others. Calling them to the witness stand, Trilling is able to get them to talk. In their own language. He interprets them in all their languages, and there are so many.

This *tri* or sorting out between the mother and maternity is at once inevitable and impossible. It condemns the matricide to impotence but also to the repetition of the murder, to the *attempted* murder in writing. We are given a demonstration of this in the course of an exercise whose musical virtuosity, to mention only this among its many virtues, consists most often in an oscillation, a beat, or, better, an accelerated vibration between adjacent but distinct notes. It is enough to have heard, as I once had the chance to do, Jacques Trilling play piano, whether alone or accompanied by the voice of Jacqueline Rousseau-Dujardin, and then to listen to a few notes of this text, to have the word *trill* on the tip of one's tongue. This book plays like a trill.

My wish, however, goes beyond an invitation to the concert or to the voyage[9]: it is that one may return over and over to this masterpiece of Jacques Trilling, as I myself returned to it, for a second time, after a long period of latency and reflection, overwhelmed precisely by the art of *return*, by the polytropic and polyphonic multiplication of anamnesis (so many memories in one and so many other memories in oneself), as by an Odyssean nostalgia. Everything is here reinaugurated, indeed augured, through this anticipation in the interpretation of signs that is the hallmark of augurs. Everything is reinvented following in the tracks of Ulysses, the written tracks, of course. Those of Homer and, in a brilliant superimposition, those of Joyce. Then those of the author. Between the two voyages, the two Ulysseses, there is the daring of a psychoanalytic invention: the discovery of a law. Freud reread and disturbed by Trilling. Beginning, perhaps, by Jacques Trilling as a child, Trilling as a schoolboy. But the schoolboy knows how to listen to himself and knows how to read; he is a writer at school, and he is disobedient, a writer who knows everything but makes fun of the lessons learned, a schoolboy who has become a *scholar*[10] and who ventures forth—self-analytically, as we naïvely say—there where he understands that we must no longer place our trust in accredited knowledge, in the canon, in consensual normality. For example, in Freud, in Oedipus, in parricide, in the name of the father, in the symbolic order and other reassuring stories of filiation.[11]

I reread *James Joyce ou l'écriture matricide* (1973) with a sort of jubilation tinged with a melancholic fervor. This piece of writing watched over [*veillait*] the birth of a friendship. Jacques Trilling generously sent it to me more than a quarter of a century ago, no doubt so that I might recognize, among so many other things, a few complicitous winks, particularly with regard to the *Phaedrus* and "Plato's Pharmacy," not far from a nod toward our friend Hélène Cixous, who was already the author of the first great reading of Joyce in France. We had not yet met, Jacques and I (or as I would wish to say, as elsewhere, James and I). Joyce was our common friend, like a secret between us, turning each of us into a sort of *secret sharer*,[12] to cite the title of a novella on the spectral double, the novella of another foreigner who knew how to make English his own. "The Secret Sharer" is not only "a secret companion"—"un compagnon secret" (as the title of this story of Conrad has been translated into French); I would prefer to speak of an acolyte, a secret guardian, or else—for the syntax of the title, "The Secret Sharer," allows it, "secret" being at once a noun and an attribute, the secret of the subject who shares and the secret as the object shared, kept or guarded by the two of them—a guardian who knows how, in secret, to watch over the secret that is shared: a secret partaker or sharer of the secret. I immediately expressed my admiration and gratitude to Jacques, and from that time on we never stopped sharing a sort of irony, always just a bit criminal, with regard to all the most frequented places, all the *commonplaces*,[13] where so many crossings still seemed forbidden, unknown, in truth *unnavigable*. How could I have known that one day I would be entrusted with this formidable task: *to attempt*, after Jacques' death, to preface this work without, unfortunately, being able to avoid privileging an interpretation, a speculation, a hypothesis, *a try*,[14] one that would risk betraying the inheritance, as if the truth could never but be betrayed by the inheritance, by the simple experience of the wake [*la veillée*], of legacy or filiation. Rousseau was keenly aware of this inevitability or fatality in the sorting out [*tri*] of letters. In the *Confessions* (XI) he confides that what troubled him most was "the want of a literary friend whom I could trust, in whose hands I could deposit my papers, so that, after my death, he might pick and choose from them [*triage*]."[15]

Unnavigable, I said. The unnavigable [*impraticable*] here becomes the very decor of this theater, the setting [*praticable*] for all the displacements of matricidal writing at work right here in *James Joyce ou l'écriture matricide*: the inventive clearing of a trail on the trail of another trail, following the trace of another trace, steps ventured at dangerous crossroads (between the reefs, I should say for this Homeric navigation), the risky crossing of an autobiography after Freud (an interminable self-analysis, if you prefer, the most tender, playful, teasing, the most implacable as well, the very school of self-analysis, that of a schoolboy who also reads "the book of himself"). All this boldly puts to work a very refined Joycean knowledge, one worthy of what is called in the academy a *Joyce scholar*—drawing so precisely, and so surely, from one of Jacques Trilling's mother tongues. And this knowledge is always put in the service of the revolution within the psychoanalytic revolution: the matricide rather than Oedipus, the matricide who weaves his ruses into the act of writing, a matricide who hounds the mother since he cannot have his way with maternity.

A certain Jacob is never very far away, all you have to do is go up a bit, toward the association of Freud's dream related to the death of Jacob Freud, his father: "we are asked to close $\frac{\text{our eyes}}{\text{an eye}}$."[16]

> This association indeed calls for a reader who has set out with Telemachus-Stephen in search of paternity. But what is singular (for these two dreams of gazes and of light no doubt govern the very particular writing of the immortal *Interpretation of Dreams*) is that with Joyce light and the gaze appear above all to be scrutinizing maternity. It is by means of a detour through Hell, with Freud, that we have found, in Homer, the specter of a mother who has

died of love for her absent son. What is being questioned here is the link between the giving birth of writing and maternity (this latter being more or less absent from the *Traumdeutung*), that is, the ineluctability of birth, of the marked hour, always already inscribed, and what the association of the dream "Father can't you see I'm burning" implies about the desire for the child's death. For Joyce, the place for such a link seems unlocatable between shadow and light, the ghost of the mother and the absent father. . . . Stephen already assailed by the specter of the mother in Ithaca in Martello Tower. . . . The mother rises up again. . . . As if the mother's womb—which one always wishes to be without a navel—arose here and there throughout the entire book, an uncircumventable re-presentation that language would run up against and turn around.[17]

You will have noticed—and I underscore this so as to justify my speculation—the *trill* of a rapid alternation between what denotes the supposedly real *mother* ("the mother's womb") and what connotes *maternity* (defined by "the ineluctability of birth, of the marked hour, always already inscribed").

One can already imagine the stakes of this *tri*—and its remainder, which will endlessly reanimate, which will always make rise up, as its leaven, as its ferment, the ineluctability or fatality of matricide: it is indeed possible to kill the mother, to replace her, to substitute one "womb" for another. This is more possible today than ever, though the possibility is ageless. But what is impossible to expunge is birth, dependency upon an originary date, upon an "act" of birth before any birth act or certificate. One can of course curse this act of birth, this act without act, this act before the act, this act before the first act. But the curse remains powerless, from Job ("Why did you bring me forth from the womb?" Job 10: 18) to Shakespeare—so important for Joyce and for Trilling, and right here in this text—to Baudelaire and so many others.[18] There is a curse because in cursing one does no more than confess that some evil or some accursed thing has taken place, without any possibility of remission. In confessing, the curse confirms, repeats, reproduces, and makes endure that which it would like to repress. There is no sense in wanting to expunge this evil [*mal*] insofar as it remains the very condition for such a wanting. The wanting inscribes denegation within it: I do not want, I cannot want what I say I want: not to be born—or to die. Like suicide, matricide (the curse of being born) bears within it this contradiction. But far from paralyzing matricide, the contradiction motivates it. Compulsively, interminably—and writing comes to be inscribed in this repetition. It signs it and countersigns it. What appears *impossible* through this curse or malediction, but also through every blessing or benediction, through every -diction, is to expunge, contest, or even confirm the contingency of my being-born, which always presupposes some denegation of being-born, and the simple thought of my virtual "not being born." Yet this impossible remains the only possibility I have of gaining access to the experience of existence, to the "I am," as well as to time, to the temporality of time inasmuch as it is always and first of all *my* time, my "living present." This access to the experience of the "I exist" is of varying intensity, no doubt, but the intensity is to be measured against that of an "I might have not been born"—which is presupposed by every "I should not have been born"—and against the correlative "I could die," which is presupposed by every "I should die."

How could one want not to be born? The curse of birth seals the powerlessness, protests against an irreversible *being-born*, an unforgivable, intransitive, unthinkable *being-born*: more or less, something other in any case, than a being or an origin.[19] Matricide puts us on the path of a birth irreducible to all ontology, to all ontological or phenomenological thinking about originarity. Being born, the event of "being born," has *already* come in place of the origin. Not only is the question no longer, not only is it already no longer, "to be or not to be," but it is even too late for the question "to be born or not to be born." Too late, then, for the question. Yes, the question comes too late, *being born* has taken place, namely, what comes to me—in short, me—from the other. From the other me. Before me the other me. Who is, without being my double, another *secret sharer*. That is what is pursued, that is who is hounded, under the name of "maternity," through the attempted murder. The desperate attempt that races and races to the rescue, as in Conrad's "The Secret Sharer," to save what it loses, its other double. Out of breath after such a delay, that is the race of matricidal writing. Not its source, for it has no source, and for good reason, but its endless race. A race without end because without origin. Birth, being born (not the being born *nothing* or *from* nothing, but always the *being born from . . . or in two's*, me and before me the other me): this is neither the beginning nor the origin nor even, save the phantasm, a point of departure. A dependency, no doubt, but not an origin or point of departure. A generation, perhaps, but without origin. The word *generation* is big with all these ambiguities. It's a ventriloquial word.[20]

Matricidal desire can thus become insatiable; it can oscillate, vacillate, vibrate very quickly, like a trill, between two notes, between the mother and maternity; but as we have already said, if it has any chance of succeeding with the mother, it cannot but fail, it cannot but persist, going from one failure to another, in its pursuit of maternity. On its shore [*rive*], without ever arriving there [*arriver*] or touching shore, without ever succeeding [*arriver à*] to touch it, if only to kill it. That is why—and those who write know this well—writing is a killer; one is never done with it. Even if the mother dies, even if a son kills her—for Trilling does not speak, it seems to me, of the matricidal daughter, or at least he doesn't make of her the decisive or specific focus of his analysis, of an analysis concerned instead with "mothers of certain male writers"[21]—the mother reappears in maternity, and it is no doubt for this reason that Trilling must so often evoke the "specter of the mother," the "ghost of the mother."[22] This spectrality would be what remains of a necessary but impossible *tri* or sorting out between existence and essence, between a (real) mother and an (essential) maternity, between a mother who appears and the appearing of this appearance.

The fact that Trilling insists on the son's matricide rather than the daughter's—in other words, on the desire or phantasm of the son rather than that of the daughter—does not prevent him from putting the difference between the sexes at the center of his analysis. Were one to follow, through all these learned meanderings, two decisive lexical elements or two intersecting guiding threads (on the one hand, "grammaire," "grammer," "grammar," "grandmother," and so on, and, on the other, "to remake [*refaire*]": "to remake oneself," "to make oneself anew," "you will not do [*feras*] that again," "to remake oneself by oneself," meaning without the mother, "I want to be my own ancestor," said Freud), then one will come to understand that the murder of maternity *bears* in itself, so to speak, as one bears a child, infanticide. "Must we," asks Trilling, "in order to 'remake' (a word that bears the sign of desire . . .) go by way of the murder of the child?"[23] One speaks in English of a *rhetorical question*[24] when the answer "yes" is known in advance. Matricide forms a pair, so to speak, with infanticide. And since we are talking about a child who tries to kill his mother, the matricide-infanticide leads on to suicide. Carnage is the response to the "rhetorical question." The inflexible cruelty of the law that condemns Iphigenia to death, the virgin daughter as the potential for childbearing:

> Sacrifice her while she is still virgin, only potentially childbearing (that is in fact what the name *Iphigenia* means). May this virgin womb remain forever virgin! That is what a womb that has given birth can never be again, no matter what one does. . . . Virgin womb or virgin white sheet, untouched by writing? Everything happens as if the maternal womb were the sheet already blackened beneath its surface by previous writings, the irrefutable proof of an engendering that is already that of the Other.
>
> The two murders—of the virgin daughter by the father, of the mother by the son—reflect, as in a mirror, the impossible condition of the wish symbolized by the effacement of Troy: the center of gravity, the driving force of tragedy.
>
> This effacement, placed at the heart of the polysemic tragedy, would be a response to the only assignable goal of omnipotence,

namely, to deny the only reality: the difference between the sexes. In the double murder are inscribed the limits that the child, on the one hand, and the mother, on the other, assign to desire. (Not just any child, a virgin, "Iphigenia": born in power.) In this writing, woman enjoys a special privilege: that of making colossuses.[25]

If one translates "omnipotence" by sovereignty, or rather by the phantasm of sovereignty, one will conclude from this that the denegation of sexual difference is part of the program of sovereignty itself, of sovereignty in general. And the political stakes—among others—of such a thought would be difficult to circumscribe. Trilling in fact notes in passing: "Knowledge about the word [*mot*] is knowledge about the death [*mort*] of sovereign speech. . . ."[26]

If one then follows Trilling's reading of the *colossus*,[27] here interpreted as a substitute for the penis and, especially, as a figurine of replacement, the child being the ideal example of this since it uses its voice to console the woman for "presence/absence," one will question a whole series of equivalences: the "psychoanalyst-colossus," the fusion of the mother with the voice of the substitute, here the son-writer ("Perhaps particularly 'consolable' mothers, . . . those sensitive to the fusion of their voices with the *phōnē* of the substitute, would be the mothers of such writers? As for man, he would not be able to give birth to such figurines . . .") and especially the couple *remake/grammaire*, which refers at once to desire and to the two murders to which a desire is destined, "to the all-powerful desire, to the murder of the mother and the murder of the child."

It is impossible to underestimate the spectral dimension of matricide. Spectral, which is to say, phantasmatic. In Greek *phantasma* also means phantom, ghost. This maternal spectrality is no doubt one of the privileged ways of gaining access to what "phantasm" is and means. Before being the spectrality of the dead or murdered father (see the treatment of Hamlet by Joyce, by Freud, and by Trilling), spectrality is essential to matricide, that is, at once to the desire and failure of the murder, to an interminable *attempted murder*. For maternity always survives, by coming back, by returning to its haunts [*en revenante*]. It has the last word, and it remains vigilant, it wakes [*y veille*].[28] It is watchful [*veille*], this night watch, this vigil light, this nightlight [*veilleuse*], to use the word Trilling puts in capital letters ("*La Veilleuse*"!).[29] It never sleeps; it not only keeps watch [*veille*] over the survivors but keeps vigil for them [*elle veille les survivants*]; it surveys them and survives them because those who come after it are also dead children, children who are already, like it, in the process of dying. Yes, matricide forms a pair with infanticide. The specter of the night watch or vigil light is a phantasm that fantasizes, that phantasmates, transforming into phantasm everything that would like to touch it. Maternity is generative of the phantasm as such, it is the genitor—I dare not say the mother—of the phantasmatic. And we will not be able to think this phantasmatic except by *departing from* it, or, more precisely, except by *parting from* it. And thus by risking to repeat here again an attempted murder.

"Phantasm" is what counts here. Trilling will have said this better than anyone: "What is seen-read [*vu-lu*], if not wished [*voulu*], up until now, is indeed a phantasm of the murder of maternity. . . . Perhaps, when it is a matter of writing, this death must be constantly denied in order for it to have access as it would wish to a rebirth."[30]

If there were a denunciation here, it would not just be of the crime or the attempted murder, the hounding of the mother or of maternity; there would also be a denunciation, indeed a ruthless denunciation, of writing, and, above all, that of Joyce. The exorcism, the supplication, the conjuring away of the death or murder of the mother ("this death must be constantly denied") is a denegation. And just as we would be holding here the key to a logic of the phantasm, we would also be approaching, in the same step [*pas*], with the same not [*pas*], the essential mechanism of what is called "denegation." In the beginning, before the *logos*, before the act, there would have been this originary denegation, this denegation of origin, or rather the denegation of this *being born* [*naître*]. Writing, literary writing, writing of writing, the signature—which is always exceptional, always the signature of a law of exception, the writing of Joyce according to another exemplary privileging—such would be, in their respective places of generality or singularity, the paradigms, illustrations, symptoms, and *verifications* of the truth [*vérité*]. Of a truth that always betrays itself in the symptom, a truth-of-the-symptom that always betrays maternity in the phantasm. And thus spectralizes it. A betrayal of truth, an unfaithful faithful betrayal, which reveals by deceiving. This betrayal *of* the truth would be—and this is my reading hypothesis—matricidal.

I must give up in advance giving an account here. Each sentence is a treasure trove of metonymies and metaphors—so rich that we risk losing it in the abyss. It is a tropics, in truth, from which one never returns and which one can never get over. Its matrix is an odyssey without return. What Trilling says of the stratagems of writing, of the writing of Ulysses, of the *Ulysses* of Joyce, could surely be said of his own writing: "All the processes of writing are put to work in *Ulysses* with a desperate, unequaled, and deliberately inimitable virtuosity."[31]

I said Homer and Joyce. We must also say Freud and Joyce. Both exiles. There is only exile without return in this milieu of writing, "the exile of the psychoanalyst and the exile of James Joyce"[32]—along with a few others. As for Jacques Trilling, he is the polyglot student of a certain

Monsieur Crevet, he of the vulnerable eyes whose name will watch over all the blind men of history, all those whose eyes have been gouged out [crevés]. And if Trilling reads *Ulysses* in English, if he himself lost his mother only a few months before discovering this book, this extraordinary story signs or rather assigns the name of Freud, countersigning and contravening *in the name of Freud*. Countersigning and contravening at once, faithfully, unfaithfully. Unfaithful: how can one not be unfaithful, always unfaithful, in the name of a more intense fidelity? For this is a psychoanalytic theory in narrative form, an autobiography whose author, Jacques Trilling, "reading the book of himself," will have sealed a theorem within. A sort of abbreviation or acronym incorporated into a knowledge. One will no longer be able to dissociate the body of the signature from the theoretical gesture, the singularity of the signatory from the formalization of a universal law.

The name of Freud thus becomes the name of an "imaginary father." Another sort of "legal fiction."[33] Before untangling all these tangled threads, Trilling in fact evokes the homonomy of patronyms. We all know what was said to Joyce when Jung wrote a nasty preface to the third edition of *Ulysses*: "There can be only one possible explanation. Translate your name into German."[34]

Among all the threads [*fils*] and filiations of this patient weave, of this enormous Penelopean genealogical web, one would thus be able to follow, though this is just an example, a certain "Jewish question." At once with Bloom, at the heart of *Ulysses*, as we well know, and, at the navel of the analytic movement, between Freud and Jung. The author was not in a bad position to speak of this, and to untangle without mincing words everything that ties these threads [*fils*] together, for example, in that curious event that was Jung's preface to *Ulysses*. It was submitted to Joyce who replied: "Ridicule it by making it public."[35] Right in the middle of the book, then, certain pages revolve around Jung, pages that might draw into the knot or noose of a certain Jewish question the synchrony or, better, the historical systemy [*systémie*] between the analytic movement and the history of literature (Freud and Jung, Freud and Joyce, Joyce and Jung, etc.). (French surrealism locates a completely different place for this same co-incidence in misunderstanding.)

Perhaps this would be just one metonymy or one kind of knot among others. No doubt, but I would risk granting some privilege to this trinomial or this trilogy (Freud, Jung, Joyce) inasmuch as it becomes readable today, in France, only by virtue of a trilingualism. With a certain Jewish question exercising here, as it often does, a magnetic attraction, it is appropriate to insist both on the proper name and on music, without forgetting that Jacques Trilling was himself a musician or a musicologist.[36] In Europe, in the Europe of psychoanalysis and of literature, it is the same field of magnetic attraction. Let me cite the following, and ask the reader to reconstitute what is woven and signed around it:

> Nothing surprising in the fact that this diver for Zurich pearls, after a late denunciation, attributes the Hitlerian catastrophe to a revolution in writing, that is, to Joyce and Schönberg: "Atonal music, the enormous ripple effect of that abyssal work called *Ulysses*. There is already there, *in nuce*, everything that took on a political form in Germany."
>
> It is hard to forgive Freud his weakness for Jung, a certain reverse racism that would have made him cling so tightly, he and psychoanalysis, to this fair-skinned Swiss . . . Aryan. Just as it is hard to forgive a father who has failed to defend a son fallen victim to the patriotic-religious schemes of a mother who also assured the order of repression with the help of Swiss-German mercenaries. . . . What must be denounced, and eternally taken back up to be taken to task, is a nostalgia for the infantile all-powerfulness of the ideal father, all-powerful, that is, without fault or weakness; a reaction, no doubt, to his own infantile romanticism, to flights of fancy, to military identifications: Hannibal, the Hebraic saga, the Irish saga, the maternal saga, echoes of fratricidal struggles, etc.
>
> This titanic enumeration ⟨in *Ulysses*, cited a bit earlier⟩ recalls the Homeric catalogue: four hundred lines devoted to the catalogue of the ships in the *Iliad*, comprised almost exclusively of proper names, "which entails a veritable training of memory."[37]

Memory of the proper name *in general*, that is, of a proper name that is not necessarily the name of the father—or the mother. As we know, this memory calls for what is referred to here as "training," namely, the mechanics of the "by heart." Mnemonics to the extent, at least, that the proper name remains aleatory and in-significant, a pure signifier, if you will, received or imposed *at birth*, *by birth*, before any possible choice on the part of the subject who bears it. This in-significant, non-signifying mark can then later, as we know, be reinvested with meaning or sense, and with common sense, opening the field to all kinds of interpretations, some of which can play the role of a mnemonic device or memory aid [*pense-bête*].

All this is well known, and has been explored by many of us for some time now, but in order to support my interpretation of the text of Jacques Trilling I would like to underscore this single trait: what remains of the in-significant, un-signifying, aleatory, pre-semantic mark in the proper name, and which thus entails some "training in memory," would be that which is connected to "maternity," rather than [*plutôt*], earlier than [*plus tôt*], the mother and the father, the name of the father or name of the mother. Or it is at least connected—with or without umbilical cord—to a phantasm of this maternity, which, as we have been underscoring, is defined by Trilling as "the ineluctability of birth, of the marked hour, always already inscribed."

I will return yet again to this possible-impossible *tri*, this necessary and forbidden sorting out, between the mother and maternity. But if I insist on the memory and survival of the proper name, if I sometimes seem to be playing in earnest on the name of Jacques Trilling in the languages that were his, it is not in order to offer an "interpretation"—something I would never do—of his name or his signature.[38] It is simply in order to distinguish at one go between *two stakes*: in order to recall, *on the one hand*, the importance of the proper name in general in this dramaturgy of matricide—of double matricide, or of an always divisible matricide, of the attempted murder that aims at both the mother *and* maternity but always falters or fails at this latter. But it is also in order, *on the other hand*, to recall something rather obvious. The text I am prefacing is, like the preface itself, signed. And my signature is only there—and I would wish it to be there, as much as possible, and in its own way, only in this way—to countersign that of my friend Jacques Trilling, whose surviving proper name could not but obey and at the same time *illustrate* in an exemplary fashion the law or the theorem that this work, *James Joyce, ou l'écriture matricide*, puts to work.

For who would dare to present himself as the authorized cartographer of this post-Joycean, post-Freudian odyssey? Such a pretension would be excessive, and thus indecent. My old indictment of the genre of the preface is here reinforced by an additional argument.[39] If it already seems difficult, in truth absurd and illegitimate, to preface a novel, as well as a philosophical treatise, how is one to introduce a signature? How is one to explain it? To give an account of it? "Signature" means first of all a *work* [*oeuvre*], that is to say, the survival of a trace whose content can no longer be separated from the process of writing, from the singular, dated act or gesture, irreplaceable like a body, like a bodily struggle, untranslatable in the end, precisely as that which refers to maternity, to birth, to "the ineluctability of birth, of the marked hour, always already inscribed." This is the case for every work worthy of the name. In an even more singular fashion here, beyond the patronymic name, the signature situates the place of a trace exempt from substitution. It can be read as an idiomatic writing, already big with certain other writings (Homer, Joyce, Freud, etc.). It thereby becomes inseparable from an adventure of interpretative reading that is itself unique, irreplaceable, untranslatable: the story of Jacques Trilling himself. By his "story" we should understand not only the abyssal manufacturing of his family story [*roman familial*] ("he who listens to himself listening to the other, in search of a family story to be reconstituted in the very movement that relentlessly tries to reveal it . . ."[40]) but the story of his formation or education (*Bildungsroman*), his years of apprenticeship as a schoolboy who lost his mother a few months before reading *Ulysses*, as a child who knew how to free himself in order to invent his signature through reading and writing, who left school without leaving it, the school of Crevet, of Homer, Joyce, Freud, Proust, and a few others.

I must thus renounce yet again trying to describe the richness of the "content." The reader will discover it for him- or herself at each and every step. To hail the work, to bless the fortunate encounter with the signature (in short, the birth of Jacques Trilling), and everything that is thereby given to us, indeed that is destined for us, by an inventive writing capable of measuring up to the contingency of signifiers, names, dates, works, births, others, I will allow myself simply to privilege, and perhaps to force—please excuse me for this—what is to my eyes one of the major consequences, we might even say the major scale, of this thesis or this theorem, that is, of what remains formalizable beyond the proper name and the signature. For this I return to my initial hypothesis, to the essay (*try*[41]) or the *tri*, the sorting out, with which I began. That is, between the mother and maternity.

Two "logics" seem to me to contend with one another over Trilling's remarkable demonstration. Two competing but also strangely allied logics, almost indistinguishable in their dynamic rhythm. One of them is classic, or more precisely "Freudian" or "Joycean." Then Lacanian. And, in the end, *commonsensical*.[42] While paternity would always be a problematic attribution, a conclusion reached through inference and reasoning (Freud),[43] a "legal fiction" (Stephen's well-known phrase in *Ulysses*, cited in fact by Trilling[44]), and thus a sort of speculative object susceptible to substitution, the maternity of the mother is unique, irreplaceable, an object of perception, like the "womb" we so often speak of as the place of conception and birth. The other logic, the one toward which I myself would risk leaning here, would subject the mother (I'm not saying "maternity" in Trilling's sense of the word) to the *same* regimen as the father: possible substitution, rational inference, phantasmatic or symbolic construction, speculation, and so on. If today the unicity of the mother is no longer the sensible object of a perceptual certitude, if maternities can no longer be reduced to, indeed if they carry us beyond, the carrying mother, if there can be, in a word, more than one mother, if "the" mother is the object of calculations and suppositions, of projections and phantasms, if the "womb" is no longer outside all phantasm, the assured place of birth, then this "new" situation simply illuminates in return an ageless truth. The mother was never only, never uniquely, never indubitably the one who gives birth—and whom one sees, with one's own eyes, give birth. If the word "maternity," as it is interpreted and deployed by Trilling, gestures toward the unicity of a mark and of a birth date that has already taken place, if there is, undeniably, maternity in this sense, then every determination of this maternity by the figure of a mother, indeed of a date, of an indisputable trace (this one and not that one), becomes the effect of a phantasm and a speculation. The mother is also a speculative object and even a "legal fiction." In the passage I am about to cite, and from which I have already taken a phrase, a passage whose argumentation and consequences I ask the reader to reconstitute with great care, it seems to me that these two "logics" cross or rather follow upon one another rapidly, as in a trill. Almost simultaneously, it seems at once necessary, urgent, decisive, but also impossible to decide, to sort things out [*trier*], between the mother and maternity. The mother can be replaced—or killed—and substitution, fiction, and thus phantasmatic speculation is possible. As for maternity, it would resist replacement, because birth, the date or the mark of birth, has *taken place*, undeniably, even if its determination is given over to calculation, speculation, or phantasm. Maternity thus cannot be reduced to the mother ("One can always murder the mother, but one will not for all that have done away with maternity"). But what are we to make of a maternity that would not be the maternity of a mother? And why necessarily associate with the maternity of the mother "the ineluctability of birth, of the marked hour, always already inscribed"? The reader will have to come to terms with this passage, the riskiest in the entire work, the boldest, the most trilled or trilling, the most *thrilling*,[45] fantastic, sensational, exciting, provocative:

> If we have come to the *word* (grammar) it is because an appropriation had conferred upon the word "remake" a determining role in the theatralization implied in every writing-reading. It is indeed "remake" that referred back to the *Oresteia*. In its place, in its time, is inscribed a reference . . . to tragedy where maternal language is the traitor on stage. But what, or whom, does one want to remake, to redo or do in? As we will never tire to point out, it is to remake oneself, or more precisely to wipe out any trace of the first fabrication . . .
> (Responding to Midas, who is questioning him about Dionysian euphoria, the Silenus says: "Wretched race of men, child of chance and of misery! Why do you want to hear what will do you no good? You cannot attain this greatest of goods: not to be born, not to be, to be nothing . . .") In these lines—and the length of the citations attests to this—one can make paternity play all kinds of roles on the stage of the symbolic and the imaginary. But this does not seem to be the case for maternity. Each of us comes out of a mother's womb, from one womb and one womb only, and each is thus forever marked. Like a remainder, a trace that would resist and

exist a little more irreducibly than any other. With regard to this liminal representation of the biological, father and son are brothers, or, more exactly, sons. One can always murder the mother, but one will not for all that have done away with maternity, no more than with Troy, or the maternal language of desire.[46]

Trilling seems at once to believe and not believe. He believes without believing in a discernible difference between a mother and maternity. What indeed would a mother be, how would one speak of her, how would one address her, without the presupposition of a maternity of the mother? And what would a maternity of the mother be, an essence of the mother *as such*, without a mother, without the singular, absolutely unique existence of a mother? If matricide is at once one and double, and thus forever frustrated, and thus always renewed, repeated, hounded (the lure of this dogged pursuit being sometimes the mother, sometimes maternity), it has to do with the fact that *there is* both the mother *and* maternity. As soon as one believes one has killed the mother, maternity remains—to be killed. Isn't writing a killer? Inversely, it is because maternity and the mother are one (maternity is the maternity *of* the mother, its essence and its "as such") that the matricidal pursuit remains the same and without end. Between the mother and maternity the ontological difference *is not*; it is not a difference between two (beings). This must be said, as we all know, about any ontological difference. There is thus no possible *tri*, no real sorting out, between the mother and maternity. And yet this sorting out is necessary, for maternity will never be reducible to the mother and this ontological difference opens up the possibility of a *tri* or a sorting out in general. That is, in just a couple of words, the *raison d'être* of interminable matricide: an *ontological difference* between the mother and maternity, almost nothing, nothing that is.

One would not kill, that is, what we call "kill," there would be no murder *as such*, without this nothing of a certain ontological difference. And without that which secretly links—an enormous task for meditation—this nothing of the ontological difference to the nothing of the phantasm. This nothing makes one return over and over again to the scenes of the crime in order to kill again what one believed one had already killed. The essence of the mother, her appearing *as such*, is maternity. Nothing, almost nothing. Nothing other, no one other, than the mother, a single mother. And yet maternity remains, and it keeps watch [*veille*], the Night Watch or Nightlight [*Veilleuse*]—absolutely indefatigable [*increvable*]. Thus: like everything that is indefatigable, beginning with God, it does not appear as such, in its own light, in the light of its nightlight, except to the murdering desire to be done with that which is never over and done with. To be done, as Job would have wanted, with light itself. With what there was. To be done with the

trace of the trace, with birth itself. To kill oneself by killing one's birth, in other words, the maternity of one's mother. So as to entertain the suicidal illusion, yet again, of giving birth to oneself. On one's own, freely, to oneself.
   —Yeah, right.
   —Auto-parthenogenesis of a writing, for example, that would like to deny or—for this amounts to the same thing—to appropriate without remainder the entirety of one's heritage. One writes, but it would be necessary to do otherwise in order to redo or remake oneself. In order to be in the end, as Joyce would have wanted, "father and son of his works."⁴⁷ Even if it means running the risk—for who could deny it?—of finding oneself at the end of the road, at the moment of signing, done in [*refait*].

P.S. July 15, 2000. Take my word for it—Ulysses' honor. From Homer to Joyce, Ulysses will have been the hero of *James Joyce ou l'écriture matricide*. In *Memoirs of the Blind: The Self-Portrait and Other Ruins* (1991), I used and abused the "name of nobody" (*outis*), which Ulysses gives to himself or remakes for himself.⁴⁸

Why recall this here? It so happens that I am finishing this preface just after the meeting of the States General of Psychoanalysis.⁴⁹ I there spoke of a beyond of cruelty, a beyond of sovereignty, a beyond of the death drive—and thus a beyond of the beyond of the pleasure principle.

It is as if I had thought I could hear a silent lesson from Jacques Trilling, the one whose hypothesis I just advanced. As if I had said to myself, in short, yet one more time but once and for all, for good and forever: from now on, no more writing, especially not writing, for writing dreams of sovereignty, writing is *cruel*, murderous, suicidal, parricidal, matricidal, infanticidal, fratricidal, homicidal, and so on. Crimes against humanity, even genocide, begin here, as do crimes against *generation*.

Whence my definition of withdrawal [*le retrait*], my nostalgia for retirement [*la retraite*]: from now on, before and without the death *toward which*, as I have written elsewhere, *I advance*—to begin finally to love life, namely birth. Mine among others—notice I am not saying *beginning* with mine. A new rule of life: to breathe from now on without writing, to take a breath beyond writing. Not that I am out of breath—or tired of writing because writing is a killer. No, on the contrary, I have never felt so strongly the youthful urgency, dawn itself, white and virgin. But I want to want, and decidedly so, I want to want an active and signed renunciation of writing, a reaffirmed life. And thus a life without matricide. It would be a matter of beginning to love love without writing, without words, without murder. It would be necessary to begin to learn to love the mother—and maternity, in short, if you prefer to give it this name. Beyond the death drive, beyond every drive for power and mastery. Writing without writing. The other writing, the other of writing as well, altered writing, the one that has always worked over my own in silence, at once simpler and more convoluted, like a counterwitness protesting at each and every sign against my writing through my writing.

If the *tri* or the sorting out between the mother and maternity remains at once ineluctable and illusory, if matricide becomes so inevitable [*fatal*] that it exonerates the one guilty of it, wouldn't one have to be an absolute monster of innocence to go on writing? A child? An ingénue? Better, an *innate* monster of innocence?

Is writing without matricide still possible?

I began with a wish. Here is another one, and it may always strike you as being pious, and little more than a pipe dream [*vœu . . . pieux*]⁵⁰: to write and kill nobody (signed Ulysses).

Jacques Derrida

Notes

1. TN: "La Veilleuse," the title of Derrida's essay, has a wide range of meanings in French that cannot be captured by one or even a couple English words. Capitalized in the Trilling text that Derrida is prefacing, the feminine noun suggests first of all a woman who keeps watch, who remains vigilant, who holds vigil—a "Nightwatchwoman" or "Waking woman." But a *veilleuse* is also a little candle or light that in certain Jewish families is kept lit for seven days after the death of a loved one. In other contexts, a *veilleuse* is a light or lamp that dimly lights a child's room at night—a nightlight. One also speaks of the *veilleuse* of an appliance, a pilot light, for example, which remains lit even when an appliance is off, or else of an appliance being *en veilleuse*, that is, illuminated or turned on but not fully functioning, in "standby mode." From these various contexts, we can see that the semantic kernel of the word suggests a keeping watch, a standing by, a remaining awake or vigilant when everyone else has forgotten or gone to sleep, a remaining lit or illuminated when all other lights have been extinguished.

2. James Joyce, *Ulysses* (New York: Random House, 1961), 595. TN: We have followed Derrida in capitalizing "Grammer," even though it is in lowercase in the edition of *Ulysses* cited here. The Gabler edition corrects this line to the reading found on the Rosenbach manuscript: "Aha! I know you, gammer!" (U 15.4581). The incorrect form appeared in all editions from 1926–1961.

3. U 9.112–15.

4. TN: "Try" in English in the original

5. TN: Jacques Trilling, *James Joyce ou l'écriture matricide* (Belfort, France: Éditions Circé, 2001), 119.

6. TN: In English in the original.

7. TN: In English in the original.

8. Trilling, *James Joyce*, 50.

9. TN: Derrida is here playing on the title of Baudelaire's poem in *The Flowers of Evil*, "Invitation to the Voyage."

10. TN: In English in the original.

11. The law governing the relationship to Freud or the distance vis-à-vis him is rather complex. Most often it is out of fidelity to a Freudian inspiration, or even to Freud's own dissatisfaction, that Trilling moves away from the "imaginary father." For example, concerning identification, "a thorn in the side of psychoanalysis, the keystone of a theory that makes of the Superego the heir of the Oedipus complex. A concept that always left Freud dissatisfied" (Trilling, *James Joyce*, 61).

12. TN: In English in the original.

13. TN: In English in the original.

14. TN: In English in the original.

15. Jean-Jacques Rousseau, *Confessions*, ed. and trans. P. N. Furbank (New York: Alfred A. Knopf, 1992), 209.

16. Trilling, *James Joyce*, 92.

17. Ibid., 93–94.

18. Even if he does not cite him, Trilling might well have been thinking of Job. The curse of birth brings condemnation upon the day, upon "seeing the day," upon giving birth or "bringing to the light of day." The curse is thus inspired by matricide, sometimes quite literally. What Job curses is phenomenality itself, life as visibility, the light of being. What must seek atonement, what must be redeemed by a sort of forgiveness, is light. And light begins with the mother. There was light, light took place, and thus remains inexpiable. "After this Job opened his mouth and cursed the day of his birth. Job said: 'Let the day perish in which I was born, and the night that said, 'A man-child is conceived.' Let that day be darkness! May God above not seek it, or light shine on it. Let gloom and deep darkness claim it. . . . Why did I not die at birth, come forth from the womb and expire? Why were there knees to receive me, or breasts for me to suck?'" (Job 3: 1–5, 11–12; New Revised Standard Version of *The New Oxford Annotated Bible*).

19. Trilling—and we will return to this—does not dissociate matricide from a certain infanticide. We earlier heard Job cursing his birth and the womb of his mother; let us now recall "The Blessing" (*Bénédiction*) that opens *The Flowers of Evil*. It is the Poet's mother, this time, who curses birth, the birth of the one who writes, that is, the birth of the matricide. And as in the book of Job, what experience signs is the inexpiable. Or rather the expiation of an inexpiable that has remained inexpiable: "When, by a decree of the sovereign powers, / The Poet comes into this bored world, / His mother, terrified and full of blasphemy, / Clenches her fists toward God, who has pity on her: 'Ah, why didn't I litter a nest of vipers, / Rather than give birth to this mockery? / A curse on that night with its fleeting pleasures / When my womb conceived my expiation!'"

Everything should really be reread and cited here in the light of this matricidal light, including the response of the son, of the Poet, who has been turned in advance into an object of "mockery" by his mother and who himself blesses, but blesses evil, the flower of evil: "Be blessed, my Lord, who give suffering / As a divine remedy for our impurities." Charles Baudelaire, *Flowers of Evil*, ed. and trans. Wallace Fowlie (New York: Bantam Books, 1964), 20–23.

Yes, everything should be reread and cited, without forgetting that this is, precisely, a poem, literature. It is thus the writing of a son who *verifies* matricide. He signs it and feigns to absolve himself of it in the very gesture whereby the poetic signature repeats the evil. The final blessing seals the crime and takes away any possible alibi from the attempted murder—which is already criminal. It makes of the inexpiable the condition of literature.

20. TN: "Ventriloqual" comes from the Latin *ventriloquus*, meaning "speaking from the belly," or, perhaps, as Derrida here seems to be suggesting, from the womb.

21. Trilling, *James Joyce*, 122.

22. Ibid., 93.

23. Ibid., 120.

24. TN: In English in the original.

25. Trilling, *James Joyce*, 120–21. With regard to the "virgin white sheet, untouched by writing," or to its being "already blackened beneath its surface by previous writings," one will recall *Inhibition, Symptom, and Anxiety*: "As soon as writing, which entails making a liquid flow out of a tube on to a piece of white paper, assumes the significance of copulation, or as soon as walking becomes a symbolic substitute for treading upon the body of mother earth, both writing and walking are stopped because they represent the performance of a forbidden sexual act" (trans. Alix Strachey, in Sigmund Freud, *The Standard Edition of the Complete Psychological Works of Sigmund Freud*, 24 volumes [London: The Hogarth Press, 1999], volume 20, 77–175, 90). I bring up this quote only in order to indicate a possible connection between an Oedipal (patricidal) analytic and a matricidal analytic of writing. Not to mention the phantasm and taboo of virginity.

26. Trilling, *James Joyce*, 87.

27. See Trilling, *James Joyce*, 121. If the colossus is here placed on the side of the figurine of the child ("an ideal figurine since it is born with *phōnē*"), which is also to say on the side of the writer-son, earlier in the text (Trilling, *James Joyce*, 88 and following)—and there is no contradiction here—Trilling analyzes the colossus around "the substitute of the absent cadaver" and "the place of the deceased." "Is the colossus-book the colossus of the dead mother, whom one wished to be a virgin?" (Trilling, *James Joyce*, 92).

28. "Last word" is also the last word of Trilling on the subject of the last word. He recognizes in it (in order to give credence or not—I don't know how to decide this here—to a tradition that runs up to at least Hegel, but in a place where I believe one must be particularly suspicious of this tradition) the law of the mother as the law of the night, as opposed to the law of the Father as the law of the day: ". . . in the penumbra that follows the occultation of the lamps by the Nightlight or Night Watch [*la Veilleuse*]. If the Father's word makes of the day the law, that of the mother, who has the last word, makes of the evening the occult law, night language, *nighty language* [in English in original], whose silent listening is, like the foam left behind by the black vessel in the depths of the night, this fine, white wake inscribed on the sea, always perceptible, a sign of life, and, whether one be

a navigator or a pirate, a sign to follow" (Trilling, *James Joyce*, 123). That is the conclusion of the book.

29. "Like the child who had to sleep. Not in the collapsing darkness but, rather, in the penumbra that follows the occultation of the lamps by the Nightlight or Night Watch [*La Veilleuse*]" (Trilling, *James Joyce*, 123). With spectrality invading the entire field of his analysis, Trilling is hardly playing when he writes this about, precisely, *analysis*, which is always busy sorting out [*trier*] or triturating the undecidable in order to detect within it the crisis and the criterion of a secret decision: "A color that only analysis could then decompose *spectrally* as if condensing in some way love and hate, defeat and exile, English and Hebrew, life and death, the object of the murder and the lost passion" (Trilling, *James Joyce*, 42, my emphasis).

30. Trilling, *James Joyce*, 118.

31. Ibid., 94.

32. Ibid., 54.

33. TN: In English in the original.

34. TN: This story is recounted in Richard Ellmann's *James Joyce*, revised edition (New York: Oxford University Press, 1982), 628–29. The preface itself can be found in: Carl G. Jung, "*Ulysses*: Ein Monolog," *Europäische Revue* 8 (September 1932): 547–68, and is reprinted in Jung's *Wirklichkeit der Seele* (Zürich: Rascher, 1934), 132–69. English translation: "*Ulysses*: A Monologue," trans. R.F.C. Hull, in *The Spirit in Man, Art, and Literature*, vol. 15 of the *Collected Works of C. G. Jung* (New York: Pantheon, 1966), 109–34.

35. Trilling, *James Joyce*, 98.

36. Trilling reads always as a musician. For example, when he deciphers a love that "lets itself be read on two registers where the voice of love and the voice of death are woven together and respond to one another in an implacable counterpoint (and not a canon). The reading of such a score requires heart, the heart [*cœur*] of a musician, of a reader, an ancient chorus [*chœur*]" (Trilling, *James Joyce*, 68).

This recommendation follows a determining moment in the scansion of the analysis: the "lethal identification" of Joyce and his mother, who called the birth of her son "the most beautiful day of her life." The blind man, Joyce, "hates her to death [*lui en veut à mort*] for having abandoned him for her illness. It is necessary to kill her a second time, an unspeakable wish."

"En *vouloir* à mort à quelqu'un"—to resent someone or hate them intensely, to hate them to death; "*vouloir* du mal à quelqu'un"—to *wish* someone ill, to *wish* them harm. Who will ever translate these idioms?

37. Trilling, *James Joyce*, 99–100.

38. Permit me simply to note this: one can apply to the name of Trilling what Trilling says about the name of his teacher, Crevet, especially as concerns the consonants, which are "like javelins threatening the pale blue eyes of a rival (in literature) who has a certain knowledge (and whom the student also seduces)" (Trilling, *James Joyce*, 40). If "death and consonants are accomplices" (ibid., 41), how can one not notice that in these two proper names, Crevet and Trilling, a single redoubled vowel (e, i) finds itself closely surrounded by consonants. Under surveillance. The consonants of death watch after [*veillent sur*] the vowel, and watch over [*surveillent*] the voice of their writing.

39. TN: On the preface, see "Outwork," DI 1–59/7–67.
40. The expression "roman familial" comes up regularly in this text.
41. TN: In English in the original.
42. TN: In English in the original.
43. I am thinking here, to cite just one example, of a note in *The Rat Man* that I devoted a great deal of attention to elsewhere (in a seminar on witnessing). What we find here in a very condensed form, I would argue, are the most salient limits and credulities of a certain Freudian discourse. Indeed, of its patriarchal phallogocentrism. Concerning "omnipotence," and especially concerning the penchant of "obsessional neurotics" for doubt and uncertainty (for example, regarding the length of life, survival after death, though also paternity), Freud notes (and I am just quoting him here): "As Lichtenberg says, 'An astronomer knows whether the moon is inhabited or not with about as much certainty as he knows who was his father, but not with so much certainty as he knows who was his mother.' ⟨That makes already two errors by Lichtenberg, both accredited by Freud: the astronomer knows in all certainty *today* that the moon *is not* inhabited, but he could *today* doubt the identity of his mother. Freud continues, as he often did, after having found the approbation of Lichtenberg.⟩ A great advance was made in civilization when men decided to put their inferences upon a level with the testimony of their senses and to make the step from matriarchy to patriarchy.—The prehistoric figures which show a smaller person sitting upon the head of a larger one are representations of patrilineal descent; Athena had no mother, but sprang from the head of Zeus. A witness who testifies to something before a court of law is still called '*Zeuge*' [literally, 'begetter'] in German, after the part played by the male in the act of procreation; so too in hieroglyphics the word for a 'witness' is written with a representation of the male organ" (Sigmund Freud, "Notes Upon a Case of Obsessional Neurosis," trans. Alix and James Strachey, in *The Standard Edition of the Complete Psychological Works of Sigmund Freud*, 24 volumes [London: The Hogarth Press, 1999], volume 10, 151–318, 233 n.1).
44. Even if paternity is founded upon a lure [*leurre*], upon an illusion that needs to be contested, it retains an incontestable privilege. But in the eyes of those who deem it indisputable (in short, without any possible illusion), the mother's maternity deprives the mother of this privilege. Simply "denouncing the lure or illusion of paternity" doesn't get you out of the system (Trilling, *James Joyce*, 118). "The lure or illusion of paternity is to be denounced," says Trilling himself (ibid., 102), after a paragraph that seems to follow a Lacanian logic (a second birth at the time of entering a symbolic order governed by the name of the father, in short, by a "legal fiction" that would be reserved for the paternity of the father). This is the phallogocentric credulity of Freud we spoke of in the preceding note. A learned discourse on the mother's phallus or on the phallic mother changes little in this regard.
45. TN: In English in the original.
46. Trilling, *James Joyce*, 118–19.
47. Ibid., 47–48.
48. *Memoirs of the Blind: The Self-Portrait and Other Ruins*, trans. Pascale-Anne Brault and Michael Naas (Chicago: University of Chicago Press, 1993), 87–88, translation of *Mémoires d'aveugle: L'auoportrait et autres ruines* (Paris: Éditions de

la Réunion des musées nationaux, 1990), 88–90. Cruelty is named there: ". . . the ruse of Odysseus, who then drives a fire-hardened stake into his eye: a *single, unique* eye, a *closed* eye, an eye *gouged out*. By ruse rather than by force (*dolō oude biēphin*), and by someone who calls himself "Nobody." The *mētis* of *Outis*: the deception that blinds is the ruse of *nobody* (*outis, mē tis, mētis*); Homer plays more than once on these words. . . . By presenting himself as Nobody, he at once names and effaces himself: like nobody, like nobody else—the logic of the self-portrait."

49. "Psychoanalysis Searches the States of Its Soul: The Impossible Beyond of a Sovereign Cruelty," in *Without Alibi*, ed. and trans. Peggy Kamuf (Stanford: Stanford University Press, 2002), 238–80, translation of *Etats d'âme de la psychanalyse: l'impossible au-delà d'une souveraine cruauté* (Paris: Galilée, 2000).

50. TN: Derrida is playing on the expression "*vœu pieux*"—literally, a pious wish, but, figuratively, a hollow or empty wish. Read as a noun rather than an adjective, *pieux* is the plural of *pieu*, a stake or sharpened stick of the kind Ulysses used to strike out the eye of the Cyclops.

II
Returns

I

JOYCE—EVENT—DERRIDA—
EVENT—JOYCE

Jed Deppman

> The great sweep of life has actually always shown itself to be on the side of the most unscrupulous *polytropoi*.
>
> —Friedrich Nietzsche, *The Gay Science*[1]

> Historical incarnation sets free the transcendental, instead of binding it.
>
> —Jacques Derrida, *Edmund Husserl's Origin of Geometry: An Introduction* (77/71)

Key: JD = Jacques Derrida (1930–2004)
      JJ = James Joyce (1882–1941)
      EH = Edmund Husserl (1859–1938)
      DJ = Derrida's Joyce(s)
      CJ = The Critics' Joyce(s)
      DH = Derrida's Husserl(s)
      JD - Joyce's Derrida

According to JD, the community of JJ critics was right to accuse him of incompetence, of not mastering the material, of speaking out of turn before audiences of specialists. As a novice in the field, every time he wrote or said anything about JJ he ran the risk of recirculating *idées reçues* without substantiating or improving upon them through research. At the same time, as a philosopher, he ran a parallel risk of casting JJ into contexts and vocabularies that were neither expected by nor intelligible to the literary community. His long reliance on EH and JJ as counterpoints for each other has proven especially intractable: no robust critical tradition exists that includes both of these figures, and now that phenomenology has been thoroughly superseded it seems unlikely that one will form. There are many good reasons why Joyceans have never been very well versed in EH's texts, including the fact that the landmark *Logical Investigations* was not available in English until the J. N. Findlay translation in 1970, by which point, one might argue, it was already too late. Still, just as JD was attracted by EH's reflections on the origin and historical transmission of the special case of geometrical thought and activity, so am I attracted by JD's reflections on the origin and historical transmission of the special cases of EH and JJ.

It is not just that Joyceans have ignored EH. For their part, few philosophers have ever thought of themselves as knowledgeable enough about JJ to evaluate JD's claim that JJ and EH represent "two great models, two paradigms with respect to thought, but also with respect to a certain 'operation' of the relationship between language and history" (TW 27/27). For philosophers, the problem with this claim is not that it is linguistically unfamiliar, unverifiable, non-thetic, or any of the other complaints JD inspired throughout his career. In fact, one could hardly ask for anything more reassuring, traditional, and "disciplined": models, paradigms of thought, operations, the relationship between language and history . . . it is all perfectly negotiable except for the part about JJ. Why is an Irish modernist crashing into this venerable collection of philosophical topoi, and what does it mean that he is? To answer this, it is necessary to look very closely at how JD thought and wrote about the great JJ and EH paradigms for thought and writing.

In a 1987 interview for *Le Nouvel Observateur*, journalist Didier Eribon proposed the idea to JD that some of his writings seemed like "literary" attempts to write about literary texts. JD replied that he always tried to be "demonstrative," but that sometimes his demonstrations took "forms of writing that have their own, sometimes novel rules" (PI 188/200). Those rules can be "produced and displayed," he noted, but they could not be expected to "correspond, at every point, to the traditional norms" that the literary texts were themselves "questioning or displacing" (PI 188/200). Not quite conceding this point, Eribon replied that, even so, he found "Ulysses Gramophone" to be "rather disconcerting." JD's brisk response:

> I was writing about Joyce. It would be a shame therefore to write in a form that in no way lets itself be affected by Joyce's languages, by his inventions, his irony, the turbulence he introduced into the space of thinking or of literature. If one wants to take the event named "Joyce" into account, one must write, recount, demonstrate in another fashion, one must take the risk of a formal adventure. (PI 188/200)

Resisting formal adventures, Eribon's line of questioning reflects the inertial force of a tradition that unashamedly respects the laws of genre. JD's approach picks up from JJ and departs from the platitude that valid critical thought must take the form of truth claims conventionally presented. JD does not seem to regret any potential diminution in demonstrativeness or epistemological consistency.

Surfacing in the Eribon exchange are several of DJ's central elements: he knew many languages, was supremely inventive and ironic, and was responsible for bringing a unique "turbulence" to twentieth-century thought and literature. More than just a gifted and influential writer-thinker, DJ was a singular "event," the effects of which some writers and thinkers irresponsibly failed to account for even as they were influenced by them.[2] The DJ effects took many shapes across the great sweep of JD's lectures and written texts: polytropic DJ variously appears as an image, a cipher, a symbol, a spirit, an interpretation, a thesis, a messiah, a force, a problem, an argument, a voice, a network of voices. Today anybody can produce a new version of DJ simply by mixing the attitudes, voices, and discourses JD brought to JJ to the ones we bring to any of them.

This may seem to open up a useless infinity of possible JJs, as if any and all interpretations of JJ were equal, but in fact DJ is not easy to confuse with the CJ created by Ellmann, Senn, Rabaté, and thousands of other critics and scholars. Although DJ and CJ both tend to be erudite, innovative, confident modernists, DJ, unlike CJ, is never particularly Irish, European, youthful, (post)colonial, exile, or male. Even when DJ is interpreted as a human subject, the pronoun "he" can be misleading, for DJ speaks and writes with voices and languages that originate from many times, places, and subject positions. DJ's literary works do not noticeably derive from the realism of Dickens, Balzac, Flaubert, Zola, or Ibsen, nor are they reliably identifiable as heirs to the European *Bildungsroman* tradition or, for that matter, to any literary tradition as such. In fact, it is not always certain that DJ is the author of *Exiles*, *Chamber Music*, *Dubliners*, or even *A Portrait*, although he is very much the originator of *Ulysses* and *Finnegans Wake*. In fact these last two texts of DJ often form one, as if they were a singular event of writing, the culmination of forces that had been gathering in Western culture for a long time.

These striking differences between DJ and CJ are one reason that JD's contribution has not been very prominent in JJ studies. Another is that, to Joyceans, JD sometimes seems to have exaggerated the importance of DJ to his own thinking. The index of the English edition of the 192-page *Edmund Husserl's Origin of Geometry: An Introduction*, written in French in 1961, shows that the discussion of JJ is limited to only three pages. This can seem *fort peu* to justify JD's later, enthusiastic descriptions of JJ's role in the book. In a typical 1987 question-and-answer session, JD explains:

> In my first book on Husserl, I tried to compare the way Joyce treats
> language and the way a classical philosopher such as Husserl treats
> it. Joyce wanted to make history, the resuming and the totalization
> of history, possible through the accumulation of metaphoricities,
> equivocalities, and tropes. Husserl, on the other hand, thought
> that historicity was made possible by the transparent univocity
> of language, that is, by a scientific, mathematical, pure language.
> There is no historicity without the transparency of the tradition,
> Husserl says, while Joyce says there is no historicity without this
> accumulation of equivocality in language. It is from the tension
> between these two interpretations of language that I tried to address
> the question of language.[3]

For literary scholars, some of JD's assumptions about JJ seem both too cryptic and too quickly stated, such as that JJ intended to make history "possible" by accumulating equivocalities in texts like *Ulysses* and *Finnegans Wake*, or that those two books can be characterized or summarized by reference to their "metaphoricities, equivocalities, and tropes."[4] And for philosophers, the obvious question is: why JJ? History is full of more canonical philosophical sources for writing about the philosophy of history.

Only a close look at JD's earliest writings on JJ can explain why he thought EH and JJ together in a way that turned them into DH and DJ. I set aside the speculative question of what and how JD interpreted, received, intuited, or otherwise conceived of JJ when he *first* heard about or read him. EH, as JD points out, also passed very quickly over questions of *Erstmaligkeit*, which in his case dealt with seizing the *very first inklings* of geometrical sense in the world. EH saw himself as methodologically limited by the necessity of beginning his reflections with the geometry he knew, the science that had already been constituted, so instead of trying to describe the birth of geometrical ideality or abstraction, he "repeatedly and obstinately" returned to the question of how the "subjective egological evidence of sense" could become "objective and intersubjective (EH 63/52)?"[5] How, that is, did the first geometers render the earliest geometrical structures and idealities communicable? How did individual conscious activity produce an "ideal and true object" characterized by "omnitemporal validity, universal normativity, intelligibility for '*everyone*,' uprootedness out of all '*here and now*' factuality, and so forth (EH 63/52)?"[6] How, as EH puts it, did "the intrapsychically constituted structure arrive at an intersubjective being of its own as an ideal object which, as 'geometrical,' is anything but a real psychic object, even though it has arisen psychically"?[7]

If I return at length and with similar questions to the Derridean scene of writing in which JJ first appeared, it is in order to examine how JJ might have become DJ, how he might have emerged as a philosophical doppelganger of EH, how the name "Joyce" might have become the event and geometrical object. From within an arguably idiosyncratic and arcane corner of French culture—an "introductory" book devoted to a late, little-known fragment of EH's writings—DJ emerged and became a central problem for a thinker who would himself become a central problem for late twentieth-century thought in all corners of the world.

As JD tells it, the intervention of the Joycean model-text-event into his consciousness dates to 1956–1957, and the first text reflecting that intervention is his *L'Origine de la géométrie de Husserl: Introduction et traduction*, published in 1962.[8] This book unfolds as a scrupulous and methodical commentary-critique some six times longer than the text on which it comments, JD's appended translation of EH's 1939 "Der Ursprung der Geometrie als intentional-historisches Problem." JJ is not mentioned early in the book and is not otherwise woven deeply into its fabric. "In the introduction we now attempt," notes JD quietly at the outset, "our sole ambition will be to recognize and situate one stage of Husserl's thought, with its specific presuppositions and its particular unfinished state" (EH 27/5). Characterizing EH's project on the origin of geometry as an innovative and "seductive" one, he follows through by describing its place in the overall trajectory of Husserlian phenomenology.

JD's willingness to take *all* of Husserl into account is a distinguishing feature of his approach in this *Introduction*. Françoise Dastur notes that although he was working at a time when most research on phenomenology was influenced by Merleau-Ponty's method of looking "for Husserl's 'unthought' in the direction of a rehabilitation of the sensible and of the body," JD was willing to accept much of Husserl's "critique of empirical and even transcendental anthropologism."[9] So instead of giving "unilateral privilege to the late Husserl, the thinker of the *Lebenswelt*, of history and intersubjectivity," JD tried instead to understand a profound tension or "apparently contradictory double gesture" that traverses many of EH's writings: a simultaneous commitment to a Platonist/Cartesian idealism and to a philosophy of history.[10] JD emphasizes that EH's chief concern throughout the "Origin of Geometry" and other writings during the period of the *Crisis in European Sciences* was to escape an unreflective Platonism on the one hand and a blind empiricism on the other, for neither philosophical approach could adequately describe the origin and historical transmission of a purely axiomatic science. JD himself wondered whether it was really possible to provide, as EH had hoped, a transcendental reduction of the world and an understanding of genesis that obeyed the requirements of transcendental philosophy, all while rendering intelligible the murky empirical givens of specific cultural histories.

It is easy to agree in a general way that JJ's last two works are characterized by a radical accumulation or superabundance of "presence," murky empirical givens, and complex referencing systems, but why was this so important to JD, and how did he relate it to EH? We might begin with Jean-Luc Marion's analysis of EH's most far-reaching contributions to thought. The distinction to make, says Marion, is one between "presencing" and "givenness":

> It seems permissible to suppose that Husserl, submerged by the simultaneously threatening and jubilatory imperative to manage the superabundance of data in presence, does not at any moment (at least in the *Logical Investigations*) ask himself about the status, the scope, or even the identity of that givenness. This silence amounts to an admission (following Jacques Derrida's thesis) that Husserl, leaving unquestioned the givenness whose broadening he nevertheless accomplished, does not free it from the prison of presence, and thus keeps it in metaphysical detention. Heidegger, to the contrary, seeing immediately and with an extraordinary lucidity that the breakthrough of 1900–1901 consists entirely in the broadening of givenness beyond sensible intuition, assumes precisely the Husserlian heritage by making the entire question bear on what such a givenness means—and therefore in being careful not to reduce it too quickly to presence, even under the figure of categorical intuition.[11]

It seems permissible to suppose as well that JD celebrates DJ's tropes and equivocalities because, like Heidegger, he seeks to turn from the limiting question of "presence" to the opening question of "givenness."[12] Marion goes on to show that JD accepted "the notion of the 'metaphysics of presence' as an overarching framework into which to read EH," but rejected "Heidegger's conclusion that Husserl represented a "new beginning" for philosophy; on the contrary, JD finds EH to be the completion or pure example of Western metaphysics.[13] The question is how and why DJ's texts became the privileged platform to critique the metaphysical commitments of EH's phenomenological approach to history.

When we interpret texts and other inherited cultural objects, we inevitably meet with givenness in the form of plurivocity (or equivocity; as JD often uses these terms interchangeably): cultural artifacts are traversed by different voices, embedded in local conditions, and guided by patterns of signifying that have since been transformed. Yet if, as JD notes, on the one hand a "radical equivocity" precludes the possibility of writing history by constantly plunging deep into "the nocturnal and ill-transmissible riches of 'bound' idealities" (EH 102/104), then, on the other, an absolute univocity would sterilize or paralyze it in selfsame iteration. In the first case there is the mess, the darkness, the shifting meanings of contingent linguistic and cultural uncertainties that overwhelm any attempt at historiographical narration or reduction. In the second case there is the ever-renewed repetition of purified concepts in ideal linguistic or symbolic structures, a *mathesis universalis* endlessly and identically reinscribing itself beyond all temporal contingency.

After describing EH's struggle to navigate between unacceptably empiricist and idealist extremes, JD presents DJ as an inspiring methodological counterexample for how to bring both the contingencies and the guiding structures of history into language: DJ comes into the *Introduction* dramatically and unexpectedly, as an equal and opposite reactive force à la Newton's third law or a *deus ex machina* à la Greek tragedy. To prepare for his arrival, JD begins by noting EH's distinction between "contingent" and "essential" kinds of plurivocity (EH 102/104).[14] The former does not generally pose a philosophical problem: certain words mean more than one thing, but the ambiguities arising from the conventions of natural language can always be reduced, clarified, and controlled. "Essential" plurivocity, however, has origins in the subjective sphere of an intending consciousness. Mental acts that bring life to objective meanings—for example, the acts that reawaken and repeat geometrical proofs—always originate along with individual and idiosyncratic experiences that force meanings into unpredictable configurations: at the same time that I recognize, or re-cognize, the Pythagorean theorem, I generate other associations and pursue other reflections. Essential plurivocity is inevitable, and although it cannot be eliminated it is precisely the kind, notes JD, that EH asks science and philosophy to overcome. Describing a form of historical transmission that would remain uncontaminated either by the private associations of individual geometers or by the broader historical transformations of language and culture, EH strains for a univocal, transcendental language that would have worldly origins and yet stay the same throughout time.

The question of historical memory becomes acute: if you want to acquire, preserve, and transmit the memory of a culture—JD likens this project of interpretive internalization to the Hegelian *Erinnerung*—then what options are there? JD finds two extremes: equivocity and univocity. The latter option is familiar as a Husserlian dream of transparent cultural transmission uncontaminated by empirical language, but the former needs elucidation and so JD introduces, one hundred pages into the book, "J. Joyce," a name, event, or philosophical option that triggers a fluvial 198-word sentence representing both a stylistic intensification of the *Introduction*'s generally patient and expository mode and a seed for disseminations in later books. Its gathering pace and process contrast so sharply with the surrounding pages that it must be quoted in full:

> L'une ressemblerait à celle de J. Joyce : répéter et reprendre en charge la totalité de l'équivoque elle-même, en un langage qui fasse affleurer à la plus grande synchronie possible la plus grande puissance des intentions enfouies, accumulées et entremêlées dans l'âme de chaque atome linguistique, de chaque vocable, de chaque mot, de chaque proposition simple, par la totalité des cultures mondaines, dans la plus grande génialité de leurs formes (mythologie, religion, sciences, arts, littérature, politique, philosophie, etc.); faire apparaître l'unité structurale de la culture empirique totale dans l'équivoque généralisée d'une écriture qui ne traduit plus une langue dans l'autre à partir de noyaux de sens communs, mais circule à travers toutes les langues à la fois, accumule leurs énergies, actualise leurs consonances les plus secrètes, décèle leurs plus lointains horizons communs, cultive les synthèses associatives au lieu de les fuir et retrouve la valeur poétique de la passivité; bref, une écriture qui, au lieu de le mettre hors jeu par des guillemets, au lieu de le *"réduire"*, s'installe résolument *dans* le champ *labyrinthique* de la culture *"enchaînée"* par ses équivoques, afin de parcourir et de reconnaître le plus actuellement possible la plus profonde distance historique possible. (104–5)

> One would resemble that of James Joyce: to repeat and take responsibility for all equivocalization itself, utilizing a language that could equalize the greatest possible synchrony with the greatest potential for buried, accumulated, and interwoven intentions within each linguistic atom, each vocable, each word, each simple proposition, in all worldly cultures and their most ingenious forms (mythology, religion, sciences, arts, literature, politics, philosophy, and so forth). And, like Joyce, this endeavor would try to make the structural unity of all empirical culture appear in the generalized equivocation of a writing that, no longer translating one language into another on the basis of their common cores of sense, circulates throughout all languages at once, accumulates their energies, actualizes their most secret consonances, discloses their furthermost common horizons, cultivates their associative syntheses instead of avoiding them, and rediscovers the poetic value of passivity. In short, rather than put it out of play with quotation marks, rather than "reduce" it, this writing resolutely settles itself *within* the *labyrinthian* field of culture "bound" by its own equivocations, in order to travel through and explore the vastest possible historical distance that is now at all possible. (EH 102/104–5)

Reluctant to stop, the French sentence stands out for its length, rhythms, enumerations, semicolons, parentheses, and pressured syntax. Although one can easily understand why John P. Leavey, in his English translation, divides it into three and adds several connecting phrases, the French has an impressive structural progression and overall four-part unity. At first it patiently doubles and repeats: "répéter et reprendre [repeat and take responsibility]"; "accumulées et entremêlées [accumulated and interwoven]"; "la plus grande puissance [greatest potential]" and "la plus grande génialité [their most ingenious forms]." Then it builds speed: "de chaque [each]," "de chaque," "de chaque," "de chaque." Then it accelerates with a string of active verbs: "circule [circulates]," "accumule [accumulates]," "actualise [actualizes]," "décèle [discloses]," "cultive [cultivates]," "retrouve [rediscovers]." Finally, it reaches an apotheosis or climax of fused JD-DJ: "bref [in short]" this is an "écriture" capable of recognizing and traversing "the vastest possible historical distance" in the most immediate way, "le plus actuellement possible [that is now at all possible]." This bursting sentence not only argues vehemently for a radical, "Joycean" mode for interpreting cultural memory but also exemplifies it. Eager to enact "the generalized equivocation of a writing that [. . .] circulates throughout all languages at once, accumulates their energies," JD has momentarily but unmistakably committed to a style with plurivocalizing philosophical consequences.

Thus DJ's first existence in prose is excessive and performative, and from this point forward he will always require hyperbolic presentation. He will remain the powerful modernist par excellence, the Bloomian strong poet among strong poets, the figure who leaves descendants no chance for originality. In "Two Words for Joyce," Derrida describes himself as a prisoner of "this admiring resentment" (TW 26/24) and speaks of Joyce's text as a computer so powerful that it would always be there "to compute you, control you, forbid you the slightest inaugural syllable. For you can say nothing that is not programed on this 1000th-generation computer" (TW 25/22). There is a "quasi-infinite speed of the movements on Joyce's cabling" (TW 25/22). This Joycean hypermnesia "indebts you in advance [. . .] and forever it inscribes you in the book you are reading" (TW 24/22). "It is very late, it is always too late with Joyce" (TW 22/15); "you have only one way out: *being in memory of him*. Not only overwhelmed by him, whether you know it or not, but obliged by him, constrained to measure yourself against this overwhelming" (TW 24/21). Overgoing and overflowing everything, destining the culture in his wake, inaugurating an epoch in which inaugural acts are no longer possible, DJ is always already the *most* X, the *absolute limit and more* of Y, the one who denies *any* possibility for Z.[15]

Compared with DJ, Google is the slow, thick-witted student Cyril Sargent from the "Nestor" chapter of *Ulysses*. JD concludes that one can only dive willingly into DJ's wake: "I decided to surrender myself along with you to a chance encounter. With Joyce, chance is always recaptured by law, sense and the program, according to the overdetermination of figures and ruses" (UG 42/60).

From the sober standpoint of literary criticism, JJ may be influential but he is not a binding, necessary, or "destining" force in any grand historico-metaphysical sense, especially not in a post-canonical world republic of literature. Critics wonder how JD can speak so confidently, without quoting any of JJ's letters, of a "Joycean project" that would include but recalibrate the historicist and anti-historicist commitments he finds in the Husserlian project he more meticulously presents. DJ's project, claims JD, "also proceeded from a certain anti-historicism and a will 'to awake' from the 'nightmare' of 'history' [U 2.377], a will to master that nightmare in a total and present resumption, could only succeed by allotting its share to univocity whether it might draw from a given univocity or try to produce another" (EH 103/105). Even though JD argues that DJ, in order to triumph over history, had to concede something to some kind of "univocity," he does not pause to try to identify those putative structures of univocity in any conventional way. He does not, for example, locate the nightmare of history quotation—the only quotation from JJ in the whole of his *Introduction*—in the embittered and resentful mind of Stephen Dedalus, nor does he discuss it as a silent quotation of Jules Laforgue, nor note that it speaks to Ireland's long history of subjugation by the English empire and the Roman Catholic church, among others.

Perhaps like Borges, who often assumed in his stories that many vast intellectual projects had been completed without him needing to do more than refer glancingly to them, JD assumes the existence of all the critics' itineraries through JJ. JD's very idea of a "generalized equivocation" seems to depend upon them and he is, after all, trying to describe DJ's writing as one that "resolutely settles itself *within* the *labyrinthian* field of culture" (EH 102/104). If so then JD does not follow individual critical perspectives into detail because they would draw him into a perspectivism and empiricism that would jeopardize his performative exposition and distract from his ongoing critique of EH. DJ, JD suggests—with proof lingering in the background in the form of the Joycean community—is just as absolute as DH in demanding a totalizing repetition of history, but instead of trying to purify language so as to protect meaning—the ongoing total presence of ideal objects—from the contaminations of cultural embeddedness, he multiplies contaminating linguistic resonances so radically that he produces a "total and present resumption" (EH 103/105), a *hypermnésie*, a virtual network of connections.[16]

DJ and DH ultimately become *comparable* because their textual events depend upon those who come along to reawaken meanings through intentional mental acts. Within phenomenology, the Western metaphysical privilege of "presence" takes the form of consciousness, and EH's scientists and geometers reawaken identical, ideal systems through the medium of a wakeful, living present. DJ's readers, on the other hand, never encounter the "same" texts or reawaken the "same" sets of ideal objects, both because the texts are hideously complex and because the essential plurivocity readers bring to them codetermines the connections available to be activated. JD struggles repeatedly to describe DJ's regional associative infinities by providing long lists—which usually end with "etc."—of vast categories such as religion, culture, philosophy, etc. The Joycean event is paradigmatically strong—strong enough for JD to equate it hyperbolically with metaphysical necessity—because of the way it awakens and structures infinite connections.

It is clear that JD on DJ can sound very much like a postmodernist genuflecting before a great modernist, but there are more precise explanations for DJ's hyperbolic shroud. The absolutist rhetoric can be seen, first, as borrowed from EH, with JD simply but strikingly taking the language EH uses for scientists and geometers and applying it to a cultural figure. EH distinguishes sharply between, on the one hand, "de facto historical culture," in which "sense-sedimentation" takes place in such a way that its validity, "rooted in a language, terrain, epoch, and so forth," can "become dated," and, on the other, "the culture of truth, whose ideality is absolutely normative" (EH 59/47). JD's idea that with JJ "chance is always recaptured by law, sense, and the program, according to the overdetermination of figures and ruses" (UG 42/60) reads like a Husserlian formula for the latter's scientific project. More broadly, the rhetoric JD uses to present DJ transposes DH's puristic descriptions of the origins and transmission of scientific truth. DJ's texts repeat the processes by which geometric and other ideal entities enter into language and transcend individual cultural circumstances to achieve omnitemporal validity, apodicticity, and normativity.

Why does JD rewrite DJ as one of DH's geometers? Most obviously, the gesture enables him to pursue a retroactive exercise in writing a preface to postmodernity. If JJ is a primal cultural geometer, then JD can describe the event of his writings as a massive software installation that subsequently governs and delimits basic modes of writing and thinking in the West. Is it possible that just as EH wanted to provide a confident vision of geometry and other axiomatic disciplines for an age of crisis in the European sciences, JD wanted to reassure his dedivinized, nihilistic, decentered, poststructuralist contemporaries by redivinizing DJ? Did he create a Romantic cultural hero whose paradigmatic decisions would supposedly be broadcast and accepted across an entire epoch?

Such a homogenizing hypothesis, reminiscent of Horkheimer and Adorno's worst fears for an age of mass media, would sound all but absurd to anybody who credits JD with helping provoke the plurivocalizing tendencies of postmodernity. A less paradoxical idea would be that JD construed JJ as an antipode to EH because he needed a new, post-geometric figure for the possibility of mastering the vertiginous possibilities of dissemination that he himself most thoroughly articulated. DJ's "mastery" over such possibilities would be unlike DH's over conscious phenomena, that is, not the mastery of the confident epistemologist discovering and describing preexisting truth but the mastery of a creative hermeneutic virtuoso. Perhaps one could even measure the strength of JD's need for such a figure by interpreting it as proportional to the strength of his disbelief in the possibility for it. As JD's readers know, the *hors livre* that opens *Dissémination* is clear that precisely the strong metaphysical prefacing JD identifies in DJ is absolutely impossible:

> If the preface appears inadmissible today, it is on the contrary because no possible heading can any longer enable anticipation and recapitulation to meet and merge with another. To lose one's head, no longer to know where one's head is, such is perhaps the effect of dissemination. If it would be ludicrous today to attempt a preface that was really a preface, it is because we *know* semantic saturation to be impossible; the signifying precipitation introduces an excess facing [*un débord*] ("that part of the lining which extends beyond the cloth," according to Littré) that cannot be mastered; the semantic after-effect cannot be turned back into a teleological anticipation and into the soothing order of the future perfect; the gap between the empty "form," and the fullness of "meaning" is structurally irremediable, and any formalism, as well as any thematicism, will be impotent to dominate that structure. They will miss it in their very attempt to master it. The generalization of the grammatical or the textual hinges on the disappearance, or rather the reinscription, of the semantic horizon, even when—especially when—it comprehends difference or plurality. In diverging from polysemy, comprising both more and less than the latter, dissemination interrupts the circulation that transforms into an origin what is actually an after-effect of meaning. (DI 20–21/17)

Somehow, DJ would supplement the logic of *dissémination*, exemplify it, and escape it. JD may therefore deliberately claim too much for and about DJ because, despite great effort, he can envision no non- or post-Joycean play between univocity and plurivocity, no post-Husserlian mastery other than DJ's.[17] In this case his "resentment" would be real, and DJ would be the author-text-event who exhausted the possibilities between these limiting asymptotes.

Or maybe JD is employing a more Nietzschean strategy. Feigned or real, his resentment of DJ recalls Nietzsche's of Socrates, as does his argument that Western culture has been transformed by the Joycean event. And JD's enthusiasms for DJ echo the breathless styles Nietzsche used to sketch out the creative possibilities he envisioned for the historical phase following the death of God. According to Alexander Nehamas, Nietzschean hyperbole is not ornamental, not a "dispensable means of accomplishing an independently accessible goal," because his "writing, and his thinking, is *essentially* hyperbolic."[18] If Nietzsche's modes of interpretation are not primarily intended to extract meanings or construct adequate representations but to inquire into the interests that are served by a particular view, then hyperbole is necessary whenever his goal is to vivify the character or type of life he seeks to promote.[19] This two-pronged process involves arguing that those characters already exist and working to create their existence through writing. Throughout *The Gay Science*, for example, Nietzsche describes, narrates, argues, and lyricizes into existence such robust, dedivinized, better-adapted characters as "we free spirits," "we godless ones," "we fearless ones," "we who are homeless," among others. If JD's hyperbole is Nietzschean, then his inflated claims for DJ are not simply fawning, pro forma, pomo bromides or transposed EHisms. Rather they are a deliberate "saying too much" that identifies and helps create a type, the need for which is deeply felt. From the point of view of the critic, a Nietzschean inquiry into the origin of DJ would therefore not try to generate a picture, story, or version of Joyce to compare and contrast with existing CJs; rather it would aim to see what type of Derridean thinking DJ inspired, identified, enabled, and promoted.

If JD hyperbolizes DJ into existence as a Husserlian antipode, the author of a unique *écriture*,[20] then perhaps DJ marks, in JD, the onset of the necessity for essentially hyperbolic thought? In this case DJ would be the name for a certain kind of impossibility made possible: a text utterly devoted to equivocalities, metaphoricities, and tropes could also function as a successful semantic saturation, a pure text that would simultaneously realize EH's phenomenological dream for total presence and his nightmare of completely uninterpretable plurivocity.[21] DJ would function as the event, signature, and context of a paradigmatic writing uncannily able to *geometrize* both contingent and essential plurivocities: his texts would define a geometry of plurivocality.

I propose that JD's Nietzschean, hyperbolic presentation of JJ is the rhetorical result of his attempt to think together the creative postures of both DJ and the Husserlian phenomenologist. To understand the details of this essentially comparative analysis, it is therefore necessary to examine the ways JJ and EH themselves articulated the processes of creating with inherited cultural traditions. If we recall that DJ is an artist who, like EH's primal geometer, is capable of being the first, idiosyncratic empirical site for an activity whose paradigmatic results would transcend later changes in culture and language, then we must still ask: what distinguishes JJ's understanding of literary creativity from EH's of geometrical activity? First of all, it is not any distrust in the idea that creativity is guided by systematic, interconnected, hierarchized architectures of thought. On the contrary, JJ often drew upon the language of engineering to characterize his writing: his letters are studded with metaphors of construction and assembly. In fact, JJ sometimes employed a geometrical language for the genetics of writing that shares core elements with the scientific ideal envisioned by EH. "Each adventure" explained JJ to Carlo Linati in one famous letter of 1920, "(that is, every hour, every organ, every art being interconnected and interrelated in the structural scheme of the whole) should not only condition but even create its own technique. Each adventure is so to say a person although it is composed of persons—as Aquinas relates of the angelic hosts" (LI, 147). Here JJ envisions each *Ulysses* episode as a "unit" of a larger "whole" and each of these units as a composite of interconnected elements. In fact those elements are themselves recognizably units of extratextual systems: each chapter's "hour" participates in wider circadian and calendrical rhythms, each "organ" in networks of the human body, each "art" in the field of sister arts.

Beyond this, it could be argued that JJ, perhaps even more than other modernist writers, shared the basic commitments of phenomenology. JJ's faith in the iterability and ideality of his techniques—famously, JJ thought James Stephens could take over and finish writing *Finnegans Wake* once he got the hang of it—align him with an EH who relentlessly returned to the *forms* of genesis in order to keep truth protected from the empirical associations of actual cultural conditions. One could also point to JJ's and EH's shared reliance on versions of the interior monologue to render the complexities of egological activity or their determined return to "the things themselves" in their writing. When JJ attempted to write a Dublin that could be recreated, reimagined, or reconstituted in every detail of life from his text alone, or when he developed the universal family in *Finnegans Wake* and spoke of that book as a "universal" history, he laid Husserlian univocal foundations beneath his plurivocal experiments.

A key difference emerges in the ways they see creators reworking their media. EH argues that because systematically linked geometrical idealities are identical always and everywhere, every new geometer can reawaken and recombine portions of the handed-down system and thereby turn them to new uses. The medium of the geometers' innovations, however, the language in which they express their new composites, must be univocal or else those advancements cannot come forth both as genuinely new geometrical acquisitions and as integral parts of an existing system. For JJ, on the other hand, the presencing medium of each unit, and *a fortiori* of collections of units entitled *Ulysses* or *Finnegans Wake*, must be plurivocal. In the case of *Ulysses*, each adventure, each echoing-yet-differentiating reprise of the Homeric epic, should "not only condition but even create" new techniques of givenness or coming to presence.

JJ emphasizes but does not explicate this distinction. Borrowing an Aristotelian line of thinking that he occasionally invoked, where different methods are suited to different parts, we might say that each adventure "conditions" its own technique when it employs forms that follow functions, when modes of presentation are somehow suited to content. The artist would establish a weak, "conditioning" causality between each adventure's featured units—hour, organ, and art, for example, but eventually the list will extend well beyond those—and its style, medium, visual disposition, and other interfacing elements. Such a method might produce an unprecedented poetics, but philosophically it will always be conservative (in another vocabulary one would say "beautiful" rather than "sublime") to the extent that it allows readers to keep three things simultaneously in view: the units, the mode of presentation, and the intelligible reasons for correlating them.

JJ's sharp distinction between "conditioning" and "creating," however, raises the possibility of a stronger causality *requiring* the adventures to bring new techniques into the world. It is not immediately obvious how this will happen, and Aristotle can no longer be the touchstone. Will the hours, organs, arts and other units interact within an existing medium (language) or media (since *Ulysses* and *Finnegans Wake* work visually, gesturally, graphically, musically)? Does a poetics of conditioning *cum* creating demand that the author do something besides arrange references (to hours, arts, organs, etc.) into allusive, allegorical, or otherwise plurivocal layers? JJ does not describe the difficult moment when the combined units pass from abstract to material, when the transformative poiesis produces formal adventures with unique stylistic features, but everything suggests that he means more than recombining inherited acquisitions à la the Husserlian geometers, more than redeploying the existing toolbox of narrative and lyric techniques, and that the new techniques will affect the medium itself.

Much has been and remains to be said about the way the artist-craftsman JJ created literary techniques, but his formulation to Linati suggests a Whitmanian model in which the self-absenting but omnipresent artist "allows" new forms to emerge organically. Such a portrait descends genealogically from other "passive" Joycean artists acting as sites of reception, fertilization, and inscription, for example, the epiphany-recording, villanelle-producing poet in *A Portrait*. Subordinating, or bracketing, his inherited literary tradition and own inspirations, the artist would allow such ideal, repeatable, geometric units as hour, organ, and art to interact so as to create technique. And what is the time or terrain in or on which units transform into technique? How can one describe the activities of a consciousness that "lets itself be affected" (to recall JD's phrase) by the idealities of units like hour, organ, and art? Joyce does not speak of the writing process as something that takes place word-by-word, sentence-by-sentence, in the mind, or on the page. The writer's primary activity lies not in choosing words, shaping sentences, applying style, or otherwise giving form to content. Before any of that, creating a technique in (for) *Ulysses* means choosing units, and the consequences of these decisions will control the text's modes of givenness: the distribution of letters, words, typographies, narratives, characters, and so forth. From this perspective, what is often considered the originary act of writing, when the pen traces the paper, is actually a late and derivative stage. Although allowance must be made for the play of the signifier, for the arbitrariness that can overtake or qualify earlier decisions—and such late-stage play can always become the principle of new techniques—even in those cases the technique has always already been fixed before the act of writing.

In Husserlian terms, then, DJ's conditioned *and* created techniques have a paradoxical and provocative double status: as the conceptual by-products and passive syntheses of determinate units, they are in principle ideal and repeatable, and can be reawakened and intuited by new readers the same way geometrical objects maintain their pure ideality and self-identity despite being reawakened and reused by different geometers. And yet, each of DJ's created techniques is also inevitably caught up in the text that it creates and can be identified only *ex post facto*. A text that has been conditioned by a technique is conceptually separable from that technique; the technique maintains its transcendental status. When a text has been conditioned *and created* by a technique, the text and technique are partly separable and partly inseparable.[22]

Thus the windy journalism of "Aeolus," the hallucinatory histrionics of "Circe," the "fizzing new" commercialese of "Nausicaa," the catechistic anthropology of "Eumaeus," the monological yet quintessentially plurivocal meanderings of "Penelope," and the many other *Ulysses* techniques paradigmatically delimit new modes of givenness and thereby negotiate the Scylla and Charybdis of Idealism/univocity and Empiricism/plurivocity. They manifest what JD called in 1989 an "economy of exemplary iterability" in literature, one uniquely able to condense the "greatest potentiality" of history and culture:

> A text by Joyce is simultaneously the condensation of a scarcely delimitable history. But this condensation of history, of language, of the encyclopedia, remains here indissociable from an *absolutely* singular event, an *absolutely* singular signature, and therefore also of a date, of a language, of an autobiographical inscription. In a minimal

autobiographical trait can be gathered the greatest potentiality of historical, theoretical, linguistic, philosophical culture—that's really what interests me.[23]

JD's hyperbolic appreciation of DJ's "absolute" singularity returns us to the question of how JJ could become the hermeneutic basis for a *community* of critics.[24] Recall that EH, JJ, and JD are all names for events of writing and thought that ultimately inspired hordes of researcher-interpreters, and that DJ represents a "landmark in the history of deconstruction" because he catalyzed precisely the one that he did.[25] Once again it helps to contrast EH and JJ. On the one hand, each member of EH's ever-renewing community of geometers starts from handed-down propositions that are transcendental and everlasting, although the historical origins of these ideal objects have long since been forgotten. On the other hand, Joyceans begin their study with a singular mixture of autobiography, encyclopedia, religion, tropes, history, *sui generis* styles, "conditioned and created" techniques, etc. Whatever Joyceans may think of DJ, few escape the Derridean imperative of characterizing JJ's texts with lists of categories ending in "etc."

Surely this means that the community of JJ researchers has no common language and must pursue its studies in a necessary plurivocity that always already destabilizes the basis of its own community? Among other basic questions: how do Joyceans communicate their results? How do they agree on an object of study, a set of texts or editions? And yet: both imagined communities—JJ researchers and EH's geometers—are exemplary cases of communal subjectivity in which participants sense that they are working together and sharing responsibility with others. One could even risk saying of individual Joyceans what EH says of geometrical investigators: each "not only feels himself *tied to* all the others by the unity of an object or task—but the investigator's own subjectivity is constituted by the idea or horizon of this total subjectivity which is made responsible in and through him for each of his acts as a scientific investigator" (EH 61/49–50). From this perspective, the singularity of the community of JD researchers is that they start from formally adventurous text-events that derive from both communities, that is, from the impossible, hyperbolic simultaneity of JJ and EH.

Notes

1. Friedrich Nietzsche, *The Gay Science*, trans. Walter Kaufmann (New York: Vintage, 1974), 282.

2. One of JD's chief examples of a thinker/litterateur who avoided JJ is Sartre, who JD understood to have resisted the Joycean turbulence by conceiving of literature too narrowly as sociopolitical activity. Without ever mounting any systematic

critique of Sartre's *Qu'est-ce que la littérature*, JD noted in interviews that Sartre did not—and suggested that he *could* not—read JJ.

3. John Caputo, ed., *Deconstruction in a Nutshell: Conversations with Jacques Derrida* (New York: Fordham University Press, 1997), 26.

4. JD's position fits squarely within the critical tradition inaugurated by T. S. Eliot's 1923 review essay on JJ's "Ulysses, Order, and Myth." Eliot argues that in *Ulysses* the artist uses ancient myth as a way of "controlling, of ordering, of giving a shape and a significance to the immense panorama of futility and anarchy which is contemporary history" (*Selected Prose of T. S. Eliot*, ed. Frank Kermode [New York: Harcourt Brace and Company, 1975], 175–78; 177).

5. In a longer essay, it would be necessary to draw out the distinction between JD's analysis of EH and JJ's of Giambattista Vico, who wrote that it is "beyond our power to enter into the vast imagination of those first men, whose minds were not in the least abstract, refined, or spiritualized, because they were entirely immersed in the senses, buffeted by the passions, buried in the body. That is why we said above that we can scarcely understand, still less imagine, how those first men thought who founded gentile humanity" (Giambattista Vico, *The New Science*, trans. Thomas Goddard Bergin and Max Harold Fisch [Ithaca: Cornell University Press, 1968], 118).

6. EH describes the basic problem that gives rise to his analysis of geometry: "The inheritance of propositions and of the method of logically constructing new propositions and idealities can continue without interruption from one period to the next, while the capacity for reactivating the primal beginnings, i.e., the sources of meaning for everything that comes later, has not been handed down with it. What is lacking is thus precisely what had given and had to give meaning to all propositions and theories, a meaning arising from the primal sources which can be made self-evident again and again" (Edmund Husserl, *The Crisis of European Sciences and Transcendental Phenomenology*, trans. David Carr [Evanston: Northwestern University Press, 1970], 367).

7. Husserl, *Crisis*, 359.

8. Here is how JD tells the story of meeting JJ: "A long time ago, in 1956–57, I spent a year at Harvard, and what I did there was to read Joyce in the Widener Library, which provided my encounter with *Ulysses*. Since then, Joyce has represented for me the most gigantic attempt to gather in a single work, that is, in the singularity of a work which is irreplaceable, in a singular event—I am referring here to *Ulysses* and to *Finnegans Wake*—the presumed totality, not only of one culture but of a number of cultures, a number of languages, literatures, and religions. This impossible task of precisely gathering in a totality, in a potential totality, the potentially infinite memory of humanity is, at the same time and in an exemplary way, both new in its modern form and very classical in its philosophical form. That is why I often compare *Ulysses* to Hegel, for instance, to the *Encyclopedia* or the *Logic*, as an attempt to reach absolute knowledge through a single act of memory. This is made possible only by loading every sentence, every word, with a maximum of equivocalities, virtual associations, by making this organic linguistic totality as rich as possible" (Caputo, *Nutshell*, 25).

9. Françoise Dastur, "Finitude and Repetition in Husserl and Derrida," *Jacques Derrida: Critical Assessments of Leading Philosophers*, ed. Zeynap Direk and Leonard Lawlor (New York: Routledge, 2002), 267–82; 268.

10. Ibid., 268.

11. Jean-Luc Marion, "The Breakthrough and the Broadening," in Direk and Lawlor, *Critical Assessments*, 313–38; 334.

12. DJ has unique abilities to manipulate and maximize the referential powers of signifiers. A single word or phrase can "contain" other words, myriad competing and contradictory meanings, whole languages, disciplines, the histories of language, the entire history of every world culture. JD's long analysis of "He war" in *Finnegans Wake* culminates a series of analyses of special, overperforming words—*pharmakon* in Plato, "hymen" in Mallarmé. (For a discussion of *cendre*, see PI 208–11/221–24). These words are words but also more than words: they are magic, talismanic, dizzying synecdoches.

13. Marion, "Breakthrough," 317. In *Speech and Phenomena*, JD will say more bluntly that despite Husserl's reliance on "presence"—"ultimate court of appeal for the whole of this discourse" (SP 9/8)—and "the living present" as grounds for his philosophies of time and intersubjectivity, nonpresence in fact plays a constitutive role in both: "phenomenology seems to us tormented, if not contested from within, by its own descriptions of the movement of temporalization and of the constitution of intersubjectivity. At the heart of what ties together these two decisive moments of description we recognize an irreducible nonpresence as having a constituting value, and with it a nonlife, a nonpresence or nonself-belonging of the living present, an ineradicable nonprimordiality" (SP 6–7/5).

14. JD criticizes Heidegger for his dismissive attitude toward plurivocity. "Concerning Trakl, it is true, Heidegger acknowledges the plurivocal (*mehrdeutig*) character of poetic language; but this plurivocity has to be gathered up in a higher univocity, which is the condition of great poetry. Heidegger then shows himself to be rather contemptuous of lightweight poets who play with plurivocity" (PI 305/315). In 1983, Derrida explained that he had also written "books with several columns or several voices" but that "for this multiplicity of levels or tones, one would have to invent still other forms, other kinds of music" (PI 130/138–39). The problem is that they are not accepted because too many people are willing to believe in the dominance and necessity of linearity, univocality, and so forth. For one account of Husserl's significance to Joyce, see Alan Roughley, *Reading Derrida Reading Joyce* (Gainesville: University of Florida Press, 1999), 1–8.

15. Sometimes DJ appears as a spirit, a messiah who has already come. In "Two Words for Joyce," DJ exemplifies two "grandeurs," that is, vastnesses or greatnesses. The first is that of "the idea of a writing that gives" (TW 24/21). "Once the gift is received, the work having worked to the extent of changing you through and through, the scene is other and you have forgotten the gift and the giver. Then the work is 'loveable,' and if the 'author' is not forgotten, we have for him or her a paradoxical gratitude, which is however the only gratitude worth its name if it is possible, a simple gratitude without ambivalence" (TW 24/21). "As for the other greatness, I shall say, with some injustice perhaps, that for me it's like Joyce's greatness, or rather that of Joyce's writing. Here the event deploys such plot and scope that henceforth you have only one way out: *being in memory of him*" (TW 24/21).

16. In "Two Words for Joyce," JD abandons himself to an uncharacteristically empiricist approach: counting the yeses in *Ulysses*. Abandoning himself to the randomness of an encounter, in a gesture of exploratory naïveté, JD assumes—as useful,

if not as true—that he can recognize the "yeses" in the first place, that they form a connective tissue, a structure, or a collection of data points. Knowing from the start how unscientific and unauthoritative such a study will be—among other things, he uses the French edition—it is as if he were experimenting with the empiricist pole of interpretation, the pole of plurivocity and the play of the signifier. Ultimately, DJ becomes the figure who most aggressively restores the nonderivative character of signs, follows and performs their indefinite drift, and exaggerates the errancy and *Verwandlung* of language in general. In "Ulysses Gramophone," JD tries to show how the "virtual infinity" of wakeable, repeatable associations in the text of *Ulysses* can predict and help create those of a human life. He follows associations through the text—for example, postcards, Tokyo, lakes, the "yes" as used and mentioned, typewriters, telephones, circumcision, Elijah, perfumes—and then weaves them into a narration of some recent experiences in his own life.

17. "Paradoxical logic of this relationship between two unequal texts, two programs or two literary 'softwares.' Whatever the difference between them, to the point of incommensurability, the 'second' text, the one which, fatally, refers to the other, quotes it, exploits it, parasites it and deciphers it, is no doubt the minute parcel *detached* from the other, the offspring, the metonymic dwarf, the jester of the great anterior text which would have declared war on it in tongues. And yet (one can see this precisely with Joyce's books which play both roles, the ancestor and the descendant), it is also another set, quite other, bigger and more powerful than the all-powerful which it drags off and reinscribes elsewhere, in another sequence, in order to defy, with its ascendancy, genealogy itself. Each writing resembles not the grandson as grandfather, but, beyond the Oedipus, *both* a detached fragment of a program and a more powerful program than the other, a part derived from but already bigger than the whole of which it is *a part*, from which it is apart" (TW 26/25).

18. Alexander Nehamas, *Nietzsche: Life as Literature* (Cambridge: Harvard University Press, 1985), 31.

19. Nehamas notes that hyperbole, precisely because it is so "unscholarly," can provoke very different reactions in readers, including indifference, indignation, and discipleship in readers (Nehamas, *Nietzsche*, 23). These categories characterize a lot of JD's readers, too.

20. Later, in a 1982 *Le Monde* interview with Christian Descamps, JD recalled that "the last text of Husserl seduced me first of all by what it has to say about writing, in a way that is at once novel and confused, a little enigmatic: graphic notation is not an auxiliary moment in scientific formalization" (PI 78/84).

21. As JD notes: "Every time this element of presence becomes threatened, Husserl will awaken it, recall it, and bring it back to itself in the form of a telos—that is, an Idea in the Kantian sense. There is no *ideality* without there being an Idea in the Kantian sense at work, opening up the possibility of something indefinite, the infinity of a stipulated progression or the infinity of permissible repetitions" (SP 9/8).

22. JD argues that DJ's encyclopedism defies the totalizing hermeneutics of the community of Joyceans and produces for it a mood or dominant affect whose status is "quasi-transcendental": "Once we recognize in principle that in *Ulysses* the virtual totality of experience, of sense, of history, of the symbolic, of languages and writings, the great cycle and the great encyclopedia of cultures, of scenes and affects,

the sum total of sum totals in sum, tends to unfold and recompose itself by playing out all its combinatory possibilities, with a writing that seeks to occupy there virtually all places, well, the totalizing hermeneutic that constitutes the task of a global and eternal foundation of Joycean studies will find itself before what I hesitate to call a dominant affect, a *Stimmung* or a *pathos*, a tonality that re-traverses all the others, but which nonetheless does not belong to the series of the others since it just re-marked them all, adding itself to them without letting itself be added up or totalized, like a remainder that is both quasi-transcendental and supplementary" (UG 68/116).

23. Jacques Derrida, "An Interview with Jacques Derrida," *Acts of Literature*, ed. Derek Attridge (New York: Routledge, 1992), 33–75, 43.

24. Jean-Luc Marion recalls Husserl's "troubled and almost anguished appeal to 'teams' of investigators, to 'generations' of phenomenological workers who would busy themselves in all the available 'regions'" (Marion, "Breakthrough," 314).

25. "What I tried to show also in my work on Joyce is that [. . .] the writing of these works functions as an injunction to the academy, that is, to literary critics to come, to the institution of Joycean scholarship, to build a sort of beehive, an infinite institution of people working as interpreters and philologists, people deciphering Joyce's signature as a singular signature. From that point of view I think that Joyce is a great landmark in the history of deconstruction; that's why the reference to Joyce is important to me" (Caputo, *Nutshell*, 25–26).

2

Joyce's Resonance in *Glas*

Sam Slote

Derrida's *Glas* is an elaboration of Hegel, or, if you will, a gloss (with all the disingenuousness that word implies). To be sure, Derrida's text, in its arrant strangeness, is hardly a limpid elucidation of Hegel. Derrida introduces a certain complexity into the dialectic in order, perhaps, to maintain it and carry it forward. To take a quote from Nicolas Sarkozy, Derrida's stance toward Hegel is "solidaire mais différent."[1] Even though he is cited explicitly only exactly once in the text, Joyce occupies a very specific albeit fuzzy locus within this intervention of differentiation into the Hegelian corpus. I would like to examine what comes and remains of this singular Joycean resonance within Derrida's *coup de glas*.

The title *Glas* has multiple valences. On the one hand, it derives from the poem "Le Glas" by Georges Bataille, which is cited in the text (G 220b–21b/245b). It also echoes from and in a poem by Mallarmé, "Aumône," which exists in or across four versions with different titles: the word *glas* occurs in all versions except the earliest.[2] Derrida teases out a pattern of tintinnabulations between the *glas* of the different versions that destabilizes the existence of the "poem" in the singular: "The poem is always also the active 'translation' of another poem that rings within it" (G 153b/173b). This enfolded plurality is pronounced in the word *glas* itself, a word whose plural is indistinct from its singular: "There is—always—already—more than one—*glas*" (G 150b/170b). And, likewise, as the word *glas* in French means bell or klaxon, it resonates multiply in other languages. For example, seemingly *apropos* nothing in particular, Derrida notes that the Slovene translation of the title of his earlier work *La Voix et le phénomène* is *Glas in phenomen* (G 79bi/92bi). In this way, the word *glas* would be an inverse correlate to Mallarmé's nonce word "ptyx," from the sonnet "Ses purs ongles," a word that he claimed did not exist in any language.[3] *Glas* announces, rings, resounds multiplicity.

Derrida also breaks up the word *glas* into constitutive phonemes to which he ascribes interlapping significances that are emblematic of the book-as-a-whole; *to wit*: "The title lays out, more a sign of fatigue, the appeased, glorious integrity of one entire word, the verbal body *glas*. Interposed before the disseminating mark, the vowel is seen no longer, no longer scaffolds. It sings [*chante*] or blackmails [*fait chanter*] the bit (the dead) [*le mors*]" (G 234b/261b). The word *glas* thus performs the text *Glas*.

The text of *Glas* consists of two parallel columnar texts—one, on the left, consecrated to Hegel and the other, on the right, concerning Jean Genet—each of which is offset by occasional marginal interruptions. The marginalia are called, variously, "tattoos" (G 3bi/8bi–9bi), or "Judases" (G 216bi/242bi), in that through glossing they betray the text they are enmeshed within (PI 7/15–16). Each columnar text is circular: like *Finnegans Wake* the last sentence can feed into the first. Furthermore, both columns form a Möbius strip as the last sentence of the Hegel column can equally well plug into the first sentence of the Genet column, and, unsurprisingly, vice versa (PI 49/56). The reversibility of the columns is an apparently perfect dialectic process: "Both processes are inseparable; they can be read in any sense, any direction whatever, from right to left or left to right; the relief of one must value [*faire cas*] the other" (G 241a/269a).

The two-column format derives directly from a short text by Genet, "Ce qui est resté d'un Rembrandt déchiré en petits carrés bien réguliers, et foutu aux chiottes" ("What remained of a Rembrandt torn into small, very regular squares and rammed down the shithole"), a fiction about finding identity in difference. This piece could also be construed as Genet's rejoinder against Sartre's *Saint Genet*. Sitting in a third-class train car, the protagonist of Genet's left-hand column stares at the unkempt man sitting across from him and realizes that "every man *is worth as much as* every other."[4] The right-hand column is seemingly unrelated although it carries certain terms from its consociate column. The situation between the men on the train thus reflects the situation between the two columns. Derrida writes, "'What remained of a Rembrandt' develops over its two columns a theory or an event of general equivalence: of subjects [. . .] of the infinite exchange between two columns that regard themselves in reverse" (G 43b/52–53b). This process of *equation* is not without relevance to Derrida's consideration of Hegel.

Quite literally, since the title of Genet's piece appears in the first paragraph of the right-hand column, *Glas* exfoliates out from "What remained of a Rembrandt." When the right-hand column describes the bi-columnar Genet text, it is also describing *Glas* itself. The right-hand column begins with "'*what remained of a Rembrandt torn into small, very regular squares and rammed down the shithole*' is divided in two" (G 1b/Gf: 7b). Obviously the statement refers to the Genet text, but also, plausibly, to whatever did remain of that torn-up Rembrandt and, by extension, to *Glas* itself. Such self-referentiality is, of course, a dialectical move par excellence. Derrida writes: "The dialectical law bends and reflects itself, applies itself to its very own statements" (G 10a/16a). In this way, the two columns are both model and metaphor for some kind of fungible inter- and intratextuality, which is itself some kind of dialogism, which is also, as Lou Reed would have it, some kinda love. For, in Hegel's works the possibility of dialectic presupposes separation and thus begins with love; as Stephen has it in *Ulysses*, Socrates learned dialectic from Xanthippe (U 9.235).

Likewise, Derrida's foray into Hegel begins with love (G 6a/12a) in that the first term of the Hegelian "concept family" is the family, which is itself founded on the bond of love between husband and wife (see also G 34a–36a/43a–44a). In the *Philosophy of Right*, Hegel describes the surrender of being-in-love: "Love means in general terms the consciousness of my unity with another, so that I am not in selfish isolation but win my self-consciousness only as the renunciation of [*Aufgebung*] my independence and through knowing myself as the unity of myself with another and of the other with me."[5] Derrida comments on this passage: "The movement described is thus the relief [*la relève*] of a dispossession, the *Aufhebung* of an *Aufgebung*" (G 18a/25a). In other words, love is an act of self-redefinition *entre deux* that nullifies the alterity of the other in the loving embrace of the *Aufhebung*. In this way, *Glas* might be construed as a *loving* reading of Hegel: taking the Hegelian corpus out of its isolation by coupling it with Genet.

Because of its funky format, *Glas* is frequently compared with chapter II.2 of *Finnegans Wake*, if not the *Wake*-as-a-whole, although the resemblance is little more than superficial. To wit, Geoffrey Hartman: "I am sufficiently convinced that *Glas*, like *Finnegans Wake*, introduces our consciousness to a dimension it will not forget."[6] One strong congruity would be that, like *Finnegans Wake*, *Glas* essays to be an encyclopedic work, albeit primarily through the filter of its linguistically fecund title. Derrida has variously affirmed and denied any contiguity between *Glas* and *Finnegans Wake*. His affirmation, in the essay "Two Words for Joyce," is somewhat less than resounding: "And I pass quickly over *Glas*, which is also a sort of *Wake*, from one end to the other, the long procession in two columns of a joyful theory, a theory of mourning" (TW 28/30). So any rapport exists only in the most general sense, the sense of a wake, the sense of the exuberance at a funeral or a "funferal" (FW 120.10), as Joyce has it in a neologism that splits the difference between joy and mourning through lexical synthesis. On the other hand, Derrida's denials have been a little more forceful. At the *Glas* seminar in Kolding in 2000, he steadfastly denied that the *Wake* was a model for *Glas*.

Essentially, *Glas* concerns the possibility of thinking apart from philosophical idealism, or, more precisely, the possibility of thinking apart from Hegelian *Aufhebung*. In a remarkably pellucid note in the *Encyclopaedia Logic*, Hegel glosses his use of the one word *Aufheben* by noting its two seemingly contradictory senses: on the one hand, "to clear away" or "cancel" and, on the other hand, "to preserve."[7] Derrida raises or brings about this double sense when he describes the two overlapping functions of *Glas*' two columns: "The first assures, guards, assimilates, interiorizes, idealizes, relieves the fall [*chute*] into the monument. [. . .] The other lets the remain(s) fall" (G 1b–2b/7b–8b). In a generalized sense, the two columns recapitulate themselves thereby enacting a process of *Aufhebung*.

Concomitant with the question concerning *Aufhebung* is the possibility of something, anything, that might not be susceptible to the play of dialectic. The problem is acute because, essentially by definition, dialectic absorbs alterity. The rule of the dialectic is the perpetual reconciliation without remainder and so the problem thus concerns the possibility of a remainder or residue within the economy of *Aufhebung*. At one point Derrida asks, "And what if what cannot be assimilated, the absolute indigestible, played a fundamental role in the system" (G 151a/171a).[8] Through *Aufhebung*, the concept "reduces difference to nothing" (G 43ai/52ai). *Aufhebung* is nothing if not restrictive. If there can be nothing alien to the steady, speculative march of Hegelian *Aufhebung*, what difference can difference make (if difference were to make a difference)? As Derrida opens the left-hand column, "one will not have been able to think without [Hegel]" (G 1a/7a); in light of such strict, inevitable solidarity what possibility can there be for difference, disruption, displacement?

In the line I would like to follow, Derrida looks at Hegel's early work *The Spirit of Christianity* wherein he posits, in "a kind of theoretical fiction" (G 37a/46a), the biblical flood as the originary loss of the state of nature. As a consequence, postulates Hegel in this charming narrative, if "man was to hold out against the outbursts of a nature now hostile, nature had to be mastered [. . .]. It was in a thought-product that Noah built the distracted world together again."[9] The conceptual ordination of the world is thus a product of Noah's survival gambit. Derrida writes:

> In all the senses of that word. Noah is the concept. By a bad wordplay, Jewish-Greek, à la Joyce, and mixing in a little gallicism Noé, one would say noesis. In effect, in order to control maternal nature's hostility in her unleashed waters, she had to be thought, conceived, grasped. Being thought is being controlled. The concept marks the interruption of a first state of love. [. . .] The concept busies itself around a wound. [. . .] Noah chose to gather together

the world torn apart, to reconstitute in sum the *Gleichgewicht* in the being-thought. (G 38a/47a)

Unsurprisingly, one can find in the *Wake* Joyce's own wordplay for conflating Noah with the originary concept: "noarchic" (FW 80.25). Now, figuring the, let's just say, "birth of the concept" through a wordplay is hardly an innocent or transparent move.

It's not just the self-styled bad wordplay that makes Derrida call up the name Joyce. Derrida had closed an earlier essay on Levinas with a proposition that feeds into the noetic column:

> Are we Greeks? Are we Jews? But who, we? Are we (not a chronological, but a pre-logical question) *first* Jews or *first* Greeks? And does the strange dialogue between the Jew and the Greek, peace itself, have the form of the absolute, speculative logic of Hegel, the living logic which *reconciles* formal tautology and empirical heterology after having *thought* prophetic discourse in the preface to the *Phenomenology of Mind*? Or, on the contrary, does this peace have the form of infinite separation and of the unthinkable, unsayable transcendence of the other? From whence does it draw the energy of its question? Can it account for the historical *coupling* of Judaism and Hellenism? And what is the legitimacy, what is the meaning of the *copula* in this proposition from perhaps the most Hegelian of modern novelists: "Jewgreek is greekjew. Extremes meet"?[10] (WD 153/227–28)

The Cap's famous equation of Greek and Jew from "Circe" (U 15.2097-98) occupies a position one could almost call Derrida's own "kind of theoretical fiction" about an originary concept. Following from Hegel, the Hellenic stands as a sigil for totality and completion; as Hegel has it in *The Philosophy of History*, "Among the Greeks we feel ourselves immediately at home, for we are in the region of Spirit."[11] Whereas, and in contradistinction, in Derrida's reading of Levinas, the Hebraic is eternally incomplete, errant, and exiled from closure.[12] Therefore, reconciling Greek and Jew would be the most formidable, if not redoubtable, *Aufhebung*: a unification of totality and fragmentation, the *Aufhebung* of *Aufhebung*.

Derrida notes that Hegel considered the Jewish background to the spirit of Christianity in terms of how *logos* was thematized as the divine character (specifically in the Gosepl of John): "John writes in Greek. The Gospel undersigned John is by a Greek Jew. How have the Jewish categorical constraints been able to ligate, to make obsolete [*vieillir*] in advance the writing of the good news?" (G 75a/88a). Unsurprisingly, Hegel attempted to extirpate this Jewish contamination of the "good news" by not entrusting its decoding to merely hermeneutics: "Nowhere more than in the communication of the divine is it necessary for the recipient to grasp the communication with the depths of his own spirit."[13] The *language* of revelation may be tainted but a reader armed with appropriate spirit can see beyond that to attain divine *logos* (see G 76a/89a). In this way, Hegel has decided the *Aufhebung* of "greekjew" in favor of a certain spirit, one that bypassed or ignores language's inability to be an *ideal* language.

Before his Joycean "greekjew" wordplay, Derrida had commented that Hegel distrusted mere etymology as a means of philosophical clarification. "That the same word or two words of analogous root can have two conceptually different, verily opposite significations proves that the word is never a concept" (G 7a/13a).[14] In other words, for language to elevate itself to the level of concept (that is, ideal interior signification), it must jettison, among other things, the possibility of the pun, which is to say the possibility consociating ideas solely on the basis of lexical congruity (such as, say in French, Noah and noesis).

Derrida addressed this problem of the pun with the essay "Proverb: 'He that would pun . . . ,'" published on the occasion of the English translation of *Glas*. He begins the essay with the seemingly glib claim that "there is not one single *pun* (in English in the text)."[15] The parenthetical addition is, of course, crucial and quite sly: whatever punning may not or may have been in the *soi disant* French version of the text is liable to be lost in translation. Derrida is not simply traducing his translators here, but rather is bringing up a problem endemic to translation. The ambiguity, such as it is, in the line "there is not one single *pun* (in English in the text)" is entirely a function of syntax, whereas puns are semantic creatures. Since the task of translation, almost always never fully realized, is to regulate gaps and anomalies, translation *suppresses* gaps by not allowing them to pass forth into another language. A pun merely provides several different possible meanings whereas syntactic looseness allows for an indeterminacy that cannot necessarily be adjudicated, or, if you will, *régler*.[16] As Derrida writes, "a translation returns [*rend*] the text to its readability, returns the text to an intelligibility that perhaps remains enveloped in its original version."[17] One example of a simple paranomastic effect lost in English is the constant play Derrida gives between (the French pronunciation of) *Hegel*, *aigle*, and *règle* (Hegel, eagle, and rule). Obviously, this effect cannot be rendered in English, although a creative translator might do something with Hegel, finagle, and bagel.

Of course, Derrida's play with the homophonous (French) couple *Hegel* and *aigle* does not betoken any significance other than the (simple) fact that it is linguistically possible. The paranomasia is significant precisely because it is meaningless; were it to be otherwise, the soaring Hegel would be triumphant.[18] In other words, its importance lies in indicating how language is not restrictive, despite Hegel's attempts to make it so: the restrictive *règle* of *Hegel* flies away as an *aigle*. Despite Hegel, language can be equivocal. Indeed, in *Glas*, Derrida finds a possibility of equivocation through Hegel's strictures and re-strictures.

The dialectic sweep of *Aufhebung* is a *re-stricture* in that it binds and delimits through a continuous suppression of difference. "But to say re-stricture—under its name repression—today remains a confused imagination, that is perhaps only to designate, in regard to philosophy, what does not let itself be *thought* or even arraigned [*arraisonner*] by a question. The question is already strict-uring, is already girded being" (G 191a/215a). In other, kinkier, words the lordship of *Aufhebung* is bondage. The *re-stricture* is strict, that is, it does not allow for free play or, if you will, equivocation. However, Derrida notes that because of language's lack of ideality the *re-stricture* is necessarily asymmetrical, which allows for a counter movement, or contra-band, that cannot be assimilated dialectically: "The contra-band is *not yet* dialectical contradiction. To be sure, the contra-band necessarily becomes that, but its not-yet is not-yet the teleological anticipation, which results in it never becoming dialectical contradiction. The contra-band *remains* something other than what, necessarily, it is to become" (G 244a/272a). On the one hand, a contradiction would be subsumed within *re-stricturing* in that it would simply be an antithesis awaiting (its own proper) *Aufhebung*. On the other hand, the contra-band is a third term that lies in the crossing over of the one into the other, the slackness of the stricture, the free-play of equivocation: "This 'theory,' to be sure, is called for by a thinking of writing (in *Of Grammatology*) but it is better thematized and formalized (with *Dissemination*, *Glas*, *Parages*) in its relation to the *double bind*, to the *stricture of the double band* and, especially, of a *remaining* that is *not* and does not stem [relève] from ontology any more than it lends itself to dialectical sublation [la relève dialectique]" (RP 29–30/44). In other words, within the stricture of *Aufhebung* lies its undoing in a nondialectical opposition, within the certainty of *Aufhebung* lies indeterminacy.

The *Wake* is, of course, filled with examples of syntactic indeterminacy. As a brief example, which will serve as a rejoinder to Derrida's use of a self-styled Joycean wordplay in *Glas*, I will take this sentence from III.4: "Here is onething you owed two noe" (FW 561.04–5). There are several different layers of wordplay in effect here. First, the sentence is homophonous with the expression "There is one thing you ought to know." But, there is more than "onething" in this sentence. The obligation of knowledge ("ought to know") is here rendered as a debt ("owed two noe"), with a word not unlike Derrida's *Noé* in *Glas*. However, the real complication here is the substitution of the preposition "to" with the number "two," especially since this acts in conjunction with the word "onething." In other words, the numeration of this one sentence is already multiple, with no resolution (or possible hermeneutic adjudication) between the different senses, or, as the next sentence has it: "This one once upon awhile was the other but this is the other one nighadays" (FW 561.05–6). Beyond the act of merely glossing these lines, something else remains. And this brings us back to *Glas*.

A translation is not unlike a gloss in that both are invariably *in other words*. In other words, translation, even in the best of circumstances, transforms, mutates, re-creates the text it translates, such as, say, *Glas*. Derrida writes, "Even in its so-called French version, translation devours *Glas*, which exhibits in a way a *passion* for the foreign tongue."[19] The act of translation is thus a metaphor—which is itself a kind of translation (*metapherein*, to translate, transport, transpose)—of dialectic assimilation itself, that is, of *Aufhebung*.[20] Translation is a mode of *Aufhebung*. In *Glas*, Derrida teases this point, briefly and brilliantly, out of French translations of the word *Aufhebung*: "the death of singularity is always an *Aufhebung*. The so frequent translations of *Aufhebung* by abolition and cancellation [*suppression*] precisely effaces this" (G 137a/155a). The singularity of *Aufhebung*'s double meaning is suppressed by its translation and this suppression is itself re-marked in the word *suppression*.

Of course, one wee problem for English readers of *Glas* is that Derrida is referring to French translations of *Aufhebung* by the word *suppression*; Jean Hyppolite generally rendered *Aufhebung* as *suppression*, as did Alexandre Kojève.[21] A few years ago, Derrida noted with some pride that French translations of Hegel now follow his suggestion from the 1960s that the French word *relever* perfectly captures the double sense of *Aufheben* that was previously thought to be untranslatable.[22] *Relever* is thus, as Derrida points out, "une traduction 'relevante'"—an event of translation that re-marks translation as *Aufhebung* both in and into another language (in this case, French).

English translations of *aufheben* and *Aufhebung* have followed a different tradition. Ever since J. H. Stirling wrote *The Secret of Hegel* in 1865, the most common English translation for *Aufhebung* has been, for better or worse, *sublation*;[23] although A. V. Miller uses the word *supersede*.[24] So, bizarrely, Leavey's translation of this passage in *Glas suppresses* translation by effacing the point Derrida makes about *French* translations of Hegel. In the English translation of *Glas*, the *suppression* of *Aufhebung* is thus *doubly* suppressed, making it, if you will, an *irrelevant* translation. In this way, the English translation of *Glas* raises the possibility that there is no escape from *Aufhebung*, that the *relève* is *huis clos*.

Of course, what is being suppressed in (the word) *Aufhebung* across these translations is the fact that, with its double meanings, it is a pun. *Aufhebung* is thus the pun that is a concept, a concept born of *lexis*. Even though Hegel distrusts etymology, he endorses the semantic duplicity of this one word in his pellucid note in the *Encyclopaedia Logic*: "The ambiguity in this linguistic usage, through which the same word has a negative and a positive meaning, cannot be regarded as an accident nor yet as a reason to reproach language as if it were a source of confusion. We ought to recognize here the speculative spirit of our language, which transcends the 'either-or' of mere understanding."[25] In this particular case, Hegel allows a confusion on the level of signification to somehow bring about a certain ideal truth. This confusion is not accidental, but, rather, essential. In other words, in at least this specific instance, signification is an *Aufhebung*; that is, the *true* meaning of the word *Aufheben* is the result of an *Aufhebung* of dual meanings.[26] The very process of signification is at its root both pun and *Aufhebung*. As Derrida puts it in *Glas*: "That it [*Aufhebung*] is subject to the law of what it is the law of, that is what gives to the structure of the Hegelian system a very twisted form so difficult to grasp" (G 121a/139a). Furthermore, the double meaning of *Aufhebung*, which embodies the speculative spirit of the German language, is untranslatable, that is until Derrida *l'a relevé* in French. At its heart, Hegel's speculative philosophy rests upon a wordplay not entirely dissimilar from Derrida's *soi disant* Joycean figuration of the birth of the concept as *Noé*.

For Derrida, Joyce has a very specific force in all this. Jean-Michel Rabaté characterizes this quite precisely by claiming that Joyce "precipitates a problem philosophy cannot solve. [. . .] Joyce comes to allegorize writing as that which obstinately resists philosophy."[27] In other words, for Derrida, Joyce *presents* language's lack of ideality, a lack evinced in the intertwining slipperiness of the very word *Aufhebung*. Derrida first articulated this in his lengthy introduction to *Edmund Husserl's Origin of Geometry* where he posited Joyce as an alternative to the Husserlian project to regulate philosophical thinking into univocity where language is transparent to or coterminous with history (EH 102–3/104–5). I will cite Derrida's reformulation of that argument (if you will, its *Aufhebung*) in "Two Words for Joyce":

> The other great paradigm would be the Joyce of *Finnegans Wake*. He repeats and mobilizes and babelizes the asymptotic totality of the equivocal. He makes this his theme and his operation. He tries to bring to the surface, with the greatest possible synchrony, at top speed, the greatest power of the meanings buried in each syllabic fragment, subjecting each atom of writing to fission in order to overload its unconscious with the whole memory of man: mythologies, religions, philosophies, sciences, psychoanalysis, literatures. (TW 27/28)

For Derrida, Joyce is literature par excellence. The Joycean text is not necessarily reducible to a singular determinant of meaning; it *equivocates*, and it does so by incorporating all sorts of meanings from many different languages across the widest number of possible fields unordinated by a single syntax. The implication here is that the task of reading Joyce will not be fulfilled by simply glossing away the references, by *explications du texte*, since these would reduce Joyce to a simple plurivocity, that is, to the realm of a singular determinant of meaning. Furthermore, any genre of thematic reading—whether through the optics of politics or biography or psychoanalysis or postcoloniality or nationalism or ideology or textual genetics or cultural production or comparative studies, in short the whole apparatus of the field of Joyce criticism—would be equally reductive; not that there's anything wrong with that. In "Two Words for Joyce," Derrida suggested that our readings of Joyce have not gone beyond the realm of the merely Hegelian (TW 26/24), whereas the Joycean oeuvre may be something that is apart from the strictures of dialectic in that it "rediscovers the poetic value of passivity" (EH 102/104), as Derrida phrased it in his Husserl essay. The Joycean text rests silent to the critical noise around it in its "hegelstomes" (FW 416.33).

By naming Joyce, even if only once, in *Glas*, Derrida suggests an introduction of *equivocation*, or, if you will, *whimsy*, into the dialectic march of *equation* without remainder (*Aufhebung*). Joyce, or rather a function of literature that Joyce embodies for Derrida, overloads the possibility of dialectic resolution. In *Glas*, Derrida glosses Hegel by bringing in Joycean whimsy; and what could be more whimsical than coupling Genet with Hegel? Joyce, then, for Derrida would be resonance: the silent resounding of many languages, in many overcathected words, and not just one (or two) *glas*:[28] the "collideorscape" "in the panaroma of all flores of speech" (FW 143.28 and 03–4), neither binarism (collide or scape) nor synthesis (kaleidoscope), but an altogether separate possibility, a whimsical third term that escapes the collision of synthesis.

Notes

1. Quoted in Philippe Ridet, "La crise du CPE incite M. Sarkozy à préparer sa sortie," *Le Monde*, March 23, 2006, Online. Accessed March 23, 2006.
2. Stéphane Mallarmé, *Oeuvres complètes*, vol. 1, ed. Bertrand Marchal (Paris: Gallimard, 1998), 1162–63.
3. Ibid., 1190. Mallarmé may have been bluffing about this word's uniqueness as there is a potential Greek precedent (see Paul Allen Miller, "Black and White Myths: Etymology and Dialectics in Mallarmé's 'Sonnet en yx,'" *Texas Studies in Literature and Language* 36, 2 [Summer 1994]: 184–211).
4. Jean Genet, "Ce qui est resté d'un Rembrandt," *Oeuvres complètes*, vol. 4 (Paris: Gallimard, 1968), 21–31; 21. English translation: "What Remains of a Rembrandt Torn into Little Squares All the Same Size and Shot Down the Toilet," trans. Charlotte Mandell, in *Fragments of the Artwork* (Stanford: Stanford University Press, 2003), 91–102, 91.

5. G.W.F. Hegel, *Philosophy of Right*, trans. T. M. Knox (Oxford: Oxford University Press, 1967), 261. I seem to remember reading something like this in one of Kim Casali's "Love is . . ." cartoons in the 1970s.

6. Geoffrey Hartman, "Crossing Over: Literary Commentary as Literature," *Comparative Literature* 28, 3 (1976): 257–76, 268.

7. G.W.F. Hegel, *The Encyclopaedia Logic*, trans. T. F. Geraets, W. A. Suchting, and H. S. Harris (Indianapolis: Hackett, 1991), 154.

8. The sentence is interrupted by a lengthy insert concerning Hegel's relationships with his sister and his wife that reprises the theme of love.

9. G.W.F. Hegel, *Early Theological Writings*, trans. T. M. Knox and Richard Kroner (Philadelphia: University of Pennsylvania Press, 1975), 182–83.

10. Derrida's reading of Joyce as Hegelian follows from Jean Paris' study of Joyce, which proved to be quite influential on French writers on Joyce in the 1960s (Jean Paris, *Joyce par lui-même* [Paris: Seuil, 1957], 56–57).

11. G.W.F. Hegel, *The Philosophy of History*, trans. J. Sibree (Buffalo: Prometheus Books, 1991), 223.

12. See WD 320–21 fn. 92/228 n.1 and G 44a–45a/54a–55a; see also Emmanuel Levinas, "How is Judaism Possible?" in *Difficult Freedom: Essays on Judaism*, trans. Seán Hand (Baltimore: Johns Hopkins, 1990), 245–54, translation of "Comment le judaïsme est-il possible?" in *Difficile liberté*, 3rd ed. (Paris: Albin Michel, 1976), 341–53.

13. Hegel, *Theological*, 256.

14. Derrida is here referring to this passage from the *Philosophy of Right*: "But even if 'moral' [*Moralität*] and 'ethical' [*Sittlichkeit*] meant the same thing by definition, that would in no way hinder them, once they had become different words, from being used for different conceptions" (Hegel, *Right*, 36).

15. Jacques Derrida, "Proverb: 'He that would pun . . . ,' " *Glassary*, John P. Leavey Jr. (Lincoln: University of Nebraska Press, 1986), 17–20; 17.

16. In *Dissemination*, Derrida argues that Mallarmé arrests meaning not through word games, but rather through syntax: "This displacement is always an effect of language or writing, of syntax, and never simply of the dialectical overturning of a concept (signified)" (DI 211/240).

17. Derrida, "Pun," 19.

18. "If one finds the fact, e.g., that the French often pronounce 'Hegel' as if it were *aigle*—the French for 'eagle'—of little interest, one will not be likely to watch the dance for long. But it is, I think, clear why it is being danced. It is because Derrida thinks that the ability to see writing as writing is what we need to break the grip of the notion of representation, of getting things accurately pictured" (Richard Rorty, "Derrida on Language, Being, and Abnormal Philosophy," *The Journal of Philosophy* 74: 11 [November 1977]: 673–81; 678).

19. Derrida "Pun," 17.

20. "Above all, the movement of metaphorization (origin and then erasure of the metaphor, transition from the proper sensory meaning to the proper spiritual meaning by means of the detour of figures) is nothing other than a movement of idealization. Which is included under the master category of dialectical idealism, to wit, the *relève* (*Aufhebung*), that is, the memory (*Erinnerung*) that produces signs, interiorizes them in elevating, suppressing, and conserving the sensory exterior" (MP 226/269).

21. Perhaps alluding to English translations of Hegel, Kojève uses the collocation "overcome dialectically [suppression dialectique]," which he defines as "overcom[ing] while preserving what is overcome; it is sublimated in and by that overcoming which preserves or that preservation which overcomes" (Alexandre Kojève, *Introduction to the Reading of Hegel*, assembled by Raymond Queneau, ed. Allan Bloom, trans. James H. Nichols Jr. [Ithaca: Cornell University Press, 1980], 15, translation of *Introduction à la lecture de Hegel*, ed. Raymond Queneau [Paris: Gallimard, 1947], 21).

22. Jacques Derrida, "Qu'est-ce qu'une traduction 'relevante'?," *L'Herne Derrida*, ed. Marie-Louise Mallet and Ginette Michaud (Paris: Éditions de l'Herne, 2004), 561–76; 573. He had first made the suggestion in MP 88/102.

23. W. A. Suchting, "Translating Hegel's *Logic*: Some Minority Comments on Terminology," in Hegel, *Logic*, xxxii–xlviii, xxxv.

24. G.W.F. Hegel, *Phenomenology of Spirit*, trans. A. V. Miller (Oxford: Oxford University Press, 1977), 111 passim.

25. Hegel, *Logic*, 154.

26. "Since the sign is the negativity which 'relifts' (*relève*) sensory intuition into the ideality of language, it must be hewn from a sensory matter which in some way is given to it, offering a predisposed nonresistance to the work of idealization" (MP 90/105).

27. Jean-Michel Rabaté, "Comment c'est: un déconstruire inchoatif, allégorique," in Mallet and Michaud, *L'Herne*, 385–91; 389. See also Rabaté's essay, chapter 11 in the present volume.

28. An alternate way Derrida posits this counter-band is through the resonance of a bell: "the difference between what does not resonate starting from (it)self, the bodies [. . .], and what resonates with (it)self" (G 249a/277a). The possibility of voice and signification (signification which is doomed to *re-stricture*) is predicated upon this difference in the sounding of a bell, the quiver of resonance.

3

Meaning Postponed:
The Post Card and *Finnegans Wake*

Andrew J. Mitchell

To ask what *Finnegans Wake* means presupposes an understanding of how the book means. The frustration given voice in such a question arises from the fact that *Finnegans Wake* dashes the hopes and expectations that we, as readers, have learned to bring to the texts we read. To engage with the *Wake*, therefore, we have to learn how to read anew. This has less to do with what is happening in the elusive language of the *Wake* than with how it is happening in, through, and as that language itself. Such language will not stand for a univocal reading or for a translation into unambiguous narrative statements. It does not, in fact, stand at all but instead is sent and is constantly traveling toward meaning, though never arriving at a meaning. To ask how this language means is to inquire into the nature of sending and reception, destiny and meaning, or what Jacques Derrida, in *The Post Card*, calls the "postal effect" (PC 3/7). After a brief rehearsal of some of the "postal theses" of Derrida's text, I will turn to the role of postality within *Finnegans Wake* as it concerns the figure of Shaun the Post. Shaun is charged to deliver a message that is not his own, and the entirety of his character can be read as so many attempts to avoid the upsetting postal situation that this involves. This avoidance is most evident in his nationalism and his thrift, which I will address in turn. *Finnegans Wake*, however, does more than depict a character vainly resisting the disruptions of postality, for the book itself is written in direct confrontation with these issues. In the concluding section of this essay, I will consider the way that *Finnegans Wake* confronts the problems of postality in its very language and explore the consequences of this postality for any meaningful reading of the *Wake*.

The Postal Principle

The first section of Derrida's *The Post Card*, entitled "Envois," presents a lacuna-filled series of letters supposedly written on the back of postcards and dealing in one way or another with questions of sending and nonarrival. In their content as well as their form, these postcards position themselves at the borders of signification,[1] proliferating around the difficulties of communication: the distance between parties, the contingencies of delivery, and the impossibility of the transmission of messages without a remainder. But "postality" for Derrida is also a matter of being as he claims to compose a "post card ontology" (PC 22/27). What this means is that Derrida will think of everything as "sent," his postal exchange operating as an examination of the effect of distance upon presence. What *is* is nothing present; instead it is what has been sent. This change in the conception of beings unsettles them from their supposedly fixed position of pure presence and self-containment and sets them into motion. They are now understood as destined to be here, as sent, and as subject to all the difficulties and obstacles that come with transmission. Two issues of importance for a reading of the *Wake* emerge from this: 1) the postal principle: for everything sent, there is the ineradicable possibility of non-arrival; and 2) the problem of legacy: the postal principle operates at every distance, including the temporal.

Derrida's early work explores the independence of the written message from its author and recipient. *The Post Card* undertakes a prolonged analysis of this independence, now emphasizing the transitional or mediate nature of what is sent. Rather than start from the position of author or recipient, Derrida does not start at all but is rather already underway, in *media res*, between the poles of sender and recipient. To even speak of "poles," however, is already a misnomer when it is precisely these fixed positions that have been "posted." Consequently, there are no poles for the letter to travel between; they are only an effect of the letter. The indeterminate space of the letter is the space of sending where there is neither sender nor recipient as fully constituted and preexistent parties of the communication. The letter is not a consequence of the distance between poles; instead, the situation is the reverse. The supposedly discrete poles are themselves the abstractions of a prior distancing.

It is with this in mind that we should understand Derrida's claims that nonarrival is always a possibility for what is sent. This is not a complaint against the accuracy of any particular postal system since no amount of security or vigilance can defend against this possibility. Nonarrival is always possible because the message itself is not wholly present. What is sent is already inhabited by nonarrival and nonbelonging to such a degree that, even when it "arrives" safe and sound, its nature is not completely present.

Consequently, a concept of complete arrival is contradictory, for it would indicate the complete assimilation of what was sent with its destination. If I receive something from someone, then it is precisely this "from someone" that separates me from the object received. The thing received still maintains a connection with its sender, which prevents the message from ever being completely my own, or, rather, this inescapable remainder will condition all appropriation and owning. As long as the missive retains this connection with its sender, I cannot wholly possess it, but neither can the sender wholly give it. There is a withdrawal coincident with sending that forces the work of appropriation on both recipient and sender.[2] Complete arrival is impossible. The message would have to be received in such a manner that both message and recipient would coincide with one another. There could be no space between them, not even a temporal one. Having received the message long ago would already disrupt this attempted coincidence. Both author and recipient must work at establishing themselves in their respective places in regard to the message. Neither is essential to the message "as such."

The postal principle is thus inherently upsetting and alienating. The appropriation and incorporation of something sent as something of one's own can never take the place of an innate quality or inherent attribute. We are faced with a self-constitution whereby the subject must appropriate its predicates (S is p). There is no identity, in other words, but only the owning up to one. This is indicated by the space between the subject and the predicate (S and p), which is yet another distance and yet another space of sending. There is a distance to every belonging and a postal effect across all such distances.

This is equally true of the temporal distance between heir and ancestor. Much of the correspondence in "Envois" concerns a postcard reproduced on the book's cover. Socrates, who wrote nothing but appears as a character in Plato's dialogues, sits at a writing desk and writes under the direction of Plato, standing behind him. The postcard depicts everything in the reverse of how it has been handed down, complicating the seemingly self-evident issue of legacy. For Socrates to establish a legacy across the generations, there must be a legatee who takes up that inheritance and makes it his or her own. The adoption of this inheritance is nothing that can ever be over and done with since, as we have seen, there is no complete transmission to be appropriated. Instead, the inheritance is always arriving. Further, by a taking up of the mantle of heir, the inheritor is kept at a step removed from the inheritance, and his or her life remains indebted to the other. This debt can never be repaid, especially since it has never been fully received.

Plato is not a legatee of Socrates unless he takes up his mission, but Socrates has no legacy if Plato does not take it up. If Plato needs Socrates to inherit from, Socrates needs Plato to receive his inheritance. Plato must be able to receive his legacy, and Derrida thinks of this as an activity; Plato "calls" for Socrates to send his legacy.[3] With this, Plato assumes the active role in the transmission and Socrates the position of recipient for the call to transmit. Derrida thus upsets the temporally linear transmission of inheritance and the chronological priority of ancestor over heirs, as postality puts Plato behind Socrates, and even Freud behind Plato.[4]

If the flow of time may be conceived as the transmission of now points and discrete moments, then the postal upsetting of chronology is similarly an interruption of such an effluence. Numerous temporal directions and dimensions now intersect and intercept the flow. Unidirectional time is a strategic arrangement to establish and maintain the lines of inheritance against the proliferation and detours of such alternate times. The past will be handed on to the present and this, later, to the future, as Derrida notes: "everything is constructed on the protocolary character of an axiom . . . : The charter is the contract for the following, which quite stupidly one has to believe: Socrates comes *before* Plato, there is between them—and in general—an order of generations, an irreversible sequence of inheritance" (PC 20/25). The unidirectional flow of time makes possible and is, in turn, secured by the causal determination of events occurring in time. Only in linear time can we guarantee that the effect will follow the cause, even to the point of a prediction of effects.

The Anti-Postal Shaun the Post

In *Finnegans Wake*, the postality provoked by Derrida is despised by Shaun the Post whose pained efforts to avoid it reveal the various contexts in which it operates. Shaun himself is not so much a character as a textual effect of the *Wake*.[5] Traditionally, and perhaps in a somewhat caricatured way, the word "character" refers to a fixed essence that maintains itself across the varieties of literary experience. This is not to say that literary characters do not change in that they can certainly become whom they are intended to be or fail to live up to their potential, but, in either case, the same underlying character suffers the events: the I who can claim that it is not the same as it was before. The "characters" of the *Wake*, however, do not underlie anything; they are found right there at the words on the page.[6]

Setting the word "character" off in quotation marks in an attempt to postpone the postal effect unfortunately only serves to multiply the characters upon the page. As an effect of distance, postality cannot be put off in this manner, but the inability of these quotation marks to accomplish their assigned task is instructive. They would return order to the text, provide assurance, and allow us to admit our fears of applying an inappropriate term, while proclaiming our fearlessness of such impropriety. The quotation marks are able to function regardless of content. They carry their term, providing a *prima facie* assurance that they, at least, are not involved in the affairs that they mention.

To bear a message and establish order: these are the roles of Shaun the Post, and he is those quotation marks. Their problem is his problem. Each attempts to contain postality and yet maintain separation, to envelope it and limit the extent of its effect. Insofar as character designates a steady presence persisting throughout the book, Shaun is not a character; he has already been torn apart by his message and surrendered to possibilities of nonreturn, misrecognition, and disconfiguration.Shaun's Commission
Throughout the text and especially in book III, Shaun is a mediator:[7] he is a postman charged with delivering a letter, a medium at a séance channeling the voice of HCE, Christ bearing God's message and "in reality . . . only" a barrel rolling down the Liffey.[8] He is a receptacle, the vehicle for another. The meaning that he bears is the meaning that defines him, and it is not his own. He himself is "unwordy" (FW 408.10). To be true to his post, he must deliver a letter that would thereby arrive, but we have already seen that the constant arrival of what has been sent uproots any sense of a final destination and institutes a reign of appropriation and belonging.

Shaun, however, for all his injunctions to work, is unwilling to commit to this work of appropriation. He considers himself impotent in regard to the letter: "since it came into my hands I am hopeless off course to be doing anything concerning" (FW 410.17–19).[9] His arrogance and pride conceal the inadequacy of his powers, and he begs for forgiveness of his debt and to be done with the never-ending labor of appropriation: "Forgive me, Shaun repeated from his liquid lipes, not what I wants to do a strike of work" (FW 409.33–34). His post is a torment, he himself a "hastehater of the first degree" bearing "postoomany missive" for delivery (FW 408.11, 13). The message is so upsetting to Shaun because it is not his own. It is a rift in his being that divides him from himself, and it distances him from himself by interrupting his identity with himself.

In the first chapter of book III, Shaun discusses how he received his permit as a postman: "it was condemned on me premitially by Hireark Books and Chiefoverseer Cooks in their Eusebian Concordant Homilies [H . . . C . . . E, E . . . C . . . H] and there does be a power coming over me that is put upon me from on high" (FW 409.34–410.01). That Shaun sees the message as "condemned on [him]" provides a first clue as to how he relates to his postal profession as a burden he would rather not bear. The order has fallen upon him, saddling him with a debt that he is desperate to discharge.[10] The order's reception has dislodged him from house and home and set him adrift in errancy as he is driven by divine messengers (angels) along random paths: "holy messonger angels be uninterruptedly nudging him among and along the winding ways of random ever!" (FW 405.07–9). He is underway among the ways, *unterwegs*, and "hopeless off course" (FW 410.18).

Shaun's assumption of his office irremediably separates him from the uninterrupted life he would rather lead. This interruption, however, is constitutive of his "character." Shaun is who he is, in effect, the Post, only because of the presence of another within him that he has to bear. His various attempts to claim authorship over it are just so many futile attempts to eradicate its alterity. Not only will he claim that the letter is a forgery ("Every dimmed letter in it is a copy and not a few of the silbils and wholly words" [FW 424.32–33]) but also that it was plagiarized from him ("Ickick gav him that toock, imitator!" [FW 423.10]). He could have written it himself, of course, if only he had the time for that sort of thing (he is indulged by his questioners—"if only you would take your time so and the trouble of so doing it" [FW 425.07–8]). He wishes to be rid of the foreign letter and to exist again in an untroubled and self-sufficient manner.

Shaun's Nationalism

Shaun's nationalism, evident throughout the text, is a direct response to his dislocated condition, and it is another symptom of his generally "antipostal" position that he seeks the solace of a natural home and the stability of a fixed identity (he is "dogmestic Shaun" [FW 411.23]). Condemned to an uprooted and wandering existence by his reception of the message, he desperately attempts to ground and reattach himself, as a citizen, to the national soil: "I heard a voice, the voce of Shaun, vote of the Irish" (FW 407.13–14). For Shaun identity must be something fixed and in place, not requiring any sort of dialectical severance and return in order to be itself; for him, it should be enough for identity to simply be itself naïvely. At the heart of Shaun's resentment of his brother is the idea that there can be no life apart from the home. Shem, Mercius, has not taken up his birthright (rendering it a "birthwrong" [FW 190.12]) and thus fails to "fall in with Plan, as our nationals should, as all nationists must, and do a certain office (what, I will not tell you) in a certain holy office (nor will I say where) during certain agonising office hours" (FW 190.12–15). Shaun, on the contrary, insists that a person should fulfill his or her obligation to the native land by taking up one's given place in it. This is what it means to be a citizen for Shaun—to belong to a nation, but not belong to it in any sense requiring the work of appropriation. Rather, Shaun wishes to belong so completely to the nation that he would literally be a part of it, just as much as its mountains and rivers. What he fails to see, however, is that the various actions he undertakes, supposedly on account of his nationality, are ultimately so many moments in the construction of that identity. His Irishness does not precede these various acts but is constituted through them; such is the nature of belonging.

A nationalism of Shaun's sort, therefore, would be better termed isolationism, for it is more an anti-inter-nationalism than a nationalism in any positive sense. His position entails an elimination of the other or, at the very least, a denial of alterity. Shaun thus sets about a program of painting the postboxes green ("you have while away painted our town a wearing greenridinghued" [FW 411.23–24]): a superficial attempt at grounding postality that fails to produce freedom. As Shaun says, "it just seemed the natural thing to do" (FW 411.26–27). Painting postboxes cannot eliminate their dangerous opening onto alterity, yet even with intranational mail there is still the distance of postality and still room for errancy. The post is always an outlet onto the other, and the otherness of this other prevents her or him from receiving a national designation *a priori*.

This rejection of alterity on the part of Shaun is nowhere more clear than in his relationship with Miss Enders, Mrs. Sanders, P. L. M. Mevrouw von Andersen, and/or Miss Anders (FW 412.23, 413.05, 413.14–15, 414.02). As so many plays on the German word *andere* ("other, different"), what is most striking here is that Mrs. Sanders is dead (or "late" [FW 413.12]). There are no others for Shaun. If he "acquired her letters," as he puts it (FW 413.09), then this only again attests to an act of appropriation or acquisition operative at the origins of identity, an affirmation of the fact that there is no natural origin for the post, just as there is no final, ineluctable destination.

There is an important coincidence in Shaun's thinking about both nationalism and the natural. One is born into a nation, and this means that the channels of birth serve the nationalist agenda. Sexual reproduction must be monitored and controlled if the nation is to remain pure, but purity is equated with chastity and virginity. The land that Shaun loves is virgin (he plops down for a nap "upon the native heath he loved covered kneehigh with virgin bush" [FW 408.07–8]), and his advice to the schoolgirls is also to maintain their chastity: "Keep cool your fresh chastity which is far better far" (FW 440.31–32). The problem is that, for the pure, virgin land to perpetuate itself, there must be a sullying of that purity through intercourse. Sex after marriage does not change this fact; it only recreates an illusory purity of the nation through the legal fiction of marriage. This use of the artificial, or the legal, marriage, as necessary for the preservation and continuation of the natural, virginity, is also lost on Shaun. He consistently fails to see the role of what we might call the "supplement" in the constitution of the natural.

Sexual intercourse must be protected as the only route for the perpetuation of the natural Irish bloodline, and corruption of the race must be prevented by any means necessary. Shaun cautions Izzy against all interactions and intercourse with foreigners and urges her especially to protect herself against all "affairs with the black fremdling" (FW 442.01). His desire to maintain identity in these matters leads to numerous threats of violence against the foreigner who would impose upon Izzy and against Izzy herself who might succumb to seduction. To insure the purity of the nation, Shaun even advises the girls in sex acts other than coitus should they find themselves unable to resist their own or their partner's desires. Numerous references to anal sex, along with other modes of nonreproductive sexuality, are thus prevalent throughout Shaun's chapters.[11]

When the four old men question Shaun (Yawn) in chapter 3 of book III, it is suddenly St. Patrick who is being asked about the passing of another vessel, a ship. It is not just any ship, however, but is "the parent ship" (FW 480.07), which must be boarded if one is to take part in the steady passing of generations. Shaun would like to be born and live as an Irishman with never a thought or a question as to what that could mean, but this is impossible. To belong to a nation is to make oneself belong; it is never something innate but an achievement, a reception and a boarding of the parent ship. In this, all ships are subject to drifting off course and to foreign overtaking, and what matters is how doggedly one remains aboard. National identity must be appropriated, and this fact already disrupts any claim to a natural national identity. As Shaun bemoans, in regard to his order, it is "becoming hairydittary" (FW 410.02). The biological national origin to which he so starkly clings is, from the outset, disrupted by postality. It is an origin that can only come after this appropriation, a *post*-origin.

Shaun's Thrift

The text unflatteringly portrays Shaun's thrift from his advice to the schoolgirls—"Deal with Nature the great greengrocer and pay regularly the monthlies"—to his condemnations of Mercius (FW 437.16–17). In Shaun's eyes, Shem/Mercius suffers from a "horrible awful poverty of mind," for he gives his money to "bearded jezabelles you hired to rob you" and saves nothing: "Where is that little alimony nestegg against our predictable rainy day?" (FW 192.10, 25, 32–33). There are two sides to Shaun's own economic existence, one of intake and preservation, the other of expansion and growth, and both work together to insure the stability of Shaun's identity. Even though he grows, he remains ever the same; he is redundantly himself.

The first moment of Shaun's thrift concerns an emphasis upon intake and consumption, and his voracious appetite is a testament to this: "twentyfour hours every moment matters maltsight" (FW 405.22–23; German,

Mahlzeit, "meal time"). He is always eating—"Oop, I never open momouth but I pack mefood in it" (FW 437.19–20)—and his clothes are stained with food.[12] When Shaun received his commission, the presence of the letter establishes a "gap" or "split" in his identity. Similarly, his grotesque consumption is an impossible attempt to fill that gap and return to wholeness. For Shaun to be whole, there would have to be no contact with an other, even in what he eats. His ideal would thus be to eat "home cooking everytime" (FW 455.31–32) and to achieve the self-identity of an HCE ("His hungry will be done!" [FW 411.11]). Shaun must support himself upon himself, in the same way that HCE—"Massa Ewacka"—was "secretly and by suckage feeding on his own misplaced fat" (FW 79.05, 12–13). Shaun, too, enjoys this same kind of cannibalism as he strives to be self-identical: the same at home in the same, sustained by and feeding on the same.[13] This, in fact, explains Shaun's braggadocio ("Jaun the Boast" [FW 469.29]), which is part and parcel of this emphasis upon intake. The self-satisfied subject views itself as complete and whole, and Shaun wants to be done with his obligation to the post in order to *be* himself as self-identical. He attempts to free himself from the responsibilities of his office and his duties to others, which makes him a particularly bad postman, to be sure.

Shaun's thrift also emerges in his concern with gain and economic growth. As he puts it in advising the schoolgirls, "mony makes multimony like the brogues and the kishes" (FW 451.12–13). What he retains may garner interest (multimony) but is itself only more of the same (more "mony"). The multimony will be compounded with the mony, and the new total will serve as mony for the production of still more multimony. Shaun does not use his money to purchase other things but instead uses it to make more of the same. That his money would only come into contact with more of itself and then, from that union, produce still more money could be seen as either another instance of his inability to produce something different (impotence) or as another image of his homo-sexuality (as absence of difference). Shaun's accrual of interest further entrenches him within his self-satisfied subjective position since his only growth is a growth of the same.

For Shaun's mony to earn interest, there must be a time across which it perdures. When the Gracehoper concentrates his charges against the Ondt into the single question, *"why can't you beat time?"* (FW 419.08), the point of attack is precisely the Ondt's self-imposed impotence before the unidirectional and linear time he requires for interest. The interest that Shaun would earn—his multimony—requires a regular and serially progressive time, one completely formal in character and operative independently of content. Shaun cannot beat this time. The content of such a time is made up of the events that are said to take place within it. These in no way alter the form of the time, since the space between form and content is again regarded as free from postality. Each of these events is stamped by this time with a particular place (or, rather, time) according to which it is infinitely comparable with other points along this timeline, preceding some and succeeding others. Such a time conducts events in an orderly manner (if only chronologically so) and thereby guarantees progress. By its simple formality, chronological time guarantees that events will succeed one another and, in effect, that there will be succession, if not directly success. This formal promise of chronological time (the assurance of success) issues in advance all "loans through the post" (FW 514.29) and makes possible the prediction of events. The success of succession (formal progression) is the essence of interest, simply put. When Shaun's mony makes multimony, it only makes more of the same because what appears has been structured in advance by time. Time bears events like Shaun bears his letter, formally. Shaun cannot beat this time because it is impossible for him to achieve an outside position from which to strike it. Thus, Shaun's demand for stability and fixity, his refusal to see in identity a matter of appropriation, and his fear of alterity all seek to deny the postal character of the world. In this, he remains opposed to Joyce himself, who accepts and negotiates with postality in *Finnegans Wake*.

Postal Meaning in *Finnegans Wake*

Language

The scholarship on *Finnegans Wake* and *The Post Card* focuses almost exclusively upon the ways in which Derrida's work exhibits a structural logic embedded in Joyce's book. Shari Benstock's 1984 essay "The Letter of the Law: *La Carte Postale* in *Finnegans Wake*" shows how both texts "illustrate the various ways that the communication of desire can go astray, be lost, be delayed, or transferred."[14] Desire runs in an orbit around an absent center, and this is not only something played out in the postal systems prevalent in these texts but is also their "frame." In "The Example of Joyce: Derrida Reading Joyce," Murray McArthur does not find a frame so much as a "metonymic bit" that forms the hinge between "the part and the whole" for a reading of the *Wake*.[15] McArthur's "bit" is the place of the example, and his essay tries to come to terms with Derrida's claim that Joyce's writing provides a necessary example of deconstruction. Finally, Alan Roughley's chapter, "Postcards to Joyce," is largely a detailed summary of the previous two articles framed by a consideration of the "double structures" operating between Joyce and Derrida.[16] Roughley finds deconstruction's distance from metaphysics to be an ironically doubled one, where the metaphysical would already prepare for its own deconstruction and the deconstructive can never assume a position completely outside the text.

In each of these cases, what is at stake is a structural matter between the texts. To be sure, postality as a "principle" is to be found in the *Wake*, but each of the forenamed commentaries omits a treatment of postality in the language of the *Wake*. Without such a treatment, structural concerns merely serve to reiterate the metaphysical opposition between form and content, precisely the sort of rigid dualism that postality is to undo. *Finnegans Wake* must be taken literally and this marks something of a difference between *Finnegans Wake* and *The Post Card*. Joyce takes postality literally, in fact, to the letter of his language, whereas it seems to operate largely at the structural level for both Derrida and his commentators.[17] For example, in *Of Grammatology*, Derrida stresses deconstruction's internal position in regard to structure:

> The movements of deconstruction do not destroy structures from the outside. They are not possible and effective, nor can they take accurate aim, except by inhabiting those structures. . . . Operating necessarily from the inside, borrowing all the strategic and economic resources of subversion from the old structure, borrowing them structurally. . . . the enterprise of deconstruction always in a certain way falls prey to its own work. (OG 24/39)

Such a "structural" role might also seem avowed in *The Post Card*, where we read: "If I say that I write for dead addressees, not dead in the future but already dead at the moment when I get to the end of a sentence, it is not in order to play" (PC 33/39). With Joyce, however, one need not wait until the end of the sentence for the posting of meaning, as Derrida himself is aware. Joyce's work breaks up the words themselves and subjects "each atom of writing to fission" (TW 27/28). It consequently exhibits a "subatomistic micrology (what I call 'divisibility of the letter')" (UG 61/100–1). Postality operates in the language of the *Wake* itself.

Thus, there is no better example of postality as it operates in literature than *Finnegans Wake*. And while *The Post Card* itself cites the *Wake* numerous times, Joyce's own text is not simply *about* deferment, distance, and loss, but it is written in direct confrontation with these problems, as a consideration of the *Wake*'s use of the portmanteau word will show.

The portmanteau is a traveling word derived from a piece of luggage which, according to the *Oxford English Dictionary*, "opens like a book."[18] A portmanteau word, then, is a case or box packed with letters. It is not, for all this, a mailbox, for it is not fixed to an address or destination. Rather, it is a piece of luggage to be carried, a satchel full of letters, a postman's satchel. On every page of *Finnegans Wake*, there is a carrying of letters by the post. These letters that make up the portmanteau words would seem to jumble together and eliminate the distance separating one word from another, but this elimination of distance only serves to open up another contextual space of meaning.

The context can so determine a word that it is pigeonholed into a single meaning. Puns escape this fixity and operate meaningfully in two separate contexts in each of which the word's meaning is fully present. Derek Attridge makes this clear in his *Peculiar Language*, which provides an elegant treatment of the pun and portmanteau.[19] To take Attridge's example of a pun from Alexander Pope (190), "When Bentley late tempestuous wont to sport / In troubled waters, but now sleeps in port," it is clear that, in one case, "port" refers to a harbor and in the other it refers to a wine.[20] The two discrete meanings do not come into contact with each other and each of them can be catalogued.

The portmanteau, however, undoes the stability of the pun since it has no fixed meaning and is not to be found in dictionaries. The delightful oscillation of the pun is set awhirl in the portmanteau. There is never one meaning that would be present in the portmanteau word but instead a constellation of meanings and echoes. The portmanteau does not *have* a meaning; it is not even the sum of the meaning of all its parts since, unlike a pun, the component meanings influence one another. Attridge views this as the creation of a "contextual circle" whereby "plurality of meaning in one item increases the available meanings of other items, which in turn increase the possibilities of meaning in the original item" (202), but we should take greater care in the location of meaning here. The portmanteau does not possess a meaning that would lie "in" it; instead meaning *touches* it at the site where the word affiliates itself into a context. Were meaning to continue to reside within the portmanteau, it would simply remain another word, ready for its dictionary entry, while, as Attridge himself points out, "[t]he portmanteau word is a monster, a word that is not a word" (196).

That the portmanteau must be understood in context is true of all words, but that it can only be understood in context is not. In collapsing the space between words, the portmanteau forces us to address the referentiality of language: for there to be meaning, we must abandon the thought of the word as a fixed reference (the portmanteau is not "in" a context like clothes are in a suitcase). Instead, meaning will occur precisely at the edge of the word, where it veers out onto its various constitutive relations. Meaning is the very stretching of the word out beyond itself, there being nothing any longer interior to the word but its own expulsion of itself onto the page. Meaning in this case becomes a matter of limit, exposure, and interstices. By moving away from the word as a fixed point embedded in a context, the portmanteau presents us with a view of contextuality not as an enveloping linguistic field but as an extrapolated, exposed, and often disappointed conglomerate of interpretive directions. It is language in motion, where no word stands alone but is already itself only a movement out to another. Meaning cannot be found in the termination of this motion or in the arrival at a destination, for this movement is endless. Rather, meaning is located at the very entrance of the word onto its context, in the unique way that each word is both shaped by its exposure to context and reflectively constitutive of that context as well. Sending itself across the mediate space of context, the portmanteau word issues into postality.

Plot and Character

The language of the *Wake* requires that we read differently. As a counter to Shaun, Joyce's language is both international and uprooted as well as excessive and exposed. It is anything but nationalistic and thrifty. These transformations bring about a concomitant change in the traditional structures and structuring principles of the novel itself, interrupting both character and plot.[21] The two postal theses isolated from Derrida's *The Post Card* and shown to motivate the characterization of Shaun the Post—the impossibility of complete arrival and the reversibility of the time of inheritance—similarly provide us with clues as to how to read *Finnegans Wake* or how not to read it.

Shaun's unaccomplished nationalism offers a Joycean view of the postal whereby the separation from natural identity is experienced by Shaun as a situation in need of restoration. Postality will be denied in favor of pure presence. Shaun's appearance to Izzy as Christ is perhaps his most literal attempt to identify himself with the letter (the word) that he is forced to bear and thus to eradicate the division within himself that the letter inaugurates. Shaun's frustrations, however, make painfully clear the futility of any attempted flight from the post. How does one distance oneself from distance itself? The attempt is always in vain, especially when the distance of the letter already separates oneself from oneself.

This division of the self reveals the ideal of self-presence to be the greatest fiction, the same ideal that motivates traditional conceptions of character. When character is taken as an instance of literary subjectivity and this is understood as a fictional self-present identity, then it serves to name an object separable from its surroundings. Such a character could be isolated from its contexts without consequence to its integrity. Characters would be so many marbles in the box of the book. When the shell of character is no longer present to contain its "contents," these are free to spill all over the page. The reader is confronted with a book of characteristics, containing no characters. Thus, there are no characters in *Finnegans Wake*, since the sending of language is a sending of character.[22]

Joyce's literal deconstruction of character in the *Wake* has serious consequences for the reader. To read *Finnegans Wake* is to learn to read anew. Through the preponderance of portmanteau words, readers become habituated to reading differently, since words that would otherwise not seem portmanteau are now read and heard in this manner. This is more than to say that *Finnegans Wake* creates its own audience: it is to say that Joyce characterizes his reader. We adopt a new characteristic in our relation to this text. Its reader is as much (and as little) a character as Shaun.

If Shaun's nationalism stages for us the self-identity of the self-present subject, then his thrift provides us with insight into the temporal order of this subject. The time of the subject is the time of security, prediction, and justice (as revenge and equivalence), not the time of grace, hope, or mercy. Shaun's calculation opposes Shem's serendipity at a temporal level. The time of Shaun is the traditional time of the plot, which strings scenes together toward a culminating moment of recuperation and justification. Plot calculates time and uses it for the greatest effect (suspense, boredom, ecstasy, and so forth). *Finnegans Wake*, however, has no such plot. Those who are concerned with strategically guaranteeing the transmission of meaning are obligated to employ a linear time; it is itself the time of employment and use. Shaun's thrift and the temporal order it proposes are ways by which he again attempts to secure meaning and perfectly understand it, without loss or remainder.

The excessive language of *Finnegans Wake* ensures that there will be no reception of a message, and Joyce's move to characterize his reader is at the same time a move of deauthorization. The sending of language is not a transmission according to the channels of plot or the identities of character but a multivalent dispersal.[23] His words produce audible effects and accidental sparks, igniting other connections, other contexts for interpretation. The path through *Finnegans Wake* is not that of a preestablished plot. Instead, the reader is slowly characterized, while the author begins to recede. *Finnegans Wake* does not occupy the place of a book, between the author who wrote it and the reader who reads it. Instead, both of these poles of the literary relationship are subjected to the postal effect. Reader enters text, and text becomes the author. *Finnegans Wake* communicates through the formation of just this literary community. This mediate position of *Finnegans Wake* is the place of language and the letter. To suffer postality so thoroughly as to undo the supposed separation between us is not only what *Finnegans Wake* has to mean but also how it can mean anything at all.

Notes

1. The cards concern traveling to conferences, sending postcards to an un-

named recipient, examining a thirteenth-century fortune-telling book, considering the problems of inheritance, and constantly worrying about whether or not the entire correspondence should be burned. In a formal sense, there are no postcards here at all but rather the opening pages of a book authored by Derrida. It should also be noted that the cards are equally preoccupied with whether they will make up the preface of *The Post Card* or not—calling to mind Derrida's earlier analysis of the preface in "Outwork, prefacing" (DI 1–59/7–67). All of these aspects play a role in Derrida's principle of postality developed in the text.

2. I have addressed this conception of a withdrawal inherent in sending through another reading of Derrida's *The Post Card*, this time in conjunction with *The Post Card*'s critique of Martin Heidegger and the notion of essence in Heidegger's *Contributions to Philosophy: From Enowning*, trans. Parvis Emad and Kenneth Maly (Bloomington: Indiana University Press, 1999), in "The Extent of Giving: Sending in Derrida and Heidegger," *Pli: The Warwick Journal of Philosophy* 14 (2003), 89–105.

3. The situation is presented as follows in *The Post Card*: "Example: if one morning Socrates had spoken for Plato, if to Plato his addressee he had addressed some message, it is also that p. would have had to be able to receive, to await, to desire, in a word to have called in a certain way what S. will have said to him; and therefore what S., taking dictation, pretends to invent—writes, right? p. has sent himself a post card . . . he has sent it back to himself from himself, or he has even 'sent' himself S" (PC 30/35).

4. Derrida writes in *The Post Card*: "Plato, who is the inheritor, for Freud" (PC 28/33).

5. On the role of characters in the *Wake* and *Ulysses*, the panel "Character and Contemporary Theory" from the Ninth International Joyce Symposium is instructive—see Bernard Benstock, ed., *James Joyce: The Augmented Ninth: Proceedings from the Ninth International James Joyce Symposium, Frankfurt 1984* (Syracuse: Syracuse University Press, 1988), 135–64. Derek Attridge's contribution to this panel will be addressed in the concluding section of this chapter. In another contribution to the panel, "Some Prefatory Remarks on Character in Joyce," James A. Snead sees the characters of the *Wake* as reader-manipulable—"These fictional subjects have as their density the very act of recombination and not any one constellation" (145)—which functions for him as part of a social critique. For Snead, Joyce "explicitly reveals that the reader's and author's capacity to arrange micro-units is the power of society, and that characters to some extent allow themselves to be manipulated, and let their individual characteristics fade precisely in order to merge with the power to array" (146). This idea of Joyce's characters as merging with the power of arrangement will be taken to mean that the characters of the *Wake* blend with the operations of the text. The difficulties of Shaun are the difficulties of the language of the *Wake*.

6. Attridge makes a similar claim in his *Peculiar Language: Literature as Difference from the Renaissance to James Joyce* (Ithaca: Cornell University Press, 1988), 207: "Characters, too, are never *behind* the text in *Finnegans Wake* but in it." Further references will be cited parenthetically in the text. Nothing underlies the language of the *Wake*. For this reason, the intense scholarly effort currently devoted to Joyce's

Wake notebooks is not directed at discovering anything beneath the *Wake* since there is nothing there to be found. Rather—and this is another postal effect—the notebooks will only serve to show the presence of the *Wake* in them, the expanse of its command and territorial effect. What is of concern, then, is not what contents of the notebooks have made it into the *Wake* but rather the opposite—how the *Wake* has made itself into the notebooks and beyond. The editors of the notebook project, Vincent Deane, Daniel Ferrer, and Geert Lernout, in their *The "Finnegans Wake" Notebooks at Buffalo: A Reader's Guide to the Edition* (Turnhout, Belgium: Brepols Publishers, 2001), do not speak of the notes and drafts as behind, beneath, or underlying the *Wake*. They do, however, speak of "source material" (3), and with this notion of a "source," already engage with transmission and sending. The notebooks are no genotype, the *Wake* itself no phenotype.

7. On the relationship between postality and the media, see Gregory L. Ulmer, "The Post-Age," *Diacritics* 11, 3 (Fall 1981), 39–56.

8. See Joyce to Harriet Shaw Weaver (24 May 1924): "the copying out of Shaun which is a description of a postman travelling backwards in the night through the events already narrated. It is written in the form of a *via crucis* of 14 stations but in reality it is only a barrel rolling down the river Liffey" (LI 214).

9. Perhaps this noncreative nature of Shaun accounts for the presence of what seem to be numerous allusions to nonreproductive sex acts around him, especially anal sex (see endnote 11 in this chapter). We should note further, however, that the postal effect is itself something of a reversal whereby the predecessor comes to stand before the inheritor and the inheritor behind the forefather. There is a certain "sodomy" to postality and a turn away from established methods and lines of reproductive descent. This is another sense in which we might, with Jean-Michel Rabaté, speak of sodomy in Joyce's writing, though now as postal effect: "Joyce's purgatorial and comic sense of sodomy locates it primarily in language"—see Jean-Michel Rabaté, *James Joyce and the Politics of Egoism* (Cambridge: Cambridge University Press, 2001), 172.

10. For an analysis of the role of debt in *The Post Card*, see Samuel Weber, "The Debts of Deconstruction and Other, Related Assumptions," in *Taking Chances: Derrida, Psychoanalysis, and Literature*, ed. Joseph H. Smith and William Kerrigan (Baltimore: Johns Hopkins University Press, 1984), 33–65.

11. After an injunction to "never lay bare your breast secret (dickette's place!)" and a description of "comepulsing paynattention spasms," Shaun advises the partners to "please sit still face to face" (FW 434.26–27, 28–29, 32), which I take as advocacy of the missionary position in intercourse. Oral-sex references can be found at FW 441.15–16 ("unless she'd care for a mouthpull of white pudding") and FW 415.35 ("Suckit Hotup!"), among others. The majority of references, however, point to anal sex as the preferred avenue of nonreproductive sexual activity. Shaun counsels, "Love through the usual channels," by which he means "not love that leads by the nose as I foresmellt but canalised love, you understand, does a felon good" (FW 436.14, 17–19); he later speaks of "your weak abdominal wall" (FW 437.10); there is talk of a woman standing behind a man (with him after her) in order to satisfy the *verge* ("the man to be is in a worse case after than before since she on the supine satisfies the verg to him" [FW 468.06–8]); and there is a desire for a certain "back haul": "Well, I beg to traverse same above statement by saxy luters in their back

haul of Coalcutter" (FW 492.14–15). We also find a description of an ejaculation related to the blowing of his postal horn ("blew off in a loveblast" [FW 471.13]), which "narrowly missed fouling her buttress for her but for he acqueducked" (FW 471.17–18). In this context of antireproduction and identity, we should also consider his outrage over his homosexual encounter ("Homo! Then putting his bedfellow on me!" [FW 422.11]). The advocacy of sodomy in these passages is a means of avoiding a contamination of the bloodline by the foreigner, thus adding a further wrinkle to Rabaté's treatment of hospitality and sodomy—see "Hospitality and Sodomy," chapter 9 of his *James Joyce and the Politics of Egoism* (153–78).

12. Shaun's overshirt has food "embrothred over it in peas, rice, and yeggyyolk" (FW 404.29–30).

13. In this, he stands in opposition to Shem. Shem is covered with the writing of an ink composed of feces through which he expresses himself. The ink itself is composed of something given out, excreted, but Shaun neither gives anything back nor puts anything out; he only eats and takes in. If Shem is Jacob to Shaun's Esau, then Joyce expresses this reciprocal relation with the unsavory names "Jerkoff and Eatsup" (FW 563.24).

14. Shari Benstock, "The Letter of the Law: *La Carte Postale* in *Finnegans Wake*," *Philological Quarterly* 63, 3 (Spring 1984), 163–85; 184.

15. Murray McArthur, "The Example of Joyce: Derrida Reading Joyce," *James Joyce Quarterly* 32, 2 (Winter 1995), 227–41; 238.

16. Alan Roughley, "Postcards to Joyce," *Reading Derrida Reading Joyce* (Gainesville: University Press of Florida, 1999), 32–43; 32.

17. Certainly one might object that "Envois" presents many literal renderings of postality, from the prescribed number of spaces between omissions in the postcards to the strange series of abbreviations offered without a key. On the whole, even these remain formal expressions of postality, challenges to a traditional reading of the text, but not themselves very far from traditional challenges to that reading. Joyce's text may well be the "example" for Derrida, as McArthur argues, precisely because his text is weathered by postality like no other, all the way to the language. It should also be noted that while the tradition does, in fact, gesture to the importance of language in postality, this never becomes a central concern.

18. See the first definition (1.a.) of "portmanteau": "A case or bag for carrying clothing and other necessities when traveling; originally of a form suitable for carrying on horseback; now applied to an oblong stiff leather case, which opens like a book, with hinges in the middle of the back." *The Oxford English Dictionary*, 2nd ed., volume 12: Poise–Quelt (Oxford: Oxford University Press, 1989), 157.

19. See especially chapter 7, "Unpacking the Portmanteau; or, Who's Afraid of *Finnegans Wake?*" in Attridge's *Peculiar Language*, 188–209.

20. See lines 201–2 of the fourth book of Alexander Pope, *The Dunciad in Four Books*, ed. Valerie Rumbold (New York: Pearson Education Limited, 1999), 301. Attridge discusses the pun in *Peculiar Language*, 190–91, and compares it with the portmanteau word at 201–2 and 206.

21. Attridge draws the connection between Joyce's revolutions in language and the understanding of character in his essay "Joyce and the Ideology of Character," in *Joyce Effects: On Language, Theory, and History* (Cambridge: Cambridge University

Press, 2000), 57: "The disappearance of the word as a self-bounded, consistent, and unique entity marks the disappearance of language as the communicator of clear and distinct meanings; or rather, it puts in question that model of language, just as the disappearance of character in the other sense puts in question the model of the subject as consistent, undivided, unique, and immediately knowable and self-knowable." Sam Slote emphasizes the manner in which narratology fails before the "fundamental incompletion to the work of the work in progress" in "Nulled Nought: The Desistance of Ulyssean Narrative in *Finnegans Wake*," *James Joyce Quarterly* 34, 4 (Summer 1997), 531–42, 538. As he laments, "*Finnegans Wake* is still read as though it were *Ulysses*" (531).

22. Jed Rasula, in "*Finnegans Wake* and the Character of the Letter," *James Joyce Quarterly* 34, 4 (Summer 1997), 517–30, 523, 524, carries this point to the letter of the text itself in his claim that "*Finnegans Wake* not only proposes but enacts a reunion between the two senses of the word 'character,' psychological and calligraphic," in order to claim that "[t]here is no character, no scene, no setting, no incident in the book not tainted by insinuations of the letter." The conclusion to be drawn from this, one omitted by Rasula, is that *Finnegans Wake is not a book*.

23. In *Joyce Effects*, Attridge speaks of this in terms of "fireworks" (xiii). As he puts it in the essay "The Postmodernity of Joyce: Chance, Coincidence, and the Reader," included in *Joyce Effects*, "Rather than attempting to control the mass of fragmentary detail to *produce* meaning, Joyce's major texts *allow* meaning to arise out of that mass by the operations of chance" (120).

4

The Mother, of All the Phantasms . . .

Michael Naas

In memory of Grant Forsberg

In "Two Words for Joyce" Derrida leaves little room for doubt about the privileged role Joyce plays in his work. "Every time I write," he says, "Joyce's ghost is always coming on board" (TW 27/27). Not sometimes, not often, or most often, but "every time I write," he says, "and even in the most academic pieces of work," a ghost or phantom of Joyce comes to haunt his writing. And if this avowal or confession were not enough, Derrida goes on in this essay to document this haunting, tracing the presence of Joyce in texts as early as his *Edmund Husserl's Origin of Geometry: An Introduction* in 1962 to "Plato's Pharmacy" and *The Post Card*, which, he says, is "haunted by Joyce, whose funerary statue stands at the center of the *Envois* . . . ," a haunting that "invades the book, a shadow on every page" (TW 28/30). Even if, as Derrida admits, he is not always sure he likes Joyce, the ghost, phantom, or perhaps even the phantasm of Joyce never fails to make its spectral appearance aboard the *Good Ship Derrida*.[1]

Whether he liked it or not, then, the phantom of Joyce, Jacques' Joyce, was always there, ambiguously there, precisely like a phantom, at once overseeing and captaining the voyage from some invisible wheelhouse and calling out for a unique response, in the language of Derrida, for a "countersignature." "*He war*," to be sure, Derrida might have said, but also "*Je suis*." Hence the *S.S. Derrida* at once followed in Joyce's wake and took a course of its own, and we can now track the itineraries of these two enormous oeuvres and plot the multiple points of contact between them: Joyce and Derrida, first of all, on language, on polysemy and translation, on the performativity of language, on the speech act, on teletechnology and telecommunication (from the newspaper and the telephone to the gramophone), or else Joyce and Derrida on generation and the generations, on inheritance and legacy, on different ways, precisely, of countersigning a tradition, or else, to end a list that could go on interminably, on specters and ghosts, on phantoms, fictions, and phantasms. For while Derrida confesses to being haunted throughout his work by a phantom *of* Joyce, it is perhaps the phantom *in* Joyce, that is, the notion of spectrality, fiction, or phantasm in Joyce, that returns most regularly in Derrida's work. Whether in "Ulysses Gramophone," where the theme of teletechnology in Joyce is always in communication with the notion of spectrality, as Derrida listens to the telephonic voice of Bloom or the gramophonic voice of Paddy Dignam from beyond the grave, or in "Two Words for Joyce," where the phantasm of Joyce *as* father, and the father as an all-knowing and all-powerful God, haunts every page, it is not just the phantom of Joyce that comes on board but all the phantoms and phantasms *in* Joyce, the theme in Joyce of the specter or the ghost, the spectral or the speculative fiction. It is thus perhaps no coincidence that the one phrase of Joyce that most conspicuously haunts Derrida's work, the one phrase that returns to the Derridean corpus with the regularity of a specter, is a phrase about the spectral, phantasmatic, or fictional nature of the father: "paternity may be a legal fiction."[2]

Whenever Derrida writes, then, it is not simply the phantom of Joyce as father that comes on board but the phantom, ghost, fiction, or phantasm of the father *in* Joyce, the father, as Stephen Dedalus argues, as a sort of speculative or legal fiction, the father as opposed to the mother. Or so it stood up until a couple of texts from the final decade of Derrida's life, and, in particular, in what will no doubt turn out to have been Derrida's final text dedicated to Joyce, in "The Night Watch." For it is in this text that Derrida refutes or at least refines the Joycean thesis regarding the speculative nature of the father by extending it to the mother. If Joyce is, then, for Derrida, a sort of father on the subject of the phantasm (among so many others things) it will be precisely on the subject of the mother that Derrida will come to mark his distance from Joyce. Indeed one of the main conclusions of "The Night Watch" will be that maternity is just as much a fiction or a phantasm as paternity. In opposition, then, to the "commonsense" view of Joyce and others who maintain that while paternity is always the result of calculation and speculation, and so always a "legal fiction," maternity is beyond such speculation because we can see the mother give birth with our own two eyes, Derrida will claim that recent developments in reproductive technology have helped to reveal this ageless truth: the mother too is an object of calculation and speculation, in short, as much a "legal fiction"—indeed, as we will see, as much a *phantasm*—as the father.

Apparently written during the summer of 2000, "La Veilleuse"—translated in this volume as "The Night Watch"—was originally conceived as a preface to the reedition of Jacques Trilling's 1973 work *James Joyce ou l'écriture matricide*. In this psychoanalytically inspired analysis of Joyce, Trilling traces the importance of the mother—and especially the death of the mother—in Joyce's work for the birth of the writer. The themes of the mother, of maternity, and of matricide, were thus determined in advance for Derrida by Trilling's work, already programmed, in some sense, by it, already bequeathed to Derrida by Trilling. And yet, as we might expect, Derrida inherits and countersigns these themes in his own inimitable way, tracing a hesitation—a wavering, an alternation, a vibration, a "trill"—in the work of Trilling not just between the commonsense thesis that only paternity is a legal fiction and the more radical and daring thought that the mother is as well, but between a conception of the *mother* that is always subject to phantasm and a quasi-transcendental notion of *maternity* that perhaps is not.

Though we must not lose sight, then, of the original context of Derrida's argument regarding the mother and maternity—a preface to the republication of the work of a friend after his death on the themes of maternity and matricide in Joyce—we are given license to put this argument into the context of Derrida's other writings on ghosts, specters, phantoms, and phantasms. As we shall see, "The Night Watch" is not the only and not even the first text to speak of the mother as a phantasm, but it is surely the one in which this thesis is most forcefully and fully developed. And it is in this text that Derrida most clearly develops a logic of the phantasm in relation to a logic of denegation, the impossibility of doing away with either the phenomenon of birth or the phenomenality of the day, an impossibility that reigns over every day, to be sure, but that appears in a most clear and exemplary way on one's birthday.

APPARITION I

> Silently, in a dream she had come to him after her death, her wasted body within its loose brown graveclothes giving off an odour of wax and rosewood, her breath, that had bent upon him, mute, reproachful, a faint odour of wetted ashes. (U 1.102–5)

Specter, ghost, phantom, phantasm: up to this point I have used these terms more or less interchangeably. But a close analysis of such terms in Derrida would demonstrate, I believe, that the last of these comes to have a rather different meaning than the others. Without being able to make the case here by citing chapter and verse, let me attempt to present in a rather schematic way the essential characteristics of the phantasm in Derrida so that we can then see how Derrida's analysis of the phantasm of the mother (or of maternity) at once contributes to and displaces this configuration.

At the risk of gross simplification, it appears that while the terms ghost, phantom, specter, spectrality, and so on all tend to suggest a repeated or iterable appearance or apparition that calls into question or disrupts any notion of a stable, unchanging reality or identity behind or before those appearances, the notion of the phantasm in Derrida, while also always the *result* of a series of phenomenal iterations, nonetheless suggests some abiding reality or identity behind or before these phenomenal appearances. From *Speech and Phenomenon* to *Glas*, *Monolingualism of the Other*, "Faith and Knowledge," *H. C. for Life*, "The Night Watch," and so on, the phantasm can best be identified in precisely this way—as the phantasm of identity. Several traits can then be distinguished on the basis of this minimal definition.[3]

First, the phantasm always involves a coincidence, or an assumed coincidence, between the self and itself, that is, an identity between the self and itself. In several texts of Derrida, and particularly in the final decade of his life, this assumed self-identity or self-coincidence goes by the name of "ipseity." The phantasm is always a phantasm of ipseity, a phantasm of self-identity and of the power generated from a being that is or is assumed to be identical to itself.

The second characteristic of the phantasm of the selfsame, of a self that coincides with itself, is thus the phantasm of a self that can act, that has power, that is, in a word, *sovereign*—over itself first of all but then also potentially over others. To say that the self-coincidence or self-identity of a being is a phantasm is thus not at all to suggest that it is some powerless illusion. On the contrary—and this is no doubt one of the reasons why the phantasm so interested Derrida—the phantasm of ipseity is always a phantasm of power, the phantasm of a source or origin with the power to decide and to act. Even if such a source or origin is itself a phantasm, this phantasm is the source of all power and all sovereignty.[4]

Third, this phantasm of sovereignty, of an indivisible and inviolable sovereignty, tends to present itself as naturally given, as part of the order of things, as organic or as a part of nature. As such, it tends to present itself as that which comes before and excludes all artifacts and machines, all language and all culture, even though its identity and its power are always the result or the effect of these. Though the phantasm is always historically conditioned, linguistically coded, and culturally determined, it always presents itself as ahistorical, prelinguistic, and precultural. It at once calls for the exclusion of these conditions and presents itself as what is already beyond them.

Related, then, to this phantasm of a purely natural formation of sovereign power is the phantasm of purity itself—a fourth trait of the phantasm. The phantasm presents itself always as pure or as the call for purity.

Fifth, in its putatively pure and sovereign self-identity, through its power and autonomy, the phantasm *presents itself* as a force of nature to be observed or denoted but never produced. There is thus in the phantasm always an elision of the phantasm's performative or even "fictive" origins and its real effects. While always the result of a performative of some sort, while always legitimated by a performative context that precedes and exceeds it, the phantasm always attempts to elide or conceal these origins, to present itself as self-generated, as naturally and purely given. Or rather, to put it in terms other than those of the performative—since to say that the phantasm is the result of, say, a performative utterance risks saying that it is the result of the performative power of another phantasm (namely, the speaker or performer of the utterance)—the phantasm always attempts to elide, subsume, or appropriate its *event*. The phantasm would present itself as that which is beyond the event, or as that which is master or sovereign over it—sovereign even, as we shall see, over its own birth, over the "maternity" that marks its event.

Sixth, because of this emphasis on power, legitimation, and productivity, on sovereignty and mastery, the phantasm would appear to be a decidedly *masculine* formation. Though not always necessarily or even essentially produced by men, the phantasm is most often identified with a certain masculine, phallogocentric power.

Seventh, and finally, it seems that Derrida considers the phantasm to be an essentially *reactive* formation, a sort of safeguard against the very forces that make it possible and against the undeniable though unacknowledged truth of its own phantasmatic or fictional character. Quite apart from the ontological question of the being or reality of the phantasm, the *power* or *authority* of the phantasm is the result of a reaction to everything that makes the phantasm possible. For Derrida, this would be a long list, beginning with difference, language, culture, history, time, performativity, technicity, the other, and the event.

On the basis of these seven traits or characteristics of the phantasm— the phantasm as self-identical and self-coincident, as powerful, natural, pure, self-given or self-produced, phallogocentric, and reactive—it is not hard to imagine the kinds of things Derrida will identify or label phantasms. Though varied, they might be grouped under three headings, all phantasms of sovereign power: the phantasms of a sovereign self, a sovereign state or nation-state, and a sovereign God. Hence the self or ego, from *Speech and Phenomenon* onward, though always a phenomenon and an effect of the phenomena, presents itself as a sovereign, self-coincident identity (a self that hears itself speaking in a meaning-to-say) that would go beyond all phenomena.

As for the state or the nation-state, though it is always produced by a kind of performative (as one *declares*, for example, that "these united Colonies are and *of right ought to be* free and independent states"), the phantasm of the nation-state is that it existed or was ordained to exist before it did (as one *notes* even before the declaration that "these united Colonies *are* and of right ought to be free and independent states"). In accordance with the putative purity of its origins, the nation-state thus often appeals, as Derrida shows, to a language of naturalism and of purity and often presents itself as an organism threatened from without by nonnatural, contaminating elements.

The third form or level of the phantasm is thus that of a sovereign and all-powerful God. Though I present it as third, it is in some sense the model or perfected image for all the other formations of sovereignty, an ultimate phantasm of what is perfectly self-identical, unlimited and indivisible in its power, a self before all phenomena, language, time, and others.

The self, the nation-state, God: three formations of sovereign power, three forms of ipseity, three forms of phantasm that feed, among other things, notions of Fatherlands and Father gods, but then also, three reactive formations that can themselves be reacted against, revealed precisely as phantasmatic, the "father," for example, being declared by Joyce or Derrida to be the result of language, culture, and the other, in short, no longer simply natural but a "legal fiction."

But then what of the mother in all this? Would she be, as Joyce—or at least Stephen—claims in the same passage in which paternity is said to be a "legal fiction," "the only true thing in life" (U 9.843)?

APPARITION II

> In a dream, silently, she had come to him, her wasted body within its loose graveclothes giving off an odour of wax and rosewood, her breath bent over him with mute secret words, a faint odour of wetted ashes. (U 1.270–72)

If the phantasm is an essentially "masculine" formation, though one that can be shared by women, this does not exclude the possibility of the masculine phantasm being precisely a phantasm of female purity and naturalness, of a female nature that must be protected from external aggression and impurities. In his 1994 essay "Faith and Knowledge," an analysis of the relationship between religion and technoscience leads Derrida to develop a logic of autoimmunity according to which one appropriates the instruments of impurity and contamination in order to purify and purge one's family, state, and religion of these very same elements.[5] It is this "autoimmune logic," as Derrida calls it, that leads those on the front lines of our new wars of religion to appropriate the most sophisticated forms of teletechnology (cell phones, videos, satellites, computer networks, and so on) in order to protect or purify, for example—though this is more than a mere example—a putatively natural, organic, and intact female body.[6] The "new archaic" violence being turned against women would thus be but the most visible sign of the autoimmune logic whereby technoscience is deployed to produce and protect the phantasm of a pure and intact female nature.[7] To return to our previous set of characteristics, the most sophisticated forms of technoscience would be appropriated *in the name* of what is claimed to be pure, natural, precultural, ahistorical, and intact, that is to say, self-identical, self-coincident, protected from impurities and foreign aggression. The only characteristic that would seem to be missing from this phantasm of a pure and ultimately *vulnerable* female nature that needs protection would be power, the power to act, to be autonomous and sovereign.

But in an important passage in "Faith and Knowledge" (see section 39) on the etymology of the Greek word *kurios*, translated by Derrida following Benveniste as "sovereign," Derrida speaks of the phantasm of an autonomous or spontaneous and thus powerful "swelling" (*kuein* means to "inflate" or to "swell") of *both* the erect penis *and* the swollen belly.[8] There is a phantasm, a phallogocentric phantasm, that involves the spontaneous, self-engendering *power* of *both* the tumescent, engendering phallus *and* the swollen, pregnant belly. Moreover, the self-engendering power of the latter can easily appear more intact and less suspect than that of the former, for while ancient fertility cults commonly represent the engendering power of the phallus in that detachable prosthesis known as the fetish, it can sometimes appear as if there is no such fetish, no technical support, for the swollen belly. In other words, while the engendering power of the phallus is easily suspect because of its replaceability and substitutability, the belly or the womb can appear irreplaceable and unsubstitutable and, as a result, purely natural and sufficient unto itself, able to engender on its own. Hence—and we would have to insert here a long reading of one of the central themes of *Glas*—the phantasm of woman can always give rise to the phantasm of an Immaculate Conception. According to Derrida, Joyce may have himself ceded to this phantasm of a mother who, unlike the father, would not be a legal fiction, who, at the limit, would be natural, beyond all doubt or speculation, in a word, the "only true thing in life."

There is, it would seem, plenty of evidence for this view in *Ulysses*. If Stephen is indeed, as Mulligan quips, "Japhet in search of a father" (U 1.561), he is himself pursued and haunted throughout by the ghost or phantom of his dead mother. Begotten, he says, by "the man with my voice and my eyes and a ghostwoman with ashes on her breath" (U 3.45–47), Stephen is surrounded from the opening page on by a series of more or less "natural" mothers, from the sea, "our great sweet mother," "our mighty mother" (U 1.80, 3.31–32), to "old mother Grogan" (U 1.357), to the silhouette of Cyril Sargent's loving mother who becomes confounded with the ghost of his own (U 2.139–50), to all the mothers Mulligan sees "pop off every day in the Mater and Richmond" (U 1.205–6), to the ever-pregnant, ever-birthing Mina Purefoy (U 8.281–92, 8.373–76, 8.479–83, 10.586–90, 11.903, 11.1102–3, 14 *passim*), to, of course, Molly (U 8.391–92), mother of Milly and Rudy, but also, like Eve (U 3.41, 9.541), mother of us all, to, finally, the ghost of Stephen's own dead mother, who returns, or whose memory returns, with the periodicity of a tidal nightmare (U 1.102–10, 1.242–79).

Though this very multiplicity and proliferation of mothers should give us pause in offering the mother as *the* "only true thing in life," since they seem to suggest that the mother too can be replaced, that she is neither as unique nor as natural as we might have thought, though there is, in addition to all these mothers, an emphasis in *Ulysses* on what Trilling will call the "ineluctability of birth, of the marked hour," an emphasis not just on the natural mother but on the cutting of the cord and the knot of the omphalos (U 1.176, 1.544, 3.38), the mother still seems to enjoy a certain privilege in Joyce's eyes, or at least in Stephen's (and the difference between these may in the end be crucial). Even if this privilege can turn into a prejudice, since it is the mother's naturalness that would shut her out of the symbolic order, the mother still seems to be presented as "the only true thing in life." Though the search for a father is paired in *Ulysses* with the memory of a mother, and the Bloomsday burial of a father (Paddy Dignam) is paired with a mother's giving birth to a son (Mina Purefoy's Mortimer Edward), paternity and maternity are hardly symmetrical.[9] Whereas paternity would be a matter of calculation and speculation, this man or that one, a man or a bird ("My father's a bird" [U 3.164]), the mother would be beyond question because her giving birth is an object of perception. Whereas it is (only) "the wise child that knows her own father" (U 6.53), as Stephen's father Simon says, even the daftest child would seem to know her own mother.[10]

Having inherited his eyes and voice from Simon Dedalus, Stephen seems to have inherited this view as well. In the famous passage containing the line Derrida cites with such regularity throughout his work—"Paternity may be a legal fiction" (U 9.844)—Stephen opposes maternity and paternity in the starkest of terms. He begins by stating, "Fatherhood, in the sense of conscious begetting, is unknown to man. It is a mystical estate, an apostolic succession, from only begetter to only begotten" (U 9.837–39). Working through his own Nicene Creed, Stephen goes on to say that "On that mystery"—that is, on that mystery of God the Father and his only-begotten son—"the church is founded and founded irremovably because founded, like the world, macro- and micro-cosm, upon the void. Upon incertitude, upon unlikelihood" (U 9.839–42). Only God begets as a father, says Stephen, which comes down to saying that only God is a father.

But that still leaves the mother's begetting of a child, and especially of a son. Continuing reflections occasioned earlier in the day by his student, Cyril Sargent, and by the thought that he, Stephen, was once "like him," that is, loved by his own mother, Stephen says just after these claims about fatherhood: "*Amor matris*, subjective and objective genitive, may be the only true thing in life" (U 9.842–43; see 2.165–66). The love of the mother: a mother's love for her child (Cyril Sargent, Stephen Dedalus) and a child's love for his mother—that would be, Stephen speculates, "the only true thing." Turning his thoughts back to the father, Stephen continues in the very next line, implicitly opposing the "only true thing in life" to a "legal fiction": "Paternity may be a legal fiction. Who is the father of any son that any son should have him or he any son?" (U 9.844–45) After Stephen's speculations about an *amor matris* that would be the only true thing in life, doubt is cast on both sides of the genitive *amor patris*—the love of a father for a son and that of a son for a father. By suggesting that *paternity* is a legal fiction, Stephen seems to be claiming that *maternity* is not, that it is not something to be established through evidence and testimony, through inference and calculation, through a reasoned *judgment*.

Such a view about maternity is, or at least was, as widely held as commonsense itself. For how can one not think along with Stephen that whereas the father is known only to the wise child, that whereas he is in essence a "legal fiction" and, as Stephen says at the start of this passage, "a necessary evil" (U 9.828), the mother, the mother who is *seen* giving birth, is unique and so unquestionable as to be "the only true thing"?[11]

APPARITION III

> She was no more: the trembling skeleton of a twig burnt in the fire, an odour of rosewood and whetted ashes. (U 2.144–46)

It would appear that the phallogocentric phantasm of an Immaculate Conception, of the self-engendering power of the womb, of the naturalness and purity of women, is even more resistant to interruption, questioning, or critique than the phallogocentric phantasm of the sovereign, engendering power of men. Though a certain overcoming of resistance is surely required to deflate the phantasm of the phallus, to begin to think that paternity is never simply naturally attributed, the phantasm of the mother appears even more resistant, less readily deflatable or defeatable, less easily demonstrated to be a "legal fiction." A reading of *Glas* or "Faith and Knowledge" would suffice to show the resistance of this phantasm, that is, precisely, the resistance of this phantasm to being seen *as a phantasm* or a fiction. In the 1990s, however, Derrida begins laying out the logic of this phantasm in very explicit terms, bringing it to light at a time when, he argues, certain developments in reproductive technology were bringing it to light of their own accord. In a lecture of 1994 later published as *Archive Fever*, Derrida criticizes Freud's error or naïveté in *Totem and Taboo* regarding the possibility of identifying the mother by extending the Joycean thesis regarding the replaceability and substitution of the father to the mother, that is, by claiming that it is not only paternity but maternity that must be determined by calculation, speculation, and performativity.[12] Derrida there writes:

> [Freud] makes a mistake in affirming that there can be no doubt about the identity of the mother, insofar as it depends on the witness of the senses, while the identity of the father always remains doubtful since it depends, and it alone, on a rational inference, as that "legal fiction" of which Stephen speaks in Joyce's *Ulysses*. However, better than ever today, if only with the possibility of surrogate mothers, prosthetic maternities, sperm banks, and all the artificial inseminations, as they are secured for us already and will be secured still more for us in the future by bio-genetic techno-science, we know that maternity is as inferred, constructed, and interpreted as paternity. And as paternal law. In truth, it has always been thus, for the one and for the other. (AF 47–48/76–77)

As in "Faith and Knowledge," it is through a confrontation with the latest developments of technoscience that an ageless truth or law is discerned or discovered. This was, it should be noted, always Derrida's way of proceeding, one of the "laws," if you will, of his own corpus or of that "practice" called "deconstruction." Thus it was, for example, in large part as a result of certain technological developments in the production, recording, and dissemination of vocal and written traces (from the printing press to the phonograph to the tape recorder) that Derrida in *Of Grammatology* and other early texts was able to discover or disclose an ageless law concerning the "priority" of writing or archē-writing over speech. The historically determined, empirical, or contingent development in technoscience thus gave rise to the inscription or reinscription of an ageless law. So it is here, then, that recent developments in surrogate motherhood, *in vitro* fertilization, and so on, gave rise to the articulation of what has *always* been the case, namely, that maternity too is a legal fiction, since the mother, like the father, can always be replaced, supplemented, and supplanted, and so must be determined and declared. Which means that the mother's identity is not simply given, not simply a natural phenomenon to be observed and declared through a constative, but an attribution that is *produced* through a performative. The mother is not outside all fiction and speculation, all calculation and substitution. In a word, the mother, like the father, is a phantasm that technoscience has begun to dispel or to reveal as a phantasm, a phantasm that several high-profile legal battles over the past couple of decades have shown to be not nearly as natural or self-evident as it once appeared.

In "The Night Watch," Derrida continues these reflections on the phantasm or legal fiction of maternity *and* takes them in some new and radical directions. For "The Night Watch" is more than your typical preface, or rather, it is a typical Derrida preface—a veritable *countersignature* that at once honors and draws attention to the work being presented *and* draws from it something rather unexpected. Following just the themes that interest me here—for there are so many others—"The Night Watch" develops the argument regarding maternity in three stages. First, continuing the reflections from *Archive Fever* cited previously, Derrida reiterates and expands on the notion of maternity as well as paternity as a "legal fiction." Second, by following what he will call an alternation or a "trill" between the mother and maternity in Trilling's reading of Joyce, Derrida will rethink the crucial and yet almost indiscernible difference between the mother and maternity in relationship to his long-standing interest in and discourse on the "phantasm." To put it in a word to anticipate, it just may be that for Derrida as well as before Trilling—and for both of them as well as before a certain Joyce—it is not the mother, not the love of the mother, but *maternity*, maternity as the ineluctability of birth, that is "the only true thing in life." Third, and finally, this rethinking of maternity and the phantasm gives Derrida what he calls a "privileged" mode of access to a logic of denegation. If what Trilling calls "matricidal writing" is an attempt to do away not simply with one's mother, with a particular mother, but with maternity as such, with one's having been born, one's having been born at a certain time and one's having been marked by that time, then matricidal writing is always a kind of desperate and doomed attempt at suicide. This is a logic of denegation *par excellence*, for what must be affirmed in the attempted suicide of matricidal writing is precisely the desire to do away with all desire, the desire to be done with the maternity that inscribes one into a language and a history, that marks one not only by birth in general but by birth on a particular day and not another.[13]

In "The Night Watch" Derrida argues that there is in Trilling's argument about "matricidal writing" an alternation or "trill" between two "logics," "two competing but also strangely allied logics." The first of these is, says Derrida, "'Freudian' or 'Joycean.' Then 'Lacanian'" as well as—and Derrida here uses the English word—"commonsensical" (NW 99/26). According to this commonsensical, widely shared logic, paternity would always be a "problematic attribution, a conclusion reached through inference and reasoning," "a sort of speculative object always susceptible to substitution," in short, "a 'legal fiction,'" whereas maternity would *not* (NW 99/27). For opposed to the substitutability of paternity, the maternity of the mother would be "unique, irreplaceable, an object of perception, like the 'womb' we so often speak of as the place of conception and birth" (NW 99/27). According to this first logic, then, paternity would always be attributed, the result of a performative utterance, we might say, at the end of a more or less long process of speculation, inference, reasoning, and judgment, while the maternity of the mother would be simply noted or observed as an object of perception and declared as an undeniable truth.[14]

Opposed to this commonsensical logic opposing maternity and paternity would be another logic, "the one," says Derrida taking sides, "toward which I myself would risk leaning here" (NW 99/27). According to this other, less commonsensical but perhaps today more and more easily recognizable logic, the mother would be subject "to the *same* regimen as the father: possible substitution, rational inference, phantasmatic or symbolic construction, speculation, and so on" (NW 99/27). The reason given for leaning toward this other logic, or rather, the reason why more and more of us are finding it more compelling, the reason why it is today perhaps *becoming* the more commonsensical of the two, is more or less the same as that given in *Archive Fever*. The "unicity of the mother is no longer the sensible object of a perceptual certitude," for the today's reproductive technologies "carry us beyond the carrying mother." "There can be, in a word," says Derrida, "more than one mother" (NW 99/27), as many recent court cases have demonstrated. Hence the mother, too, the mother as well as the father, the mother like the father, is "the object of calculations and suppositions, of projections and phantasms" (NW 99/27). In other words—and we can hear the dramatic conclusion coming to the light of day from the very beginning of the argument—"the mother *is* also a speculative object and even a 'legal fiction'" (NW 99/28; my emphasis).

The use of the present tense here reinforces the point made some six years earlier in *Archive Fever*. It's not that surrogate motherhood, *in vitro* fertilization, and so on, have caused maternity to *become* a "legal fiction." It is, rather, that these technoscientific developments have helped reveal what was always already the case. Derrida continues:

> if the "womb" is no longer outside all phantasm, the assured place of birth, then this "new" situation simply illuminates in return an

ageless truth. The mother was never only, never uniquely, never indubitably the one who gives birth—and whom one sees, with one's own two eyes, give birth. (NW 99/27–28)

To return to our previous reading of the phantasm in Derrida, it is as if the phantasm of a womb that is natural, pure, beyond speculation and calculation, before any speech act, has given way to the revelation of the phantasm, to the womb now understood *as* a site of phantasm and "fiction," a site of substitution, speculation, even contamination, which is to say, not quite a phantasm at all anymore. For as soon as the phantasm begins to appear *as* phantasm, *as such*, it is already no longer simply itself. For the more it appears the less it appears—and vice versa. Is there, then, anything that escapes the logic of the phantasm, any "one true thing in life" to be opposed to all these legal fictions?

APPARITION IV

> The Mother: (*Comes nearer, breathing upon him softly her breath of wetted ashes.*) All must go through it, Stephen. More women than men in the world. You too. Time will come. (U 15.4181–84)

In the passage I cited earlier in which Derrida tells us which of the two logics in Trilling he prefers or leans toward, a brief parenthesis orients us toward a critical distinction.

> The other logic, the one toward which I myself would risk leaning here, would subject the mother (I'm not saying "maternity" in Trilling's sense of the word) to the *same* regime as the father: possible substitution, rational inference, phantasmatic or symbolic construction, speculation, and so on. (NW 99/27)

The reason for this parenthesis is that, on Derrida's reading, Trilling alternates or "trills" not just between two logics of the mother, that is, between the commonsense logic and the logic that is today becoming more and more common, but between these two logics of the mother and a very different notion of maternity. This distinction can be heard most clearly in a passage from Trilling that Derrida quotes near the beginning of "The Night Watch" and will repeat throughout the essay, a passage that scans Derrida's essay and returns at various intervals to give it its own "trill." Derrida quotes Trilling: "One can always murder the mother, but one will not for all that have done away with maternity" (NW 100/28). It is on the basis of this passage distinguishing the mother from maternity that Derrida will try to rethink both the logic of the phantasm and the logic of denegation. Though he will ultimately question such a distinction, Derrida sees the necessity of following it to its logical conclusion.

A first parsing-out of these two terms in Trilling would seem to oppose the particularity of the mother, the phantasm of the mother or of *a* mother, to maternity as something like the *fact* or *necessity* of being born, the *givenness* of birth, the undeniability of this givenness or this event. Derrida relates this notion of maternity as that which marks but does not yet signify to a proper name that would remain "aleatory and insignificant, a pure signifier, if you will, received or imposed *at birth, by birth*," an "in-significant, non-signifying mark [that] can then *later* be reinvested with meaning or sense, and with common sense" (NW 97/23, my emphasis of "later"). Meaning or sense would thus come *later*, after the fact, to reinvest the proper name (and the event of maternity) with meaning, to link it to a language and a lineage, to a mother and a father. *Before* this reinvestment, however, the proper name (and maternity) would point toward something like the mark itself, the ineluctable itself, before or beyond all phantasm.

But how exactly are we to think this maternity *before* the mother, a maternity that would be, it seems, the only thing not susceptible to phantasm? How are we to think this maternity in light of the fact that this givenness is always immediately inscribed in language and in history, the givenness of the event, of birth, always immediately marked and thus *always immediately related* to some mother, which is to say, to the possibility of some phantasm? Moreover, as Derrida asks in "The Night Watch," "what are we to make of a maternity that would not be the maternity of a mother?" (NW 100/28).

What Derrida seems to find so fascinating, so "thrilling," about Trilling's work is the necessity *and* impossibility of thinking maternity *apart* from the mother. Derrida writes:

> If the word "maternity," as it is interpreted and deployed by Trilling, gestures toward the unicity of a mark and of a birth date that had already taken place, if there is, undeniably, maternity in this sense, then every *determination* of this maternity by the figure of a mother, indeed of a date, of an indisputable trace (this one and not that one), becomes the effect of a phantasm and a speculation. (NW 99–100/28; my emphasis of "determination")

It is, as we have seen, the *determination* of maternity, the determination of the mother's identity, that leads to or is the result of a phantasm. Derrida continues a few lines later:

it seems at once necessary, urgent, decisive, but also impossible to decide, to sort things out [*trier*], between the mother and maternity. The mother can be replaced—or killed—and substitution, fiction, and thus phantasmatic speculation is possible. As for maternity, it would resist replacement, because birth, the date or mark of birth, has *taken place*, undeniably, even if its *determination* is given over to calculation, speculation, or phantasm. (NW 100/28; my emphasis of "determination")

Two times, then, Derrida relates the phantasm not to maternity *as such* but to the *determination* of maternity, the identification of and with a particular mother, date, and so on. The phantasm thus passes by way of the supplement, by means of speculation and calculation, sense and commonsense, even if it appears—for that is the phantasm!—to precede these and to be independent of them. Hence Derrida speaks of a rapid alternation or "trill" in Trilling between what denotes the supposedly real *mother* (the "mother's womb") and what connotes *maternity* (defined by Trilling as "the ineluctability of birth, of the marked hour, always already inscribed" [see NW 100/28]) and he goes on to argue that it is impossible for Trilling to distinguish between these in the end, impossible to sort them out and keep them separate, since the phantasm of some mother comes always and immediately to haunt the very notion of maternity. While a particular mother can thus always be denied, ignored, forgotten, done away with, even murdered, her phantasm exposed and, thus, deflated, maternity—of all the phantasms!—keeps on coming back, promising not simply a certain undeniable givenness or facticity but an origin and a lineage, not simply a birth date but the beginnings of a history. There can be no denying this maternity, this givenness or ineluctability, since denying it just reaffirms and reinscribes it, brings it back on board. Though one can kill the mother, as Trilling says, one will never be done killing off maternity, for, like a fatal attraction, or, better, like fatality or necessity itself, it keeps on coming back—inexhaustible, inexorable, inexorcisable. Though one might thus succeed, writes Derrida, "in murdering some particular mother or figure of the mother," "maternity itself, maternity in its phantasm, survives. . . . Maternity goes on, and will always go on, defying the matricide" (NW 88/8).

It is, argues Derrida, in this discernible/indiscernible, believable/unbelievable difference between the mother and maternity—a difference that, like every ontological difference, *is not* because it is not a difference between two beings—that we are given a privileged means of access not just to the logic of the phantasm but, says Derrida, to the logic of denegation. Matricidal desire, the endless, dogged pursuit of matricide, stems from the fact that "there is [*il y a*: to be distinguished in Derrida from *il est* or *ils sont*] both the mother *and* maternity" (NW 98/24). Matricidal desire is a desire to efface *at once* the determination of our origins, our particular mother, *and* the very givenness or ineluctability of the origin, the always-already-givenness of the mark. A logic of denegation thus comes to be superimposed upon this logic of the phantasm. In attempting to do away with the ineluctability of birth, with a maternity that returns in every matricide, one is attempting to do away with the very desire that makes this attempt possible. In attempting to do away with one's very birth one is attempting to do away with the ground or foundation of every attempt. Like Job—whom Derrida evokes in a footnote—matricidal desire, suicidal desire, is the desire to be done with the light of "phenomenality itself, life as visibility, the light of being" (NW 104/14 n. 7). For Trilling in *James Joyce où l'écriture matricide*, this matricidal desire is related precisely to writing, to the attempt to "redo" or "remake oneself," to give birth to oneself in writing by killing off not only the mother but maternity. Matricidal desire is thus a desperate, phantasmatic attempt to remake oneself, to generate oneself all by oneself through writing, to use one's birth and the light of day to be done with both birth and the day, to fabricate one's own birthday. Doomed to fail and doomed to recommence, Derrida asks—in writing—"Isn't writing a killer?" (NW 101/30).

APPARITION V

"Mother, why do you slip away when I try to embrace you? . . . Are you a phantom sent by Persephone to make me groan even more in my grief?" (*Odyssey* 11.211–15)

"No, mother! Let me be and let me live." (U 1.279)

Derrida ends "The Night Watch" with a postscript, dated July 15, 2000. It is a postscript about violence and metaphysics, or violence and writing, about the impossibility of writing without violence, the desire and the impossibility of doing away with the violence of writing through writing. It is also a postscript that marks, it would seem—unless there are other surprises waiting for us in the archive—the end of a certain relationship to Joyce. At the end, then, of his preface to Trilling's book on Joyce, Derrida begins and ends with a reference to Ulysses, not the novel, this time, but the man himself, the man of "many turns and devices" who once called himself "nobody" and whose portrait begins to resemble the self-portrait of the artist himself as a now not-so-very-young man, that is, the writer Jacques Derrida on his seventieth birthday. Derrida begins the postscript after the inscription of the date—which is to say, *his* "marked hour":

Take my word for it—Ulysses' honor. From Homer to Joyce, Ulysses will have been the hero of *James Joyce ou l'écriture matricide*. In *Memoirs of the Blind: The Self-Portrait and Other Ruins* (1991), I used and abused the "name of nobody" (*outis*), which Ulysses gives to himself or remakes for himself. (NW 102/31)

And he ends this postscript several paragraphs later:

I began with a wish. Here is another one, and it may always strike you as being pious, and little more than a pipe dream [*voeu . . . pieux*]: to write and kill nobody (signed Ulysses). (NW 103/32)

In this postscript full of ruse, Derrida speaks of the necessity of beginning to write differently, the necessity of beginning again, at the age of seventy, "to learn to love the mother—and maternity, in short, if you prefer to give it this name," "beyond the death drive, beyond every drive for power and mastery. Writing without writing" (NW 102–3/32). At the end of this remarkable text on maternity, on denegation, and on writing, Derrida imagines—and he knows it is little more than a phantasm, a pipe dream—a writing that would be without power and without violence. The point of the play on *vœu . . . pieux*—meaning "hollow wish" or "pipe dream," or, if *pieux* is taken as a noun, "stake," such as the stake driven by Ulysses into the eye of the Cyclops (*Odyssey* 9.387)—could not be sharper: every writing, every desire or wish in writing, and even the desire or wish to write without violence, merely inscribes violence, another violence—more or less violent but a violence nonetheless—in its turn. Violence, then, always against violence: Ulysses against Polyphemus, Bloom against the Citizen. With every stroke of the *mokhlos* the countersignature becomes a counter-stigmature, every penman a postman, right up to the point of trying to do away not only with the father but with the mother, a violence inscribed even in the desire to begin again to "learn to love the mother . . ." (NW 102/32).

And yet, for Derrida, or for Derrida as a reader of Joyce, the inevitability of this violence, undeniable and irrepressible as it is, never seems to have the last word—or, rather, even if it has the last word it is always conditioned, yes, by a first word. For Joyce too seemed to suggest not quite that maternity like paternity is a legal fiction but that the mother or the maternity of the mother is not something to be observed, noted or connoted, but, more essentially, *affirmed*. The mother or the maternity of the mother would be not only the most resistant of all phantasms but that which is most resistant *to* phantasm insofar as it is nothing more than the originary affirmation that closes the book by opening up the world (yes, yes), nothing more than the originary or pure faith (Purefoy) that brings one into a world by inscribing one into a language. In two words from Joyce, two words of Stephen spoken early on in *Ulysses*, "No, mother! Let me be and let me live." These words suggest that behind or before the denial, before the constative—"no mother"—there is the performative, the affirmation and the apostrophe, the address to the other, "No, mother! Let me be and let me live." The silence of a pause, the hesitant punctuation between two phrases, silently opens up the space of affirmation and of writing.[15]

"Silently, in a dream she had come to him . . . ," "In a dream, silently, she had come to him . . .": between "no mother" and "no, mother!," denial and affirmation, there where the mother is denied and yet still conditions every denial, the phantasm of the mother hangs on a silent, never totally silent, mark.

In "Two Words for Joyce" Derrida reads the vowel play in *Finnegans Wake* of "Ha he hi ho hu. Mummum" in terms of this very same affirmation, as an affirmation of maternity that is at once a silencing and an avowal. He there writes:

> The final "Mummum," maternal syllable or infant's apostrophe of the mother could, if one so wished, be made to resound with the final *yes* [*oui*] of *Ulysses*, said to be feminine, the "yes" of Mrs Bloom, of ALP, or of any "wee" girl . . . (TW 37/49–50)

Yes, for in a dream she comes, always silently, impossible to deny, impossible because even the silence must be spoken, the violence inscribed and affirmed, because even to keep silent "Mummum's" still the word.

Notes

1. Derrida writes: "One can admire the power of a work and have, as they say, a 'bad relationship' with its signatory, at least the signatory as one projects his or her image, reconstructs, or dreams, or offers him or her the hospitality of a haunting" (TW 23/19–20).

2. U 9.844; see, for example, *For What Tomorrow* . . . , trans. Jeff Fort (Stanford: Stanford University Press, 2004), 41, translation of *De Quoi Demain . . . : Dialogue* (Paris: Fayard/Galilée, 2001), 75, or HC 109/95.

3. I treat this question of the phantasm in much greater detail in chapter 10 of *Derrida From Now On* (New York: Fordham University Press, 2008), 187–212.

4. Derrida speaks in *H. C. for Life* in reference to Freud of "a phantasm of animist and infantile omnipotence" (HC 108/94). Though Derrida takes this passage in a somewhat different direction, it might be said that for Derrida all phantasms are phantasms of omnipotence, of an all-powerful performative. Later in the same text Derrida writes provocatively, "The phantasm is, like faith, the best proof of God's existence, the only one in truth. And one must draw all the consequences from this" (HC 157/135).

5. Written in 1994–1995, "Faith and Knowledge" was originally published in French in 1996 and in English translation two years later in *Religion*, ed. Jacques Derrida and Gianni Vattimo (Stanford: Stanford University Press, 1998), 1–78. *La Religion*, ed. Jacques Derrida and Gianni Vattimo (Paris: Éditions du Seuil, 1996), 9–86.

6. Derrida, "Faith and Knowledge," 42/56.

7. Ibid., 52/70.

8. See ibid., 48–49/63–65.

9. On the rinse cycle of birth and death: "Nature. Washing child, washing corpse. Dignam" (U 13.955–56). Recall too that it is in the "Oxen of the Sun" episode, in the maternity ward, that Stephen and Bloom, whose paths have crossed throughout the day, really come together, the recognition of a kind of paternity coinciding with the cries of maternity: "Hoopsa boyaboy hoopsa!" (U 14.5).

10. This formula gets inverted in the "Oxen of the Sun" episode, where it is said of Bloom, "Now he is himself paternal and these about him might be his sons. Who can say? The wise father knows his own child" (U 14.1063). But the inversion of the formula is not its reversal, just its flipside. It takes a certain wisdom, knowledge, speculation, or judgment for the child to recognize his or her father and the father his son or daughter. Unlike *amor matris*, the love of the father must go by way of this speculative supplement. In this particular chapter, it is the narrator, speaking in the style of English essayist Charles Lamb, who has this knowledge of Bloom's paternity: "No son of thy loins is by thee," says the narrator in a rhetorical address to Bloom, "There is none now to be for Leopold, what Leopold was for Rudolph" (U 14.1076–77).

11. To the universal rule that dictates that on those rare occasions when two people from the same family die at the same time they are buried separately, Bloom notes this single exception, "Only a mother and deadborn child [are] ever buried in the one coffin" (U 6.819–20).

12. It is worth noting in passing that Freud's *Gradiva* (Sigmund Freud, *Delusions and Dreams in Jensen's* Gradiva, trans. James Strachey, in *The Standard Edition of the Complete Psychological Works of Sigmund Freud*, 24 volumes [London: The Hogarth Press, 1999], volume 9, 3–95)—a seminal text on the phantasm—plays a significant role in *Archive Fever*, and a no less significant, even if initially less obvious, role in "Faith and Knowledge."

13. Derrida argues in *H. C. for Life* that we must try to think denegation or denial on the basis of *Anankē* (HC 116/101).

14. While one might be tempted to see this "privileging" of the mother as a sort of contestation of phallogocentrism, the opposite is really the case. Derrida writes: "Even if paternity is founded upon a lure [*leurre*], upon an illusion that needs to be contested, it retains an incontestable privilege. But in the eyes of those who deem it indisputable (in short, without any possible illusion), the mother's maternity deprives the mother of this privilege." Derrida thus goes on to speak of a Lacanian logic whereby a "second birth at the time of entering a symbolic order governed by the name of the father, in short, by a 'legal fiction'," "would be reserved for the paternity of the father" (NW 107/27 n. 27). This is, says Derrida, "the phallogocentric credulity of Freud" evoked above.

15. Derrida writes in "How to Avoid Speaking: Denials" (PSII 167/169): "When Jeremiah curses the day he was born, he must still or already *affirm*."

5

MATRICIDAL WRITING: PHILOSOPHY'S ENDGAME

Christine van Boheemen-Saaf

the measure [. . .] by which our Outis cuts his truth.
—James Joyce, *Finnegans Wake* (493.24)

Derrida's most recent publication on Joyce, "The Waking Woman: '[Reading] in the Book of Himself,'" is a preface to Jacques Trilling's psychoanalytic reading of *Ulysses*, entitled *James Joyce or Matricidal Writing* (1973).[1] Although an occasional piece, this preface is important. It bears on the contamination of philosophy by literature in Derrida's writing. It is important for feminist philosophy, because it hinges on sexual difference. In the piece Derrida makes a claim regarding the need to separate the mother from motherhood; but its emancipatory intention is undermined because the concept of "matricidal writing" lures the philosopher into a self-deconstructive struggle with the specter of the (m)other. The piece is also important to Jewish studies, because it reveals Derrida's attempt to escape the bond to the mother in relation to the "Jewish question" of psychoanalysis (at a time when Derrida was also writing his plenary address on Freud's *Beyond the Pleasure Principle*). Repetition compulsion and the splitting of the ego—self-consciously performative—enact the ineluctability of the bond. The suggestion of the following analysis will be that Derrida's close identification with Joyce's modernity effectuated a process of transferential self-analysis which eventually produced the articulated desire to relinquish the truth claims and drive for power characteristic of philosophy since Plato staged Socrates in dialogue with the bard Ion. Derrida's piece, dated on Derrida's birthday, playing on the signature, shows philosophy in a fatal struggle with the materiality of inscription: the mark.

Derrida begins with a claim. He will speculate on a working hypothesis, which, while it entails a risky act of differentiation, he will nevertheless sign. At issue is the difference between the figure of the mother and maternity: "To distinguish between the mother and maternity, to sort them out [*trier*], to draw an infinitely fine but indivisible line between them, even when the thing seems undecidable—that, I would say, is Trilling's decisive gesture, his critical operation, his *krinein*. And this operation takes place at the very moment he reminds us of the inevitability or fatality for the one who writes, and par excellence for Joyce, of a certain matricide" (NW 88/8).

While Derrida here speaks of the distinction between mother and motherhood in relation to the signature style of writing, he elsewhere speaks of it as a sociopolitical issue, relating to the peculiar construction of maternity in contemporary, technological society. In *For What Tomorrow . . . : A Dialogue* with Elisabeth Roudinesco, the distinction between motherhood and maternity receives extensive attention. And there, with a reference to Joyce and to "The Waking Woman," Derrida brands his attempt to differentiate between the mother and motherhood as emancipatory. "[T]he identity of the mother (like her possible juridical identification) depends on a judgment that is just derived, and on an inference that is just as divorced from all immediate perception, as this 'legal fiction' of a paternity conjectured through reason (to use a phrase from Joyce's *Ulysses* referring to paternity)."[2] In a patriarchal culture, understanding motherhood, like paternity, as a "legal fiction" might undo social inequality. The Joycean reader will recall that, in *Ulysses*, Joyce's character Stephen Dedalus had spoken of paternity as unverifiably a "legal fiction," in contrast to maternity, which is materially evident.

To contextualize Derrida's surprising turn to motherhood, our discussion must return to "Ulysses Gramophone: Hear Say Yes in Joyce." There Derrida, citing Molly Bloom's repetitive "yes, I will yes," had affirmed the Becoming Woman of Joyce's modernity—in recalling the figure of woman in *Spurs*. Both *Spurs* and "Ulysses Gramophone" received substantial scholarly discussion, especially from feminist critics. The main critical question was whether Derrida/Joyce's recourse to female figuration to denote the difference of their signature style of writing did not, in fact, amount to a double dispossession of women, rather than an emancipatory advance?[3] Derrida's recent essay also employs gendered figuration, the mother rather than the woman, and it moves beyond Nietzschean affirmation to isolate the interminable drive to undo maternity as the motor of performative writing. From identification with the positionality of the female figure, the relationship has shifted to the desire for differentiation and the undoing of the bond, but the connection with Joyce's *Ulysses* remains. Significant here, is that

"The Waking Woman," which is preoccupied with the cluster-theme of the inability to deny the gift of birth, with repetition and the death drive, as well as with "a certain 'Jewish question'" (NW 96/21) should have arisen from Derrida's rereading of Trilling's psychoanalytical work on Joyce, and be inscribed by Derrida as the effect of a certain written trace of the story of Odysseus throughout different disciplines: literature, psychoanalysis, and philosophy. Although his filiation to Joyce appears to have mutated into the criminal shape of an Orestes rather than the yea-saying Penelope / Molly Bloom, the trajectory keeps circling Joyce *and* always relates to the process of "reading . . . [the] . . . self," as the subtitle of Derrida's preface indicates.

As we know, from the first, Derrida saw Joyce as the embodiment of an absolute or pure form of writing that fuses autobiography with representation, and the general law with the singularity of the individual writer. Such writing undermines the self-presence of ontological claims to a full truth. Hence the recourse to the gendered figuration of *Spurs*: "Woman is but one name for that untruth of truth."[4] As "The Waking Woman" indicates, however, over the years Derrida's thinking about writing, representation, and truth has evolved. The recent title would seem to continue the theme of hauntology (of "the state of debt, the work of mourning"), which became noticeably present in *Specters of Marx* of 1994;[5] but note that the ghost has turned female, ahistorical, and denotes, as we shall see, the effect generated by a certain self-conscious, linguistic-phenomenological wish to be free of contingency and the debt of generation. From an oedipal and parricidal understanding of writing, Derrida has moved to a matricidal construction of it. "The Waking Woman" confirms my analysis in *Joyce, Derrida, Lacan, and the Trauma of History* (1999), which outlines the phantasmatic drive to undo the debt to mother/materiality in Joyce and Derrida.[6] In addition, the later Derrida shows himself fascinated by the lure of the reaffirmation of a reason "without alibi," without metaphysical/religious or material grounding, which might transcend the will to power and sovereignty, as his address to the States General of Psychoanalysis in July 2000 indicates.[7] The conclusion of "The Waking Woman," which celebrates transcendental homelessness and ends in enunciation without an enunciated, is pointed toward the foreclosure of the "alibi" of motherhood, as well as of the tradition of metaphysics.

Derrida is writing in the wake of Trilling, as the waking friend who lends Trilling's text a ghostly second life. He performs a close reading of Trilling's text that unquestionably accepts Trilling's suggestion of matricide as the phantasmatic aspect, which explains the peculiar nature of Joyce's *Ulysses*, extending the application to other modern masters: Baudelaire, Proust, Mallarmé (and himself, of course). The essay is very personal, reminiscing about musical performances, their mutual love of Joyce as the "secret sharer" in their lives. The autobiographical nature of Trilling's study is also emphasized.

His interest in Joyce's text dates to the loss of his own mother, just as Stephen Dedalus and his creator James Joyce had been in deep mourning.

First note, then, that the cast, here, is all male, and that the drive of Derrida's writing is, as always, the filiative effect of linking masculine signatures. What Jacques Trilling and Jacques Derrida have in common, apart from their "secret sharer" James Joyce, is, obviously, their first name, which comes in for considerable comment, and which is in turn linked to the English translation of "Jacques" as "James." This play on the masculine first name, which traces the transferential intersubjectivity of this all-male cast of authors, is added upon by Derrida's play on the family name of the bilingual Trilling. This allows him references to Trilling's musical abilities, as well as to his tendency to attempt to "*tri-er*" (to "separate out") what cannot be disunited (mother and motherhood). This discussion of the name follows from Derrida's reminder that Trilling's text belongs to that genre of signature writing to which Joyce and he himself also belong. By "signature" Derrida means "a *work* [*œuvre*], that is to say, the survival of a trace whose content can no longer be separated from the process of writing, from the singular, dated act or gesture, irreplaceable like a body, like a bodily struggle, untranslatable in the end, precisely as that which refers to maternity, to birth" (NW 98/25). The reader will have noted that the incontrovertible material bond of motherhood (although Derrida is here and elsewhere engaged in trying to turn it into a "legal fiction") precisely functions as the model and figure for the very special nature of the performative style of the writing of Joyce and of himself. This might seem to confirm earlier feminist accusations of appropriation of sexual difference, but closer inspection will show that, here, Derrida is actually engaged in the demonstration that patriarchy, in its desire for purity and exclusion of the other, precisely *produces the spectral power of the materiality of motherhood.*

A New Scene of Writing

Since Derrida makes his points by quoting Trilling, let us begin with one of those quotations. Trilling claims:

> What is being questioned here is the link between the giving birth of writing and maternity (this latter being more or less absent from the *Traumdeutung*), that is, the ineluctability of birth, of the marked hour, always already inscribed [. . .]. Stephen already assailed by the specter of the mother in Ithaca [. . .]. As if the mother's womb—which one always wishes to be without a navel—arose here and there throughout the entire book, an uncircumventable

re-presentation that language would run up against and turn around. (NW 186–87/12; Derrida citing Trilling, 93–94)

Derrida repeats Trilling's definition of "maternity" as "the ineluctability of birth, of the marked hour, always already inscribed" to remind us that Trilling's reading of Joyce extends beyond an individual case study to a theory about writing-marking. He also points out that Trilling's analysis is noncanonical, always aimed at being revolutionary within the revolutionary discipline of psychoanalysis. As I said, the focus is on matricidal desire rather than on the parricidal Freudian Oedipus complex. This revolutionary gesture, revising the central patriarchal tenet of orthodox Freudianism, is related by Derrida to the figure of the wily Ulysses, more precisely, his written trace in the works of Homer and Joyce. "Between the two voyages, the two Ulysseses, there is the daring of a psychoanalytic invention: the discovery of a law. Freud reread and disturbed by Trilling" (NW 89/9). In other words, Derrida finds in Trilling's revision of the phallogocentrism of Freudianism a revolutionary opening up of a textual space for the desire to kill the mother/maternity, hitherto untheorized. Of course, in following Trilling, Derrida is also rewriting his own scenario of the scene of writing as parricidal, in which Plato, the son figure, had been writing out of the death of Socrates (*Dissemination, The Post Card*). Here: "Before being the spectrality of the dead or murdered father [. . .] spectrality is essential to matricide, that is, at once to the desire and failure of the murder, to an interminable *attempted murder*. For maternity always survives, by coming back, by returning to its haunts [*en revenante*]. It has the last word, and it remains vigilant, it wakes [*y veille*]" (NW 94/18). Thus the literary/psychoanalytic Joycean pre-texts bring Derrida to share/articulate a new scenario of the scene of writing.

From Hamlet to Job

As we saw, the subtitle of Derrida's essay carries a reference to Hamlet from *Ulysses*. The question with which the ghostliness of the father is usually identified is Hamlet's question: "To be, or not to be."[8] In Trilling this question is shifted to a more fundamentally existential level, and voiced as the ancient lament: "I wish that I had never been born." This malediction of birth echoes the figure of Job in the Old Testament. It is this fantastic wish to never have existed, the fiction of having never been born, which Derrida ties to the spectrality of the mother. Crucial is the fact that such a curse of one's existence may be possible as speech, but cursing cannot alter our existential condition. The words are at once a denial of their own claim.

In saying we wish we had not been born, we confirm that we have been born. I quote Derrida directly:

> Like suicide, matricide (the curse of being born) bears within it this contradiction. But far from paralyzing matricide [as in *Hamlet*], the contradiction motivates it. [. . .] What appears *impossible* through this curse or malediction, but also through every blessing or benediction, through every -diction, is to expunge, contest, or even confirm the contingency of my being-born, which always presupposes some denegation of being-born, and the simple thought of my virtual "not being born." Yet this impossible remains the only possibility I have of gaining access to the experience of existence, to the "I am," as well as to time, to the temporality of time inasmuch as it is always and first of all *my* time, my "living present." (NW 91–92/13–14)

The curse protests against the ineluctability of being born, which is unforgivable, unthinkable, but, and here Derrida becomes didactic, "more or less, something other in any case, than a being or an origin" (NW 92/15). Matricide brings us on the trail of a birth "irreducible to all ontology, to all ontological or phenomenological thinking about originarity. Being born, the event of 'being born,' has *already* come in place of the origin" (NW 92/15).

This may seem a blow to orthodox Freudian patriarchy, since patriarchy places the father, alive or dead, as the *archē* (beginning/origin). Here the place of the *archē* is occluded by a female ghost, and this phantasmatic spectrality, the haunting presence of what is dead and absent, is crucially related to the wish to undo one's beginning, because matricide can never succeed. It is an *unending* attempt of at once desiring and failing to kill. One can kill the mother, she may have died, but one cannot kill motherhood. "Between the mother and maternity the ontological difference *is not*; it is not a difference between two (beings) [. . .]. There is thus no possible *tri*, no real sorting out, between the mother and maternity. And yet this sorting out is necessary, for maternity will never be reducible to the mother and this ontological difference opens up the possibility of a *tri* [cut] or a sorting out in general" (NW 101/30). It is a cut which, as we shall see, Derrida will prove unable to make, however. Motherhood always survives to haunt. Motherhood has the last word, and motherhood wakes, "And yet maternity remains, and it wakes [*veille*], the Waking Woman [*Veilleuse*] does—absolutely indefatigable" (NW 101/30; tm). If paternity is a "legal fiction"—and as such it is more easily denied or foreclosed—motherhood, the fact of generation is undeniable, and will insist on entering consciousness and writing, albeit phantasmatically. The murderous intention of matricidal writing, then, Derrida argues, has to do with the fact that when we conceive the notion of "never having been born,"

> Yes, the question comes too late, *being born* has taken place, namely, what comes to me—in short, me—from the other. From the other me. Before me the other me. Who is, without being my double, another *secret sharer*. [. . .] The desperate attempt that races and races to the rescue . . . to save what it loses, its other double. Out of breath after such a delay, that is the race of matricide writing. Not its source, for it has no source, and for good reason, but its endless race. A race without end because without origin. (NW 92/15)

From Affirmation to the Death Drive

If we compare the deployment of gendered figuration in this essay to that in Derrida's earlier work (*Spurs, Glas, The Post Card*, "Ulysses Gramophone") we note that it has a similar function although it has changed shape. While the question concerning (the) mother(hood) vitiates the self-presence, the totalizing grasp of embodied consciousness, just as Nietzsche's "Woman" had signaled the untruth of truth, there is a new and very interesting aspect to matricidal writing. The new figuration is linked to the *act* of writing, not just to the truth-claims of writing. In Derrida's words: "the contradiction [in the question regarding the mother] *motivates* it" (NW 91/13; emphasis added). It produces its own repetition. Compulsively, interminably, "writing comes to be inscribed in this repetition. It signs it and countersigns it" (NW 91/13). Thus the rise of the specter of the mother may diminish patriarchal self-presence, or vitiate ontological notions of truth; it also guarantees the continuity of writing (and writing, we remember, had been the patriarchal prerogative. Paternity is "legal" [that is: "written"] fiction). In Joyce, the night language of the waking women/mothers circulates the text back to its beginning. Indeed, the waking woman is the central but crucially ambivalent linchpin of Joyce's interminable writing. Between dusk and dawn, between waking and dreaming, life and death, outside the story but inside the text, her spectrality or marginality is the uncanny countersign to the singularity of Joyce's signature. Like (some versions of) psychoanalysis, matricidal writing is interminable, an endless Odyssey without possibility of return because the beginning, the origin, the starting point is not fixed, only present as shadowy trace, a perpetual exile from full self-presence. Derrida concludes this passage with the claim, deliberately phrased so as to bring out the self-reflexiveness of such writing rising out of the question regarding the mother: "writing is a killer; one is never done with it [*l'écriture est tuante, on n'en finit jamais*;

which could also be rendered as: writing is a killer; one is never done with oneself]" (NW 92/15). Derrida's wordplay signals to the reader that the bondage to articulation and text production, which the question of the mother initiates, is not just a burden or curse. It may, as in his case, and that of Joyce, be a joyful and unending trajectory of productivity as well.

Without Alibi

Although the text does not mark a new chapter in Derrida's career, "The Waking Woman" does shift the problem of the untruth of truth away from its association with Nietzsche, perhaps owing to the presence of Freud in the text. It relinquishes the identification of femininity and affirmation, however much a matter of "hearsay," to bring out the other side of the coin: that of denial and *Verneinung*. It also brings into the discourse a theme, the notion of "a certain 'Jewish question'" (NW 96/21), related to Freud's concern with repetition compulsion and the death drive. Indeed, the former identification with Joyce's Penelope has now shifted to the "secret sharing" of the band of brothers who, like Orestes, need to kill the mother. The problem of modernity's relationship to truth here gains a different articulation, perhaps more psychoanalytical than philosophical, certainly more primal, which Derrida repeatedly links to what he calls "a certain 'Jewish question.'"

What can that mean? Let us first see how the adjective "Jewish" features here. Trilling presents the Jewish mother as the parent who demands that he learn Hebrew, just as Stephen Dedalus' mother had insisted that he do his Easter duty. The mother lays a claim on her son in the name of faith and tradition, and the Jewish mother is the privileged *locus* of the continuity of the race. From the dialogue with Roudinesco, we know that Derrida understands his own Jewishness primarily as a bond: "some One marked my destiny even before I had a word to say. [. . .] I am marked even before being able to speak"[9]—indeed, we may have here the predominant impetus of Derrida's writing, of his sense of belatedness. In his reading of Trilling, too, Derrida understands the figure of motherhood as that of a "one" who lays a claim and who effectuates a doubling (secret sharing) without having existential identity and presence. The figure of the (Jewish) mother implies the son's lack of self-determination, the claim of the bond, and the inability to father oneself. It is an old issue, in many respects. As Derrida reminds us, even Freud claimed he would have liked to have been his own father (NW 93/16). But should we see this as "Jewish"? In Derrida's earlier work the conundrum of belatedness had always reared its head without reference to Jewishness. Moreover, even the Irish Stephen Dedalus thinks of Shakespeare as becoming "the ghost of his own father" (as Mulligan jokingly puts it [U 1.556–57]). Although Joyce promoted a vaguely Jewish figure, Leopold

Bloom, to the role of protagonist in his version of the Odyssey, it remains hard to define what Derrida means by "a certain 'Jewish question.'" He links the fantasy of controlling one's own prehistory to Jewishness, and then turns it into a general cultural symptom comprising an Irish novelist. It is certainly not a racial trait, but must be something that, he implies, brings with it a certain effect of secret sharing, a lack of self-presence, which may be hard to tolerate, and which stimulates cultural productivity.

Derrida also links "Jewish" to modernity. When he speaks of "the Jewish question" in "The Waking Woman" (NW 96/21), it is also to point to the historical configuration of overlap between the rise of psychoanalysis (the Jewish science that pointed to the presence of the unconscious) and modernist literature. He recalls the antagonism that Freud's psychoanalysis inspired in the Nazis, and links it to the antagonism that Joyce inspired in Jung. In mentioning Freud's trials with the Aryan Carl Gustav Jung, Jung's vile comments on *Ulysses*, and even the rise of Surrealism in France, Derrida sketches a modern movement of outsiders and exiles, a band of brothers whose common denominator is their inability to return to full self-presence: "an odyssey without return," an "exile without return" (NW 95/20, 21). This configuration he in turn attaches to the signature style of writing, discussed earlier, in which one "will no longer be able to dissociate the body of the signature from the theoretical gesture, the singularity of the signatory from the formalization of a universal law" (NW 96/21). Thus the term "Jewish" is increasingly diluted. Its ultimate referent seems to be a condition of perpetual dispossession (the wandering Jew), of being in exile without possibility of return because the original point or place of departure has disappeared from the earth. It is as if Derrida wishes to claim Joyce for a more Hebraic inscription: the Abrahamic exile who will never settle. But note that that is a falsification of his earlier view of Joyce as Hegelian. He had ended "Violence and Metaphysics," which contrasts the Hebraic and the Hellenic, arguing that we live in the difference between them, with a question regarding Joyce: "And what is the legitimacy, what is the meaning of the *copula* in this proposition from perhaps the most Hegelian of modern novelists: 'Jewgreek is greekjew. Extremes meet'?" (WD 153/228).

The term "Jewish" in "Jewish question," then, can have as its referent only the notion of a certain positionality in the inscription in twentieth-century cultural practice that effects a spectralizing effect on the illusion of full truth or full self-presence. The puzzling thing is: How does the figure of the Greek Odysseus, invoked again and again as a link between Trilling, Joyce, Homer, Freud, and Derrida, become the icon or star figure of such transcendental homelessness? He is neither Jewish, nor Irish, nor contemporary, nor, and this is what Derrida seems to repress here, *perpetually exiled*. In "Violence and Metaphysics" he had contrasted the circularity of the

Odyssey with Abraham's exile. What prods Derrida to contradict himself, to overlook, or deny the cultural difference between Jew and Irishman, Hebraic and Hellenic, and to foreclose the fact of Odysseus' safe return to his Penelope in Ithaca? While James Joyce, commenting on *Ulysses*, wanted the "Penelope" episode, necessary as *clou* to the text, nevertheless to be understood as placed *outside the story* of *Ulysses* (an ambiguity that has generated ample discussion in Joyce studies), Derrida is now even more radically exclusionary. Joyce, ambivalently, locates the feminine matrix of origin and return both inside and outside. The "Penelope" episode, which stages the stream-of-consciousness of the half-dreaming heroine, functions as a *ricorso* to the beginning. Derrida, however, just lops off Ithaca and Penelope, castrating any return, origin or matrix. In "The Waking Woman," the circularity of the *Odyssey* appears restyled as the endless forward flight of the subject—seemingly in order to enlist Odysseus as avatar "Jew."

Note that the important quality related to Odysseus in "The Waking Woman" is his wiliness, his success in escaping from traps. In the *Odyssey* traps are laid especially by designing females like Calypso or Circe, but this is not central to Derrida's thought. To him Odysseus is primarily the figure who escapes from the Cyclops through the revision of the name as "No-one" (*outis*). Also remember Odysseus as the hero whose wiliness defeated proud Troy. In Derrida/Trilling, the defeat of Troy/Ilium takes on symbolic meaning. It stands for the war on the self-sufficiency, the arrogance, and denial of those (like Jung, or the Nazis) who wage war on the "Jewish question" of psychoanalysis and deconstructive philosophy. In other words, psychoanalysis or deconstructive philosophy wages war on the supremacy of the Ego; and the wiliness of Odysseus is the totem quality of such discourse. Meanwhile, the Homeric plot is subjected to more radical censorship than even Joyce had envisioned. Derrida's signature style rudely suppresses the return to Penelope in order to endorse its own singularity and otherness. It homogenizes the Jew and the Greek, perhaps in an act of loyalty to his friend Trilling, perhaps out of belated obedience to his own upbringing, similar to Freud's supposed deferred obedience in writing *Moses and Monotheism*.[10]

Now we would seem to know what "matricide" means in terms of textual production. In focusing on "matricidal" writing, and drawing a thin line between the mother and motherhood, the philosopher may hope to strike a blow for equality, but he enacts patriarchal exclusion, while arrogating the privilege of motherhood, the materiality of its mark, to the signature style of writing. Presenting itself as "matricidal" or "Jewish" in relation to the master discourses of ontological philosophy or even Nazism and Jungian psychology, the foreclosure of Penelope enacts and repeats the plot of patriarchy on a textual level. In order to move beyond the question mark and the ambiguity that had concluded "Violence and Metaphysics," Derrida condemns Penelope to being a lonely and forgotten "waking woman" forever.

Is this a (Freudian) slip of the pen? Or is Derrida following a trace in the writing on Odysseus that might explain the self-contradiction? Let us return to the *Odyssey*. There Orestes, the classical figure of the matricide, does not feature as matricide. The murder of the mother is elided, Orestes is praised for his decisiveness and held up to a Hamlet-like Telemachus as example. Thus the history of matricide is edited out from the representation, and Orestes turned into a model to be followed. Although Homer precedes Derrida in an act of foreclosure, then, Homer nevertheless allows Penelope a star performance. So, in claiming that the signature style of writing follows "in the tracks" of Odysseus (NW 89/9), what might Derrida mean? On the one hand he edits out the female and the point of origin in styling Odysseus and matricidal writing as exilic without possibility of return, on the other hand he appears to wish to highlight the haunting presence of the mother's ghost, all the while inscribing himself in the masculine heroic tradition. Is this a contradiction? I do not think so. Let us remember what Trilling said about Joyce and the mother: He wants to kill her, again, for having deserted him. Is modernity, perhaps, a mourning for the mother who has long since been silenced, killed even? Yet such an original "murder," if murder it was, was apparently, not definitive. The mother survives as a "question [. . .] from the other" (NW 92/15) that deprives us of self-presence. She haunts modernity as a ghost. She must be killed again, and again, because she has deserted us without granting us full command of ourselves. Here I must return to Derrida's words on the difference between Hamlet and Job. The difference between the phrases "To be or not to be" and "I wish I had never been born," is the rise of spectrality. The latter question, wishing the mother as always already not-a-mother, raises the suggestion of an "other me. Who is, without being my double" (NW 92/15). The ghost emerges from the unwishing of the fact of generation itself. Wishing the mother as nonmother, going beyond the patriarchal strategy of relegating the female to the subservient role, and attempting to let even her memory vanish, the subject spectralizes his or her very own subjectivity—he gains a secret sharer (the term litters the pages of Derrida's essay). What Derrida's "The Waking Woman" implies about the supposed positioning of signature writing within twentieth-century cultural production, is that it is not an undoing of patriarchal repression, nor an opening up to the other, but an attempt to arrogate the privilege of generative materiality to a certain style of writing or cultural production. It offers a transcendentalization, a repetition at a more mediatized level, of the classic patriarchal gestures of foreclosure and appropriation. Post-structuralism (and perhaps Trilling's version of psychoanalysis) is, indeed, more matricidal than Freud's patriarchal discourse. It grew to be so, and here is the paradox, because the so-called signature style of writing depends, much more so than traditional classic realism, on the materiality of the medium itself, on textuality, inscription, layout, print, and so forth.[11] In its attempt to fuse style with referentiality, form with content, the general with the particular, the archive with the singular, the practitioner of this style ineluctably enmeshes him- or herself in the materiality of the mother/medium. Indeed, the signature style of writing highlights the debt to materiality, the bond to the medium. It lends prestige and power to what remained invisible and foreclosed in classical realism and in Freudian psychoanalysis. "Killing the mother" thus becomes necessary to safeguard the spirit.

Derrida's Endgame

It seems to me there is something at work, then, a struggle between spirit and matter, which is best addressed by means of a scrutiny of Derrida's own stylistic practice—reading him as if he were Joyce. We may recall Derrida's words about *Finnegans Wake* in "Two Words": "something essential in it passes the understanding as well as the hearing, hear in that a graphic or literal dimension, literally literal, a muteness that one should never pass over in silence" (TW 36/46). Here I would like to show Derrida engaged with that mute "dimension." Beginning the essay, Derrida had promised that he would sign the attempt to separate the mother from motherhood, in his own name. Let us see how he works himself up toward that moment.

> The essence of the mother, her appearing *as such*, is maternity. Nothing, almost nothing. Nothing other, no one other, than the mother, a single mother. And yet maternity remains, and it wakes [*veille*], the Waking Woman [*Veilleuse*] does—absolutely indefatigable [*increvable*]. Thus: like everything that is indefatigable, beginning with God, it does not appear as such, in its own light, in the light of its nightlight, except to the murdering desire to be done with that which is never over and done with. To be done, as Job would have wanted, with light itself. With what there was. To be done with the trace of the trace, with birth itself. To kill oneself by killing one's birth, in other words, the maternity of one's mother. So as to entertain the suicidal illusion, yet again, of giving birth to oneself. On one's own, freely, to oneself.
> —Yeah, right.
> —Auto-parthenogenesis of a writing, for example, that would like to deny or—for this amounts to the same thing—to appropriate without remainder the entirety of one's heritage. One writes, but

it would be necessary to do otherwise in order to redo or remake oneself. In order to be in the end, as Joyce would have wanted, "father and son of his works" [Trilling, *James Joyce*, 47–48]. Even if it means running the risk—for who could deny it?—of finding oneself at the end of road, at the moment of signing, done in [*refait*; literally "remade"]. (NW 101–2/30; tn)

Interesting here is not only the content of the message, to which we will return, but the sudden shift in genre, evident in the materiality of its inscription. From discursive text, essay, we shift into the dialogue of drama. The direct speech in this dialogue is in turn indicated by the dashes that Joyce insisted be used to denote direct speech in his texts. Who is/are speaking here? Is Derrida talking to himself, to his secret sharer, to the memory of Trilling? Is he the only speaker? The break in the generic convention affects the status of the message. Although the last part of the quotation appears to present a personal confession of the speaker, there is no guarantee that that speaker is Derrida. The signature itself becomes spectral. The statement appears histrionic, play-acting, pretending to conclude in the name of Derrida, while deferring to a dramatic alter ego or secret sharer.

The reader's uncertainty mounts when we reach the conclusion proper. Derrida adds a "P.S. June 15, 2000. Take my word for it—Ulysses' honor" (NW 102/31). This postscript, a full page and a half, ends: "(signed Ulysses)" (NW 103/32). At the bottom of the page, however, one notes another signature: "Jacques Derrida" (NW 103/32). Is Derrida, born June 15th, ventriloquizing as Ulysses/*Outis*, the wily exile? Again the authority of the signature is deferred and spectralized, but that effect can only be created because the different names are held together by the mute, material medium of the printed page. The material substrate is indispensable. What does this mediatized spectralization imply about the status of the surprising turn this postscript takes?

What we see happen here, at the moment when the text must conclude and make its point, is philosophy's coy gesture of hiding itself in the guise of (post)modernist literature, spectralizing its own discursive authority. Moreover, philosophy encrypts itself in the materiality of writing (the conventions of dashes, abbreviations, postscripts) that marks the difference between literature and philosophy. Thus it takes the shape of what, since Plato, has been the *mother*-discourse, while subsuming the difference between the disciplines in the invention of a signature style and the concept of singularity. The reader of Joyce is quite familiar with Joyce's exploitation of the materiality of the text and his increasing tendency to make the process of writing itself, the play with the materiality of language, the aim of his signature style of writing, turning the author into Shem the Penman who uses his own body to write on, with ink made from his own excrement, materializing himself as one "continuous present tense integument" (see FW 185.14–26). With regard to Joyce, the substitution of writing for living and the inability to come to a full stop are well documented. Whether/how this applies to Derrida, remains to be seen; just as we need to decide whether the term "fetishism" is at all appropriate to denote such a linking of energy to textual production.[12]

Whether Derrida is playing the role of wily Ulysses/No-one whose revision of the name effectuates escape, or is marking his inability to escape the net of Joyce and the mother-discourse, his essay inscribes writing as repetition compulsion. It testifies to the persecuting effect of the mother's ghost. In Homer's epic, Odysseus, calling himself "*Ou-tís*" (No-one) had escaped from being devoured by the Cyclops. The play on a name, which unnames, is the play of the philosopher who desires a cut but cannot effectuate it without committing suicide (also one of the themes in "The Waking Woman"). Perhaps the *clou* to this ambivalence resides in the peculiar content of the "P.S." Reminding us that he had (ab)used the play on the personal name "No-one" in *Memoirs of the Blind: The Self-Portrait and Other Ruins* (1991),[13] Derrida then mentions his address to the States General of Psychoanalysis, dealing with a "beyond of cruelty, a beyond of sovereignty, a beyond of the death drive" (NW 102/31). It is as if he had understood a silent lesson from Jacques Trilling and made the resolution once and for all:

> from now on, no more writing, especially not writing, for writing dreams of sovereignty, writing is *cruel*, murderous [. . .]. Crimes against humanity, even genocide, begin here, as do crimes against *generation* [. . .]. from now on, [. . .] to begin finally to love life, namely birth. Mine among others—notice I am not saying *beginning* with mine. A new rule of life: to breathe from now on without writing, to take a breath beyond writing . . . I want to want an active and signed renunciation of writing, a reaffirmed life. And thus a life without matricide. [. . .] It would be necessary to begin to learn to love the mother—and maternity [. . .]. Beyond the death drive, beyond every drive for power and mastery. Writing without writing. The other writing, the other of writing as well, altered writing, the one that has always worked over my own in silence. [. . .] I began with a wish. Here is another one, and it may always strike you as being pious, and little more than a pipe dream [*voeu . . . pieux*]: to write and kill nobody (signed Ulysses). (NW 102–3/31–32)

The passage echoes *Specters of Marx*, which had begun: "*to learn to live finally.*"[14] One critic reads this as an Odyssean return to Husserl, the beginning of Derrida's career.[15] However, this reimposes the circular model of return that precisely contradicts the exile without alibi, which Derrida highlights in "The Waking Woman." Derrida's conclusion is, of course, self-contradictory. It is an active demonstration of the effect of the spectrality of the mother/desire for mastery/need of survival of the spirit that forces one to keep writing, even to confess to the matricidal desire in writing, while foreclosing the possibility of the full stop. The contradiction, the paradox of the wish to have never been born, reappears here as the paradox of the signature style of writing. Derrida cannot just leave off writing. In order to make that act significant, *to mark it*, he must *write down* that he stops writing; but that act belies the intention of renunciation. Such a paradoxical message can only be signed by an *alias*: "Odysseus." What proves inescapable, then, is the material mark. Writing is a killer, indeed.

Notes

1. I have translated "La Veilleuse" as "The Waking Woman" rather than "The Night Watch" in order to bring to the fore the sexual dimension at stake in the essay itself (a sense noted by the translators of this essay in this volume in their endnote to the title). My reasons should be clear from the analysis that follows. Derrida's essay is the preface to Jacques Trilling, *James Joyce ou l'écriture matricide* (Belfort, France: Editions Circé, 2001).

2. Jacques Derrida and Elisabeth Roudinesco, *For What Tomorrow . . . : A Dialogue*, trans. Jeff Fort (Stanford: Stanford University Press, 2004), 41, translation of *De Quoi Demain . . . : Dialogue* (Paris: Fayard/Galilée, 2001), 75.

3. See *Feminist Interpretations of Jacques Derrida*, ed. Nancy J. Holland (University Park: Pennsylvania State University Press, 1997); Christine van Boheemen, *The Novel as Family Romance: Language, Gender, and Authority from Fielding to Joyce* (Ithaca: Cornell University Press, 1987).

4. Jacques Derrida, *Spurs: Nietzsche's Styles / Éperons: Les Styles de Nietzsche*, trans. Barbara Harlow (Chicago: University of Chicago Press, 1979), 51/50.

5. Jacques Derrida, *Specters of Marx: The State of Debt, the Work of Mourning, and the New International*, trans. Peggy Kamuf (New York: Routledge, 1994), translation of *Spectres de Marx: L'État de la dette, le travail du deuil et la nouvelle Internationale* (Paris: Galilée, 1993).

6. Christine van Boheemen-Saaf, *Joyce, Derrida, Lacan, and the Trauma of History: Reading, Narrative, and Postcolonialism* (Cambridge: Cambridge University Press, 1999).

7. Jacques Derrida, "Psychoanalysis Searches the States of Its Soul: The Impossible Beyond of a Sovereign Cruelty," in *Without Alibi*, ed. and trans. Peggy Kamuf (Stanford: Stanford University Press, 2002), 238–80, translation of *Etats d'âme de la psychanalyse: l'impossible au-delà d'une souveraine cruauté* (Paris: Galilée, 2000).

8. William Shakespeare, *Hamlet*, ed. Ann Thompson and Neil Taylor (London: Arden Shakespeare, 2006), III.i.64.

9. Derrida and Roudinesco, *For What Tomorrow*, 193ff./311ff.

10. Sigmund Freud, *Moses and Monotheism*, trans. James Strachey, in *The Standard Edition of the Complete Psychological Works of Sigmund Freud*, 24 volumes (London: The Hogarth Press, 1999), volume 23, 1–137. See Yosef Hayim Yerushalmi, *Freud, Moses: Judaism Terminable and Interminable* (New Haven: Yale University Press, 1991). Yerushalmi is criticized and called a personal friend in Derrida's discussion with Elisabeth Roudinesco.

11. I must refer to Boheemen-Saaf, *Joyce, Derrida, Lacan* for a lengthy analysis.

12. See Jacques Derrida, "Entre le corps écrivant et l'écriture: Entretien avec Daniel Ferrer," *Genesis* 17 (July 2001), 59–71.

13. Jacques Derrida, *Memoirs of the Blind: The Self-Portrait and Other Ruins*, trans. Michael Naas and Pascale-Anne Brault (Chicago: University of Chicago Press, 1993), translation of *Mémoires d'aveugle: L'autoportrait et autres ruines* (Paris: Éditions de la Réunion des musées nationaux, 1990).

14. Derrida, *Specters of Marx*, xvii/13.

15. Asja Szafraniec, *Beckett, Derrida, and the Event of Literature* (Stanford: Stanford University Press, 2007), 190.

III

Departures

6

SERO-POSITIVES: BELATEDNESS AND AFFIRMATION IN JOYCE, CIXOUS, AND DERRIDA

Laurent Milesi

How can it feel to be writing *after* Joyce? "It is very late, it is always too late with Joyce, I shall say only two words" (TW 22/15). Or, at the beginning of *Glas*, "a sort of *Wake*" (TW 28/30): "what, after all, of the remain(s), today, for us, here, now, of a Hegel?" (G 1a/7a), in a book having a tilt at Hegel's *Sa* (*savoir absolu*, but also sounding like "her"), whose bicolumnar structure is deceptively reminiscent of the catechistic format of the "Lessons" chapter of Joyce's encyclopedic *Finnegans Wake*, where the twins swop sides and roles like self-righteous or upright Hegel (left) and *sinister* Genet (right) in Derrida's death knell (French *glas*) to dialectic and absolute knowledge. Two famous beginnings not untypical of Derrida's awareness of coming after—Hegel or Joyce—and making do with writing their remains in their wake(s). Beckett's solution was to swerve to a diametrically opposite style of increasingly minimalist terseness after the pre-postmodern, yet neoclassical plenitude of the *Wake*, but what of Cixous and Derrida (the latter being somewhat curiously left out of Hayman and Anderson's 1978 *In the Wake of the "Wake"*)?[1] And what if this lateness was not already "pre-programmed" as assent by Joyce himself, to use Derrida's characterization of the Joyce effect both in "Two Words for Joyce" and "Ulysses Gramophone"? Let us listen again to two famous *endings*, this time, the second one only made up of two words, in two works by Joyce:

> and then he asked me would I yes to say yes [. . .] and yes I said yes I will Yes. (U 18.1605–9)

> Yes, tid. (FW 628.11–12)

But also, much earlier, to Gabriel Conroy's resigned double acquiescence toward the end of "The Dead," first when he imagines the death of one of the two aunts: "Yes yes: that would happen very soon," then as the final symbolic movement unfolds: "The time had come for him to set out on his journey westward. Yes, the newspapers were right: snow was general all over Ireland" (D 223).

Whether in the ironic undertones of a disappointed husband's "generous" resignation, in Molly's insistent *yeses* in the final monologue of *Ulysses*, or in ALP's more discreet, enigmatic acceptance expressed in the proclitic rhythm of her textual flow at the "end" of *Finnegans Wake* (FW 628.15–16), Joyce's fictional masterpieces close on affirmation long awaited but delivered too late perhaps since its consequences can only be envisaged in the imagined fiction, twice removed from "reality," of a post-textual world—will Gabriel Conroy indeed undertake his spiritual journey westward into the heart of a once despised nation, which the long-lost lover of his wife stands as a accusatory symbol of, and will Molly make breakfast for Bloom on 17th June 1904 and maybe resume full sexual intercourse with him?—or even fed back into Vico's eternal cyclical scheme of events—when it is not downright an equation for the unavoidable acceptance of death ("The Dead"). Foreclosed or de-finitized, Joyce's belated *yeses* raise more doubts than they fulfill promises, though of course it may be argued that they best ensure the survivability of the opus, beyond the faint glimpse of the cycle of death and life's renewal (*Dubliners*), a final full stop in an otherwise relatively depunctuated final chapter (*Ulysses*), or the pretense of a forever returning textual loop (*Finnegans Wake*).

The inscription of Anna Livia's final, yet always deferred yes may be counterpointed with its conception in Derrida's philosophy of affirmation, one of whose iterations can be found in "Nombre de oui," a short text originally published in a memorial volume for Michel de Certeau and here paying homage to his ability to make us think the significance of this peculiar performative element of language, its originary repetition as "cutting opening":

> That a *yes* should be presupposed each time, not only by every statement on the subject of the *yes*, but also by every negation and every opposition, dialectical or not, between the *yes* and the *no*, this is perhaps what immediately gives the affirmation its essential, irreducible *infinity*. (PSII 232/240)[2]

For Derrida *after* de Certeau—but also in his reading of "Penelope" in "Ulysses Gramophone"—*yes* is already a *yes yes*, and *no* already presupposes a *yes*, that of *a priori* responsibility to the Other, listening to Him/Her so that denying or refusing is already the *a posteriori* mark of a more originary acceptance. In that sense as well, Molly's emphatic *yeses*, in contrast to her "nay-slaying" of Blazes Boylan as Penelopean suitor, or ALP's timid acquiescence to rush, die, and be reborn into her father-husband's arms as a younger daughterwife, come late, too late after the originary yes that even a no would have not prevented from presupposing: perhaps their late, "final" positioning in the text also records Joyce's awareness of the impossibility of saying yes for the first time (e.g., amid the rhododendrons on Howth head)—and, in connection with adulterous Molly, confers a new meaning on the "destiny of duplicity" Derrida assigns to the yes of affirmation as well as a novel interpretive direction for Joyce's text.

Philosophizing the *oui dire* of Joyce's earthy female characters may not be such a farfetched critical move if one recalls not only Molly's role as acquiescent "*ich bin das Fleisch das stets bejaht*" in the notes for "Penelope" (SL 285), reversing Mephistopheles' identification of himself in Act I of Goethe's play as "I am the spirit that always denies," but also the larger framework of affirmation and negation in his later fiction. In an unpublished paper entitled "The Ethics of (Br)ay: Joyce's Pre-Apocalyptic Ass in *Finnegans Wake*," which I gave on the occasion of a panel on "Ethics in Joyce" at the Zurich James Joyce Symposium (1996), I chose to read the cryptic creature following the synoptic gospeller St. John, himself coming after the three others in MaMaLuJo, as a post-Nietzschean protagonist through which the issue of ethics of reading in Joyce's texts could be redeployed in relation to hermeneutics and even hermetics, taking as a cue the following excerpts from *Thus Spoke Zarathustra*, all punctuated by the return of "The ass, however, brayed 'Ye-a' ":

> He bears our burden, he has taken upon himself the likeness of a slave, he is patient from the heart and he never says Nay.
>
> He does not speak, except always to say Yea to the world he created [. . .]. It is his subtlety that does not speak: thus he is seldom thought wrong.
>
> What hidden wisdom it is, that he wears long ears and says only Yea and never Nay! Has he not created the world after his own image, that is, as stupid as possible?[3]

Whether as the Christian ass loaded down with responsibilities and memories, tied to gravity, always forever acquiescing, however ironically one may wish to hear and interpret that yea-saying in German—*I-a* or *Ja*; also *Jah* or the egocentric I of the divine graph in Angelus Silesius, recalled in de Certeau's *La Fable mystique*—or therefore as the gay dancer defying gravity and making light of affirmation in the eternal return, solar rather than earth-bound,[4] the Nietzschean animal may hold the "dombkey" (FW 20.25; also Hungarian *domb*: hill = Norwegian *aas*[5]), in his silence-as-(subtle)-stupidity, not only to the ethical need for the Joycean reader to position his hermeneutics in relation to the hermetic strategies of a given text (as I suggested then),[6] but also to the belatedness of an always duplicitous yea-saying, between the double *oui-dire* of "Oyessoyess!" (FW 488.19; also "Oyes! Oyeses! Oyeseyeses!" [FW 604.22]) and the three-plus-one negations followed by the double (br)ay-saying of "Noughtnoughtnought nein. Assass" (FW 488.25–26)[7]—and only at daybreak will another animal known as Chanticleer (FW 584.21: "shantyqueer," i.e., sings clear) invert this sequence into "yeigh, yeigh, neigh, neigh" (FW 584.22). Used alongside Shaun as medium, with whom he occasionally merges, in order to reach back to the protohero's sin in the original midden, "Hanner Esellus" (FW 478.08) "brings up the rear," as it were (cf. FW 475.30), and stands for the belated reader-interpreter-translator, the dragoman or "thass withumpronouceable tail" (FW 479.09; cf. also 486.08) that always comes after the event, especially in snatches of FW III.3, which read like a burlesque recasting of the hermetic tradition of the philosophical dialogue involving an ass, as in Giordano Bruno's *L'Asino* or in the preface to *Candelaio*, with that mixture of stupidity and authorial madness as stubborn genius that defines Brunonian and Nietzschean *asinità*.[8] His critical re-productions must be couched in "midden Erse clare language" (FW 488.25), that is, at bottom a language of mediation to reach back clearly to the text's *Ursprache* buried in the "prehistoric barrow" (FW 477.36) and prepared to indulge in verbal horseplay (affirmation in laughter or *oui rire*,[9] or the "Yes! laugh Yes!" in "The Seven Seals (or: The Song of Yes and Amen)" section of *Thus Spoke Zarathustra*)—although a keener reading would probably want to oppose the ass who (br)ays to the horse who neighs/nays (cf. Willingdone's "white harse" in the Museyroom episode of FW I.1 who says "Hney, hney, hney!" [FW 10.15]).

Thus conceived, Joyce's belated *yes (yes)* is not unlike the logic of what Fritz Senn used to call the "dynamics of corrective unrest," which manifests itself in deceptively insignificant actions, themselves occasionally the product of textual readjustments at draft stage: "[Bloom] pulled the door to after him and slammed it tight ["twice" in the Rosenbach manuscript] till it shut tight."[10] More generally, the frequency of parapraxis used as an epiphanic revealer of sorts testifies to the essential untimeliness of the "right action," whose original condition would be the belatedness of any "originary" affirmation.

So how can one write, after somebody who has pre-programmed even the sequence of malfunctioning and readjustment that preside over human and textual/scriptural activity (including the various critical interpretations of his own works in FW I.5[11]), the error and its correction whose dynamics could be said to be that of critical debates? And after somebody who has already, if belatedly, said yes for us?

In his own wake of his dead father, Derrida first sketched out the motif, which was to take on different, recurrent forms subsequently,[12] of the "logic of obsequence," or what happens when one says *je suis*: I am but also I follow a dead parent, for instance during the procession at a funeral or *obsequy*, in their footsteps, including by inheritance:

> I am (following) the mother [*je suis la mère*]. The text. The mother is *behind*—all that I follow, am, do, seem—the mother follows. As she follows absolutely, she always survives—a future that will never have been presentable—what she will have engendered [. . .]; she survives the interring of the one whose death she has foreseen. Logic of obsequence. Such is the great genetic scene: the mother secutrix denounces, then lets the son die [. . .]. (G 116bi–117bi/134bi).

> From the outset, it has been another theory-procession [*théorie*] that we follow: the logic of obsequence [. . .]. I am always (following) the dead man. (G 255bi/283bi–284bi)

> The *glas* also has to do with a war for the signature, a war to the death—the only one possible—in view of the text, then (dingdong), that finally, obsequently, remains no one's. (G 71bi/83bi)[13]

Derrida will retrospectively allude to and gloss what he sees as an "elementary kinship structure" a couple of years later, appropriately in the lecture on Nietzsche known as "Otobiographies:"

> It is not only that the son does not survive his father *after* the latter's death, but the father was *already* dead; he will have died during his own life. As a "living" father, he was already only the memory of life, of an already prior life. Elsewhere, I have related this elementary kinship structure (of a dead or rather absent father, already absent to himself, and of the mother living above and after all, living on long enough to bury the one she has brought into the world, an ageless virgin inaccessible to all ages) to a logic of the death knell [*glas*] and of *obsequence*. (EO 17–18/30–31)

This follows from a passage about the origin of the subject's life in between "life death," and identity: "In a word, my dead father, my living mother, my father the dead man or death, my mother the living feminine or life. As for me, I am between the two," and introduces a famous quotation from "Why I Am So Wise" at the beginning of *Ecce Homo*: "I am [. . .] already dead as my father [. . .], while as my mother, I am still living and becoming old," glossed as follows:

> Inasmuch as *I am and follow after* [je suis] my father, I am [*je suis*] the dead man and I am death. Inasmuch as *I am and follow after* my mother, I am life that perseveres, I am the living and the living feminine. I am my father, my mother, and me, and me who is my father my mother and me, my son and me, death and life, the dead man and the living feminine, and so on. (EO 16/28).

Derrida's major book-length study of, and tribute to, Hélène Cixous, *H. C. for Life, That Is to Say . . .* will recall this passage (HC 58/55) and establish the parallel with the writer often abbreviated to the initials H.C., whose plural biologico-textual identities oscillate between "I/me" on the side of the living mother and "the author" as the daughter of the dead fathers (HC 38/34–35)—towards the end of OR, *les lettres de mon père*, the author will declare: "I write to you. Yes of course I say, I am/follow your letter. I am/follow myself your letter to me I say [*je suis ta lettre à moi dis-je*]" (HC 42/42).[14] The author is "engendered" by, becomes the text destined to him/her by inheritance, according to a (theory-)procession of generations, which each time subsumes the (usually dead) father and the (usually living) mother, and whose elementary kinship structure can also be read in the Vichian cycles of *Finnegans Wake*, with its obsequent letter (*je suis ta lettre à moi dis-je*) forever to be written/posted/delivered by sons about dead fathers(' sins) under the dictation of a living mother.

Unlike the famous Borgesian creed, which liberatingly states that "each writer *creates* his precursors,"[15] the Derridean problematic tying together existence, text and signature, and the burdensome inheritance from a dead, foreseeing forebear who is always already there and behind—not unlike the mother's precession and procession that Stephen tries hard to resist in order to create—threatens to spell the death knell of litterature, places each singular text in the post-mortem condition of an iterative always already which the "original" may well need in order to survive—Derrida's arguments in "Living On: Border Lines" and, in relation to translation, in "Des Tours de Babel"—but which makes of any new instance of writing a (re)reading *après coup* precariously confronted with a catastrophe each time renewed.[16] To counteract what Jean Paris called *la mort du signe*[17]—to which Derrida added *la mort du signataire*[18]—Cixous's *oublire* (to forgetread), practiced by Derrida in her footsteps at least once, may be the only solution, as we shall see.

In a somewhat symmetrical text in the Derridean corpus, "Circonfession"—made up of fifty-nine periods corresponding to the age of the writer and former resident at rue des Augustins, written before the mother's death, and also a borderline text running underneath Geoffrey Bennington's "derridabase"—Derrida will declare later: "I posthumize as I breathe,"[19] a circumlocutionary gloss *après la lettre* on *je suis* (since one needs to breathe in order to live on posthumously). The idiomatic turn *comme je respire* ("as I breathe") is worth noting here at it will reappear at two crucial junctions of *H.C. for Life, That Is to Say . . .* ; the later instance, in a context dealing with forgetting, forgiving and betrayal, is neatly poised before the episode of the tallith:

> Forgetreading and betrayal—of which I will only take one example, the latest. Ever since I have known her, I have read her and I keep forgetting that she writes, and I forget what she writes. This forgetting is not a forgetting like any other; it is elemental, I probably live on it. Her work for me will remain for life like what I have always forgotten a priori: I forget it as naturally as I breathe. And not only as one forgets those canonical texts where one can find everything, like [. . .] Joyce [. . .], and so many others, all those men and women who have already said everything in the past. (HC 152–53/131)

Oublire—"To reread, that is to say read, that is to say resurrect-erase, that is to say *forgetread*"[20]—characterized the famous suspensive ending of the book it came from, tensed in the pulsating movement between reading and not reading the six hundred letters of Georges Cixous to his distant bride, from "J'avais toujours pensé que je finirais par ne pas lire ces lettres" (whose double syntax is noted by Derrida in *H.C. for Life, That Is to Say . . .* : "not letting us know if, *in the end*, she will have read them" [HC 10/14]) to "Maintenant je savais que je finirais par les lire" and, *in the end*, "Je les lirai demain, dis-je, à haute voix. C'est promis. DEMAIN CE SERA LE 24 AOUT 1995."—just before the Wakean signature giving the date away: 27 August 1996, since "[t]o date is to sign."[21] But it is also at the crux of the intertextual relationship between Derrida and Cixous,[22] in a mode reminiscent of the dialectic of forgetting and re(-)membering that presides over the eternal *ricorsi* of *Finnegans Wake*: "Begin to forget it. It will remember itself from every sides, with all gestures, in each our word. [. . .] Forget, remember!" (FW 614.20–22). After all, Cixous and Derrida had met in French "turned towards the English. [. . .] A certain French ours, a certain English that of Joyce,"[23] to whom a renewed practice of reading could be imputed, as "délire plulire surlire souslire dublire [i.e., Dublin + *lire*] doublire [i.e., *double* + *lire*] oublire."[24]

Derrida's latest instance of writing-as-forgetreading is the now celebrated episode of the tallith, the silk prayer shawl "given to me by my mother's father":[25]

> It so happens that, two years ago, in a so-called autobiographical text entitled *Un ver à soie*, I devoted a long tender meditation to my tallith [. . .], to this prayer shawl, this white silk veil that my grandfather had given to me. [. . .] You can easily imagine that if I knew or if I recalled at the moment that there was a text by Hélène Cixous on the tallith, I would have done one of two things, believe me: either I would have abstained from speaking about mine or else I would have honestly referred to hers, all the more so since *Un Ver à soie* also talks about Hélène Cixous and about another of her texts, *Savoir*. And all the more so, especially, since my real tallith remains fully mine, in life, my father too, and so our respective stories as irreducible the one to the other as possible. To each his own father and to each his own mother. The real story of my tallith [. . .], all that did not need her in any way, apparently, did not need her own memory and even less what she could have written about it.
>
> This remains true but naturally I was in a state of absolute forgetreading, and just these past weeks, as I was rereading *La Baleine de Jonas*, which I must have, should have met some thirty-five years ago, well, I found, found again where I had not found it, a tallith, which has no reason to be jealous of mine which has every reason to be jealous of it. An entirely other tallith, sewn [*cousu*] entirely otherwise, but also related [*cousin*] to mine. (HC 154–55/133)

This belated avowal of forgotten antecedence reverses the filiation (*cousin*) and *filature* (*cousu*) that the semi-palindromic texts of Cixous' and Derrida's, "Savoir" and "Un Ver à soie," had woven two years before, according to a logic of obsequence posthumously recalled in *Insister*: "Là où si tu es je—je te suis"[26]; and *"Je suis le Ver."*[27] It also retrospectively casts the whole writing of "A Silkworm of One's Own" itself into a new light, as a serigraphy of sorts, that is, not only a writing on silk and silkworms, on oneself and/ as the other as (silk)worms, but as a writing so late, too late:

> Because I feel that the time of this verdict [. . .] is so paradoxical [. . .] that it could mime the quasi-resurrection of the new year only by sealing forever the "so late, too late" in what will not even be a late conversion. A "so late, too late, *sero*" (life will have been so short) [. . .]. Was it even to Christ that my poor old

incorrigible Augustine finally addressed his "too late," "so late" when he was speaking to beauty, *sero te amavi, pulchritudo tam antiqua et tam nova* . . . ? "So late have I loved thee, beauty so ancient and so new," or rather, because it is *already* late, "late *will* I have loved thee . . ." A future perfect is wrapped up in the past, once "late" means (as it always does, it's a tautology) "so late" and "too late." [. . .] "Late" is already said in the comparative, or even the absolute superlative, "late" always means "later than . . ." or "too late, absolutely."[28]

Cixous recalls this passage in *Insister*,[29] in a context evoking one of two sealed letters given to her by Derrida with the explicit injunction not to open them until *after* a certain publication, and whose formulation *après coup* reverses or unweaves the parsing of belatedness from superlative (too late) to positive (late) to relative (rather late) in Penelopean fashion:

I had thus hardly touched this textual tallith in an envelope. Forewarned. Thus would I have indeed read it "too late," as he intimated the order, too late that is to say late, that is to say rather late. [. . .]. I have just reread page 35 [of *Voiles*] twenty times.[30]

But Cixous' later restaging of the Derridean serigraphy or "séricifilage,"[31] including in her Penelopean unweaving of *sero*, is itself "obsequent" upon her own present confession, yet belated recognition, of a blind reading of "A Silkworm of One's Own":

I must reread *Voiles*, I said to myself. This immense text [. . .] I confess to myself not to have read it "so to speak." And why? And how? How did I "manage" to read it only in my absence so to speak, distractedly?
I who read all of Jacques Derrida's texts at least three times [*before, during and after publication*], then at least read thirty times, each text [. . .]. Except *Voiles*?[32]

Perhaps the reason why the ultimate absence/disappearance (cf. FW 420.19: "Initialled. Gee. Gone") or even nonexistence of a stable, signed (initialed) proto-letter in *Finnegans Wake* is masked by countless derivations is that, not unlike the complex scene of mutual blind forgetreadings and writings between Cixous and Derrida, we too, the text's producers-as-consumers (cf. FW 497.01–2), have never really begun to read—or have read late, too late, "from the antidulibnium [i.e., antediluvian] onto the serostaatarean" [i.e., *sero*, here applied to *Saorstát Éireann* or the Irish Free State] (FW 310.07–8).

The posthumous relays of co-production and consumption turn those textual palimpsests into the dead letters of a *poste restante* (cf. "ce goût de mort en poste restante"[33]) and our critical decipherings into post-scriptums at the bottom of forgotread documents. After all, in a footnote to the famous P.S. to her momentous *thèse d'état* called *L'Exil de James Joyce, ou l'Art du remplacement* on Thoth (the God of writing and hermeticism, also death via German *Tod*) and writing as poison or cure, did not Cixous already recall, thus anticipating the dense web of "quashed quotatoes" (FW 183.22) with Derrida by some thirty years by quoting his footnote within her footnote, that "Plato's Pharmacy" was "nothing more than a reading of *Finnegans Wake*, as the reader will quickly have realised"?[34] The cross-stitching of texts does not only have the effect of a *pharmakon*, whereby an "original text" is forever lost in the intertextual maze, but also that of a *serum*, (forget)read and written late, too late . . .

Notes

1. David Hayman and Elliott Anderson, ed., *In the Wake of the "Wake"* (Madison: University of Wisconsin Press, 1978), features a translated fragment from Cixous' 1976 novel *Partie* ([Paris: Des femmes, 1976], 95–100) after a brief introduction, in which one may record the following: "Since the publication of *Neutre* (Paris: Grasset, 1971), Cixous' writing has been marked by a distortion of normal syntax and an irreverence for morphemic integrity associated with the Joyce of the *Wake*" (95).

2. See also PSII 246–48, and also, about unconditional affirmation: "It is in effect nothing other than the affirmation of affirmation, the 'yes' to the originary 'yes' [. . .]" (AF 74/118).

3. Friedrich Nietzsche, *Thus Spoke Zarathustra*, trans. R. J. Hollingdale (Harmondsworth: Penguin, 1969) 321–22 (cf. also 212).

4. See also PSII 233–34/241–42 and also UG 64–65/108–9 and 69/118–19.

5. For some of these cross-lexical weavings, see Ian MacArthur, "The Complex Ass," *A Wake Newslitter* 13, 5 (October 1976), 92–94. MacArthur establishes a final parallel between Bruno's use of the ass and Joyce's via Frances Yates' statement in *Giordano Bruno and the Hermetic Tradition* that the ass is a symbol for "[t]he mystical Nothing beyond the Cabalist Sephiroth" (94).

6. In a recent article, Anne L. Cavender likewise developed the idea of the ass functioning as an inscription of the reader as a free creator, as opposed to the sterile old four interpreters MaMaLuJo. See "The Ass and The Four: Oppositional Figures for the Reader in *Finnegans Wake*," *James Joyce Quarterly* 41, 4 (Summer 2004), 665–87, 681–84.

7. See also "Nixnixundnix" (FW 415.29).

8. Unlike Cixous' "Conversation with the Donkey," where she denies *bêtise* ("duncity") to the animal, whom she links to her own yea-saying to the work of writing: "I am only an ideal donkey, I carry and I hear [*j'ouïs*] I admit my work is of acceptance" (Hélène Cixous, "Writing Blind: Conversation with the donkey,"

trans. Eric Prenowitz, *Stigmata: Escaping Texts* [London and New York: Routledge, 1998], 142).

9. See UG 68/115–16.

10. James Joyce, *Ulysses* (Harmondsworth: Penguin, 1971), 88. Gabler's edition follows the Rosenbach manuscript and reads "twice" instead of "tight" (U 6.9–10). Fritz Senn discusses this in "Righting *Ulysses*," *James Joyce: New Perspectives*, ed. Colin MacCabe (Bloomington: Indiana University Press; Sussex: Harvester, 1982), 3–27; 4; but see also the essay bearing the title "Dynamics of Corrective Unrest" in his *Joyce's Dislocutions: Essays on Reading as Translation*, ed. John Paul Riquelme (Baltimore: The Johns Hopkins University Press, 1984), 59–72.

11. Already about *Ulysses*, Derrida had rightly claimed that "All that can be said of *Ulysses*, for example, is already anticipated, including, as we saw, the scene of the academic competence and the ingenuity of meta-discourse" (UG 60/97).

12. See especially PC 333/353–54. I have commented on other aspects of the Derridean logic of obsequence in relation to animality in "Saint-Je Derrida," *Oxford Literary Review* 29 (June 2007), 55–76.

13. French insertions added. See also G 174bi/196bi and 257bi/286bi, and John P. Leavey Jr., *Glassary* (Lincoln: University of Nebraska Press, 1986), 106–8 and 115b.

14. The citation is from: Hélène Cixous, *OR les lettres de mon père* (Paris: Des femmes, 1997), 192.

15. Jorge Luis Borges, "Kafka and His Precursors," *Selected Non-Fictions*, ed. Eliot Weinberger; trans. Esther Allen, Suzanne Jill Levine, and Eliot Weinberger (New York: Viking, 1999), 363–65; 365.

16. "It is really as if I had never before written anything, or even known how to write [. . .]. Each time I begin a new text, however modest it may be, there is dismay in the face of the unknown or the inaccessible, an overwhelming feeling of clumsiness, inexperience, powerlessness. What I have already written is instantly annihilated or rather thrown overboard, as it were" (PI 352/363).

17. Jean Paris, *Univers parallèles II: Le point aveugle: Poésie, roman* (Paris: Seuil, 1975), 223–35.

18. "When I sign, I am already dead. I hardly have the time to sign than I am already dead, that I am already dead. I have to abridge the writing, hence the siglum, because the structure of the 'signature' event carries my death in that event. For which it is not an 'event' and perhaps signifies nothing, writes out of a past that has never been present and out of a death that has never been alive. To write for the dead, out of them, who have never been alive [. . .]" (G 19bi/26bi). And about the signature in "Ulysses Gramophone": "A signature is always a 'yes, yes,' the *synthetic* performative of a promise and of a memory that makes any commitment possible" (UG 58/94–95, see also UG 74/125–26).

19. Jacques Derrida, "Circonfession," in Geoffrey Bennington and Jacques Derrida, *Jacques Derrida*, trans. Geoffrey Bennington (Chicago: University of Chicago Press, 1993), 26, translation of *Jacques Derrida* (Paris: Seuil, 1991), 28.

20. Cixous, OR, 16, translation mine.

21. Ibid., 199; cf. EO 11/23–24.

22. This was chosen as the theme of a conference in which both Cixous and Derrida were originally scheduled to take part, organized by Marta Segarra in

Aiguablava in June 2005. See *L'Événement comme écriture: Cixous et Derrida se lisant,* ed. Marta Segarra (Paris: Campagne Première, 2007), in particular my essay "Entre eux deux: le traductor," 303–14.

23. Hélène Cixous, *Insister: A Jacques Derrida* (Paris: Galilée, 2006), 16, translation mine.

24. Ibid., 24, in connection with Derrida's "Voilà lire voile à lire," referring to *Voiles*.

25. Jacques Derrida, "A Silkworm of One's Own," *Veils*, trans. Geoffrey Bennington (Stanford: Stanford University Press, 2001), 44, translation of "Un Ver à soie," *Voiles* (Paris: Galilée, 1998), 44. In *Insister*, Cixous brackets off "le père de" when she quotes this passage from their earlier double session (102).

26. Cixous, *Insister*, 40.

27. Ibid., 66. See my "Portrait of H. C. as J. D. and Back," *New Literary History* 37, 1 (Winter 2006), 65–84.

28. Derrida, "Silkworm," 33/35.

29. Cixous, *Insister*, 76–77.

30. Ibid., 76, translation mine.

31. Ibid., 17.

32. Ibid., 75, translation mine.

33. Ibid., 83.

34. Hélène Cixous, *The Exile of James Joyce*, trans. Sally A. J. Purcell (New York: David Lewis, 1972), 744, n. 8, translation of *L'Exil de James Joyce* (Paris: Grasset, 1968), 841, n. 8. The Derrida citation is DI 88 fn. 20/99 fn. 17.

7

JJ, JD, TV

Louis Armand

At the time when James Joyce's *Finnegans Wake* was published, on May 4, 1939, Europe, indeed the world, was, as we all know, on the verge of radical, unprecedented change; social, political, technological. It was to be the crisis of civilization toward which the Enlightenment and the Industrial Revolution had so inexorably appeared to be tending: the great dialectical moment of modern history, ushered in by global warfare, mass eugenics, and the comprehensive destruction of the existing order. Yet, as Walter Benjamin notoriously surmised in 1937, the most pressing crisis confronting "modern man" at the outbreak of World War II was considered in certain quarters to be one arising not from the immanence of world war, but through a transformation of critical perception announced by way of technology and the detached experience of aesthetic gratification arising from it. "This is evidently the consummation of *l'art pour l'art*. Mankind," wrote Benjamin, "which in Homer's time was an object of contemplation for the Olympian gods, now is one for itself. Its self-alienation has reached such a degree that it can experience its own destruction as an aesthetic pleasure of the first degree."[1]

With the end of World War II came the dawning of the computer age, the atomic age, the age of satellites, television, and new global networks of communication. The age, as Guy Debord would later write, of *spectacle*, whose operations would both absorb and, in a sense, compute the totality of human experience in part, as Benjamin foresaw, by means of a type of techno-aestheticism reprising, to varying degrees, the technological irrationalism of Oswald Spengler.[2] War, likewise totalizing, itself became the paradigm of a type of monstrous cognition, a matrix of nihilistic and suppressed rationales that stood in place of Civilization's "unthought." In it could be seen a technological determinism struggling with its own irrationality—the whole unconscious drama of the Enlightenment, in fact—in which the "logic of the machine" came increasingly to confront within itself a certain "logic of the event." Lewis Mumford, an important commentator on the progress of modern technology, characterized this "crisis of civilization" as the culminating evolutionary struggle of the paleotechnic and the neotechnic. "The state of the paleotechnic society," Mumford wrote in 1934, "may be described, ideally, as *wardom*. Its typical organs, from mine to factory, from blast furnace to slum, from slum to battlefield, were at the service of death. Competition: struggle for existence: domination and submission: extinction."[3]

> The machine—the outcome of man's impulse to conquer his environment and to canalise his random impulses into orderly activities—produced during the paleotechnic phase the systematic negation of all its characteristics [. . .]. With war at once the main stimulus, the underlying basis, and the direct destination of this [paleotechnic] society, the normal motives and reactions of human beings were narrowed down to the desire for domination and the fear of annihilation.[4]

For Mumford, a "neotechnic" phase had begun to emerge after 1832, the date of Fourneyron's perfection of the water turbine, anticipating the later work of Volta and Faraday on electricity, and providing the basis, ultimately, for what is sometimes referred to as post-industrialism. Broadly speaking, the neotechnic "erected a new basis for the conversion and distribution of energy"[5] whose latter-day analogue will be in the conversion and distribution of *information*—tending toward the cybernetics of Claude Shannon, Alan Turing, Norbert Wiener, and Gregory Bateson. However, the neotechnic firstly begins to be realized in "a series of complementary inventions, the phonograph, the moving picture, the gasoline engine, the steam turbine, the airplane"[6]—from the telegraph to the automatic telephone and thence onward to television and the future promise of a fully integrated, pan-sensory telecommunication and/or tele-entertainment and consumption system. Yet it is precisely at this nexus that we find "the arts of enlightened behaviour and orderly communication," as Mumford refers to them in *The Condition of Man*,[7] inwardly transformed into new arts of simulationism and of the universal language of "spectacle."

At the time James Joyce was completing *Finnegans Wake*, no certainty existed as to the future evolution of technology and the arts, and the inexorability of global crisis did not appear to be that of a historical necessity, let alone of scientific progressivism. As Mumford relates, "Right down to the World War an unwillingness to avail itself of scientific knowledge or to promote scientific research characterized paleotechnic industry throughout the world."[8] In 1935, Jean Dusailly complained about "la campaigne contra la télévision,"[9] reprising a growing indignation at the abuse of patent laws and monopolistic practice to inhibit the development of new technologies, from the automatic telephone to FM radio. And yet, despite this "paleotechnic" inertia, the implications of these new technologies were still clearly delineated in the minds of those who—like Joyce—saw in them, not future instruments of negation but rather of invention and of the *possible* per se. The "miracles of television," as they were called at the time, were already being thought of by Dusailly and his contemporaries (who coordinated early TV broadcasts in Paris from the Eiffel Tower) as directly analogous to those of Gutenberg's printing press and the advent of linotype.[10] With the addition of hindsight, postwar "media" theorists like Marshall McLuhan could also assert that, with the widespread emplacement of television and broadcast networks, Western consciousness in the second half of the twentieth century had indeed undergone a paradigm shift commensurate with that brought about by the advent of the Gutenberg printing press in the fourteenth. McLuhan's *Understanding Media* spoke of the "extensions of man" beyond the literacy-consciousness of formerly "typographical man,"[11] while anthropologists such as Bateson coined terms like "schismogenesis" to account for the broadly synaesthetic and syncretistic character of experience everywhere made evident in the structures of the new globalized media.[12]

Such is in part the context in which *Finnegans Wake*, arguably the most contestable and contesting language experiment to have been undertaken in modern times, was conceived. Indeed, the importance of this "context" and the integral relation of the *Wake* to it, had led the late Donald Theall, a former collaborator with McLuhan, to speak of a "Joyce Era" of "technology, culture and communication,"[13] while McLuhan's now canonical text, *The Gutenberg Galaxy*, "a book which redirected the way many theorists viewed the role of technological mediation in communication processes," itself had its origin in McLuhan's desire to write a book called *The Road to Finnegans Wake*.[14] For Theall and McLuhan, Joyce's writing, above all the *Wake*, is emblematic of a technopoetic transformation, not only encapsulating the sense of a new "era," but in fact mediating our understanding of this era and of its consequences for contemporary culture. In this way *Finnegans Wake* can be regarded as a type of matrix. As Geoffrey Bennington has similarly noted in regard to the work of the late twentieth century's major philosopher, Jacques Derrida: "It is not at all by chance that Derrida talks of Joyce's book in terms of supercomputers, nor that his thought should communicate in an essential way with certain discourses on so-called artificial intelligence."[15] Theall makes an analogous point:

> *Finnegans Wake* signalizes a whole new relationship with language, with audience, and with the everyday world. Joyce anticipated the age of the microcomputer and the micro's easy relationship with

telecommunications, while also dramatizing certain developments which were and would be taking place in poetry and the arts as a result of the dramatic socio-economic, cultural and technological changes which had started in the mid-nineteenth century.[16]

The *Wake* similarly figures in Claude Shannon's postwar framing of "information theory" and Charles Ogden's experiments with Basic English,[17] while Nobel physicist Murray Gell-Mann turned to the *Wake* in 1963 when seeking a name to designate the fundamental constituent of the nucleon.[18] But it is more than simply historical coincidence or literary curiosity that causes us to view Joyce's text as somehow pivotal in terms of the paradigm shift related by Mumford, McLuhan, Theall, and others. Joyce's direct interest and involvement with early cinema is well attested (in 1909 Joyce opened the first cinematograph in Ireland, named appropriately enough the Volta), while references to almost all facets of communication technology can be found throughout Joyce's writings and have been duly noted by several of Joyce's commentators. It is hardly surprising that Joyce's library (now archived at Buffalo) included the first number of the technical journal *Télévision Magazine* (subtitled *revue mensuelle de vulgarization* and in which Dusailly's article appears) published in 1935. Allusions to several other articles from *Télévision* significantly resurface—for example—in book II.3 of *Finnegans Wake* where, as Theall notes, "complex puns involving terminology associated with the technical details of TV transmission" abound,[19] including references to cathode tubes, carrier waves, "syncopanc pulses," amplifiers, transmitters, and static interference (FW 349). Nor is it surprising that the first editorial for *Télévision* should compare the advent of television in 1925 to the invention of the first stone tools, signaling the dawn of a new age and of a new awareness.

However, the significance of communication technologies for Joyce goes beyond the merely thematic or artefactual. As Theall has pointed out, along with *Ulysses*, "*Finnegans Wake* is one of the first major poetic encounters with the challenge that electronic media present to the traditionally accepted relationship between speech, script and print." Hence: "Beginning with gesture, hieroglyph and rune, Joyce traces human communication through its complex, labyrinthine development, right down to the TV and what it bodes for the future."[20] The status of communication technology is vested, for Joyce, not in the prosthetic "extensions of man" (in the sense of a technē *added* or *applied* to an existing state of affairs), but rather in the "human condition itself"—one which, constituted in and through "modes of semiotic production," is implicit to any "experience of the real."[21]

This experiential character of Joyce's engagement with the question of technology is made evident, for Theall, in the way *Finnegans Wake* presents itself as "a polysemic, encyclopaedic book designed to be read with the simultaneous involvement of ear and eye." Or as Joyce says: "What can't be coded can be decorded if an ear aye seize what no eye ere grieved for" (FW 482.34–36). Moreover, Theall argues, "it is also a self-reflexive book about the role of the book in the electro-mechanical world of the new technology."[22] In this sense, *Finnegans Wake* is taken to "function" as a metonymy of what Joyce calls the "reel world," in which technicity, mimesis, and hermeneutics are inextricably entangled in what, paradoxically, we might refer to as the essentially teletechnological character of the "real."[23]

Speaking at the Ninth International James Joyce Symposium in Frankfurt in 1984, Jacques Derrida—whose own work attests to a profound indebtedness to Joyce—opened a discussion on the particular relation of communication, transmission, and the supposed "crisis" of representation symptomatic of the contest between the paleotechnic and the neotechnic, between natural language and technology, between the real and the spectacle. Recalling his earlier work on "grammatology," Derrida's lecture—"Ulysses Gramophone: Hear Say Yes in Joyce"—elaborates a fundamental ambivalence in Joyce's texts toward the received orality/literacy dichotomy (amplified in the very structure of Joyce's language, above all in its generalized paronomasia, *as well as* in its conceptualization of a digital "telegraphic" poetics as a writing *of* radiotelevisuality) along with its co-implication in the structural logics of mimesis. Among other things, Derrida's lecture interrogated the notion of *presence* as always already a type of *tele*presence or, as he later suggested, *telepathy*,[24] whereby the significative event is put into a particular kind of remote communication with its phenomenal (phono-graphic) counterpart—its *sense*—implying that the underwriting principle of any system of sign operations is not that of a transitively intending, self-evident, self-verifying agency, but rather a "technē" of mediality and distanciation. Meaning: of *equivalence across contiguity*, and hence the investment of any essence by a generalized teletechnology.[25] For Derrida, this distanciation and teletechnology marks out a fundamental ambivalence—what Joyce calls ambiviolence ("ambiviolent," FW 518.02])—in the material structures of signification, commencing with the "verbivocovisual" effects of synaesthesia that elsewhere supply Derrida's notions of equivocation and *différance*, linked as they are to a critical conception of "virtual reality" and a Batesonian "semiotic ecology of communication."[26] Subsequently, these interrogations of structural ambivalence in Joyce have been further pursued by critics like Theall, notably with regard to Joyce's increasingly explicit play on the "tele-" prefix, particularly in *Finnegans Wake* and the coincidence of gesture and speech in Joyce's conception of writing.

Derrida, for whom "even in academic things, Joyce's ghost is always coming on board" (TW 27/27), had by 1984 already drawn extensively upon Joyce's work in elaborating a body of textual theory that has come to be known as "deconstruction," beginning in 1962 with his introduction to *Edmund Husserl's Origin of Geometry*, though most notably exemplified in later volumes such as *The Post Card* (1980) and in essays such as "Two Words for Joyce" (1982) and "Des Tours de Babel" (1985). In his lecture on *Ulysses*, however, Derrida began to take stock of the particularly technological characteristics of Joyce's language in ways that extended his previous treatment of "writing" and writing machines vis-à-vis Freud, Plato, Nietzsche, and Philippe Sollers. Coining the term "telegramophonic" (UG 51/78), Derrida attempted to delineate in Joyce's text a certain *mark* "that is both spoken and written, vocalized as grapheme and written as phoneme [. . .] *in a word gramophoned*" (UG 49/75–76). This ambivalence, in the "*double focus*" (FW 349.13) of the phonic and graphemic, comes to approximate a mechanical signal or "quasi-signal," a "mimetic-mechanical double" of what is called language, and which assumes the surface appearance of a "narrative metonymy" (UG 55–56/86–87). That is to say, in place of something like a paradigm or referent, what is called "language" mimes the recursive event of signification "itself"; of its fundamental ambivalence and arbitrary "determinism." Hence the generalized paronomasia and synaesthesia of Joyce's text counters "the hegemony or the supremacy of one sense over the other" often localized in phenomenology.[27] (Indeed, in later writings Derrida returns to the *critical* nature of this "countering" in positioning it clearly within the "humanistic struggle for power," in the neglect of the prosthetic and synaesthetic dimensions of perception, and above all in the philosophical neglect of teletechnology and "virtualization" at precisely the time these had come to invest the entire field of cultural and scientific inquiry.) Radicalized in *Finnegans Wake*, this effect implies what Derrida terms a "*remote control* technology," directed not by some rational agent or even a programed deus ex machina, but rather an implied (binary) "control mechanism," a type of "ambiviolent" homoeostat mechanism, which gives rise to an other type of "text"—one which places in question the "TELEOLOGICUM" (FW 264.R1). In this way Derrida's "mimetic, mechanical double" extends to the recurring phenomenon of twins and correlatives in Joyce's text, to the labile or "paradoxical" status of Joyce's so-called portmanteau words, and to the structural recursions and doublings of the Joycean schematic taken "as a whole."

It is with regard to the irreducibility of this ambiviolence that Derrida situates the tele-effect of distanciation, "telephonic spacing," and "remote control" characteristic of what Derek Attridge has described as the "singularity of Joyce's text" and "its encyclopaedic ambitions"; "its simultaneous foregrounding of complex connectedness and chance collocations"; and its "involvement with communication networks" that are at once "unique and programmable."[28] *Ulysses* and *Finnegans Wake* are thus jointly conceived as what Derrida terms a "hypermnesic machine capable of storing in a giant epic work, with the memory of the West and virtually all the languages of the world, *the very traces of the future*" (UG 60/98)—something that Paul Virilio, speaking elsewhere of television, has referred to as a "museum of accidents."[29]

This is not to say that Joyce's texts assume an oracular or "inspired" status—with regard to the future technological condition of man, for example—but rather that they foreground the necessary relation to futurity conditional for any type of sign operation. Equally, this does not mean a relation of a present "here and now" to what is yet "to come," so to speak, but rather, within the structure of what is gathered under the constellation of the present, the implied futurity of its own condition, i.e., of what renders it possible, or at least delineates it in relation to a *horizon of possibility*, however tentative, contingent, or speculative "it" may be. Such a forethrow, or *prosthesis*, within the logic and structure of the "present"—its singularity and encyclopedic totality—characterizes for Derrida the ambivalent status of the singular event as something simultaneously *experienced* and *signified*. Consequently, Derrida argues: "Only another event can sign, or countersign to bring it about that an event has already happened. This event, which one naïvely calls the first event, can only affirm itself through the confirmation of the other: a wholly other [*tout autre*] event" (UG 81/143).

In a series of television interviews with Bernard Stiegler, conducted in 1993 and published in 1996 as *Échographies de la télévision*, Derrida goes on to elaborate this event-state ambivalence in terms of a "technological process" that "takes the general form of expropriation, dislocation, deterritorialization."[30] Signifiability, we might say, is constituted *only* in this teleeffect, this distanciation and threat of expropriation of the present "time of the event"—i.e., of the identity, coincidence, or simultaneity of so-called signifier and signified, of transmission and reception, of medium and message.[31] "Even if this expropriation can at times produce the opposite effect," Derrida argues, "the global and dominant effect of television, the telephone, the fax machine, satellites, the accelerated circulation of images, discourse, etc., is that the *here-and-now* becomes uncertain, without guarantee [. . .]. This is nothing new. It has always been this way."[32]

The system of teletechnology has always, in a sense, been "in place"—its event testified to by the very fact that language, signification, semiosis, has always somehow been in receipt of itself, from the very first visuotelephony; the first transmission of supposed "sense data"; the first act of consciousness; the first reflex. Its recursive structure is thus also that of an "agent"—whether an agent of transmission, or the so-called initiating agent of the technological "process" itself. Moreover, as a technē of spatiotemporalization, this "agent" also describes a technē of supercession—of ellipsis and recursion—across what we might call a transmissive gap: "from one singularity to another," as Derrida says, "by way of a filiation *implying language*."³³ In other words, of a supersession and metonymic forethrow within the logic and structure of the event, of the present. Joyce writes: "Doth it not all come aft to you, puritysnooper, is the way television opes longtimes ofter" (FW 254.21–22). As though illustrating Derrida's Joycean theory, the recursive supersession implied here in the filiation of "aft" and "often" is not simply *characteristic* of a generalized technē of inscription, but marks a teletechnological *condition*—according to which the coincidence of *aft* and *oft* could be said to mime the effect of a "repetition machine"³⁴ productive of a "future writing": a "tele-vision" that is also a "Tell ever so often" (FW 338.09) and a "Till even so aften" (FW 338.14)—the visual, for Joyce, always being *synaesthetic*.

For Derrida, as for Joyce, this teletropic relation remains one of radical ambivalence—in that, between the one and the other (the event and its technological antecedence), "we" will never be able to decide for both. The transmissive "event" is in essence already an effect of the transmission "itself": it has no prior status, no prior determination, outside this mode of supersession, and remains—as Joyce says—"Inexcessible" (FW 285.28): both inaccessible as such, and always in-excess of itself. It is important to note that supersession here does not mean the lineaments of a historical, teleological process marked by successive stages of redundancy, but rather a principle of mutual exclusion which seems to affect the reduction of signifying "potential" to a determinate "state," a *one or the other*—despite this "potentiality" being, as the *Wake* says, "ambivalent to the fixation of his pivotism" (FW 164.03). What this also implies is a mode of reduction that might, though only nominally, be characterized as a decision, and according to which language would be viewed, for example, as a "montage of discrete elements"³⁵ (provided, of course, that we attend to the arbitrary and procedural nature of any *decision-making agent* implied here). Indeed, in the "multidimensional media" of Joyce's paronomastic text, it may be that there is no agent of reduction (no "will") *other* than the mechanism of ambivalence itself. As Joyce writes:

> 'by Allswill' the inception and the descent and the endswell of Man is temporally wrapped in obscenity, looking through at these accidents with the faroscope of television, (this nightlife instrument needs still some suntractional betterment in the readjustment of the more refrangible angles to the squeals of his hypothesis on the outer tin sides), I can easily believe heartily in my own most spacious immensity as my ownhouse and microbemost cosm when I

am reassured by ratio that the cube of my volume is to the surfaces of their subjects as the, sphericity of these globes [. . .] is to the feracity of Fairynelly's vacuum. (FW 150.30–151.07)

The "gramophoning," as Derrida says, of *Allswill* and *endswell*—like *oft* and *aft*—implies both an impossible phono-graphic correspondence while miming, as it were, an effect of instantaneous transmission in the intertwining of their supposed referents, in which agency or "will" approximates its own "ends," thereby defining a ratio which is no longer that of *reason* as such but of a tropic spatiotemporalization, of metaphor and metonymic recursion, or else of a stochastic "resemblance" between quasi-signifiers, ranging on a scale of coincidence between one and zero.

Like the Darwinian accidents of the *Descent of Man*—with its statistical, genetic readjustments, its implied law of averages and standard deviation, and its suggestion of a type of materialist veracity underwriting the human hypothesis—Joyce's TV analogue *operates* by ambiviolences (not a consummated, *selective* violence, but radical *ambivalence*; violence without agency, violence of the *to come*). Early in *Finnegans Wake* we find: "Television kills telephony in brothers' broil" (FW 52.18), a forecast of the "tellavicious" slapstick comedy of Butt and Taff, whose account of how "Buckley shot the Russian general" (referring to an incident of the Crimean War) descends into generalized strife among a series of unstable TV images described as a "*charge of the light barricade*" (echoing Tennyson's "Charge of the Light Brigade") on the "*bairdboard bombardment screen* [alluding to the invention of television by John Logie Baird in 1925]" (FW 349.08–10). The later fusing of Private Buckley with Bishop Berkeley, whose popularized dictum—*esse est percipi*—links a theory of haptic vision to the notion of mind-dependent ideas, and what we might call a *prosthesis of perception* or telepresence, as the underwriting of a metaphysics of being or knowing—likewise "anticipates" the advent of the moving picture and television broadcast, as direct technological outcomes of the pioneering of photography and the first wartime usage of the photographic medium during the Crimean campaign by Roger Fenton in 1855 (whose best-known print is entitled, incidentally, *The Valley of the Shadow of Death*). The genealogy of film photography—from the motion studies of Eadweard Muybridge, and by way of Étienne Jules Marey and Charles Fremont's chronophotographs of the 1880s (using a camera rifle to "shoot" multiple-exposure images of moving objects), to Frank B. Gilbreth's cyclographs, Edison's kinetoscope, and the first celluloid film projections of the Latham and Lumière brothers in 1895—can also be seen as one tied to a conception of *animation*, in which the static image firstly analyzes motion and is then serialized in order to produce an appreciable illusion of motion by way of various techniques of enframing—and later "teleframing."

As McLuhan and Theall have pointed out, Joyce's text contains numerous possible allusions to the history of communication technologies, in particular image transmission, from the myth of Butades' invention of the "mnemotechnic of drawing" (as sciagraphy or shadow-tracing),[36] to the late nineteenth- and twentieth-century inventions of radiovision, visuotelephony, telephotography, radiodiffusion, and phototelegraphy. Joyce's allusions draw upon many likely sources, including J. Davoust's 1933 *Système de la Télévision* and C. Dulac's *Télévision et Télécinéma*. Many such allusions—including references to transmissional "parasites," antennae, base-frequency transformations, receivers, Soviet animation, rates and ratios of television transmissions, optics, and Michael Faraday's experiments with vacuum discharge tubes ("Fairynelly's vacuum")—find their possible *avant-textes* in the technical literature Joyce read around 1935 and appear with highest frequency (but not at all exclusively) in the five so-called "Butt and Taff" broadcasts in the *Wake*—principally in the bracketed, italicized text beginning on page 349—including references to fades and optical transformations, Philo Farnsworth's groundbreaking sixty-line image transmission, Karl Ferdinand Braun's CRT oscilloscope, and the "electron guns" and "scanning beams" of Vladimir Zworykin's (1923) cathode tube kinescope and imaging iconoscope:

> In the heliotropic noughttime following a fade of transformed Tuff and, pending its viseversion, a metenergic reglow of beaming Batt, the bairdboard bombardment screen, if tastefully taut guranium satin, tends to teleframe and step up to the charge of the light barricade. Down the photslope in syncopanc pulses, with the bitts bugtwug ther teffs, the missledhopes, glitteraglatteraglutt, borne by their carnier walve. Spraygun rakes and splits them from a double focus: grenadite, damnymite, alextronite, nichilite: and the scanning firespot of the sgunners traverses the rutilanced illustrated sunksundered lines. Shlossh! A gaspel truce leaks out over the caesine coatings. Amid a fluorescence of spectracular mephiticism there coagulates through the inconoscope steadily a still, the figure of a fellow chap in the wohly ghast. (FW 349.06–19)

Later in the *Wake* the light storm of this bairdboard bombardment screen's static interference becomes a "claractinism" (FW 611.31)—a cataclysm and visual *cataract*,[37] as well as a reference to the Latin *clarus* ("clear") and to the thirteenth-century Saint Clare of Assisi (named, by Pope Pius XII, patroness of television, "this nightlife instrument," on the basis of Clare's supposed remote visioning, while bedridden, of a Midnight Mass performed in her convent chapel: "*a fellow chap in the wohly ghast*")—pointing to the fact that what we call "resolution," or indeed "definition," is characterized both by unverifiablity, catachresis, and a type of statistical outcome (a coagulating *fluorescence of spectracular mephiticism*); as likely and as precarious, in a sense, as language itself.

For Joyce, the "miraculous broadcast" and transmission effect of this "midden Erse clare language" (FW 448.25) always involves a "comprehendurient" (FW 611.31), a difficulty with "sense" that does not resolve itself but constantly *evolves*—which is to say, it pursues a constant and "irrational" struggle; a forethrow, a reflexive distanciation in which the "stereotypopticus" of writing is paradoxically prefigured in the "faroscope" of televisual transmissionality. (Evolution, it is necessary to recall, is not an intention directed toward some future advent, but a series of contingencies "materializing" at the horizon of possibility.) As a type of "future writing," *Finnegans Wake* not merely prefigures the radical transformations of television, but, as Derrida argues, achieves in itself a kind of teletechnological extension (hence also invention) of language itself. Between Baird's transmissions of crude outline images and the advent of TV as a global medium in the 1950s, Joyce's text "intervenes" as something like an agent of transmission. It functions, we might say, as a matrix of coincidence, accidence, and chance; a "hypermnesiac machine" productive of that "consensual hallucination," as McLuhan says, of "technological determinacy."

"Who," *Finnegans Wake* asks, "is the sender of the Hullo Eve Cenograph in prose?" (FW 488.25). As a "gramophonic" transmission that is both *without reason* and empty (*cenos*) of a determinate sense, Joyce's text points toward a radical "viseversion" ambivalence in the very structure of transmissibility—wherein the nonpresence of either sender or receiver represents not an aporia of signification, but rather its condition: the conjoint trope of equivalence and equivocation in the structure of identity as present-being. "Sending," as Derrida has suggested, in this way implies an act of expropriation, according to which the function of agency—of an assumed rational actor, or sender-as-such—is dispersed in the generality of the text "itself"—which is to say, it is *broadcast*—its filiations disseminated and generalized in the expropriation of its "own" signal identity (MP 313/372). As a type of globalized telesystem, *Finnegans Wake* is not simply a moment, as it were, in the transformation of literary or aesthetic consciousness brought about by consequence of new communication technologies, but rather itself an "agent" of transformation of the very *idea* of identity: of consciousness, of agency, and of signification as such.

Notes

1. Walter Benjamin, "The Work of Art in the Age of Mechanical Reproduction," *Illuminations*, trans. Harry Zohn (London: Fontana, 1995), 217–51; 242.
2. Guy Debord, *The Society of the Spectacle*, trans. Donald Nicholson-Smith (New York: Zone Books, 1995 [1967]), §6.
3. Lewis Mumford, *Technics and Civilsation* (London: Harcourt, Brace and World, 1934), 194–95; emphasis added.
4. Ibid., 195.
5. Ibid., 214.
6. Ibid., 214.
7. Lewis Mumford, *The Condition of Man* (London: Secker and Warburg, 1944), 412.
8. Mumford, *Technics*, 194.
9. J. Dusailly, "Vers une télévision française," *Télévision Magazine* 1 (1935), 6–8, 6.
10. Ibid., 8.
11. Marshall McLuhan, *Understanding Media: The Extensions of Man* (New York: McGraw-Hill, 1964). See also McLuhan, *The Gutenberg Galaxy: The Making of Typographic Man* (Toronto: University of Toronto Press, 1962).
12. Gregory Bateson, "Culture Contact and Schismogenesis," *Man* 35 (1935):, 178–83; rpt. *Steps to an Ecology of Mind* (St Albans: Paladin, 1973), 61–87.
13. Donald F. Theall, *Beyond the Word: Reconstructing Sense in the Joyce Era of Technology, Culture and Communication* (Toronto: Toronto University Press, 1995).
14. See Donald Theall, "Beyond the Orality/Literacy Dichotomy: James Joyce and the Pre-History of Cyberspace," *Postmodern Culture* 2, 3 (1992). Online.
15. Geoffrey Bennington, "Derridabase," in Geoffrey Bennington and Jacques Derrida, *Jacques Derrida*, trans. Geoffrey Bennington (Chicago: University of Chicago Press, 1993), 314, translation of *Jacques Derrida* (Paris: Éditions du Seuil, 1991), 290.
16. Theall, *Beyond the Word*, xiii.
17. See Claude Shannon, "A Mathematical Theory of Communication," *Bell System Technical Journal* 27 (July 1948) 379–423; 394. It is worth noting that Ogden attempted a partial translation into Basic English of the "Anna Livia Plurabelle" section of *Finnegans Wake* in *transition* 21 (March 1932). In August 1929, Ogden, an authority on the influence of language upon thought and founder of the Orthological Institute in London, had persuaded Joyce to come to the institute to record the last pages of "Anna Livia." This represents the only known recording of Joyce reading from the *Wake*.
18. The word "quarks" appears at the beginning of chapter II.4 of Joyce's text (FW 383.01), and Gell-Mann relates this episode in his own book *The Quark and the Jaguar* (New York: W.H. Freeman and Co., 1994), 180.
19. Donald F. Theall, *James Joyce's Techno-Poetics* (Toronto: University of Toronto Press, 1997), 66.
20. Theall, "Literacy/Orality," 5, 13.
21. Ibid., 32. In his 1905 Pola Notebook, Joyce disputes the notion of technē as artificial, arguing that Aristotle's *"e tekhnê mimeitai ten physin"* had been falsely

rendered as "Art is an imitation of Nature." Joyce: "Aristotle does not here define art, he says only 'Art imitates nature' and meant the artistic process is like the natural process" (CW 145).

22. Theall, "Literacy/Orality," 6.

23. This distinction echoes that employed by Edmund Husserl in the *Logical Investigations* (1900–1901), vis-à-vis the terms *real* and *reell*, "the former connoting what is actually there in the space-time world, and not abstract or ideal, the latter what is actually immanent in an experience, and not merely 'meant' by it" (*Logical Investigations*, trans. J. N. Findlay [Amherst: Humanity Books, 2000], II.437, vol. II, ch. 1, §2).

24. See Jacques Derrida, "Telepathy" (PSI 226–61/237–70).

25. According to Theall, Joyce's own use of the term technê works against any such oppositional tendency, emphasizing a "machinic" aspect inherent in nature, not as a prosthesis, as Aristotle suggests, "to produce what nature does not produce," but as the basis of production itself. Yet if Joyce viewed nature as "machinic," that is not to say that nature is "technologized," or that it is *subject* to technology, nor that technics is "organicized," which would simply introduce a reversible mimetic element, oriented, once more, by the exteriorization of one of its terms. According to Theall: "Joyce associates art as *technê* with the artist as a constructor and, recognizing the classical affinity of the arts and the proto-technology of the crafts, he carries his conception of the artist as engineer forward into the post-Enlightenment eras of mechanization and electrification. But a post-technological assembler is of necessity a comic, satiric parodist. While Joyce is intrigued by tools and machines of electricity and photochemistry, his satiric critique is directed towards the spirit of technology and the fetishization of organization" (Theall, *Techno-Poetics*, 8–9).

26. Theall, "Literacy/Orality," 33.

27. Jacques Derrida, "In Blind Sight: Writing, Seeing, Touching . . . ," *Deconstruction Engaged: The Sydney Seminars*, ed. Paul Patton and Terry Smith (Sydney: Power Publications, 2001), 13–30; 21.

28. Derek Attridge, introduction to "Ulysses Gramophone," *Acts of Literature*, ed. Derek Attridge (New York: Routledge, 1992), 253–56; 255.

29. Paul Virilio, *Unknown Quantity*, trans. Chris Turner (New York: Thames and Hudson, 2003), 58–65.

30. Jacques Derrida and Bernard Stiegler, *Echographies of Television*, trans. Jennifer Bajorek (Cambridge: Polity, 2002), 79, translation of *Échographies de la télévision* (Paris: Galilée, 1996), 91.

31. The question of transmission, so vexed in Shannon's mathematical theory of communication, and entirely omitted from Saussure's published *Course on General Linguistics* (1916), returns elsewhere in Saussure's manuscripts to further complicate the problem of communication "modeling." The "sign," as a type of homeostat mechanism, may by consequence of rethinking the status of transmission, be viewed both as an engine of information *and* of entropy—in other words of *dynamic structure*.

32. Derrida, *Echographies*, 79/91.

33. Ibid., 86/99; emphasis added.

34. Ibid., 89/102.

35. Ibid., 59/70.

36. See Jacques Derrida, *Memoires of the Blind: The Self-Portrait and Other Ruins*, trans. Pascale-Anne Brault and Michael Naas (Chicago: University of Chicago Press, 1993), translation of *Mémoires d'aveugle. L'Autoportrait et autres ruines* (Paris: Louvre, Réunion des musées nationaux, 1990).

37. "TV is 'non visual' as Joyce understood from careful analysis. . . . It is a 'blind' medium, fostering inner trips and hallucinations . . ." (Marshall McLuhan, letter to Donald Theall, 6 August 1970); Donald F. Theall, *The Virtual Marshall McLuhan* (Montreal: McGill-Queen's University Press, 2001), 218–19.

8

"MEMEMORMEE":
NOTES ON DERRIDA'S RE-MARKINGS OF DESIRE AND MEMORY IN JOYCE

Alan Roughley

Derrida responds to Joyce's call for remembrance in specific textual acts of recalling, remembering, and reinscribing. He analyzes and deconstructs Joyce's texts and then re-members them, gathering scions or slips from Joyce and grafting them into his own scenes of writing. Joyce and Derrida: not the writers themselves but the writings signed with their proper names (which are simultaneously threatened, if not ruined, by the writings to which they are appended as signatures). This chapter situates itself between, and/or *entre*, Derrida and Joyce. It follows the mapping of desire signed by Jacques Lacan as it moves between the traces of desire and memory in the language of both writers. It explores and exploits the writing sites (and citations) between Joyce and Derrida where memory and desire, and the relationships between these forces, are doubled in a remarking of the intertextual writings and textual echoing between them. Remarking the themes and the doubling(s) of memory and desire in Joyce and Derrida requires an investigative analysis of the writing(s) between them as mediating mediums of exchange and translation between the two forces as Derrida regards, remembers, translates, and remarks Joyce's desire, folding its traces back and doubling them in(to) his own writings.

Patterns of circularity and return have long been an important focal point of writings on Joyce's last two major texts. Leopold Bloom's circuitous perambulations around Dublin restage Odysseus' return to Ithaca, and the natural cycles of rainfall, river flow to sea, and subsequent evaporation and rainfall provide one of the dominant metaphors for the movements of language in *Finnegans Wake*. While it works for the diagram of ALP in "Nightlessons," the geometrical model of the circle is too precise for the circuitous patterns of repetition and return operating in the narratives of Joyce's writings, so the model of cycles, rather than circles, has frequently been used as a way of investigating these processes of return. Northrop Frye used the concept of the cycle when he considered the *Wake* in terms of the epic hero and quest in the context of a reader-text relationship:

> Who then is the hero who achieves the permanent quest in *Finnegans Wake*? No character in the book itself seems a likely candidate; yet one feels that this book gives us something more than the merely irresponsible irony of a turning cycle. Eventually it dawns on us that it is the *reader* who achieves the quest, the reader who, to the extent that he masters the book of Doublends Jined, is able to look down on its rotation, and see its form as something more than rotation.[1]

Frye explored the reader's role in certain aspects of Joyce's textual operations, and this approach continued with recent studies such as John Nash's *James Joyce and the Act of Reception*,[2] although Nash focuses upon historically real readers and groups of readers of Joyce rather than the ideal reader that Frye took from Joyce's own "ideal reader suffering from an ideal insomnia" and identified as "the critic."[3]

Umberto Eco's "The Semantics of Metaphor" explores the roles that readers take in the process of interpreting texts from the perspective of a model, rather than real, reader. His study was one of the first to identify the linguistic and semiotic circuitous patterns of return and repetition within Joyce's texts. Like Derrida's investigations of Husserl's "Origin of Geometry" and his subsequent engagements with Joyce, Eco reads the *Wake* as a model of the linguistic universe. *Finnegans Wake*, "presents itself as an excellent model of the Global Semantic System (since it posits itself, quite explicitly, as the Ersatz of the historical universe of language)."[4] Eco explores how the circuitous narrative patterns of Joyce's *Wake* produce puns sustained by metaphors, which are in turn supported by "subjacent chains of metonymic connections which constitute the framework of the [semiotic] code upon which is based the constitution of any semantic field, whether partial or (in theory) global."[5] Readers can follow the progressive straightforward narrative patterns of the *Wake* or they can trace the circuitous metonymic loops from nodal points of metaphors or paronomasias that will eventually lead the reader back to the point from which he or she started.

Examining what he calls the "pun-lexeme"[6] of the *Wake*'s term "meanderthaltale" (FW 19.25), Eco isolates the lexemes /meander/ /tal/ (German for "valley") and /tale/ as well as the pun between /meanderthal/ and /Neanderthal/ in order to trace the associative and semantic links between them.

Demonstrating how these links can be of "either a phonetic or semantic type," he demonstrates how they produce the "puns which define the book."[7] The chains of subjacent metonymies sustaining the metaphors produce and sustain the puns defining the book as a river that has, since the historical period of "Neanderthals," been "meandering" and flowing throughout history. The flowing water is a metaphor for the narratives or tales, and they wander or meander through a "valley." This metaphor for the *Wake*'s "tale" produces terminal puns and metaphors by which the reader can leave the *Wake*'s progressive linear narrative patterns and follow the text's semantic circuits. Such circuits function like the electronic ones with which Derrida describes the writings of *Ulysses* and *Finnegans Wake* as a "hypermnesiac machine" and a "1000th-generation computer" (TW 25/22). Creating metaphoric and punning "short circuits" between the metonymic chains and lexemic nodes of its circuitous meanderings, the *Wake* provides its readers with opportunities to leap from metaphor to metaphor and pun to pun in another (and an "other") way of traversing the text's narrative patterns and metonymic chains.

Following his early comparison of the linguistic philosophies and practices of Husserl and Joyce, Derrida's engagements with Joyce's texts consist of short enigmatic comments scattered among the footnotes to his own texts and longer, but no less enigmatic, explorations of Joyce's writings that repeat and remark the circuitous patterns of technical and linguistic communicative relays of Joyce beneath seemingly simple engagements of those writings.[8] Tracing the "circular movements" in Derrida's "Ulysses Gramophone" that mimic the movements in Joyce's writing and "keep returning to themselves," Derek Attridge contends that Joyce's writing "stands for the most comprehensive synthesis of the modern university's fields of knowledge, containing within itself all that can be said about itself."[9] But Derrida's essay also interrogates the relationships between chance and necessity as it begins and ends with playful allusions to the mundane worlds of Japanese bookshops and French airports. Like Joyce's writings, Derrida's replicate the differences between so-called serious philosophy and popular culture, crossing but also interrogating the borders between them even while sustaining those borders. Moving between the realms that Heidegger distinguishes as the "ontic" and the "Ontological," Derrida marks how Joyce sets advertising jingles and modern technology like telephones and gramophones to work in narratives constructed from the pretexts of classical Homeric epic.

In *The Post Card*, Derrida restages Joyce's commingling of classical and popular when he "(con)fuses" popular television and the transmission of "serious" intellectual ideas. Can the authentic voice of Heidegger's Dasein emerge from the cacophony of *gerede*, from beneath the "neutral tyranny" of the "they" or "das man"?[10] Through a simple negation, Derrida detects the oppressive voices of the dead in a popular and most unlikely academic source:

> I have just fallen asleep [. . .] watching *Charley's Angels* (four female private detectives, very beautiful, one is smart, their orders arrive on the telephone, from a boss who seems to be "sending himself" a fifth by speaking to them) and in passing I caught this: only the dead don't talk. That's what you think! They are the most talkative, especially if they remain alone. It's rather a question of getting them to shut up. (PC 246/263).

In his readings of Joyce, Derrida frequently remarks the circuitous patterns of return (of Joyce's texts and the readings of those texts) in terms of memory and desire, and he describes his own engagements in such terms: "one remains on the edge of reading [. . .] and the endless diving in throws me back onto the bank, on the brink of another possible dip, *ad infinitum*" (TW 26/24). Reading Joyce entails engaging the "hypermnesia" of his texts. The reader has "only one way out: *being in memory of him*":

> Not only overwhelmed by him, whether you know it or not, but obliged by him, constrained to measure yourself against this overwhelming.
>
> Being in memory of him: not necessarily to remember him, no, but to be in his memory, to inhabit a memory henceforth greater than all your finite recall can gather up, in a single instant or a single vocable, of cultures, languages, mythologies, religions, philosophies, sciences, histories of spirit or of literatures. I don't know if you can love that, without resentment and without jealousy. (TW 24/21–22)

Derrida sees the reading positions for Joyce's texts articulated by Joyce's writings, and Joyce's "hypermnesia" "*a priori*" places Joyce's readers in his debt even as "in advance and forever it inscribes you in the book you are reading" (TW 24/22).

The first extensive engagement of Derrida with Joyce's writing is a part of his comparison of Husserl's and Joyce's respective concepts of the historical developments of language. Husserl's arguments concerning linguistic development reveal an aspiration for a "pure ideal univocity, a univocity that is in the last resort unattainable."[11] Although it is unattainable, Husserl's model of linguistic univocity and relativity provides the model of teleology with which Derrida contrasts Husserlian and Joycean models of language. Husserl's project is to "reduce or impoverish empirical language methodically to the point where its univocal and translatable elements are actually transparent." The goal of such a reduction is to "reach back and grasp again at its pure source a historicity or traditionality that no de facto historical totality will yield of itself" (EH 103/105). In contrast to Husserl's, Joyce's writing repeats and attempts to take responsibility "for all equivocation itself, utilizing a language that could equalize the greatest possible synchrony with the greatest potential for buried accumulated and interwoven intentions within each linguistic atom, each vocable, each word, each simple proposition, in all worldly cultures and their most ingenious forms" (EH 102/104).

After comparing Joyce's and Husserl's philosophies of language, Derrida engaged with Joyce in the marginalia and footnotes of his texts. In "Two Words for Joyce," Derrida revealed the importance of his readings of Joyce in his own work with the metaphor of a ghost: "Yes, every time I write, and even in academic things, Joyce's ghost is always coming on board" (TW 27/27). As the "other" haunting Derrida's writing, Joyce's meaning is "other" and becomes part of the meaning of Derrida's own desire. The operations of Joyce as the "other" of Derrida's desire are marked in that desire by the oscillating force toward, and for, the other: Derrida simultaneously admires and resents Joyce:

> It is with this sentiment, or one should say this resentment, that I must have been reading Joyce for a long time [. . .]. Imprisoned in this admiring resentment, one remains on the edge of reading; for me this has been going on for more than twenty-five years, and the endless diving in throws me back onto the bank, on the brink of another possible dip, *ad infinitum*. (TW 25–26/23–24)

Derrida's sentiments about Joyce are characterized by the ambivalent yet admiring anxiety that characterizes the operations of desire: "I've never dared to *write on* Joyce. At most I've tried to mark in what I write [. . .] Joyce's scores [*portées*], Joyce's *reaches* [*portées*]" (TW 26/24). It is Derrida's "markings" of Joyce's "scores" and "reaches" that the rest of this chapter remarks. Derrida's "marking" of Joyce's writings is of course deconstructive or disseminative and marks the intervals between the previously high and low terms of the binary opposites in the text being marked. Like such markings, a re-marking of them can take place "only . . . in . . . a *grouped* textual field" such as the textual field assembled below.

Learning to Count to Three: Triadicity Plus One

Joyce's Catholicism provided him with a sense of the importance of the trinity, which never left him even after he started setting theological symbols and imagery to work in an artistic, aesthetic context. As a symbol of unity, his literary use of triads is apparent as early as *Dubliners*. The three strokes responsible for Father Flynn's death (D 9), the three figures who gather to read the card pinned to the crape bouquet on the door of the house (D 12), and the three characters who kneel at the foot of the Priest's coffin in "The Sisters" (D 14) reveal Joyce's early aesthetic use of the trinity in the first story of the collection. In the ironic "crucifixion" of Bob Doran in "The Boarding House," Doran has a three-day growth of beard (D 65), which adds to his Christological symbolism, and when he meets Jack Doran ascending the stairs, Jack carries bottles of Bass beer that bear the red triangle of the Bass brewery. Joyce surely enjoyed the double values of 3 and 1 provided by the Bass trademark as a triangle and the first registered British trademark. There are far too many examples of Joyce's symbolic use of the triad to note here, but Derrida was clearly familiar with many of them.

Derrida's own use of triads and tripartite patterns is apparent in the opening sentences of *Dissemination* where he solicits the structure of his own text: "This (therefore) will not have been a book. Still less, despite appearances, will it have been a collection of *three* 'essays' whose itinerary it would be time, after the fact, to recognize" (DI 3/9). In the same text, Derrida quotes a passage on the importance of the triangle in the *Wake*: "The triangle with its point downward, the lower part of Solomon's seal, is a traditional symbol of the feminine principle, exploited extensively in *Finnegans Wake*" (DI 330/367). The generative triads of HCE and ALP have made readers of the *Wake* familiar with the importance of the triad in Joyce's text, and Philippe Sollers reads the *Wake* as "one immense word" with a nucleus where "to give *one* word [. . .] there is a coming together of at least three words, plus a coefficient of annulation."[12]

Joyce "ceaselessly meditated (and played)" on the trinity to the point where he *lived* in a state of "triadicity, *plus one*." Sollers see this triadicity operating on numerous levels of the *Wake*:

> When it is noted [. . .] that the *last* word [of the *Wake*] is THE, followed by a blank, with no punctuation mark, and that this terminal THE is calculated so as to turn round to the beginning, the reading THE RIVERRUN, which is obviously the course of the river but in which can be heard and seen THREE VER UN, three toward one.[13]

The concept of three *plus one* or three *toward one* is philosophically explored in Heidegger, and this exploration provides a context for both Derrida's and Joyce's use of triadicity. In "Modern Science, Metaphysics, and Mathematics," Heidegger demonstrates how "three" may stand in "third place" in the natural series of numbers but is "not the third number."[14] "Three" is "the first number." "One" is not "really the first number":

> For instance, we have before us one loaf of bread and one knife, this one, and in addition, another one. When we take both together we say, 'both of these,' the one and the other, but we do not say, 'these two' or 1+1. Only when we add a cup to the bread and the knife do we say 'all.' Now we take them as a sum, i.e., as a whole and so and so many.[15]

For Heidegger the triadic sequence of 1+2+3 produces the concept of "all-ness" or wholeness that is often symbolized by the number "one." This concept emerges only after we count to three and emerges as something other to the first numerical sequence 1+2+3. With the emergence of the concept of "all," it then becomes possible to use the figure of "one" to symbolize the unity or all-ness of the three.

In *Finnegans Wake*, the three letters of the triads HCE and ALP produce a "whole" or complete collection of letters or characters the reader can, if he or she wishes, "read" as novelistic characters. The triad *"plus one"* and "three toward one" marked by Sollers at the linguistic and representational levels of the *Wake* also operate in the text's tenth section. This section is constituted by the set of three marginalia that operate among each other and simultaneously signify *toward* the column of text dominating the typographical layout of the pages. The three-toward-one pattern also operates in the identification of "Ainsoph," "this upright one, with that noughty besighed him zeroine" (FW 261.23). "Ainsoph" is marked with the footnote number 3, which signifies *toward* the "Ainsoph" or upright one" and the footnote, "Groupname for grapejuice" (FW 261.N3). Joyce's articulation of "Ainsoph," "noughty," and "zeroine" (1+0+0+1) and the "Ainsoph" *plus* the footnote number 3 is structured by the same "tetractys (1+2+3+4)" (DI 347/386) Derrida marks in the 10 (1+2+3+4 = 10) sections of "Dissemination," the ultimate, doubling section of *Dissemination*.

Desire between Joyce and Derrida

> I wanted to take the plane to Zurich and read out loud sitting on his knee, starting with the beginning (Babel, the fall, and the Finno-Phoenician motif, "the fall (bababadalgh) [. . .]. (PC 241/257)

Derrida's desire to sit on Joyce's knee emerges in Joyce's haunting of Derrida's work and attests to the power of Joyce's writing in Derrida's: "Above all [. . .] *La Carte postale* is haunted by Joyce, whose funerary stele stands at the center of the *Envois* (the visit to the cemetery in Zurich). The specter invades the book, a shadow on every page, whence the resentment, sincere and feigned, always mimed, of the signatory" (TW 28/30). The meaning of Derrida's desire can be marked in his ambivalent desire for Joyce as well as his willingness to allow the space for this spectral figure to haunt his own writing. Jacques Lacan's modification of Freud's notion of desire helps to re-mark the operations of desire that Derrida marks in Joyce's writing. These operations are also a part of Derrida's desire to engage with Joyce and function as the "other" of the Irish writer. Lacan's translator explains that the psychoanalyst uses "neither Freud's term, *wunsch*, nor the English translation, 'wish,' which corresponds closely to it." Lacan employs *désir* because, as his translator Alan Sheridan explains, the German and English terms "are limited to individual, isolated acts of wishing, while the French has the much stronger implication of a continuous force."[16] Such a concept of desire can help us comprehend the continual return to reading the *Finnegans Wake* Derrida describes in "Two Words for Joyce" as well as the continual force with which Derrida responds to the uniqueness of Joyce's encyclopedic project of *Ulysses* and which he marks as articulated within that project.

"Language Is a Virus from Outer Space" (William S. Burroughs)

Language, and particularly speech or vocable language, is intrinsically involved in the operations of desire. Burroughs' metaphor of the virus that is language may seem a flippant or outlandish comment, but it is no more than a simple description of the origin of language as an exterior force that penetrates the self through the ear or is apprehended through the eye in the process of interiorization, which moves from the outside to the inside of the individual. For Lacan the reverse of this process, the subject's articulation of a penetrative language, is the articulation and exteriorization of desire. He links the concept of "desire" with "need" (*besoin*) and "demand" (*demande*) in particular ways: as "an organism, a human individual has certain biological needs, needs certain objects satisfy."[17] These needs are affected by the acquisition of language. "All speech is demand; it presupposes the Other to who it is addressed, whose very signifiers it takes over in its formulation . . . that which comes from the Other is treated [. . .] as a response to an appeal, a gift, a token of love."[18] Derrida was fond of vocalizing Joyce's writing. In his public addresses he frequently made sure that he enunciated Joyce's writing extensively as he analyzed and commented on it. According to Julia Kristeva, he thus participated in the splitting of himself into the subject of [the] articulation of desire and the needful "subject of utterance,"[19] creating the gap between demand and need in which desire oscillates.

Desire does not exist in printed language, even if it is Joyce's quiet, printed text where "silence speaks the scene" (FW 13.03). The reader's engagement with that text as the articulation of an "other" desire provides the meaning of the reader's desire. The meaning of desire is always found "in the desire of the other."[20] The meaning of all of Derrida's engagements with the desire articulated in Joyce's writings is the engagement with Joyce's desire as Derrida marks it and then remarks it in the meaning of his own writing and the expression of his own desire. The operations of Derrida's desire for the meaning provided by the desire of Joyce as "other" can be marked in the ambivalence, noted earlier, which Derrida, like so many of Joyce's readers, feels about Joyce. Desire does not necessarily involve liking or pleasure as desire sustains itself in finding its "boundary, its strict relation, its limit," and finding its own limit in order to sustain itself, entails "crossing the threshold imposed by the pleasure principle."[21] Derrida holds his own writings open to the haunting by Joyce's ghost, but he does not always like it even if he desires it. While he feels our "admiration for Joyce ought to have no limit" he admits to not being sure of "loving Joyce, of loving him all the time" (TW 23–24/20).

Metaphors of Linguistic Motion

Inscribed letters or printed characters do not move. It is the desire of the reader apprehending the written text and providing the illusion of motion that produces meaning for the reader's desire. This desire and the metaphors of linguistic motion within written or printed texts are a part of how the illusion of textual motion is created: "Go on reading, but watch out for this, which should already have started to make your head spin: that each separate fragment is only readable within the well-calculated play of an extremely numerous recurrence and an innumerable polysemy" (DI 327/363). The reader's head may "spin" while reading Derrida or Joyce, but this metaphor is written or printed in the static printed characters of a text that in itself remains static and does not move. It is in the reader, and only in the reader, that such spinning may be experienced. The texts of both Joyce and Derrida produce metaphors of movement for the characters and words of the printed text. The *Wake* refers to the spaces between its lines of printed text as "ruled barriers along which the traced words, run, march, halt, stumble up again in comparative safety seem to have been drawn first of all of all in a pretty checker with lampblack and blackthorn" (FW 114.7–11). These "traced words" neither run nor march, but the reading process produces the illusion that they do. Addressing the spectral or illusionary "you" to whom he feigns to write in *The Post Card*, Derrida distinguishes between the "reality" of running or jogging and the expression of desire "running" within his text: "and me, I run. I am not going to encounter you without hoping for anything that is not chance precisely [. . .] (but when I say I run, I'm not talking about jogging [. . .]) [. . .]. Toward this fortuitously encountered encounter, I make my (a)way backward, *á rebours*" (PC 247/264).

Desire and Memory

The operations of desire are inextricably linked to memory. Even though individual desire, or the desire of each individual, is limited by its temporality, according to Freud and Lacan, desire itself is indestructible. One of the functions of desire mapped by Joyce and then re-marked by Derrida is its mnemonic role: "desire merely conveys what it maintains of an image of the past towards an ever short and limited future."[22] ALP's plaintive plea, "mememormee" (FW 628.14) on what can be read as the final page of the *Wake* but also as yet another of the 625 pages on which one can find numerous "other" beginnings, remarks an assertive triple inscription of the objective case of the subjective pronoun "me," which also puns on the lexeme /memory/. To begin at an end that is no ending entails a gamble, a risk of sending a postcard or other text to a "destination without address" and heading out, perhaps recklessly, in a direction which "cannot be situated in the end" (PC 29/34). Such a direction is nothing new, nothing more than a repetition of one of the many textual strategies that Derrida has already iterated for us, even if Derrida's iterations were reiterations of what Joyce and an entire history of philosophers and writers have busied themselves iterating and reiterating since the eras of Socrates and of God's confusion of languages at Babel. Insisting on something new and completely different under our sun, we can sometimes overlook (without really looking over) what we may already have at hand in even the most unlikely of places. The difficulty, if not the impossibility, of articulating something new about Joyce's writing is a significant theme in Derrida's engagement with that writing.

Following Roland McHugh's *Annotations*, Joyce's readers can decipher "mememormee" as the representation of a final call to be remembered: ALP's final plea for remembrance is part of the river Liffey's (and hence the pun, noted by McHugh, with the Hebrew term for water, *mem*) farewell as she flows into Dublin Bay. But it is also a part of the *Wake*'s pages, or "leaves," speaking: "I am leafy speafing" (FW 619.20). A river, a female character, a page and, because the so-called proper name of Anna Livia Plurabelle offers itself as a condensed history of Western languages, language itself also calls for remembrance. The linguistic sequence of "Anna" (Gk), "Livia" (Latin), and "Plu" (French) (or "belle," "elle," "le," etc.) articulates the major linguistic developments in Western languages as the literatures and philosophies of Classical Greek were translated into Latin and then into modern European languages.[23] Simultaneously, this call for remembrance overdetermines the objective-case signifier that represents the self: /me/ three times or mememormee: me, me, and more or "mor" mee. This overdetermination undermines representational interpretations of "mememormee," destabilizing any attempt to establish a simple representational link between "me" and a traditional reading of the term as a signifier of a unified self. The repetition of "me" and the "mor" inserted within it causes any attempt at a simple mimetic reading of the term to shudder and tremble, if not to collapse, as overdetermination does so frequently in Joyce's slipping, collapsing, falling "collupsus" of Mister Funn's "back promises" (FW 5.27–28).

In a linear, "goahead" reading of the *Wake*'s narrative, "mememormee," can be read as a terminal point of the text's hypermnesia that corresponds to the initial "riverrun" (FW 3.01), and its pun on the German "erinnerung," or "remembrance." The text thus begins and ends with signifiers of memory and remembrance, and "mememormee" articulates the three-plus-one pattern explored by Sollers: /me/, /me/, /more/, /me/. Between these two pun lexemes the *Wake*'s hypermnesiac engagement of history is played out. Derrida's "Ulysses Gramophone" replays a similar pattern. After its initial stress on the spoken nature of the paper as it was delivered to the 1984 International James Joyce Symposium in Frankfurt—"*Oui, oui*, you are hearing me well, these are French words" (UG 41/57)—the essay locates its own genesis in the city of Tokyo, the city that features in the "Eumaeus" episode of *Ulysses*, one of the episodes that Derrida's essay explores. The numerous pretexts explored and remembered by *Finnegans Wake* originate outside of that text but are brought within it by Joyce's hypermnesic writing. Derrida's (possibly) "real" visit to the Okura Hotel in Tokyo provides an initial link with an extratextual locus that Derrida doubles with the Tokyo, or "Tokio," of the cabman's shelter in the "Eumaeus" episode and then uses to introduce the element of chance into his conclusion: "I decided to stop here because I almost had an accident as I was jotting down this last sentence, when, on leaving the airport, I was driving home returning from Tokyo" (UG 81/143).

What Derek Attridge describes as the "long, detailed, circuitous" exploration of *Ulysses* in "Ulysses Gramophone" imitates some of the patterns of Joyce's text at the same time that it self-reflectively describes its own creation: "it weaves together the story of its own composition" and "mimes both Joyce's novel [. . .] and a crucial aspect of its own argument: the necessary connection between chance and necessity."[24] The essay mimes or mimics the relays of the postal systems and telephone circuits that feature in Joyce's writing, but the essay also allows Derrida the opportunity to position his own readings of Joyce in relationship to those made possible by members of the International James Joyce Foundation. Derrida finds an ambivalent force at work in Joyce's participation in laying the groundwork for this foundation. Joyce "has done everything, and said so, to make it indispensable and to make it function for centuries" (UG 50/77). But this institution is also one "he did everything to render impossible and improbable in its principle, to deconstruct in advance, to the point of undermining the very concept of a competence on which an institutional legitimacy could be based" (UG 50/77).

Using his explorations of *Ulysses* to solicit the concept of institutional legitimacy, Derrida playfully explores the text's repetitions of "yes," and its metaphors of postal systems and electronic modes of communication such as telephone systems and gramophones. He uses one strand of his address to the Frankfurt Symposium in order to playfully explore his own desire concerning the notion of competence in readings of Joyce. The opening rhetorical gambit in this particular relay of his talk is the adoption of a traditional rhetorical *apologia*: "For a long time I have thought—and this is still true today—that I would never be ready to give a talk on Joyce to an audience of Joyce experts." He follows this apparently humble confession with a question about Joycean competency that he develops into a major question in his address: "What is an expert, when it comes to Joyce, this is my question" (UG 48/73). Derrida feigns to acknowledge the competency of his audience of Joyceans: "All of you are experts, and belong to the most singular of institutions," an institution that can be seen as "a powerful reading, signing and countersigning machine in the service of his name, of his 'patent'" (UG 50/77).

After acknowledging the competence of his audience of Joycean experts, Derrida begins a frequently comic, rhetorical tour de force in which he assaults the very concept of Joycean competency by invoking Joyce's own attempts to undermine the institution set up in his name. He interrogates the possibility that there could be such a thing as competency in Joyce studies. He continues his subversive strategy by again acknowledging the competency of Joyce scholars: "the Joycean experts are the representative as well as the effects of the most powerful project to program over centuries the totality of research in the onto-logico-encyclopedic field—while commemorating his own signature. [. . .] He or she has the mastery over the *computer* of all memory, plays with the entire archive of culture" (UG 59/97). Following this ironic acknowledgment of the competence of Joyce scholars and members of the International James Joyce Foundation, Derrida removes his gloves and makes a series of points that call into question the very notion of Joycean competence: "In the end, there cannot be a Joycean competence, in the strong and rigorous sense of the concept of competence, with the criteria of evaluation and legitimation that are attached to it. There cannot be a Joycean foundation or family. There cannot be a Joycean legitimacy" (UG 60/98–99).

While asserting that there can be no Joycean competency or legitimacy, Derrida prepares to deliver the coup de grace of his assault on Joyce scholars by claiming that he, like other outsiders, has been invited to address the symposium in order "to be humiliated" and, perhaps, to bring good news that might liberate the members of the foundation of the "hypermnesic interiority" from which they suffer:

> When you call on incompetent people, such as myself, or on allegedly external competences, even though you know that they aren't any, isn't it in order to both humiliate them and because you are expecting from these guests not only some news, some good news that would come to finally free you from the hypermnesic interiority in which you run in circles like madmen in a nightmare but also, paradoxically, a legitimacy? (UG 62/104)

Invoking his own Judaic heritage, Derrida hints that his birthright might qualify him, a self-confessed "incompetent" in matters Joycean, to hold a chair of Joycean studies. Declaring that his audience will not believe him, Derrida employs the affirmative "yeses" from Joyce's text (thus countersigning that text) to assert that his audience of Joyceans doesn't "believe a word of what I am telling you right now. And even if it was true and even if, yes, it is true, you would not believe me if I told you that my name is also Elijah: That name is not inscribed, no, on my birth certificate but it was given to me on my seventh day" (UG 62/104–5).

"That's why I'd rather hear your voice
than see your face" (Laurie Anderson)

> So you are out of my sight. And [. . .] where do you "see" me [. . .] when you have me [. . .] on the telephone? [. . .] Me, I look out for the noises in the room around you. (PC 19/24)

Who is the "you" addressed in Derrida's *Envois*? Doubtless some biographer or bibliographic critic will assert an answer without convincing everyone of its validity. The answer in any case could only ever be partially correct for at least two reasons, a double reason. The first is that this "you" has different names (even though these names will always be the names of a dead person according to a logic we will see later). Plato as P. "is the law, is you, is me" (PC 35/41); "of course it is to Socrates that I am addressing myself at this very moment" (PC 67/75). The pronoun, "you," like the noun, is another name "made to do without the life of the bearer, and is therefore always somewhat the name of someone dead" (PC 39/45). The second reason is that the "you" like the "I" that addresses the "you" as well as the "us" of "we readers" is not an "author," nor a "reader," nor a "deus ex machina" (DI 325/361). These pronouns are positions in language that are "both part of the spectacle and part of the audience." They function not to refer to some unique, living individual but as "pure passageway[s] for operations of substitution." None of the pronouns signify "some singular and irreplaceable existence, some subject or 'life'" (DI 325/361), but, like the pronouns in *Finnegans Wake*, they operate as part of "the identities of the writer complexus" (FW 114.33) within the "order" that Joyce's writing makes "othered" (FW 613.14).

If, as Derrida states, "Above all [. . .] *La Carte postale* is haunted by Joyce," and Joyce's "funerary stele," which "stands at the centre of the *Envois*" attests to Joyce's "specter [which] invades the book, a shadow on every page" (TW 28/30), the "you" addressed on nearly every page will also be haunted, not by Joyce, the being, but by the language and writings of "a worker" and "a tombstone mason" who has carefully constructed and crafted his own tomb (FW 113.34). The Derridean voice in *The Post Card* that wants "to read out loud sitting on" the knee of Joyce's statue, is a voice that wishes to lose itself in the voice of Joyce as the other. The voice would be that of Joyce's writing (with a French accent) and his rewriting of the fall (PC 240/257–58). In adopting that voice and articulating it, Derrida finds his meaning in Joyce's desire.

Two of the terminal points from which the *Envois* of *The Post Card* are generated are the figures of Socrates and Plato as they are depicted on the "frontispiece of *Prognostica Socratis basilei*, a fortune-telling book" from thirteenth-century England by Matthew Paris (PC title page verso). This frontispiece was reproduced on the postcard from which the title of Derrida's book derives. Exploiting the spaces between the original, its reproduction on the postcard, and its presentation in his book, Derrida analyzes and deconstructs the relationships between Plato and Socrates, developing them into a series of themes that he exploits and plays much like a musician develops variations on a theme. Because the postcard is a "reproduction of a reproduction" it is a "text and a picture, indissociably," which is "in principle governed by a law and subject to *copyright*" (PC 37/43). On this postcard Plato stands behind Socrates, who sits writing at a desk. Plato is smaller than Socrates but he appears to be prodding Socrates in the back with his right hand while his left hand is stretched behind Socrates so that it appears in front of him as if guiding him. Derrida explores the historical reality that our only access to Socrates is through the writings of Plato but extends Socrates' historical antecedence beyond traditional logical limits: "S. is P., Socrates is Plato, his father and his son, therefore, the father of his father, his own grandfather and his own grandson" (PC 47/54). Plato is also Socrates' "modest widow" (PC 171/186), and Socrates, is, "on his part, Plato's widow" (PC 172/186).

S. and P. are ciphers that retain links with their philosophical proper names, but Derrida uses Joyce's technique of "doublin" (FW 3.08) their signifieds (which double again into signifiers in Derrida's bifurcating writing) and his reconfigurations of them. "S. does not see P. who sees S., but (and here is the truth of philosophy) only *from the back*" (PC 48/55). Derrida undermines the possibility of establishing any certain or stable identity for S. and P. with the suggestion that they could have changed hats so that P. may be S. and S., P. He takes them out of the traditional, philosophical contexts in which they might be "properly" situated. Looking at Plato's raised foot on the postcard, Derrida draws on a "delirious" discourse, refiguring Plato as "pushing himself on a skate board" or:

> taking tram fares in a poor country, on the dashboard pushing the young people inside as it gets underway. He is pushing them in the back. *Plato* as the tram conductor, his foot on a pedal or a warning buzzer (he is pretty much a warning himself, don't you think with his outstretched finger?), and he drives, he drives avoiding derailment. At the top of the staircase, on the last step, he rings for the elevator (PC 17/22).

This "delirious" account of Plato as a tram conductor is counterbalanced (if one may use balance in such a context) with an equally delirious account of Socrates as a gangster:

> you know the end of the detective story: Socrates knocks off all of them, or makes them kill themselves among themselves, he remains alone, the gangbusters take over the locale, he sprays gas everywhere, it's all ablaze in a second, and behind the cops the crowd presses forward somewhat disappointed that they didn't get him alive or that he didn't get out of it, which amounts to the same. (PC 252/269)

Derrida's bifurcated writing reproduces and remarks the doubling of Joyce's. It allows the ciphers of S. and P. to double and proliferate in numerous ways. S. and P. become Shem the penman and Shaun the post from *Finnegans Wake*, but before reaching this destination (which can be, for Derrida, a "destination without address" (PC 29/34), S. and P. are doubled by the proper names of Freud and Heidegger. These proper names belong to the epoch "whose technology is marked" with signifiers that dominate certain modes of the *Wake*: "paper, pen, the envelope, the individual subject addresses, etc." (PC 191/206). In the *Wake*, the proper name of Freud signifies from within a short narrative concerning Alice Liddell, the young girl who was the model for Alice in Wonderland: "but we grisly old Sykos who have done our unsmiling bit on 'alices, when they were yung and easily freudened" (FW 115.21–23).

We do not know how familiar Joyce was with Heidegger. Perhaps this is a question for our future, but the *Wake* remarks the title of his major work with its capitalized "Sein" (FW 277.18) and its "zeit" (FW 415.26) and "Zeit's" (FW 78.07) Perhaps chance and necessity can account for the appearance of the key terms from the title of Heidegger's major work in *Finnegans Wake*. They may also be a force in the parallels between the Heideggerian call of conscience summoning authentic being to turn from the neutral tyranny of Das Mann and the gerede that ensnare the fallen being thrown down into the world: "abide Zeit's summonserving, rise afterfall" (FW 78.07). "Here," Derrida declares, and perhaps one can in part localize this "here" in *Finnegans Wake*, here, "Freud and Heidegger, I conjoin them within me like the two great ghosts of the 'great epoch.' The two surviving grandfathers. They did not know each other, but according to me they form a couple, and in fact just because of that, this singular anachrony. They are bound to each other without reading each other and without corresponding" (PC 191/206). Derrida refigures them in the physical position of S. and P. on the postcard: "two thinkers whose glances never crossed and who, without ever receiving a word from one another, say the same. They are turned to the same side (PC 191/206).

Some of Derrida's re-marking of Joyce is little more than a trace, a faint echo of a doubling. To catch a glimpse of these traces one must read Derrida's "wake" ("*no my love that's my wake*" [PC 141/154]) as one can read Joyce's: create a short circuit between the linear narrative printed as if it were on a postcard and read the pages of these postcards out of sequence. Following the suggestion to "expose [an] invisible trajectory," one can jump from the identification, "And if [. . .] I called you Esther?" (PC 73/81), to the identification of the narrative "I" and "you" as "twins": "Did I tell you that we are the infant twins (heterozygous but homosexual) of those Double-doubles [*Sosie-sosie*]?" (PC 113/125; cf. PC 142/155). The echo of the *Wake*'s "sosie sesthers" (FW 3.12) may be coincidence, but it remains an echo from "Echoland" (FW 13.05).

The darkest parts of the shadow "on every page" (TW 28/30) that Joyce's haunting casts on *The Post Card* are the easiest to define, if not to apprehend (how does one apprehend the shadows cast by a ghost or its haunting?), and they are clearly identified by Derrida: the tales of Shem and Shaun, the creation of the stamp for mail, the circuits of postal services by which postcards are delivered, and "above all the Babelian motif which obsesses the "Envois'" (TW 30/32). What does not appear in Derrida's description is the refiguring of himself and Joyce as S. and P. Derrida does point out, however, the doubling of James and Jacques in "a whole family of James, Jacques, Giacomo" and declares that Joyce's *Giacomo Joyce* "runs rhythmically through the *Envois*" of *The Post Card*. Derrida's *Envois* "are sealed [. . .] by the *Envoy*" of Joyce's text (TW 29/32).

Backing Up (to) Joyce

In his account of his relationship with Joyce's texts—and even in his descriptions of his ambivalence toward the Irish writer—Derrida is looking at Joyce's texts, gazing at Joyce and his writings face-to-face as it were, reading and frequently reciting those texts. Only in doubling Joyce and himself with the figures of S. and P. does he figuratively turn his back on Joyce, and this is an extremely important trope in *The Post Card*: "Before all else it is a question of turning one's back [*dos*]." "Our great tropics: to turn the '*dos*' in every sense, to all sides" (PC 178/192). Derrida argues that after Joyce, there is "no more starting over, draw the veil and let everything come to pass behind the curtains of language at the end of its rope" (PC 240/257). Putting Heidegger's Dasein into play, Derrida uses the trope of turning one's back as a mode of being behind the curtain: "There (*da*) is behind, behind the curtain or the skirts of the crib, or behind oneself" (PC 178/192). Derrida asks "What does it mean, 'to have behind oneself'?" (PC 159/172). One way to experience the answer is to experience "being there," behind the "curtains of language" with one's back turned. A part of the desire Derrida articulates in *The Post Card*, as we have seen, is "to take the plane to Zurich and read out loud sitting on [Joyce's] knees, starting with the beginning (Babel, the fall, and the Finno-Phoenician motif" (PC 240/257). Derrida would still be reading Joyce, but in his own voice, and with Joyce at his back. He could, of course, sit facing Joyce, but as he asks, to "turn one's back is the analytic position, no?" (PC 178/192).

Notes

1. Northrop Frye, *Anatomy of Criticism: Four Essays* (Princeton: Princeton University Press, 1957), 323–24.

2. John Nash, *James Joyce and the Act of Reception: Reading, Ireland, Modernism* (Cambridge: Cambridge University Press, 2006).

3. Frye, *Anatomy*, 354.

4. Umberto Eco, "The Semantics of Metaphor," trans. John Snyder, *The Role of the Reader: Explorations in the Semiotics of Texts* (Bloomington: Indiana University Press, 1979), 67–89; 68.

5. Ibid., 68.

6. Ibid., 76.

7. Ibid., 76.

8. Derrida's marginal comments on Joyce are summarized in my book *James Joyce and Critical Theory* (Ann Arbor: University of Michigan Press, 1991), 273–74.

9. Derek Attridge, introduction to "Ulysses Gramophone," *Acts of Literature*, ed. Derek Attridge (New York: Routledge, 1992), 253–56; 253.

10. See, for example, *Being and Time* where Heidegger discusses "The Everyday Being of the 'There,'" and the "Falling of the Dasein" (*Being and Time*, trans. John

Macquarrie and Edward Robinson [New York: Harper and Row, 1962], §1.5.34.B, 210–11) and *Idle Talk* (§1.5.35, 211–14).

11. Alan Roughley, *Reading Derrida Reading Joyce* (Gainesville: University Press of Florida, 1999), 7.

12. Philippe Sollers, "Joyce & Co.," trans. Stephen Heath, *In the Wake of the "Wake,"* ed. David Hayman and Elliott Anderson (Madison: University of Wisconsin Press), 107–21; 113.

13. Ibid., 113–14.

14. Martin Heidegger, "Modern Science, Metaphysics, and Mathematics," *Basic Writings*, ed. David Farrell Krell (New York: Harper and Row, 1977), 247–8;, 253.

15. Ibid., 253.

16. Alan Sheridan, translator's note, Jacques Lacan, *Écrits: A Selection*, trans. Alan Sheridan (New York: W.W. Norton, 1977), vii–xii viii.

17. Jacques Lacan, *The Four Fundamental Concepts of Psycho-Analysis*, ed. Jacques-Alain Miller, trans. Alan Sheridan (New York: W. W Norton, 1981), 278.

18. Ibid., 278–79.

19. Julia Kristeva, *Desire in Language*, ed. Leon S. Roudiez, trans. Thomas Gora, Alice Jardine, and Leon S. Roudiez (New York: Columbia University Press, 1980), 75.

20. Lacan, *Écrits*, 58.

21. Lacan, *Concepts*, 31.

22. Ibid., 31.

23. See Barbara Johnson's translator's note: DI 182 n.10.

24. Attridge, introduction to "Ulysses Gramophone," *Acts of Literature* (New York: Routledge, 1991), 253.

9

OF CHREMATOLOGY: JOYCE AND MONEY

Simon Critchley and Tom McCarthy

Der Geist, der aus der Ornamentik der Banknoten spricht.
—Walter Benjamin, "Kapitalismus als Religion"[1]

Money makes the round go a-world, as Joyce might have said. Certainly, *Finnegans Wake*, his book of wandering and return, of "aloss and again" (FW 18.22–23), is awash with money. There are English pounds, "shelenks" (FW 8.06), and pence, American bison nickels, French louis, Russian kopecks, German grosch and "dogmarks" (FW 161.08). "Woodpiles of haypennies" (FW 11.21), the "sylvan coyne" (FW 16.31) designed for Ireland by William Wood, circulate alongside "ghinees" (FW 16.31), "tenpound crickler[s]" (FW 82.26) and "tinpanned crackler[s]" (FW 82.34). Money crinkles, clunks, and rings throughout this novel in which nothing's free, this novel in which roads have tolls, museums entry fees. Belchum solicits "tinkyou tankyou silvoor plate" (FW 9.31); Kathe barks "Tip" (FW 8.08 ff.). Before he'll tell Jute anything, Mutt must be bribed with "trink gilt" (FW 16.30); on receiving this he shows him "selveran cued peteet peas of pecuniar interest [. . .] pellets that make the tomtummy's pay roll" (FW 19.02–4)—then demands the cost of a tram fare. Money is the prerequisite for the passage of signs: "You will never have post in your pocket unless you have brasse on your plate" (FW 579.10–11). If *Finnegans Wake*'s very content is, as its first page reminds us, "retaled" (FW 3.16), then the space of recirculation in which this retaling occurs is, as Professor Jones suggests in book I, chapter 6, an "economantarchy" (FW 167.06).

Our aim in this chapter is simply to read *Finnegans Wake* by following the chains of coinage that litter the text: of credit, credibility, credence, debt, indebtedness, reneging on debt, bankruptcy, profit, loss, inflation, deflation, and counterfeit. *Finnegans Wake* opens with a prophetic allusion to the Wall Street Crash of 1929 ("the fall [. . .] of a once wallstrait oldparr"

[FW 3.15–17]), and we would like to view the text as if it were some vast financial system. We will try and establish what we call a chrematology in this economantarchy, that is, pick out the monetary logic in Joyce's text. Our deeper, darker purpose in all this is not just to show that literature is haunted by economics, in the manner of classical Marxism and contemporary Marxist mannerism. Rather, our hypothesis is that in Joyce and elsewhere (where Joyce might be seen as the index for an elsewhere of absolutely modern literary, visual, and musical art), economics is raised to the level of cultural form.[2] For us, artworks are aspects of an *agon* as to the irreducible determination of contemporary life by economics, engaging us in a process of reflection that might, at best, achieve some distance from the fact of that determination.

Joyce himself, of course, had a strange and intense relationship with money. His parents had been rich but met with financial ruin; his mother would pawn furniture to send James money while he lived in Paris. Continually poor, he nonetheless retained expensive tastes, taking his family to eat in the best restaurants when they couldn't pay the rent on their accommodation, tipping theater ushers ten pounds when the ticket had cost less than one. It is almost as though he has willed himself into debt. He borrowed incessantly. He liked to boast that he owed money to every single person he knew. His situation is reflected in that of *Ulysses*' Stephen Dedalus, who, when asked by Deasy whether he could say of himself "I paid my way," runs through a mental list of everyone to whom he is indebted: "Mulligan, nine pounds [. . .] Curran, ten guineas. McCann, one guinea. Fred Ryan, two shillings. Tempel, two lunches. Russel, one guinea, Cousins, ten shillings, Bob Reynolds, half a guinea, Koehler, three guineas, Mrs MacKernan, five weeks' board" (U 2.255–59). For Deasy, not owing is a measure of one's subjectivity, one's sovereignty. The Englishman can boast this sovereignty precisely because he can say: "I paid my way." For Deasy, this is not unconnected to the fact that England never let in the Jews, a race (as far as anti-Semites such as Deasy are concerned) of usurers and wanderers. Stasis and self-sufficiency are the lynchpins of Deasy's credo. Stephen falls very short of meeting this credo's terms, and so did Joyce, an exile living on perpetual credit, extended against or guaranteed by some vague promise that he'd one day write a masterpiece and become rich.

What better place to discuss this theme than Trieste, the city described by Joyce as "Europiccola." Is it a more Joycean city than Dublin? Obviously not, but it is intriguing to entertain the thought. As Joyce said, "Trieste ate my liver" or "Trieste était mon livre." In Jan Morris' clear, still prose, Trieste becomes many things: a crepuscular, melancholy city swept by the Bora wind and enwrapped in an ecstasy of the poignant; the capital of nowhere, of wistful meditation, a Triesticity located at the intersection of the cultural plate tectonics of Latinity, Germanity, and Slavicity.³ The place where the young Freud tried to locate the testicles of eels, from which Eichmann dragged his unexpungeable guilt away to South America, and which was described by Marinetti as "la nostra bella polveriera," "our beautiful powder-magazine." But, above all, Trieste is a money town, the port of Vienna, a place of trade, of human and inhuman cargo, of capital, of profit, and (since 1918) of loss. The monumental Hapsburg structures of the Piazza Unità and the shoreline simply testify to the wealth that poured through Trieste. Who knows, but Joyce's errant, economantarchic preoccupations might have been better served had he set *Ulysses* in Trieste rather than Dublin.

But what is money? Many things. It is, of course, the coins and notes rattling in our pockets, as well as the piles of real and virtual stuff lying in banks, or the smart money that tends toward disappearance and increasing immateriality, being shuffled electronically along the vectors of the financial networks.

This might serve as an empirical definition, but what is the logic of the concept of money? The core of money is trust and promise, "I promise to pay the bearer on demand the sum of [. . .]" on the British pound, the "In God we trust" of the U.S. dollar, the BCE-ECB-EZB-EKT-EKP of the European Central Bank that runs like a Franco-Anglo-Germano-Greco-Finno-Joycean cipher across the top of every euro note. In other words, the legitimacy of money is based on a sovereign act, or a sovereign guarantee that the money is good, that it is not counterfeit. Money has a promissory structure, with an entirely self-referential logic: the money promises that the money is good; the acceptance of the promise is the acceptance of a specific monetary ethos, a specific, yet often flexible, monetary geography.

This ethos, this circular "money promising that the money is good" is underwritten by sovereign power as its transcendent guarantee. It is essential that we believe in this power, that the sovereign power of the bank inspires belief, that the "Fed" has "cred," as it were. Credit can only operate on the basis of credence and credibility, of an act of fidelity and faith, of con-fid-ence. The transcendent core of money is an act of faith, of belief. The legitimacy of money is based on the fiction of sovereign power, and in this connection one can speak of a sort of monetary patriotism, which is particularly evident in attitudes in the United States to the dollar, particularly to the sheer materiality of the bill, and in the United Kingdom's opposition to the euro and to the strange cultural need for money marked with the queen's head.

In a deep sense, money *is* not. It exists empirically, but it is not essentially there at all. All money is what the French call *escroquerie*, swindling, it is a virtual or at best conceptual object. It is, in the strictest Platonic definitional sense (forget Baudrillard), a simulacrum, namely, something that materializes an absence, an image for something that doesn't exist. Money is delusionary and faith in money is a form of collective psychosis. In the godless wasteland of global capitalism, money is our only metaphysics, our only onto-theo-logy, the only transcendent substance in which we truly must have faith. It is this faith that we celebrate, we venerate, in commodity fetishism. Adorno makes the point powerfully:

> Marx defines the fetish-character of the commodity as the veneration of the thing made by oneself which, as exchange value, simultaneously alienates itself from producer to consumer [. . .]. This is the real secret of success. It is the mere reflection of what one pays in the market for the product. The consumer is really worshipping the money that he himself has paid for the ticket to the Toscanini concert. He has literally "made" the success which he reifies and accepts as an objective criterion, without recognizing himself in it. But he has not "made" it by liking the concert, but rather by buying the ticket.[4]

Marx describes money as the universal form of equivalence by virtue of which capitalism can exist, that goods can be exchanged. In the imperial space of what Hardt and Negri describe as "network sovereignty," money becomes the general form of life, it constitutes the fact of Empire, and money's absence defines Empire's opposite: the multitude are poor.[5]

For us, here and now, money has no outside, there is no pure form of economy, no barter system, somehow unsullied by money's circulation. You are always already locked into a monetary ethos, part of a contour line upon a financial cartography. There is only the sully of money. All money is dirty. From a Freudian perspective, money is deeply anal, it is shit rather than bread, you can use it to buy shit, and a general obsession with money is why people talk so much shit. For the infant, the little Freudian child, shit is money, which is why it is so proud of its soft, smelly currency. In the proto-Lockean world of anal sadism, shit is the first form of property ownership; the labor theory of value begins in your diapers. Let's not forget, Freud is a kind of anti-Midas: where, for Midas, everything natural was transformed into gold, for Freud, all that glitters is transformed into shit. Freud touches a familiar object and suddenly—poo!—you wonder where the smell is coming from. Our favorite Freudian neurotic, the Rat Man, is obsessed with money, with repaying a misconceived debt. He is also highly aware of money's dirtiness, and anally obsessed, his fears of Rat torture (in which a rat eats into one's anus) being verbally linked to shame about his "Spielratte," his father's gambling debts. His very neurosis is described in economic terms by Freud, who writes, "In his obsessional deliria he had coined himself a regular rat currency [. . .]. Little by little he translated into this language the whole complex of money-interests which centered around his father's legacy to him."⁶

Of course, money is also indexed to desire, and there is a strong association between money and the *dépense* of *jouissance sexuelle*, and not only when you have to pay for it. Money is power, sex is power, power is sexy and so is money. And let's not forget the profound link between psychoanalysis and payment. With the exception of Karl Marx, were there ever creatures on earth more obsessed with money than psychoanalysts? Of course, they are right and the core of the analytic pact is a monetary union, a monetary act of trust: one has to pay, whatever it is that you can afford, otherwise the analysis begins to lose credibility. One cannot do analysis for free. The faith and trust of the transference, which is the key to the analytic relationship, is guaranteed by money; the promissory trust of therapy is secured through monetary exchange.

Jouissance brings us back by a commodious vicus of recirculation to Joyce. Lacan, who was unnaturally obsessed by *Finnegans Wake* throughout the 1970s, writes, "Joyce is in relation to joy, that is, jouissance, written in *lalangue* that is English; this en-joycing, this jouissance is the only thing one can get from the text. This is the symptom."⁷ For Lacan, it is the joy in Joyce that enjoys, just as it is the *Freude* in Freud that *freut sich*. This is what one feels in reading Joyce: "Read *Finnegans Wake* without trying to understand [. . .]. One usually reads it because one can feel the presence of the writer's jouissance."⁸ It is the sheer pressure of this presence that suffocates and oppresses the reader of *Finnegans Wake* because, as is well known, Lacanian jouissance is not pleasure but suffering, an excitation or excess that is too much for the organism to bear. En-Joyce-ment, or what Joyce calls "joyicity" (FW 414.22), is not enjoyable. Perhaps this is why many people think that the *Wake* is unreadable—is it not rather simply unbearable? Its seeming trifles are traces of psychic pain. One might go a little further with Lacan and say that *jouissance* is the kernel of psychotic suffering, a kernel that is nonanalyzable and that cannot be symbolized. For Lacan, it is this writing of psychotic *jouissance* that Joyce enacts, "Joyce manages to bring the symptom to the power of language, yet without rendering it analyzable."⁹ A very common behavior of psychotics is the forging of neologisms or fresh linguistic coinages and to this extent the writing of *Finnegans Wake* might be viewed as some vast psychotic case history. Of course, the psychotic suffering here is not just that of Joyce (although Lacan asks, "When does one start to be mad [. . .]. Was Joyce mad?"¹⁰), but also that of his daughter Lucia, whose psychotic sayings and diagrams litter the literature of *Finnegans Wake* (FW 260–308).

In a wonderful formulation, Lacan remarks that Joyce was "désabonné à l'inconscient," namely, that he abandoned or gave up his subscription to the symbolic order.[11] In ugly Lacanese, this means that Joyce affirmed the lack in the big Other and experienced the *jouissance* of the Real. In more everyday parlance, we might say that Joyce progressively shed the legitimating narrative conventions and expectations of the nineteenth-century realist novel. For some, literature might be understood as the draining of the excitation of *jouissance*, the *Zuider Zee* of the unconscious in Freud, or the Dionysian womb of being in Nietzsche. Literatures symbolizes or gives beautiful Apollonian form to the chaos of desire. As such, *Finnegans Wake* is literature in reverse, a writing of the symptom that attempts to attend to the clamor of *jouissance* that subtends literary creation and that cannot be dammed up. This reversal is mirrored linguistically in Lacan's punning distinction between language (*la langue*) and *lalangue*. If the symbolic is the order of language, which is given priority in Lacan's earlier structuralist-inspired work, then *lalangue* is his nickname for an experience of language that is itself a form of *jouissance* and sheer material affect that precedes and resists symbolization, marking Lacan's distance-taking from structuralism as well. We want to read the planned Babel of *Finnegans Wake* as a monetary *lalangue*, a chain of crazy coinage that both subtends and ruins the symbolic universe of literature, reducing letter to litter.

Only one town, perhaps, could rival Trieste in its claim as ideal host for this discussion: Dublin—not Dublin, Ireland, but rather Dublin, Georgia, USA. This city, founded on the River Oconee in Laurens County by Irish emigrant Peter Sawyer, finds its way into the *Wake*'s first complete sentence, whose second clause reads: "nor had topsawyer's rocks by the stream Oconee exaggerated themselse to Laurens County's gorgios while they went doublin their mumper all the time" (FW 3.06–9). Topsawyer's rocks are a formation on the Oconee's banks; "rocks" also means both testicles and money. "Ochone!" is the Gaelic for "alas!" The image here is of mothers wailing as their sons, fruits of their father's swollen loins, depart across the waters in an effort to win wealth and status in the new world, to swell their coffers. Campbell and Robinson, always keen to emphasize the "story" of the *Wake*, interpret the passage thus: "A successful son of HCE emigrates from East to West, as his father before him. Settling in America, he begets a large progeny and bequeaths to them a decent, even gorgeous prosperity."[12]

Joyce's own son was, of course, Giorgio. Downstream of Topsawyer's Rocks, the biologic and the economic blur together, much as they do in Shakespeare's sonnets, where "from fairest creatures we desire increase," "increase" being both economic profit and physical reproduction.[13] What is "doublin their mumper"? Rocks: balls, wealth, world in the sense of place and populace. The town motto of Dublin, Georgia, is "Doubling all the time," and Joyce keeps doubling Dublin into "Dyoublong," "durlbin," and "Dybbling" (FW 13.04, 19.12, 29.22).

So many of the *Wake*'s themes are touched on in these twenty-three words. So, too, perhaps, are the workings of the novel's very text. *Finnegans Wake* is an accumulative novel, a novel in which characters, events, reports, and interpretations multiply incessantly, doublin their mumper all the time. Mutt, discussing the relation between printed "papyr" (FW 20.10) and the significations generated by it, tells Jute: "you need hardly spell me how every word is bound to carry over threescore and ten toptypsical readings throughout the book of Doublends Jined" (FW 20.13–16). Meaning itself, it seems, is an accumulation: profit, a return on a text's investment to the tune of seven thousand percent, of threescore and ten—also, coincidentally, the average return (in years) on the investment of biological existence.

What we have here, then, is a glowing annual report, a multileveled tale of profit. But lurking between the lines of this report is another, contradictory one, a tale of loss. To return to our opening twenty-three words, the Latin *exaggerare* may mean to pile up, but the English exaggerate suggests that the wealth is overstated, perhaps even nonexistent. Hiding inside the "mumper" of fertile rocks is mumps, an illness which makes men infertile. The book's next sentence shows us not aggrandizement but collapse, the fall of "a once wallstraight oldparr" (FW 3.17)—a reference to Wall Street crashes. The great crash of 1929 was lurking round the corner when Joyce wrote the passage. Values, now as then, have plummeted, "one sovereign punned to petery pence" (FW 13.02). The opulent, accumulating landscape of Laurens County gives way to a retreating one whose length "lies under liquidation" (FW 12.07), whose typical inhabitant, "livving in our midst of debt" (FW 11.32), will "loan a vesta and hire some peat and sarch the shores her cockles to heat and she'll do all a turfwoman can to piff the business on" (FW 12.09–11). The line separating gorgeous bourgeois splendor from frugal poverty, as Joyce knew all too well, is thin.

Finnegans Wake, then, is a tale of two economies, two coexisting ones: one characterized by surplus, profit, wealth; and another characterized by bankruptcy and debt. This is true semantically as well: alongside a great glut of meanings runs a continual failure to establish any: "the unfacts, did we possess them, are too imprecisely few to warrant our incertitude, the evidencegivers by legpoll too untrustworthily irreperible [. . .] our notional gullery is now completely complacent, an exegious monument, aerily perennious" (FW 57.16–22). In the *Wake*'s negational language, "Sense" becomes "sinse" (FW 83.12), without (sin) sense, *senza*; "Enquiring" becomes "unquiring" (FW 3.20); "fiat," it was thus, becomes "fuit" (FW 128.1), it eluded us, escaped, and, eventually, "pfooi" (FW 125.22), that is, "rubbish!" "In this scherzarade of one's thousand one nightinesses," we are told, "that sword of certainty which would indentifide the body never falls" (FW 51.04–6). The book fails to return its readers' investment with fixed dividends of meaning, instead "[b]orrowing a word and begging the question and stealing tinder and slipping like soap" (FW 93.25–27), sliding further and further into the red of indeterminacy.

Finnegans Wake is a tale of two economies in more ways than one. Not only do the economy of surplus and that of loss tussle with one another for supremacy: so, too, do two differing versions of economy itself. We will call these versions "economics" and "chrematistics," respectively. The distinction is borrowed from Aristotle, where, crudely stated, it is the difference between the good natural economy of the *oikos* and the bad, artificial economy that arises when money (*to khrema*) appears on the scene. Derrida, in a fascinating passage from *Donner le temps—la fausse monnaie*, summarizes Aristotle's distinction between economics and chrematistics thus: "for Aristotle, it is a matter of an ideal and desirable limit, a limit between the limit and the unlimited, between the true and finite good (the economic) and the illusory and indefinite good (the chrematistic)."[14] Economics comes from *oikos*—home, hearth, seat of the family, the household, indeed of all those things that Derrida lists under "the proper," the sovereign—and "chrematistic" from *to khrema*, money, the unlimited exchangeability of goods that occurs when money appears on the scene. The distinction between economy and chrematistics is reflected not only in that between the limited and the unlimited but also in that between, continuing the previous quote, "the supposed finiteness of need and the presumed infinity of desire."[15] Once money, *to khrema*, has appeared on the scene, the infinity of desire will always transcend the finitude of need. Money is the desire of desire itself, a priori unsatisfied by any object one might actually need—behold, the logic of shopping! The fact that Derrida's language recalls that of Levinas (need/desire, finitude/infinity) is perhaps not accidental, for in opposition to an antimonetary tradition in philosophy that begins with Aristotle and culminates with Marx (recall that a communist society would be a society without the spectrality of money), Levinas is one of the rare thinkers who reserves a privileged place for money in his work. He writes in "The Ego and Totality" and I quote at length, "Money then does not purely and simply mark the reification of man. It is an element in which the personal is maintained while being quantified—this is what is proper to money and constitutes, as it were, its dignity as a philosophical category."[16] And further on the same page,

> Money allows us to envisage a justice of redemption to be substituted for the infernal or vicious circle of redemption or pardon. We cannot attenuate the condemnation which from Amos II, 6 to the Communist Manifesto has fallen upon money, precisely because of its power to buy man. But the justice which must save us from economy, that is, from the human totality, cannot negate

its superior form, where the quantification of man appears, the common measure between men, for which money, whatever be its empirical form, supplies the category. It is indeed shocking to see in the quantification of man one of the essential conditions for justice. But can one conceive of a justice without quantity and without reparation?[17]

Connecting this line of thought with Derrida, he continues the passage with a gesture that will be familiar to readers of his work: "As soon as there is the monetary sign—and first of all the sign—that is, *différance* and credit, the *oikos* is opened and cannot operate its limit."[18] Money, in effect, is deconstruction, opening the closure of the *oikos*, what Levinas calls totality, to the unrestricted "economy" of desire where money circulates and where wealth is accumulated or squandered.

However, we would like to go a little further and think of deconstruction as a monetary sign and indeed to think of money as one of the names for that incalculable excess that precedes any restricted economy of meaning. In this sense, money might even be thought of as a quasi-transcendental structure rendering the activity of a restricted economy of the proper both possible and impossible. It is with this thought in mind that one might redescribe grammatology as chrematology, as a logic of money. Money is a kind of deconstruction, opening the totality of the proper's economy, but is not the reverse of this proposition also plausible, namely, that deconstruction is a kind of money? For what is money, if not a specter, namely, the spectrality of difference that haunts the "real" value of the notes and coins in our pockets, the spectrality that has been at the heart of so many of Derrida's texts, particularly his reading of Marx's political economy? Doesn't the force of Derrida's argument against what he sees as Marx's essentializing "ontology" of life, praxis, labor, and the organicism of community entail a commitment to what he coins the "hauntology" of money, and thereby capital itself? What is deconstruction, on this account, if not a cipher for capital?[19]

Turning back to Joyce, this movement from the *oikos* to *khrema*, breaching the possibility of Home Rule in all senses of the word, occurs constantly in *Finnegans Wake*. HCE, the patriarch, "Highup Big Cockywocky Sublimissime Autocrat" (FW 612.12), finds himself repeatedly turned inside out, "allaroundside upinandoutdown" (FW 612.14). His private life is made public, subject to speculation. He is tried, fined, bankrupted. He has to pawn his furniture, the landscape of his *oikos*. It gets auctioned off—that is, assigned value according to how much and how many other people desire it, becomes currency. He becomes currency himself: people, first blackmailing him and then selling his story, make money from him (from him, they make money).

He is coined, stamped, circulated, sent abroad and then called back again. As a fallen, broken Ur-god (Humpty Dumpty, or "Hump Cumps Ebblybally" [FW 612.15]) he becomes a tip, a scrapheap full of items of "pecuniar interest" (FW 19.03) through which other people sift. His fall, a fall into both sin and debt (the German *Schuld*, combining both these terms, crops up in several guises), makes him "oblious autamnesically of his very proprium" (FW 251.04–5): it is a fall from the limited propriety of economics into the an-economic openness of chrematistics. *Finnegans Wake* is a retale that is retailed—again and a gain—a story of "One sovereign punned to petery pence" (FW 13.2): the sovereign economy of meaning punned chrematistically into grubby public circulation.

    This rupture of the limits of economics, which are the limits of the family, hearth, and home rule, makes possible, writes Derrida, "the chance for any kind of hospitality [. . .] the chance for the gift itself. The chance for the event."[20] Derrida is suggesting here that money is the possibility of a form of an-economic giving, for a donation without return, for an event. As a long and intriguing footnote to *Donner le temps* makes clear, the word "event" is to be understood in its Heideggerian sense as *das Ereignis*. Derrida associates money, *to khrema*, with *der Brauch* or usage, *to khreon*, which, according to Heidegger, names Being as the presencing of the present in early Greek thinking. Thus, the possibility of money, that is to say, the possibility of "*différance* and credit," breaking the restricted economy of finite need, is also the possibility of the gift, of another ethicality of the gift, hospitality. What Joyce calls "creed crux ethics" (FW 525.02) might be replaced with a new "ethical fict" (FW 523.33)—and here a further series of connections with Levinas' work might be imagined.

    Finnegans Wake, like many of Shakespeare's plays—or, for that matter, Hergé's *Tintin* books—abounds in instances of host-guest encounters, often fraught. As Hosty, publican perhaps of foreign origin, HCE plays host to people who, turning on him, become an alien host; Mutt, playing host to Jute's Danish invader, "trumple[s] from rath" (FW 16.27). It also abounds in instances in which a gift is sought, a line of credit opened. One of the primal events of *Finnegans Wake* is the encounter in the park between HCE and the cad. The episode is replayed at least twice (in book I, chapters 2 and 4). It is based on a report Joyce found in a regional Irish newspaper, *The Connaught Enquirer*, which told of how a drunk accosted another man demanding money, and a scuffle followed, after which the other man agreed to lend him some. This small news item caught Joyce's eye as it echoed a story his own father had told him about being accosted by a tramp (who John Stanislaus described as a "cad") in Phoenix Park one evening. Joyce told Frank Budgen that these twin events—or, rather, twin secondhand accounts—formed the basis of the novel.[21] In Joyce's versions of the incident (or incidents, the one which "prerepeated itself" [FW 81.33]), HCE plays the lender. In the second, the accoster is described thus:

> whereupon became friendly and, saying not, his shirt to tear, to know wanted, joking and knobkerries all aside laying, if his change companion who stuck still the invention of his strongbox, with a tenacity corrobberating their mutual territorial right, happened to have the loots change of a tenpound crickler about him at the moment, addling that hap so, he would pay him back the six vics odd. (FW 82.21–27)

HCE replies:

> Woowoo would you be grossly surprised, Hill, to learn that, as it so happens, I honestly have not such a thing as the loo, as the least chance of a tinpanned crackler anywhere about me at the present mohomoment but I believe I can see my way, as you suggest, it being Yuletide or Yuddanfest and as it's mad nuts, son, for you when it's hatter's hares, mon, for me, to advance you something like four and sevenpence between hopping and trapping, which you might hust as well have, boy baches, to buy J. J. and S. with. (FW 82.31–83.03)

In the first account of the encounter, too, HCE is well-to-do, "billowing across the wide expanse of our greatest park" (FW 35.07–8)—billowing like Antonio's ships' sails, but also, like the overstretched Antonio, bill owing. The cad asks him for the time—a veiled demand, perhaps, to hand over his watch, for time is money. HCE asks the cad to "credit" him in believing that there is no truth "in that purest of fibfib fabrications" (FW 36.33–34). What fibfib fabrication? It seems HCE is giving over more than he was asked for—and, in doing so, rendering himself accountable, indebting himself.

What's at stake in this encounter? HCE's reputation, certainly, as well as his money, his watch, and his life. The cad's next drink is in the balance too: J. J. and S. denotes Jameson's whiskey. But it also denotes James Joyce and Son. There's a sense that Joyce is writing his own history, opening a line of credit, the continuum in which his mumper can be doubled. The cad's words "I have met with you, bird, too late, or if not, too worm and early" (FW 37.13–14) echo those Joyce claims to have said to Yeats on their encounter ("We have met too late. You are too old for me to have any effect on you"[22]), folding literary history itself, its struggles of succession and anxieties of influence, in which pretenders to the literary crown are recipients of "loans" unwillingly made by—and unlikely to be returned to—their predecessors, into the mix.

The cad asks for ten pounds, and is offered four and sevenpence: the encounter involves not just indebtedness and impropriety (*Schuld*) but also bartering, like the bartering Heidegger describes when discussing the Anaximander Fragment. Beings come, then go back whence they came, thus rendering justice and paying penalty to one another for their injustice, according to the ordinance of time, the fragment tells us. "Thus," Heidegger writes, "they exhibit a kind of barter system in Nature's immutable economy."[23] What the fragment, an incomplete account from deep, deep in the past—just like the *Wake*'s accounts of the encounter, or encounters, of which Joyce himself only received partial accounts—represents to Heidegger is the dawn of that destiny whereby Being, the presencing of what is present, is sent to us—the dawn, that is, of the possibility of the *Ereignis*, the event, "in which the history of the Western world comes to be born out, the event of metaphysics."[24] *Finnegans Wake*, the book of history, of knowledge and of ignorance, of rereadings, repetitions, and exegeses, turns around the possibility of the event: of the event that might have happened way back in the park, or might happen again, or maybe is continually happening and has never stopped—and round the possibility of understanding it, of finally containing it in thought. In Joyce's text, the event unfolds as possibility, as destiny. It comes round again and again; it is retaled. But what it brings round is not Being, presencing and presence—rather, it reopens all lines of difference and credit around a monetary sign, an event of economic exchange. It is a tale that is retailed, again and a gain. Joyce's *Ereignis* is not that of presence, but rather of *différance*. In it, *es gibt Sein* becomes *es gibt Geld*.

Joyce believed that *Finnegans Wake* would be the last book, the one in which the destiny of literature realized itself. We would argue that he was exactly wrong: *Finnegans Wake* is the first book, the very possibility of literature become visible: as letter and as litter. One could almost say that it is money, the currency (*to khrema*) that has haunted literature's home and hearth since its beginnings, enabling its various closed economies (the Homeric epic, the picaresque adventure, the nineteenth-century novel, etc., etc.) as it lays them waste.

The way in which *Finnegans Wake* is offered to us is economic: it is not just retailed but also entailed. The second sentence of the novel's second paragraph tells us this, with a further allusion to Wall Street crashes: "The great fall of the offwall entailed at such short notice the pftjschute of Finnegan, erse solid man" (FW 3.18–20). What is the meaning of this word "entailed"? The OED defines "entail" as "The settlement of the succession of a landed estate, so that it cannot be bequeathed at pleasure by any one possessor" (sb. def. 1), "The securing (an office, dignity, privilege) to a predetermined order of succession" (sb. def. 2a), and "To carve, sculpture; to make carvings upon, ornament with carvings; to portray or represent by carvings" (v. def. 1).[25] It seems we are being treated, right from the outset, to a drama of inheritance, a drama of inheritance engraved in writing. This drama, acted out around the struggles between Shem and Shaun, is alluded to as soon as the first paragraph, in which we are told that "not yet, but venisoon after, had a kidscad buttended a bland old Isaac" (FW 3.10–11). The reference is to Jacob ("Shem is as short for Shemus as Jem is joky for Jacob" [FW 169.01]) robbing Esau of his inheritance by bringing a lamb to his blind father Isaac while dressed in a hairy sheepskin: Isaac felt the hair, thought Jacob was Esau and gave him his estate. Wile, trickery, and subterfuge will make themselves felt throughout the struggle.

Let's take a closer look at Shem and Shaun, these twin representatives of economic poles. Shaun is dubbed "the Post," the one controlling the economy of messages, of signs, of currency. He is wealthy. Shem, by contrast, is poor, and constantly in debt. He "lives on loans" (FW 173.07). He is prodigal, a spendthrift, "foe to social and business succes" (FW 156.35–36), "making encostive inkum out of the last of his lathings and writing a blue streak over his bourseday shirt" (FW 27.10–11). As Burrus, Shaun inherits bread and honey; as the Ondt, he smokes "Hosana cigals" (FW 417.12–13). Shem, as Caseous, inherits shit; as the Gripes, he relies on "the fortethurd of Elissabed" (FW 156.33–34), the poor relief law or, as it was known, the 43rd Statute of Elizabeth. Biographically, Shem corresponds to James, Shaun to Stanislaus Joyce. Shem is a penman, a writer. He is also a forger. For Joyce, the two are synonymous: ever since *Portrait* it has been axiomatic for him that art is forgery. Shem's literary apprenticeship is one and the same as his development as a forger: perusing other writers' work, he decides to "study with stolen fruit how cutely to copy all their various styles of signature so as one day to utter an epical forged cheque on the public for his own private profit" (FW 181.14–17). The epical cheque denotes Joyce's own novel, the shady trading zone in which all literature becomes chrematized currency.

Identity and difference, twin principles of money. That money—every single penny, zloty, dinar, lira, and shekel—must be exactly the same as another, and yet different. Money's sameness is constituted through a repetition that makes it distinct: again and a gain. And Shem and Shaun are almost twins; it is suggested that what occurred in the womb was not a splitting of the egg but rather superfetation, the fertilization of a second egg while the first was already gestating: doubling mum (superfetation also means profit, accumulation). As children, they are twin-like, "jimminies" (FW 23.12). "Why do I am allok alike two poss of porterpease?" (FW 22.05–6) the Prankquean asks Jarl van Hoother/HCE as she swaps them for one another under his very nose.

This problem of identity versus difference comes to a head in book I, chapter 6, as Shaun/Jones answers his eleventh question: Would you give money to an exiled, wandering beggar to save his soul? No, replies Shaun/Jones, before launching into an elaborate explanation in which time and space are discussed in terms that are both economic and concerned with principles of equivalence and likeness. In his "cash-dime" speech Shaun/Jones starts by belittling Bergson ("the sophology of Bitchson" [FW 149.20]), Einstein ("the whoo-whoo and where's hairs theorics of Winestain" [FW 149.27–28]), and Proust ("who the lost time we had the pleasure we have had our little recherch brush with [. . .]" [FW 149.23–24]). They are all temporalists and all Jews, and hence, by "Deasian" association, wanderers, exiles. As is the Professor Levy-Bruhl ("Professor Loewy-Brueller," "Professor Levi-Brullo, F.D. of Sexe-Weiman-Eitelnaky" [FW 150.15, 151.11–12]), whose work on *les mentalités primitives* and the experience of the mystical is dispatched on the next pages, "by what I have now resolved to call the dime and cash diamond fallacy" (FW 150.23–24). This preoccupation with time, Shaun/Jones argues, is solipsistic and sentimental, in another swipe that makes Proust's madeleine crumble,

> *When* Mullocky won the couple of colds, *when* we were stripping in number three, I would like the neat drop that would malt in my mouth but I fail to see *when* (I am purposely refraining from expounding the obvious fallacy as to the specific gravitates of the two deglutables implied nor to the lapses lequou asousiated with the royal gorge through students of mixed hydrostatics and pneumodipsics will after some difficulties grapple away with my meinungs). Myrrdin aloer! As old Marsellas Cambriannus puts his. But, on Professor Llewellys ap Bryllars, F.D., Ph. Dr's showings, the plea, if he pleads, is all posh and robbage on a melodeontic scale since his man's when is no otherman's *quandor* (Mine, dank you?) while, for aught I care for the contrary, that all is *where* in love as war. (FW 151.24–36)

Which is to say the following: an intense memory of eating a madeleine does not entitle its author to claim insight into all of human experience. The fact that Proust can hold up his two bits, his tiny dime, does not mean that he owns all the world's time, its thought-wealth, for dime is money. In arguing this, Shaun/Jones claims, Shem is

> a mere cashdime [. . .] to this graded intellektuals dime *is* cash and the cash system (you must not be allowed to forget that this is all contained, I mean the system, in the dogmarks of origen on spurios

[dogmas of spurious origin, Deutschmarks of dodgy origin, dog marks, i.e., shit, and Darwin's *The Origin of Species*], means that I cannot now have or nothave a piece of cheeps in your pocket at the same time and with the same manners as you can now nothalf or half the cheek apiece I've in mind unless Burrus and Casseous have not seemaultaneously sysentangled thmselves, selldear to soldthere, once in the dairy days of buy and buy. (FW 161.04–14)

Thus, juggling the questions of likeness, self-sameness, and difference that currency brings into play, Shaun refutes Shem's claim to his wealth. It is he, and he alone, who will inherit. One Dubliner will be doubling his mumper, while the other will be doubled with mumps.

Shaun repeats this claim in book III, chapter 1. There, setting out his own "last will intesticle" (FW 413.17), he "spinooze[s]" (FW 414.16) the fable of the Ondt and the Gracehoper. Shaun reinvents himself as the industrious Ondt, a truly anti-Schellingian idealist with "a schelling in kopfers" (FW 416.04), whose "raumybult" (FW 416.03) riches contrast strongly with the Gracehoper/Shem's "jungle of love and debts" (FW 416.09). Encountering the Gracehoper while he, the Ondt, smokes "a spatial brunt of Hosana cigals" (FW 417.12–13), he mocks him with what Joyce calls his "comfortumble phullup-suppy" (FW 417.15): "Flunkey Footle furloughed fould, writing off his phoney, but Conte Carme makes the melody that mints the money. Ad majorem l.s.d! [pounds, shillings, pence] Divi gloriam [divi as in dividend paid in former time by the Co-Operative Society, a share or portion]" (FW 418.02–4).

The Gracehoper/Shem admits defeat, his capitulation also expressed economically:

> As I once played the piper I must now pay the count [. . .]
> I pick up your reproof, the horsegift of a friend
> For the prize of your save is the price of my spend. (FW 418.17–22)

He ends, though, with a caveat:

> As I view by your farlook hale yourself to my heal [. . .]
> Your genus is worldwide, your spacest sublime
> But, holy Saltmartin, why can't you beat time? (FW 418.36–419.08)

Shem/Gracehoper, down to his last dime, is countering that Shaun/Ondt may inherit space, the "sees of the deed" the exiled Gracehoper has "twicycled" (FW 416.30), the "vico[s]" (FW 417.05–6) onto which he's "tossed himself" (FW 417.05–6), but the time in which the world goes round remains the preserve of the artist.

Which of these two claims does Joyce's text prefer? Ultimately, neither. Each time Shaun and Shem's battles over inheritance replay themselves, they fade away to be replaced by Isabelle, Issy, Nuvoletta, Margareen: the sons give over to the daughter. And what does the daughter do? Long for the father, his "roturns" (FW 18.05), "I go back to you, my cold father, my cold mad father, my cold mad feary father" (FW 628.01–2). She longs not for the world to come around to her, but for the round to go a-world again, "Onetwo moremens more" (FW 628.05–6). For the ISA figure, HCE is experienced not as an economic legacy, a fortune, or a debt-mountain to be inherited, but rather as a gift, an accumulative gift, a donation without return, "Till thousendsthee" (FW 628.14–15). This is how the novel ends: with an invocation of the gift, its recirculation. The last complete sentence in the novel consists of a single word: "Given!" (FW 628.15). The next phrase tails off incomplete, unclosed, improper, entailing the pftjschute of Finnegan, erse solid man, once more, bequeathing one more time his debris, his pecuniary litter, the unconverted currency that makes the round go a-world, as gain and loss, again.

Notes

1. "The spirit that speaks from the ornamental design of banknotes." Walter Benjamin, "Capitalism as Religion," trans. Rodney Livingstone, in *Selected Writings*, vol. 1: 1913–1926, ed. Marcus Bullock and Michael W. Jennings (Cambridge: Harvard University Press, 1996), 288–91; 290, translation of "Kapitalismus als Religion" in *Gesammelte Schriften*, in collaboration with T. W. Adorno and Gershom Scholen, vol. 6: *Fragmente. Autobiographische Schriften*, ed. Rolf Tiedemann and H. Schweppenhäuser (Frankfurt am Main: Suhrkamp Verlag, 1991), 100–3; 102.

2. We borrow this formulation from Peter Osborne.

3. Jan Morris, *Trieste and the Meaning of Nowhere* (London: Faber, 2001).

4. Theodore Adorno, "On the Fetish-Character in Music and the Regression in Listening," in *The Essential Frankfurt School Reader*, ed. Andrew Arato and Eike Gebhardt (New York: Continuum, 1982), 278–79.

5. Michael Hardt and Antonio Negri, *Empire* (Cambridge: Harvard University Press, 2000), see esp. chap. 2.5, "Network Power: U.S. Sovereignty and the New Empire," 160–82.

6. Sigmund Freud, *Notes Upon a Case of Obsessional Neurosis*, trans. Alix and James Strachey, in *The Standard Edition of the Complete Psychological Works of Sigmund Freud*, 24 volumes (London: The Hogarth Press, 1999), volume 10, 151–318; 213.

7. Jacques Lacan, "Joyce le symptôme," *Le Sinthome. Le Séminaire, livre XXIII*, ed. Jacques-Alain Miller (Paris: Seuil, 2005), 161–69; 167. The translation of Lacan's address at the 1975 Joyce Symposium is by Lorenzo Chiesa (unpublished typescript). Our interpretation of Lacan's reading of Joyce is deeply indebted to a paper by Lorenzo Chiesa, "Writing Enjoyment: Lacan, Artaud," given at the University of Essex, June 2002.

8. Ibid., 165.
9. Ibid., 166.
10. Ibid., 163.
11. Ibid., 166.
12. Joseph Campbell and Henry Morton Robinson, A *Skeleton Key to "Finnegans Wake": Unlocking James Joyce's Masterwork* (Novato, CA: New World Library, 2005), 27.
13. *Shakespeare's Sonnets*, ed. Katherine Duncan Jones (London: The Arden Shakespeare, 2007), I.1.
14. Jacques Derrida, *Given Time: 1. Counterfeit Money*, trans. Peggy Kamuf (Chicago: University of Chicago Press, 1992), 158, translation of *Donner le temps: 1. La fausse monnaie* (Paris: Galilée, 1991), 200.
15. Ibid., 158/200.
16. Emmanuel Levinas, "The Ego and Totality," in *Collected Philosophical Papers*, trans. Alphonso Lingis (Dordrecht: Kluwer, 1987), 45.
17. Ibid.
18. Derrida, *Given Time*, 158/200.
19. Derrida responded to our thoughts, with skepticism but good grace, during an extensive discussion of the function of money in his work. The debate is published as "Autor des écrits de Jacques Derrida sur l'argent," in Marcel Drach, ed., *L'argent: Croyance, mesure, spéculation* (Paris: Éditions La Découverte, 2004), 201–32.
20. Derrida, *Given Time*, 158/200.
21. We are grateful to Finn Fordham for drawing our attention to this.
22. Richard Ellmann, *James Joyce*, rev. ed. (Oxford: Oxford University Press, 1982), 102.
23. Martin Heidegger, "The Anaximander Fragment," in *Early Greek Thinking*, ed. David Farrell Krell, trans. David Farrell Krell and Frank A. Capuzzi (New York: Harper and Row, 1984), 13–58, 20.
24. Ibid., 51.
25. *The Oxford English Dictionary*, 2nd ed., volume 5: Dvandva–Follis (Oxford: Oxford University Press, 1989), 285.

IV

Recollections

10

Signature/Countersignature: Derrida's Response to *Ulysses*

Derek Attridge

I

Is it possible, as a reader or critic, to do justice to Joyce's *Ulysses*? This question immediately raises another one: what would it *mean* to do justice to a literary work? In this essay I shall be discussing Jacques Derrida's response to *Ulysses* in light of the first of these questions (and in so doing attempting to do justice myself to his response), but in order to do this I will initially need to take up the second question. We don't hesitate to say such and such a review does justice to—or doesn't do justice to—the work on which it is commenting; but we don't stop to analyze what this might mean.

Derrida himself addresses the topic of justice in many places, most notably, perhaps, in the essay "Force of Law." He sums up the paradoxical nature of the just decision as follows:

> [I]f the act [by which justice is exercised] simply consists of applying a rule, of enacting a program or effecting a calculation, one will perhaps say that it is legal, that it conforms to law, and perhaps, by metaphor, that it is just, but one would be wrong to say that the decision was just. [. . .] To be just, the decision of a judge, for example, must not only follow a rule of law or a general law but must also assume it, approve it, confirm its value, by a reinstituting act of interpretation, as if, at the limit, the law did not exist previously—as if the judge himself invented it in each case. . . . it must preserve the law and also destroy or suspend it enough to have to reinvent it in each case, rejustify it, reinvent it at least in the reaffirmation and the new and free confirmation of its principle.[1]

Derrida is, of course, not talking about literary criticism, but one does not have to look far in his writing on literary texts to find similar structural paradoxes, and similar imperatives for responsible judgment, being articulated. In two essays on works of literature, the idea of the law is directly interrogated: "Before the Law," on Kafka's parable of the same name, and "The Law of Genre," on Blanchot's fiction "The Madness of the Day."[2] In each case, the problem of justice, and its relation to the law, is implicit both in the text being discussed and in Derrida's own approach to it. For the problem of justice, as Derrida insists, is the problem of the relation between the *absolutely singular* and the *wholly general*: a relation which is at once that of mutually defining opposition and necessary interimplication. "How to reconcile the act of justice," he writes, "that must always concern singularity, individuals, groups, irreplaceable existences, the other or myself *as* other, in a unique situation, with rule, norm, value, or the imperative of justice that necessarily have a general form, even if this generality prescribes a singular application in each case?" ("Force of Law" 245/39). "Each case is other, each decision is different and requires an absolutely unique interpretation, which no existing, coded rule can or ought to guarantee absolutely" ("Force of Law" 251/51).

The literary text I read is singular, yet that singularity is constituted and conveyed only by its participation in general laws: laws of genre, convention, language, discourse. My response to that text is singular—at least it's my obligation as critic to strive for a singular appreciation of its singularity, since no other response will do its singularity justice—yet it's arrived at and articulated only by means of norms and conventions. The act of literature has the structure of the *signature* (Derrida discusses *Ulysses* in these terms, and I shall come back to this), the *date* (a motif he traces Celan's poetry), the *proper name* (given particular emphasis in his work on Ponge's poetry and on *Romeo and Juliet*), and the *invention* (highlighted in his account of Ponge's poem "Fable");[3] that is to say, it's constitutively unique, but with a uniqueness itself already constituted by repetition and repeatability, what Derrida terms "iterability." And the act of criticism, the decision or the judgment whereby the reader assents to the singularity of the text (and thereby produces it *in* its singularity), is an affirmation that does not *follow* rules but rather suspends and reinvents the rules by which it is rendered readable. It passes, as Derrida says any decision must, through "the ordeal of the undecidable [*l'épreuve de l'indécidable*]" ("Force of Law" 252/53); if it did not, it would merely be the application of an algorithm; a calculable, programmable reaction.

It's impossible therefore, to do justice to a literary text; not because of the infinite richness of literary language or the sad limitations of readers, but because the act of critical judgment is an impossible, though always necessary, act. (And we might think of the several meanings of the word "act" before we attribute to it any sense of simple spontaneity or intentionality.) It's impossible because the text is other, and our reading of it is only of value to the extent that it's a response to that otherness (most readings of course are exercises in converting otherness to sameness); but there's no way we can represent, to ourselves or to anyone else, that otherness without contaminating it with, or rather without finding it *already* contaminated by, the same. That is to say, acknowledging and affirming the otherness of the other necessarily involves some limitation of its alterity: to perceive the other is to find that it has made some impression on the world with which I am familiar.

Once again, it's necessary to emphasize—since Derrida's thinking is always pursuing a difficult course along the edge of truisms, which is one reason why it has so often been recuperated by the institutions it seeks to undermine—that the otherness and singularity of the literary text is not an ineffable, inaccessible essence; indeed, it may well be in its very *readability* that a text manifests its otherness. As Derrida puts it in "'This Strange Institution Called Literature'":

> An absolute, absolutely pure singularity, if there were one, would not even show up, or at least would not be available for reading. To become readable, it has to be *divided*, to *participate* and *belong*. Then it is divided and takes *its part* in the genre, the type, the context, meaning, the conceptual generality of meaning, etc. It loses itself to offer itself. [. . .] The "best" reading would consist in *giving oneself up to* the most idiomatic aspects of the work while also *taking account* of the historical context, of what is *shared*, [. . .] of what belongs to genre and type.[4]

We must not confuse "doing justice to" a text with evaluating it, criticizing it in the sense of placing it on a fixed scale of values; the phrase suggests, rather, an affirmation, a saying "yes" to what matters most in the text. This may sound somewhat different from the characteristic operation of justice in the law courts, which *is* perhaps closer to the evaluative notion of literary criticism as it condemns or saves texts. But justice in the legal sphere as *Derrida* represents it is equally affirmative, equally responsive to what is unique in the other; he appeals to what he calls "an 'idea of justice' that is infinite, infinite because irreducible, irreducible because owed to the other—owed to the other, before any contract, because it has *come*, it is a *coming*, the coming of the other as always other singularity" ("Force of Law" 254/55). He goes on: "this 'idea of justice' seems indestructible in its affirmative character, in its demand of gift without exchange, without circulation, without recognition or gratitude, without economic circularity, without calculation and without rules, without reason and without theoretical rationality" ("Force of Law" 254/55–56). It's in this sense that I want to talk about the critic's obligation to *do justice to* the literary text, which is of course as far from what usually goes by the name of "deconstruction" as it is from New Criticism or New (not to speak of old) Historicism.

Implicit in what I'm saying, though Derrida doesn't spell it out, is that the link between legal and literary studies is in large part an ethico-political one. It's not, however, a question of the moral power of great literature as traditionally taught in humanistic criticism, nor of the detection of morally and politically suspect ideological positions concealed in literary texts, but of the supremely difficult ethical act of responding to the singularity and otherness of the unique instance—whether person, act, or text—while bringing to bear on it, without merely *applying* them, all the general laws and norms that constitute both it and the judging discourse. This is not to decry critical analysis that operates by means of the application of rules; most of what we do as critics is just such an activity, and the skills involved in this activity form the foundation of all reading. But just as no successful *literary* text is ever entirely the programmable reaction to events or experiences, but reinvents the very rules that enable it to come into being in a way that surpasses the logic of computers or psycho- and sociological rules, so no *critical* text that can be said to do justice to literature, and to the specific literary text it's answering to and affirming, can be solely a skillful application of existing rules. Its singularity affirms, and makes possible, the singularity of the other, of the text, but also necessarily betrays it, does violence to it (otherwise it could not be a singular but merely an algorithmic reaction); and we touch here on the difficult, and essential, question of the violence at the heart of any ethical relation.

II

I want to switch now to the autobiographical mode. I was among the audience in the packed hall for the opening session of the Ninth International James Joyce Symposium held in Frankfurt in 1984. We were gathered to hear Jacques Derrida speak what the program announced as "Ulysse Grammaphone [sic]: L'Oui-Dire de Joyce." Although later in his life Derrida often gave lectures in English (either reading from a translation of his original French, or translating as he went along), in 1984 he was not confident enough in this language to do so. The result was a somewhat bizarre event: Derrida gave his lecture in French, but paused from time to time to allow a translator-cum-abstracter to give a brief summary of what he had said over the previous twenty or thirty minutes. (Derrida's fifty-page script, a copy of which he gave me later, has arrows in the margins approximately every ten pages, which are no doubt the four places where he stopped for the summaries.) Those of you who know the text of this lecture, which takes the reader on a circuitous intellectual as well as geographical odyssey, will realize what a heroic task this summarizer took on. Furthermore, Derrida paid no attention to the official hour-and-a-half period allotted to his lecture: he spoke with the ease and assurance of someone who had been given no time limits whatever. I can't remember how long the lecture lasted, but it was well over two hours. Although most of the audience must have had very little understanding of what he was saying, and there was no chance that the brief summaries would convey the complex texture of the argument, let alone the subtle tonalities of Derrida's style, surprisingly few people left the room; perhaps there was a shared awareness that this was, however incomprehensible, a landmark event in twentieth-century literary studies.

At the time, I was a relative neophyte in the Joyce world. I'd been persuaded by friends to give a mini-paper at the symposium in Dublin two years before, and since then had started to teach a course on Joyce alongside my usual teaching in Renaissance and Romantic studies. I was also getting to know Derrida's work and trying to improve my French; and these three projects were coming together in a collection of essays by French Joyceans I was coediting with Daniel Ferrer. When, a month before the symposium, one of those friends who had persuaded me two years earlier to dip my toes in the Joycean ocean, Maud Ellmann, asked me if I would take her place on a panel following Derrida's address, I agreed, though not without some trepidation. The panel, organized by Ellen Carol Jones, was called simply "Deconstructive Criticism of Joyce." With little time to write the paper, I exploited the fact that both Joyce and Derrida were struck by the potential ambiguity of the genitive construction—Joyce in the phrase *Amor matris*, love of the mother, allowing interpretation, as he puts it in the "Nestor" episode, as both "subjective and objective genitive" (U 2.165); Derrida, among other places, in the title of Blanchot's *Arrêt de mort* (PC 285/385)—and that the title of our panel could be read in two ways thanks to the same ambiguity: "deconstructive criticism of Joyce" could be criticism *about* Joyce or criticism *by* Joyce. With the brashness of (relative) youth, I called the paper I presented "Of" (though in its published version it became "Criticism's Wake"[5]).

I recently listened again to the audiotape of this event, and sensed once more the palpable excitement, mixed with a certain degree of hostility, in the room. There were two other short papers, by Christine van Boheemen and Beryl Schlossman, and then the floor was open for questions. Most of them, understandably, were addressed, implicitly or explicitly, to Derrida himself, and he responded to them all in his somewhat halting English. The dominant tone of the questions was skeptical—"Doesn't deconstruction say the same thing about all works of literature?"; "Why do the panelists not take issue with one another?" "Isn't intentionalism being let in by the back door?" Listening to the discussion now, it's clear that there was a widespread feeling that deconstruction was a machine that ground down all works of art (and of philosophy, presumably) to the same uninteresting heap of rubble. Derrida's two-and-a-half-hour analysis of the specificity of *Ulysses* seemed not to have shifted this perception, and I'm not convinced that had he been speaking in English the result would have been any different. In the panel discussion, Derrida was at pains to stress, as I have also been stressing, that far from treating every text alike, a deconstructive reading attempts to do justice to the singularity of the work, and that this can only be achieved if the reading itself is a singular text.

It was in Frankfurt that I raised with Derrida later in the week the possibility of an anthology of his writings on literature—one of whose aims would be to demonstrate the variety of his readings of different works and authors—and received a gratifyingly positive response. Although space meant that I had to include shortened versions of some of Derrida's longer texts, I included "Ulysses Gramophone" in full in the volume (which after much deliberation I called *Acts of Literature*), since it seemed—and still seems—to me to be one of his most remarkable and important performances (I use the word deliberately), and one that all students of literature have something to learn from.

III

Derrida began "Ulysse gramophone" with the sentence "Oui, oui, vous m'entendez bien, ce sont des mots français," immediately announcing one of the major topics of his lecture, the *yes* in *Ulysses*, and at the same time foregrounding the occasion, an address in French to a largely Anglophone audience. The singularity of this opening lies partly in its use of perfectly normal lexical and grammatical forms to produce an untranslatable sentence whose meaning is undecidable; and it is this untranslatability and undecidability that marks Derrida's discourse from the beginning as partaking of the literary. As he says in an important footnote in the essay "Passions,"

> Something of literature will have begun when it is not possible to decide whether, when I speak of something, I am indeed speaking of something (of the thing itself, this one, for itself) or if I am giving an example, an example of something or an example of the fact that I can speak of something, of my way of speaking of something,

of the possibility of speaking in general of something in general, or again of writing these words, etc.⁶

Something of literature clearly began in Frankfurt as Derrida started speaking.

What I would like to single out from the commentary that Derrida offered on his opening sentence is the notion of the *signature*, since this becomes a crucial term in the discussion of *Ulysses*. I can develop only a few of the implications of the signature in this essay, as it is closely linked to the other topics of this long, rich text, and to follow it in all the directions in which it could lead would be to write a piece even longer than Derrida's.⁷

The two possible meanings of the words "oui, oui" with which Derrida began his lecture both involve *signing*, by which Derrida means a singular affirmation made by a subject at a specific time and place. If I *use* the word "yes," he says, "I affirm or acquiesce, I subscribe, I approve, I respond or I promise, I commit myself in any case and I *sign*" (UG 41/58, my italics); and if I *mention* the word "yes"—that is, if the word is being quoted as an instance—"the act of citing or mentioning no doubt also supposes some *signing* [*quelque signature*]" (UG 41/58, my italics). In the second case the signature remains implicit, and it is this implicit signature that will become important later in the lecture.

For the first forty minutes or so those of us in the auditorium in Frankfurt heard little more about the signature, apart from a reminder that to date is to sign (UG 43/62) (for signing is always affirming a specific here and now that is recorded for the future) and the description of the institution of Joyce scholars as a "signing and countersigning machine" (UG 50/77) (a description we'll come back to). Then, after a narrative account of his travels while writing the lecture, and of the coincidences and misunderstandings that accompanied his communication of a title to the organizers, events whose relevance only became clear to the audience in retrospect, Derrida returned to the question of the repetition of the *yes*—Molly's increasingly frequent *yeses* in the final pages of the book, of course, but also Miss Dunne's repeated *yeses* on the telephone to her employer, Hugh Boylan (U 10.389–95). In order for the *yes* to function as a signature, it must, he stated, "archive its voice to give it once again to be heard" (UG 56/90). Repetition, in other words, is not an external and optional feature of affirmation, it is internal and intrinsic: if my *yes* doesn't imply a promise of future *yeses*, if I could just as well deny next minute what I affirm now, it is not a commitment, and lacks force as a speech act. This essential requirement of repeatability, as Derrida points out, insinuates a mechanical factor into the most personal and lively *yes*. The *yes* must in some way be recorded or inscribed; it cannot be pure spontaneity, existing only in the present. Hence the importance of the many telephones in *Ulysses* to Derrida's argument, for the telephone provides a tangible example of the mechanical relays underlying what we too easily think of as "natural" speech communication, and hence, too, the significance of the gramophone Bloom imagines in "Hades" (U 6.961–66), for the gramophone testifies to the recordability of the living voice. Every *yes*, then, involves a signature, and every signature involves a *yes*.

In order to appreciate what is at stake in approaching *Ulysses* by way of the signature, let us pause for a moment to consider how the signature works successfully in our daily lives.[8] When I sign a document, I testify that I am physically (and mentally) present, here and now, and that I approve what I have signed; and I promise to acknowledge that presence and that approval at any future date. A signature represents that unique event for posterity. But as Derrida stresses, simply to write one's name is not to sign (UG 58/94, 66/111). My signature will only work as it is supposed to if it is at once unique *and* recognizable. To be unique is to be different each time; if on inspection a signature turns out to have been produced by a stamp, it fails, since it no longer testifies to the presence of the signer. (By convention, a mechanical signature is accepted in certain contexts, on a banknote, for example, or an e-mail, even though it does not testify to the presence of the signer. What such examples disclose is that a signature can always be mechanically reproduced or forged—it would not function as a signature if it could not.) But to be recognizable is to be repeated: a signature that is different from the same individual's other signatures will also fail. Hence the paradox of the signature: to function properly, it has to be both different and the same, on the one hand a unique testament to an unrepeatable here and now of an individual, and on the other a reproducible inscription participating in general codes and processes. "Usually interpreted as one's very own mark," writes Derrida elsewhere, "[the signature] is instead what I cannot incorporate, cannot make my own."[9]

Ulysses, with its many *yeses*, its telephones and telegrams, its letters and post offices, its imagined gramophone, stages in a host of different modalities the operation of affirmation as signature, as a singular commitment, here and now, bearing within it the necessary possibility of repetition. What Derrida *doesn't* do, but what his reading seems to invite, is examine the actual signatures that occur in the text. Had he done so, he would have found that Joyce provides ample evidence for the Derridean account of the signature by giving us a range of examples that highlight the logic and the limits of its operation. There are childish signatures—Cyril Sargent's babyish "crooked signature with blind loops and a blot" in the "Nestor" episode" (U 2.129–30) and Milly Bloom's adolescent "signature with flourishes capital em" catalogued in "Ithaca" (U 17.1794). It's not certain that these are able to work properly as signatures because it's not clear that the next time Cyril or Milly sign they will produce something that is recognizably "the same." Conventionally, an illiterate person can sign with a mark, another example of the signature that lacks force, as it is *too* repeatable; thus in the *United Irishman* skit read out by the citizen in "Cyclops" we hear that the Alaki of Abeakuta "signed his mark in the visitors' book" (U 12.1530). There is an example of scholarly cleverness that must also raise doubts about its effectiveness: in "Ithaca" Stephen shows off to Bloom his ability to write his "signature in Irish and Roman characters" (U 17.775). We must, however, doubt whether the Irish version is really a signature, or whether it is, rather, only a written name.

Another dubious type is the one that inscribes a fictional name (an omnipresent possibility with the signature), such as the "H" that Bloom writes on his letter to Martha Clifford (U 11.893), or, in "Circe," the "anonymous letter" Mrs Yelverton Barry accuses Bloom of having written to her, in a disguised hand, "signed James Lovebirch" (U 15.1016–18). We cannot tell if the inscription "Martha" at the end of the letter Bloom picks up in "Lestrygonians" is a genuine signature or a written pseudonym, but Bloom presumably recognizes it from previous correspondence. There may be no such thing as a private signature, but within a community of two, signatures can function perfectly well. Then there is the signature that substitutes a common noun for a proper noun, but seems to function just as efficiently: when Molly recalls getting a letter with such a signature—"an admirer he signed it" (U 18.762)—she can tell perfectly well it is from Lieutenant Mulvey. The force of the signature as an obligation stretching into the future is brought home by Bello—the transgendered form of Bella Cohen in "Circe"—when she orders Bloom, "Sign a will and leave us any coin you have!" (U 15.3206), and by Bloom himself in "Sirens" when he imagines his letter to Martha being read out in court as evidence for breach of promise: "Henry. I never signed it" (U 11.1080). (He hopes, of course, to benefit from the failure of his pseudonymous signature in the wider community.) Molly, in her Circean guise, also takes advantage of the signature's testimonial power to browbeat her husband: "I'll write to a powerful prostitute or Bartholomona, the bearded woman, to raise weals out on him an inch thick and make him bring me back a signed and stamped receipt" (U 15.3778–3881). And in "Lestrygonians," the inescapable commitment implied by the signature is the point of Nosey Flynn's gesture during a conversation about Bloom in Davy Byrne's pub, "His hand scrawled a dry pen signature beside his grog," which he then interprets for the publican: "Nothing in black and white" (U 8.986–88).

There are a number of mechanically produced signatures in *Ulysses*, which sever the bond between signer and signature and thus open the possibility of fraud and falsification. Joyce gives us the wording of a telegram sent to Buck Mulligan: "*The sentimentalist is he who would enjoy without incurring the immense debtorship for a thing done.* Signed: Dedalus" (U 9.550–51). Here there is no guarantee that the printed name actually represents an original signature (though everything else about it unquestionably points to Stephen). Another telegram is the one Stephen recalls receiving in Paris, where the signature is replaced by a family appellation: "Nother dying come home father" (U 3.199). Less successful is the printed signature at the foot of the *United Irishman* skit read out by the citizen in "Cyclops," as the drinkers' conversation reveals:

—Is that by Griffith? says John Wise.

—No, says the citizen. It's not signed Shanganagh. It's only initialled: P. (U 12.1538–39)

Lacking both the individuality of handwriting (one could imagine a handwritten P signed with a particular flourish) and the distinctiveness of a name, this signature barely deserves to be called one, as the citizen recognizes. In "Aeolus," Stephen points to the "title and signature" (U 7.517) of Garrett Deasy's letter to the press: this genuine signature will appear in the newspaper in the form of a printed name, again providing only a simulacrum that could always be false. (We are alerted later by the mangling of Bloom's name in the newspaper as "L. Boom" how easy it is for print to misrepresent a handwritten name.)

Finally, Joyce gives some sense of the many possible extended uses of the notion of the signature in the opening of "Proteus," when Stephen muses on the "signatures of all things I am here to read" (U 3.2), and in his fanciful image in "Scylla and Charybdis" of Shakespeare watching the constellation Cassiopeia, with its distinctive W shape, "the signature of his initial among the stars" (U 9.931).

Like the *yeses* in *Ulysses*, then, the signatures dramatize, in many different ways, the complex conditions that both enable and constrain the act of affirmation and commitment. We need to turn now from the signature in *Ulysses* to the signature of *Ulysses*.

IV

To speak of the signature of *Ulysses* is to refer to that which renders it unique among literary works, but also to register those many features that it shares with other works, by Joyce and by other authors, features that, from the very first word he wrote, took it out of Joyce's hands and into the space of public conventions and laws. As we've seen, for Derrida, the signature is that which one cannot make one's own, like the proper name: it is constituted as singular in the space of generality. If it were wholly unique, it would be completely unreadable, as there would be no codes and conventions by which to read it. If it were wholly a repetition of other works, no-one would bother to read it. A successful reading of *Ulysses* is one that does justice to both these dimensions.

Ulysses, then, besides staging a range of different types of signature, successful and failed, is also *itself* a signature, Joyce's signature. In "Ulysses Gramophone" Derrida writes: "Someone answering, yes, in Joyce's name, succeeded in linking the future of an institution to the singular adventure of a *signed* proper name" (UG 58/94). The name "Joyce," as it is used by Joyce scholars and critics, and for that matter by nonspecialist readers, is not just a proper name; it stands for a singular body of work underwritten by, sent out into the world by, *signed* by a particular individual. Joyce's signature is not just the scrawl to be seen on his letters and certain documents, but the distinctive corpus, the distinctiveness of the corpus, he left to posterity.[10]

Derrida uses another term, one that complicates the picture, however. He draws on the notion of the *countersignature*: a signature that affirms another signature, which would otherwise remain invalid, unwitnessed, a possible forgery. The countersignature—possessing exactly the same paradoxical properties as the signature—*constitutes* the first signature as a signature, not just a written name. (It will probably be evident that both signature and countersignature are *events* rather than objects.) The response that can be said to do justice to the literary work countersigns its signature: affirms its singularity and identity by its own singularity and identity. In fact, one could say that the work's singularity and identity do not exist as such until responded to by readers in this way. The implication, of course, is that all good readings are different, though all find ways of responding to what is distinctive about the work. A countersignature can also be a commitment that involves trust and the taking of a certain risk, as when I sign to attest to my willingness to underwrite someone else's financial obligation. Like the signature, the countersignature is both an affirmation and a promise: I affirm in the present, and I promise to stand by this affirmation in the future. It's an exercise of responsibility, and not just responsibility *to* but, in Levinas' terms, responsibility *for* the other. In affirming a literary work through my critical response to it, I am helping to keep it alive for this and future generations.

We can regard Derrida's lecture, therefore, as a countersignature affirming Joyce's signature—as he sees it—in *Ulysses*. The chain does not, of course, end with Derrida: his work, too, calls for countersignatures before it can be said to do justice to Joyce; this essay could be thought of as such a countersignature. The question that arises, therefore, is: does the lecture

Derrida gave in Frankfurt successfully affirm, in its own singularity, and through its own unmistakeable Derridean signature, the singularity of Joyce's signature? Does it, in other words, convey to the reader or listener (at least one who reads or listens with attention and understanding) a distinctive response to what is distinctive about *Ulysses*—or at least some important aspect of what is distinctive—in such a way as to bring the novel freshly to life? Or does it merely use Joyce's work as an occasion to develop certain philosophical interests that were Derrida's main concern? (There's plenty of biographical evidence that at one stage of his career reading Joyce was a formative experience for Derrida as a philosopher, so that there was a point at which Joyce was primary and philosophical thought secondary; but it's still possible that on this occasion he allowed his philosophical agenda to dominate his literary instincts.) Or, worse still, is it, as Rodolphe Gasché suggests it "could easily be construed," "an irresponsible spinning out of private fantasies, wild jokes, and totally arbitrary associations—in other words, as a text of so-called deconstructive criticism where everything goes"?[11]

V

We've already seen that Derrida's approach to *Ulysses* in terms of the doubleness of the *yes* and the signature responds to something that it is indubitably going on in *Ulysses*. (Joyce could not, of course, have put it in these terms, and would not have wanted to—but they are not the only terms in which it could be put; this is part of the point of the notion of "countersignature.") Nor is Derrida concerned only with the literal occurrences of *yes* and similar affirmatives in the work, although the subtitle, "Le oui-dire de Joyce," "Joyce's yes-saying," might first seem to suggest as much, and although he does engage in what seems like a mechanical counting exercise telling us how many *yes*es he found (though the Steppe-Gabler *Handlist* to *Ulysses* shows that he missed many instances[12]). It becomes clear, rather, that he is interested in an affirmation that is prior to any actual utterance of *yes* (it also underlies any utterance of *no*, for instance), and that he finds staged in many ways and many places in Joyce's text—this is the implicit signature I have already referred to in the second possible meaning of that opening "oui, oui." Even if *oui, oui* is a citation, an example for discussion, rather than an actual announcement, it has an unspoken affirmation underlying it—yes, I am quoting, yes, I am willing to confirm what I am putting before you.

It's an affirmation that, in order to do its work, must be countersigned by another affirmation, an answering *yes* that, paradoxically, is already implicit in the first yes. Derrida quotes Molly Bloom's words on the last page of *Ulysses*: "I asked him with my eyes to ask again yes and then he asked would I yes to say yes." Joyce doesn't present Molly's acceptance of

Bloom as a simple response to a simple question, as he might have done; he shows a surprising awareness of the complexity of this scene of request and affirmation. As Derrida says, "A certain narrativity is to be found at the simple core of the simplest 'yes'" (UG 65/110). The exercise of counting the explicit *yeses* is not dismissed: our reading, and our literary criticism, could not function without such mechanical procedures. But doing justice to the singular case, and the singular work, we recall, requires going beyond the mechanical and the computable, suspending and reinventing the laws of literature and discourse, and passing through the ordeal of the undecidable in offering a singular response.

But we haven't yet touched on the most surprising and, to me, the most significant aspect of Derrida's countersignature, which again is a response to the signature *in* as well as *of* Joyce. Well over an hour into his lecture, Derrida introduced the question of *laughter*, relating it closely to the signature and "the *yes* that it always implicates" (UG 66/113). (Thus, unlike many commentaries on *Ulysses*, his does full justice to *the humor of the work*.) A double laughter, he argued, runs through the text: a sardonic, triumphant laughter that takes pleasure in the work's totalizing power, and a light, dancing laughter that opens the work to otherness. The former arises from the encyclopedic ambition of the novel, its appearing always to preempt any response made by the reader; the latter to its ceaseless undermining of any such ambition, opening fresh spaces for inventiveness, what we might call a deconstructive laughter. The two laughters presuppose one another, ventriloquize one another, put one another at risk, make each other possible; they correspond to the two kinds of criticism, the mechanical analysis of a text and the countersignature of unique affirmation. They are both *yeses*—Derrida invents the word *oui-rire*, on the model of *oui-dire*—one mocking, the other welcoming (and welcoming the other). One is like the complicated web of communications systems that can be controlled from a single point (Derrida names this "Elijah," quoting a passage in the "Circe" episode in which the prophet appears as a telephone operator [U 15.2190–91]), the other like the chance events that such a web makes possible but which are outside its determination (and this is again "Elijah," but now the one for whom a place is set at the Passover Seder—the outsider made welcome). (We learn, too, that Derrida himself received the name "Elijah"—Elie—at his circumcision; he too is an outsider made welcome by the Joyce community.) *Ulysses*, then, is a work of such complexity and richness that it seems to preempt all critical maneuvers, yet that very complexity makes possible unpredictable coincidences, connections, and insights—not just within the work, but, as Derrida's personal narrative reveals, between the work and the lives of its readers.

Derrida's lecture is not just an argument, though, as this summary of some of its elements might suggest: to treat a critical commentary as nothing but an argument is to engage in the mechanical reading I've referred to and doesn't offer a unique countersignature to the work's unique signature. Just as the *yes* and the signature and the laughter in *Ulysses* are double, Derrida's answer is double: respecting the archival, enumerable aspect of the text he also finds a way to respond affirmatively to the affirmative, open-ended dimension. He gives us a narrative in answer to Joyce's narrative, another *Odyssey:* the story of his writing of the lecture itself and the travels that accompanied it. Moreover, countersigning the laughter that characterizes Joyce's signature, it is a *comic* narrative, full of absurd coincidences and mock-seriousness, from his choosing a title three months earlier and discovering that the scholar Jean-Michel Rabaté had used the same pun on *ouï-dire*, meaning "hearsay," in a new book on Joyce, to telephonic mishearing by Klaus Reichert (one of the conference organizers) of the title as referring to the name Louis. (Communications systems can always go wrong, which for Derrida is a necessary condition for their ever going right.) Thence to his trip to Oxford, Ohio (where he finds a brand of yoghurt called YES), to his purchasing of postcards in Tokyo in May and noticing books entitled *16 Ways to Avoid Saying No* and *Never Take Yes for an Answer*, to his deciding to stop writing—and at this point in Frankfurt he also stopped speaking—when he nearly had an accident trying to copy a Joycean sentence on his way home from the airport. It's a story full of chance accidents and correspondences, like *Ulysses*; and like *Ulysses* it is both self-absorbed and open to ever-renewed interpretation. As Henry Sussman observes, " 'Ulysses Gramophone' constitutes a literary work in its own right," and we have noted that as soon as Derrida started speaking in Frankfurt something of literature began.[13] The narrative framework is part of what makes it a unique countersignature: it is Derrida's response and nobody else's. Yet it is that singularity that makes it such a compelling commentary, and such a superb affirmation of Joyce's singularity.

There's one final comic twist, before that near-accident that brings the lecture to a close. Derrida imagines a "department of Joyce studies" using a high-powered computer to count and tabulate the *yeses* in *Ulysses* (and again indulges in a little mechanical sorting himself). There are two tasks, however, which even the most powerful computer would find impossible. It would not be able to do justice to the undecidable interlacings between the two laughters, the two *yeses*: here Joyce's signature exceeds any mechanical accounting. And it would not be able to deal with another undecidability: the program itself presupposes a *yes* that affirms the *yeses* of *Ulysses*, and this supplementary *yes* is both a part of and not a part of the corpus under examination. The act of engaging with the text, like the act of speaking, implies from the very first moment a *yes*, a *yes* that, as we've seen, is both a response to a call but at the same time a constituting gesture; it is thus both without and within that to which it appears to be responding.

No critical commentary that does justice to a work of literature, Derrida is suggesting, stands completely outside it, however positivist its methodology. To return to the signature and countersignature: the latter not only confirms the former but makes it what it is—which means that the signature that comes second has a paradoxical priority over the one that comes first.[14] If Derrida, in presenting "Ulysses Gramophone," says yes to the yeses in Joyce's work, his affirmation is part of what makes the work what it is for those who read and respond to him. A strange reversal that renders our commentaries more than just aftereffects, and *Ulysses*, for all its forbidding and totalizing power, an always open invitation, asking us to ask it to say *yes*.

Notes

1. Jacques Derrida, "Force of Law: The 'Mystical Foundation of Authority,'" trans. Mary Quaintance, in *Acts of Religion*, ed. Gil Anidjar (New York: Routledge, 2002), 228–98; 251, translation of *Force de loi: Le "Fondement mystique de l'autorité"* (Paris: Galilée, 1994), 50–51. Subsequent references will be cited parenthetically in the text.

2. Jacques Derrida, "Before the Law," trans. Avital Ronell and Christine Roulston, in Jacques Derrida, *Acts of Literature*, ed. Derek Attridge (New York: Routledge, 1992), 181–220, translation of "*Préjuges: Devant la loi*," in *La faculté de juger*, ed. Jacques Derrida et al. (Paris: Minuit, 1985), 87–139. Jacques Derrida, "The Law of Genre," trans. Avital Ronnell, in *Acts of Literature*, 221–52, translation of "La Loi du genre" in *Parages* (Paris: Galilée, 1986), 249–87.

3. See, respectively, UG 59–81/98–143; "Shibboleth: For Paul Celan," trans. Joshua Wilner, in *Sovereignties in Question: The Poetics of Paul Celan*, ed. Thomas Dutoit and Outi Pasanen (New York: Fordham University Press, 2005), 1–64, passim, translation of *Schibboleth: pour Paul Celan* (Paris: Galilée, 1986), passim; *Signéponge / Signsponge*, trans. Richard Rand (New York: Columbia University Press, 1984), passim, translation of *Signéponge* (Paris: Seuil, 1988); "Aphorism Countertime" (PSII 127–42/131–44, passim); "Psyche: Invention of the Other" (PSI 1–47/11–61).

4. Jacques Derrida, "'This Strange Institution Called Literature': An Interview," in *Acts of Literature*, 33–75, 68.

5. Derek Attridge, "Criticism's Wake," in *James Joyce: The Augmented Ninth*, ed. Bernard Benstock (Syracuse: Syracuse University Press, 1988), 80–87.

6. Jacques Derrida, "Passions: 'An Oblique Offering,'" trans. David Wood, in *On the Name*, ed. Thomas Dutoit (Stanford: Stanford University Press, 1995), 1–31, 142–43, translation of *Passions* (Paris: Galilée, 1993), 89.

7. Derrida discusses the structure and function of the signature in many places. It is considered in relation to J. L. Austin's theory of performative speech acts in "Signature Event Context" (MP 328–30/390–93), while *Signéponge* is an

extended consideration of the function of the signature in literature through an analysis of the poetry of Francis Ponge—one of the meanings of the title is "signed, Ponge." *Glas* also contains a remarkable discussion of the relation of the signature to the picture or text it signs—see Peter Mahoney's discussion in *Imagining Joyce and Derrida: Between "Finnegans Wake" and "Glas"* (Toronto: University of Toronto Press, 2007), 224–26. See also Bennington's contribution to Geoffrey Bennington and Jacques Derrida, *Jacques Derrida* (Chicago: University of Chicago Press, 1993), 148–66, translation of *Jacques Derrida* (Paris: Seuil, 1991), 140–56; Peggy Kamuf, *Signature Pieces: On the Institution of Authorship* (Ithaca: Cornell University Press, 1988), passim; and the indices to *Acts of Literature* and *A Derrida Reader: Between the Blinds*, ed. Peggy Kamuf (New York: Columbia University Press, 1991).

8. For an illuminating discussion of the signature see Peggy Kamuf, *Signature Pieces*, especially the introduction.

9. Jacques Derrida, "I Have a Taste for the Secret," in Jacques Derrida and Maurizio Ferraris, *A Taste for the Secret*, trans. Giacomo Donis, ed. Giacomo Donis and David Webb (Malden, MA: Blackwell, 2001), 1–92; 85, translation of "Ho il gusto del segreto" in *Il Gusto Del Segreto* (Rome-Bari: Gius. Laterza & Figli S.p.A., 1997), 5–108; 102. Elsewhere, Derrida asserts that "When I sign, I am already dead" (G 19b/26b); in other words, I have submitted to the general laws that operate in complete disregard of my living existence.

10. Derrida sharply dissociates himself from those who, taking Joyce's signature to be merely the name "Joyce," indulge in the "play of signifiers" and fail to appreciate the complexity of the signature's structure (UG 66/111).

11. Rodolphe Gasché, *Inventions of Difference: On Jacques Derrida* (Cambridge: Harvard University Press, 1994), 231.

12. See Wolfhard Steppe with Hans Walter Gabler, *A Handlist to Joyce's "Ulysses"* (New York: Garland, 1985).

13. Henry Sussman, *The Task of the Critic: Philosophy, Poetics, Religion* (New York: Fordham University Press, 2005), 160. Gasché, however, offers the necessary corrective: "Although 'Ulysses Gramophone' certainly performs what it establishes through its argumentative procedures and thus has 'literary' features, there is also ample evidence that this text belongs to philosophy" (*Inventions of Difference*, 231). Gasché's chapter, "On Reading Responsibly," gives an excellent account of the philosophical thrust of Derrida's essay, especially with regard to the "yes."

14. Blanchot, whom of course Derrida knew well, is also sensitive to the complexity of the two-way process between reader and work: "The reading of a poem is the poem itself, affirming itself in the reading as a work. It is the poem giving birth, in the space held open by the reader, to the reading that welcomes it. [. . .] To read is thus not to obtain communication from the work, but to 'make' the work communicate itself" (Maurice Blanchot, *The Space of Literature*, trans. Ann Smock [Lincoln: University of Nebraska Press, 1982], 198).

11

Two Joyces for Derrida

Jean-Michel Rabaté

I'll begin with a personal memory, one anecdote, the first and the last one, I promise, so as not to fall prey to nostalgia. In the spring of 1969, having made a firm decision to write an MA thesis on the concept of parody in *Finnegans Wake*, and having secured the assurance of Hélène Cixous' supervision, I went to see Jacques Derrida, as I would do weekly, since I was the one of the rare *normaliens* to take the opportunity of his office hours, and asked a stupid question, a question that had burned my tongue for a while. I blurted out: "Have you *read Finnegans Wake?*" For me at the time, such a feat seemed almost impossible, as I had barely ploughed randomly through the dense pages, never being sure whether any of it made sense or not. Not that this worried me too much: in the lingo of the period, *Finnegans Wake* was the best model approximating ideal conditions of *illisibility*, a term that had become a rallying cry for avant-garde writing. I had taken all too literally the liberal praise meted out by *Tel Quel* and similar reviews. Thus facing the philosopher I respected most, I expected at best a circumstantial response, an evasive waiver qualifying the very idea of reading such an opaque masterpiece. My rather impertinent question aimed less at checking Derrida's knowledge of the book than at seeking a confirmation of my opinion that one couldn't read it. Besides, I was looking for any sign that might help me in my progression in that impenetrable thicket.

I was thus both reassured and shocked when I heard Derrida answer simply, slowly and deliberately: "Yes, indeed, I have *read Finnegans Wake* . . ." A silence added a number of dots, all implying patience, process, perusal of guides and not simply a rapid browsing. I didn't know then that Derrida had read more on Joyce than on Husserl in the Widener Library during his stay at Harvard where he had been sent in 1956–1957, that it was in that library that he had read both *Ulysses* and *Finnegans Wake* (he was to let me know, much later, that he used Joyce to relieve the tedium and the mental cramp caused by too many pages of Husserl at one go). Since that moment, he had met Hélène Cixous before she completed her huge dissertation on Joyce's exile and would often discuss Joycean conundrums with her on the telephone. However, in the spring of 1969, in order not to leave me on the closure of a purely private moment, Derrida added: "If you are trying to tackle *Finnegans Wake*, you might use Mikhail Bakhtin as a guide." The unexpected tip allowed me to familiarize myself with the works of the Russian critic, then only recently introduced into the Parisian milieu by Julia Kristeva. This left me better equipped to deal with a Joycean parody that I saw, of course, closer to Rabelais than to Dostoyevsky. The useful advice allowed me to see in Joyce not just a modern version of Rabelais' humor but a writer who had gone back to forgotten medieval practices such as the *missa parodia* that subverted orthodoxy by deliberately blending the sacred and the profane.

It might interest Joyce scholars who have witnessed a relatively late American coupling of the names of Joyce and Bakhtin in the nineties to know that Derrida's reading, already in the late sixties, was framed and filtered by concepts like dialogism, polyphony, and the carnivalesque body. We didn't know then that Bakhtin himself considered both Proust and Joyce as the main representatives of modernist monologism, both prey to the "reification of the word." But this is another story. My simple anecdote aims only at this snapshot: Derrida's firm "yes" to a banal question bearing on the possibility of reading *Finnegans Wake*.

That such a reading was not only possible but had also been accomplished suggests that, in a sense, Derrida never ceased reading Joyce. Indeed, "Ulysses Gramophone" provides a general recapitulation of this lifelong frequentation that it is unnecessary to repeat. I would just try to catch here, on a rebound as it were, the title of Derrida's 1982 lecture, "Two Words for Joyce," so as to suggest in my turn that there are two Joyces for Derrida, or at least two modalities of reading facing Joyce. Before attempting to follow this duplication more in detail, I would like to sketch briefly the opposition: on the one hand, a Joyce presented as a destructive philosophical machine, a very male and threatening paternal figure, the author of the *Wake*, the book of all books, a technological tour de force hypostasized as the exact counterpart of Husserl's phenomenology, on the other hand the author of *Ulysses*, a seductive successor to a feminized Homer, a poet who left feminine voices to provide a final signature, who enjoys perfumes and performatives as stemming from a single seductivity of literature, the former being closer to Hegel and Heidegger, the latter closer to Hélène Cixous and her main interrogations on sexual difference, the links between writing and the body, saintliness and messianicity. One could say that the first Joyce is allegorical, the second Joyce alluvial.

If Derrida first read Joyce in an allegorical manner, we need to understand in what context. Derrida's foregrounding of writing as the concept that had not been thematized or theorized by Husserl had a few rare predecessors. To the list of usual suspects on Joyce and Mallarmé linked together by Robert Greer Cohn,[1] I would like to add the name of Walter Benjamin, who, in his wonderful *The Origin of the German Tragic Drama*, quotes at some length Johann Wilhelm Ritter, a minor Romantic writer known for posthumous essays praising the mystical properties of electricity. In fact, Ritter develops a philosophy of writing that curiously anticipates the analyses of Derrida in *Of Grammatology*. Far from thinking like most Romantics that writing copies or reproduces living speech, Ritter posits that the written and the spoken word are generated together. Here are some quotes given by Benjamin: "do we ever have a thought or an idea without its hieroglyph, its letter, its script? [. . .] the organ of speech itself writes in order to speak. The letter alone speaks, or rather: word and script are, at source, one, and neither is possible without the other."[2]

Benjamin generalizes these insights not to found a grammatology yet, but to define the baroque allegory as a foundation for his revisiting the German baroque drama (*Trauerspiel*).

> With the theory that every image is only a form of writing, [Ritter] gets to the very heart of the allegorical attitude. In the context of allegory the image is only a signature, only the monogram of essence, not the essence itself in a mask. But there is nothing subordinate about written script; it is not cast away in reading, like dross. It is absorbed along with what is read, as its "pattern." [. . .] And so the age was not entirely without some sense of those comprehensive relationships between spoken language and script, which provide the philosophical basis of the allegorical, and which contain within them the resolution of their true tensions.[3]

What is peculiar to the langage of the *Trauerspiel* is that the visual cannot be distinguished from speech for everything turns into an emblem. The implications of the last chapters in this book replete with dazzling insight seem nevertheless to contradict its beginning, the prologue in which Plato stands out as a master. In fact, the whole book is a "treatise" and as such it can accommodate huge discrepancies. Contrasting mathematics and philosophical writing, Benjamin has already warned his readers at the end of his first paragraph:

> In the canonic form of the treatise, the only element of an intention [. . .] is the authoritative quotation. Its method is essentially representation. Method is a digression. Representation as digression— such is the methodological nature of the treatise. The absence of

an uninterrupted purposeful structure is its primary characteristic. Tirelessly the process of thinking makes new beginnings, returning in a roundabout way to its original object. This continual pausing for breath is the mode most proper to the process of contemplation. For by pursuing different levels of meaning in its examination of one single object it receives both the incentive to begin again and the justification for its irregular rhythm.[4]

Obviously, Benjamin is describing his own book, but he could also have been writing about Husserl's texts, if not Derrida's later books. Thus whoever has read both Benjamin and Derrida cannot avoid being struck by deep affinities and a convergence between the anti-logocentric logic of deconstruction and the deconstruction of the Romantic symbol achieved by Benjamin's quasi-kabbalistic theory of writing seen as allegory, and of allegory seen as writing. In both efforts, a similar *allos* is at work in *logos*, whether the *logos* be that of literature or philosophy. Such a tension will be exemplified most clearly by Joyce.

Benjamin allows us to think radically the vital breath of thinking, especially when it is caught in some sort of methodological asthma that pushes it forward inchoatively. This is a pattern that struck Derrida when he translated Husserl's "Origin of Geometry", a "treatise" that he described in terms that call up those of Benjamin: "In effect these pages of Husserl, first written for himself, have the rhythm of a thought feeling its way (*d'une pensée qui se cherche*) rather than setting itself forth (*plus qu'elle ne s'expose*). But here the apparent discontinuity also depends on an always regressive method, a method which chooses its interruptions and multiplies the returns toward its beginning in order to reach back and grasp it again each time in a recurrent light" (EH 26 n. 2/4 n.1).

The progressive-regressive method is inseparable from a practice of writing that can appear as paradigmatic: thinking would thus be from the start—and one can begin anywhere, obviously condemned to start *in medias res*—writing for oneself. Writing for himself in order to hear himself think, Husserl we know will then give these pages to others like Eugen Fink who will type them, and begin the long process of transmission when they are added to the huge corpus of the Husserliana—until, one day, they are translated into French and annotated. Deconstruction begins with Husserlian phenomenology taken as a "method" of thinking or a "style" of writing that takes origins as a theme of meditation; by its readiness to take risks (such as the wish to be open to literature, even Joyce's literature) phenomenology will end up providing a wholesale critique of classical Reason. For the late piece (1936) entitled "Origin of Geometry," while contemporary with the

Crisis of European Sciences and Transcendental Phenomenology, sends us back to one of Husserl's earliest philosophical essays, *The Philosophy of Mathematics* (1891). Both treatises address the function of mathematical or geometrical ideal unities (or idealities) by returning to their foundation in consciousness—hence opening a transcendental operation. To speak of a "return" here may seem to beg the issue of the foundation, or simply of the beginning—but it is precisely a return to some point that is not an absolute beginning in the historical sense. Or rather, the main shift in Husserl's thought between the 1880s and the 1930s consists in a renewed consideration of the role of history. This reopening of the file of historical reason is based upon the awareness that the present is in a state of crisis, and that the road to transcendental idealism cannot be the same as before. The method followed will then have to be different from what traditional philosophical systems have done so far. Derrida points out a dangerous hesitation in this movement toward history: when "history itself breaks through into phenomenology [*fait irruption dans la phénoménologie*]" (EH 29/8), it is more and more difficult to contain it or assign it to a well-delimited space.

If we agree to identify Husserl's writing style and his a-systematicity, we can foresee where Derrida's trajectory will carry him: toward a thinking of Difference as undermining from the start any possibility of founding phenomenology and hence all philosophy on an absolute origin, seen as the Nowness of a Living Present (see EH 153/171). He will have in between to deal with an inevitable question (contained in the parenthesis I have skipped): is the historicity of science and philosophy the culmination of history or totally elsewhere, as a condition of possibility beyond history?

Husserl's essay on geometry is also, more or less directly, a meditation on culture and literature. Derrida will use the scattered remarks on literature used as a springboard for his analysis of "traces," or writing deployed as the practice of difference, which will be totally unleashed by Joyce. One footnote insists on the importance of keeping records of scientific inventions through language. In his discussion of scientific archives, Husserl is ready to grant literature a surprising preeminence. Husserl writes:

> But geometrical existence is not psychic existence; it does not exist as something personal within the sphere of personal consciousness: it is the existence of what is objectively there for "everyone" [. . .]. And all forms newly produced by someone on the basis of pregiven forms immediately take on the same objectivity. This is, we note, an "ideal" objectivity. It is proper to a whole class of spiritual products of the cultural world, to which not only all scientific constructions

and the sciences themselves belong but also, for example, the constructions of fine literature. (EH 160/178–79)

To which Derrida adds this footnote:

But the broadest concept of literature encompasses them all: that is, it belongs to their objective being that they be linguistically expressed and can be expressed again and again; or, more precisely, they have their objectivity, their existence-for-everyone, only as signification, as the meaning of speech. This is true in peculiar fashion in the case of the objective sciences: for them the difference between the original language of the work and its translation into other languages does not remove its identical accessibility or change it into an inauthentic, indirect accessibility. (EH 160 n./179 n. 1)

The remark about translation is crucial: Husserl is above all interested in the possibility of preserving a nucleus of meaning, which is why language is indispensable to geometry. But in fact, as Derrida stresses in his commentary, it is geometry that provides a model for literature on Husserl's view and not the reverse. "Every linguistic dimension that would escape this absolute translatability would remain marked by the empirical subjectivity of an individual or society. For Husserl, the model of language is the objective language of science. A poetic language, whose signification would not be *objects*, will never have any transcendental value for him" (EH 82/77).

However, Joyce would not be dismayed by this thesis, since he opened his collection of stories *Dubliners* with a tantalizing hint that geometry was indeed the master science. In the famous opening paragraph of "The Sisters" we hear of a *gnomon* ominously knotted with *simony* and *paralysis* and its source is acknowledged: Euclid's *Elements*. "Every night as I gazed up at the window I said softly to myself the word *paralysis*; It had always sounded strangely in my ears, like the word *gnomon* in the Euclid and the word *simony* in the Catechism" (D 9). Even if Joyce has in mind a very precise figure in which an identical parallelogram has been taken away from another bigger parallelogram, as if one corner was imply missing, it would be worth paralleling them with what Husserl has to say about Euclid, the first geometrician according to Greek tradition, who introduces a very early infinitization (which will need mathematics to be dealt with) in the science of shapes. In this movement, the whole issue of technology will engulf itself—as Heidegger has well noted. "Starting from this inaugural infinitization, mathematics cognizes new infinitizations, which are so many interior revolutions. For, if the primordial infinitization opens the mathematical field to infinite fecundities for the Greeks, it no less *first* limits the a priori system of that productivity. The very content of an infinite production will be confined within an a priori system that, for the Greeks, will always be *closed*. The guide here is Euclidean geometry, or rather the "*ideal Euclid*, according to Husserl's expression, which is restricted to sense, not historical fact" (EH 127–28/138). Indeed, as a confirmation of this insight, one can notice that a "gnomon" was not only used as a geometrical figure (the carpenter's tee) but also in mathematical relations to mean any proportion between two numbers such that one will contain the other. By opening itself to geometry, Joyce's text suggests the first trap set for the reader (and of course his characters): the lure and prestige but also the endless aporias of textual infinitization.

Derrida's commentary points out that Husserl's reliance on a strict model of translatability will meet intractable problems as soon as he tries to address the links between subjectivity and language, to the point that he quietly but firmly contradicts the text he translates especially when it seems to be seeking for a Nature that would provide an origin or a ground for all precultural identities:

> But preculturally *pure Nature* is always buried. So, as the ultimate possibility for communication, it is a kind of inaccessible infra-ideal. Can we not say, then, just the opposite of what Husserl said? Are not non-communication and misunderstanding the very horizon of culture and language? Undoubtedly misunderstanding is always a factual horizon and the finite index of sound intelligence taken as infinite pole [translation modified]. But although the latter is always announced so that language can begin, is not finitude the essential which we can never radically go beyond? (EH 81–82/77)

In this revealing aside, in which Derrida abandons the mask of the good pupil who carefully annotates and introduces the text he has translated, another tone can be heard—closer to Heidegger clearly, but also informed by Blanchot.

What is most revealing here is the idea that the pole of infinity is announced "so that language can begin," a notion that parallels the thesis of Roland Barthes in *Writing Degree Zero* (modern literature is purposely without any "style" so as to let language speak by itself—such would be the main effort of the "nouveau roman").[5] Husserl nevertheless considers language as such in his essay on geometry and takes the example of *Löwe* (lion) to show that such a word is both an "ideal objectivity" (*eine ideale Gegenständlichkeit*) and something that is given a "linguistic living body" (*Sprachleib*) in German—a language in which, moreover, it exists objectively "only in virtue of [. . .] two-levered repetitions and ultimately in virtue of sensibly embodying repetitions" (EH 161/181). Like Euclid's theorems, which remain the same in all their translations, *Löwe* belongs a commonly shared universe of human culture. Civilization is the community of those who, by speaking, can not only name the world but also share the world (EH 162/182). And writing makes this communication become virtual, anticipating on the idea that language is sedimented, and that, in spite of the requirement of pure univocity without which a science would not be rigorous, words pile up on another, and any discovery will be made not only by avoiding the "seduction of language" (EH 165/187), but also by taking into account the specific "passivity" that is implied by tradition. The rest of Husserl's essay is devoted less to geometry than to problems posed by tradition and history.

Even when Husserl keeps attacking historicism and its fascination for unanalyzed raw facts, and sees Hegel primarily as a historicist philosopher, Derrida is right to stress interesting similarities in Husserl's and Hegel's treatment of language. One footnote in Derrida's introduction stands out as quite revealing. Derrida sums up the thesis of the ideality of words:

> Thus, the word has an ideal Objectivity and identity, since it is not identical with any of its empirical, phonetic, or graphic materializations. It is always the *same* word which is meant and recognized through all possible linguistic gestures. Insofar as this ideal object confronts language as such, the latter supposes a spontaneous neutralization of the factual existence of the speaking subject, of words, and of the thing designated. Speech, then, is only the practice of an immediate eidetic. (EH 67/58)

He then adds this footnote to "eidetic":

> The linguistic neutralization of existence is an original idea only in the technical and thematic signification that phenomenology gives it. Is not this idea the favorite of Mallarmé and Valéry? Hegel above all had amply explored it. In the *Encyclopedia* (one of the few Hegelian works that Husserl seems to have read), the lion already testifies to this neutralization as an exemplary martyr: "Confronting the name—Lion—we no longer have either an intuition of such an animal or even an image, but the name (when we understand it) is its simple and imageless representation; in the name we think" (§462, this passage is cited by Jean Hyppolite in his *Logique et existence*, 1953, p. 39,[6] a work which, on many points, lets the profound convergence of Hegelian and Husserlian thought appear.)

Hegel also writes: "The first act, by which Adam is made master of the animals, was to impose on them a name, i.e., he annihilated them in their existence (as existents)" (System of 1803–1804). Cited by Maurice Blanchot in *La Part du feu*, 1949, p. 325.[7] (EH 67 n. 62/58 n.1)

Although Hegel and Husserl converge when affirming the idea that the word is the death of the thing, the dramatizing language of Hegel is foreign to the technicality of Husserl's idiom. The reference to Blanchot belongs to a somewhat different world, closer to Kojève's anthropological readings of death in Hegel. Derrida quotes "La Littérature et le droit à la mort," which closes *La Part du feu* (1949). The piece provides the theoretical core of the book and is largely based upon a reading of Hegel. Blanchot starts from Hegel to explore all the paradoxes that any writer will face, the first being, typically, the impossibility to really begin. "From his first step, as Hegel says more or less, the individual who wants to write is blocked by a contradiction: in order to write, he needs the talent to write. But in themselves, talents are nothing. So long as he has not sat at a table and written a work, the writer is not a writer and he does not know whether he has the ability to become one. He has talent only after he has written, but he needs talent to write."[8] The writer becomes, to follow another Hegelian phrase, a nothingness working with nothingness.

Beyond these Hegelian references that structure the argument, one sees another reference looming in Blanchot's text, a reference to Levinas, who provides not so much a way out than another terminology permitting to move beyond the pathos of negativity. Levinas provides a new abyssal foundation leading not so much to Hegel's "night" but rather to a "there is" deriving from Levinas' book *From Existence to Existent* (1947). If this is a text that Derrida read closely, since he quotes Hegel through it, the impact of Levinas' thought must be already perceptible. Derrida's introduction to Husserl was written just a year after the publication of Levinas' *Totality and Infinity* (1961), a superb philosophical novel in which the figure of Odysseus who only wants to return home is taken as the paradigm of a purely Greek mode of thinking: phenomenology engages in "purely imaginary adventures or undergone, as with Odysseus, only to go back home."[9]

As Derrida writes almost in echo: "This historicity or traditionality is always presupposed by every Odyssean repetition of Joyce's type, as by all *philosophy of history* (in the current sense) and by every *phenomenology of spirit*. The essences of finite totalities and the typology of figures of the spirit will always be idealities that are bound to empirical history" (EH 103/105). He would need a little more time to digest Levinas' conflation of all phenomenologies of spirit and of Greek philosophy as such; from the point of view of a radical Jewish sense of ethics, any return of the Spirit to itself is a nostalgic tautology asserting the domination of the Same, which confirms the category mistake of ontology. Derrida's reply took two more years and was published in 1964 as "Violence and Metaphysics," and it begins with a well-known reference to the "Jewgreek is greekjew" theme in *Ulysses* (WD 153/227–28; U 15.2097–98).

What Blanchot brings to Derrida is the strong awareness that any "work" will surprise its writer, and the sense that writing is the name of a process by which I "become[s] other."[10] This is not far from the remark quoted in the introduction about the possibility of considering writing as an archive, or in the words of Jean Hyppolite, a "subjectless transcendental field": "Writing, as the place of absolutely permanent ideal objectivities and therefore of absolute Objectivity, certainly constitutes such a transcendental field" (EH 88/85).

A question remains: it is after having stressed the convergence of Husserl and Hegel in their idealizing strategies that Joyce, "the most Hegelian of all writers" is quoted as a radical alternative to phenomenology's idealizing gesture. Why not, instead of Joyce, use Heidegger as an internal questioning of phenomenology? Why is it that the name of a novelist, poet, and polyglot mythologist is needed at this juncture? In the introduction to *Edmund Husserl's Origin of Geometry*, Joyce is called upon as much as the author of interconnected puns that make *Finnegans Wake* a perfect pastime for retired linguists as the launcher of an "Odyssean repetition" (EH 103/105). However, Derrida is reluctant to identify Joyce's project with that of pure historicism, and notes that Stephen Dedalus' deepest wish is to wake up from "the nightmare" constituted by history. From that turning point in the introduction to *Edmund Husserl's Origin of Geometry*, Joyce acquires a monumental and emblematic stature. He seems to embody by himself a radical alternative to phenomenology, while Husserlian phenomenology condenses the fundamental desire of philosophy, a desire to reduce the equivocation of everyday speech to the univocity of a concept. As Derrida recalls it in a very condensed manner in "Two Words for Joyce"—a talk presented twenty years after the introduction—Joyce calls up for Derrida much more than a "great novelist of the modern period" but sketches an entire philosophical program:

> The other great paradigm would be the Joyce of *Finnegans Wake*. He repeats and mobilizes and babelizes the asymptotic totality of the equivocal. He makes this his theme and his operation. He tries to make outcrop, with the greatest possible synchrony [*faire affleurer à la plus grande synchronie*], at top speed, the greatest power of the meanings buried in each syllabic fragment, subjecting each atom

of writing to fission in order to overload its unconscious with the whole memory of man: mythologies, religions, philosophies, sciences, psychoanalysis, literatures. (TW 27/28)

Only a hyperbolic style can render the violent impact of a no less hyperbolic project. The admiration granted to the unheard of idea—since Dante at least—of creating a new language from some seventy idioms calls up less Babel than the Flood. In this torrential downpour, Joyce the demiurge is replaced by an almost nightmarish version of a totality that calls up an evil Doctor Mabuse. In his own way, Roland Barthes had also attacked the "monster of totality" in his own *Roland Barthes*.[11] Besides, Joyce does not limit his enterprise to "mobilizing" the totality of culture, he both demobilizes and immobilizes (which is how Levinas described the effect Derrida has produced on him: he was compelled to go back to the time of the *drôle de guerre* when he was mobilized in the army with nothing to do, and then was disbanded soon after). What distinguishes Joyce is that he refuses the nuclei of meaning that for Husserl are necessary when a language is translated into another without, apparently, believing as Heidegger does that truth follows the tangled path of folk etymologies. "This generalized equivocality does not translate one language into another on the basis of common nuclei of meaning. It talks several languages at once, it parasites them" (TW 27/28).

In 1962, Joyce was mentioned at the end of a series of other literary references: after Goethe's *Faust* already quoted by Husserl as an example of literary ideality, one also meets Valéry, Mallarmé, and Blanchot (EH 67 n.62/58 n.1). This leads to an allusion to what Gaston Bachelard has called the *bibliomenon*: "This "being of the book," this "instance of *printed* thought" whose "language is not natural," Gaston Bachelard calls a "*bibliomenon*" (EH 91/90). Husserl was aware that writing "defines and completes the ambiguity of all language" (EH 92/90). In the long sequence of philosophical writers who bring literature to bear on thinking, Joyce brings to Husserl the counterweight of a writing not just bound in culture but also "unbound" in the sense that its chains of links belong to a purely empirical system, from that of spelling to the empirical hazards of local myths, religions, and historical narratives:

> And, like Joyce, this endeavor would try to make the structural unity of all empirical culture appear in the generalized equivocation of a writing that, no longer translating one language into another on the basis of their common cores of sense, circulates throughout all languages at once, accumulates their energies, actualizes their most secret consonances, discloses their furthermost common horizons,

cultivates their associative syntheses instead of avoiding them, and rediscovers the poetic value of passivity. In short, rather than put it out of play with quotation marks, rather than "reduce" it, this writing resolutely settles itself *within* the *labyrinthian* field of culture "bound" by its own equivocations, in order to travel through and explore the vastest possible historical distance that is now at all possible. (EH 102/104–5)

In spite of all this, I would suggest that what Derrida proposes here is not a philosophical reading of Joyce; more precisely, it is a reading of Joyce for philosophy, it is a reading of Joyce as allegory for philosophy. A systematic philosophical reading of *Finnegans Wake* remains to be done, and it would for instance probe the consequences of Joyce's Aristotelianism, of his Hegelianism, or of his medievalism. At one point of his introduction, Derrida seems on the verge of launching such an investigation when he quotes Aristotle on color and transparency. He is discussing how the impossibility of providing a phenomenology of the Idea opposes Husserl to Hegel. A "phenomenology of the Idea" cannot be "given in person, nor determined in an evidence, for it is only the possibility of evidence and the openness of 'seeing' itself" (EH 138/151–52). Such a phenomenology would reduce itself to "the horizon for every intuition in general, the invisible milieu of seeing analogous to the diaphaneity of the Aristotelian Diaphanous, an elemental third, but the one source of the seen and the visible" (EH 138/152). Then Derrida quotes Aristotle: "by diaphanous I mean what is visible, and yet not visible in itself, but rather owing its visibility to the colour of something else. 'It is thanks to this alone that the colour of a thing is seen' (*De Anima*, 418b)" (EH 138/152). For readers of Joyce, it looks as if Derrida was going to embark on a commentary of the most "phenomenological" passage in *Ulysses*, Stephen's famous meditation on the act of seeing, which quotes exactly the same passage from the *De Anima*:

> Ineluctable modality of the visible: at least that if no more, thought through my eyes. [. . .] Snotgreen, bluesilver, rust: coloured signs. Limits of the diaphane. But he adds: in bodies. Then he was aware of them bodies before of them coloured. How? By knocking his sconce against them, sure. Go easy. Bald he was and a millionaire, *maestro di color che sanno*. Limit of the diaphane in. Why in? Diaphane, adiaphane. (U 3.1–8).

It is very likely that it was his reading of *Ulysses* that brought Derrida to this beautiful echo between Stephen's "phenomenology of the Idea" and a pre-Berkeleyan meditation on the conditions of possibility of visibility.

Derrida does not engage Joyce in this way, via his philosophical sources, precisely because he wants to introduce "Joyce" into the field of philosophy as a dangerous Trojan horse, an exorbitant and radical exemplification of "writing" in action. Joyce as an author of "inventor of discursivity" thus gives his name to a sort of antiphilosophy that traverses philosophy and makes it shudder or stutter. For the polyglottism and antihistorical historicism, the generalized equivocation and the encyclopedic hubris are factors that Joyce condensed to a high degree but that would also be shared by high modernist writers like Pound, Lewis, and Eliot. The point here is not to establish a philosophical dialogue (as one sees on the same page of the introduction in which Derrida notes that the "dialogue between Husserl and Heidegger could go on indefinitely" [EH 138 n.164/151 n.1]). The reference to Joyce is more powerful because there is no way of grasping a concept behind the unleashing of the writing process.

I would like to insist on a major shift that justifies my title: without significantly altering his general thesis on Joyce, Derrida evinces a subtle shift between 1962 and 1982. The 1962 reading lumps *Ulysses* and *Finnegans Wake* together, they define a single project that could be called "Joyce as an alternative to phenomenology," while twenty years later, Derrida tends to differentiate between *Finnegans Wake* (which had by then been canonized as an archetype of the avant-garde textual production) and *Ulysses*, a novel that he takes as the pretext for a quasi-autobiographical exploration of several key themes: the feminine affirmation of life as a redoubled yes-yes saying; the links between organic death and death by the letter; the interactions between Jewishness and the ways of the Gentiles, including circumcision; male circumnavigations, periplums, and perambulations, in short, odysseys. This is why in 1982, Derrida makes the revealing qualification: "The other great paradigm would be the Joyce of *Finnegans Wake*" (TW 27/28), as we have seen. Does this mean that one can forget the megalomania of a totalizing program of hypermnesic strategies because one comes closer to the riddle of femininity embodied by Molly Bloom? Or are the two novels still conceptually linked in Derrida's mind?

In order to progress along this investigation, it seems to me that the series of theses on Joyce elaborated from the introduction to *Edmund Husserl's Origin of Geometry* to "Ulysses Gramophone" overlap partly with Eliot's definition of a "mythical method"—a thesis that underpins most modernist visions of literature. Eliot had claimed that *Ulysses* worked on two planes and presented a systematic parallel between classical antiquity and the "present" of Dublin 1904. The handling of such a parallel would be for Eliot a way of controlling the uneasiness facing the "chaos" observed in contemporary history. Joyce, like Einstein, would have produced a scientific discovery bridging the gap between a cultural or "ideal" order and the irrelevance or confusion of present-day events. Derrida's thesis about a Joyce seen as an antiphilosopher of writing can appear as a variation on Eliot's fundamental thesis about tradition and order. Eliot's 1923 article on "*Ulysses*, Order, and Myth" expands the theses launched in "Tradition and the Individual Talent," an essay published in 1919 to define what constitutes the "historical sense" and its links with a global tradition.[12] Like Husserl in the "Origin of Geometry," Eliot sees the consciousness of history in the present: "What is historically primary in itself is our present" (EH 176/207) Husserl says, while Eliot admits that culture builds a quasi-organic system that any new masterpiece, as soon as it is introduced, will radically modify in all its relationships. Thus when *Ulysses* is introduced into the field of Western culture, it is the whole of Homer's works that change. For instance, we will read the *Odyssey* differently, we will be looking for puns differently, and will pay more attention to certain racial stereotypes, and so on . . . In the same way, the election of Joyce to the role of synthesis of universal culture and history will have important consequences for the creation of a new reader. This has been perceived by Derrida and expressed in an interview with a very competent Joyce scholar, Derek Attridge:

> *Ulysses* arrives like one novel among others that you place on your bookshelf and inscribe in a genealogy. It has its ancestry and its descendants. But Joyce dreamt of a special institution for his oeuvre, inaugurated by it like a new order. And hasn't he achieved this, to some extent? When I spoke of this as I did in "Ulysses Gramophone," I did indeed have to understand and share his dream too: not only share it in making it mine, in recognizing mine in it, but that I share it in *belonging to the dream* of Joyce, in *taking a part* in it, in walking around in *his* space. Aren't we, today, people or characters in part constituted (as readers, writers, critics, teachers) *in* and *through* Joyce's dream? Aren't we Joyce's dream, his dream readers, the ones he dreamed of and whom we dream of being in our turn?[13]

Going further than the main modernist writers who all dreamed of creating a new audience by a new mode of writing, Derrida postulates the birth of a new subject in the wake of Joyce's works. Thus Husserl and Eliot seem to working together at redefining an ethical relationship to tradition: "To meditate on or investigate the sense (*besinnen*) of origins is at the same time to: make oneself responsible (*verantworten*) for the sense (*Sinn*) of science and philosophy, bring this sense to the clarity of its 'fulfil(ment),' and put oneself in a position of *responsibility* for this sense starting from the total sense of our existence" (EH 31/11).

This, coupled with the intuition that any writer should feel an entire European tradition in her or his "bones" sketches a program to which Husserl would have entirely subscribed: ". . . the historical sense compels a man to write not merely with his own generation in his bones, but with a feeling that the whole of the literature of Europe from Homer and within it the whole literature of his own country has a simultaneous existence and composes a simultaneous order."[14] Eliot supposes that the apparition of a new masterpiece always redistributes the esthetic values of the past according to a logic of minimal differences (the *whole* ideal order of culture must be, "if ever so slightly," altered each time something really new occurs in it[15]). Similarly, Derrida posits that the totalizing masterpiece modifies not only our reading and writing habits to the point that a new model of subjectivity is created. And we will be this subject provided we accept recognition of ourselves as read in advance by the author, traversed by Joyce's reading. A double genitive is at play, both objective and subjective, in a hesitation inevitably triggered by this new writing as it writes us, in us, without our being aware of its unconscious inscription. In *Ulysses*, Stephen Dedalus spoke of Shakespeare as the father of his grandfather and his own grandson, presenting him as the paradigm of the self-generating artist who thereby constitutes a world we happen to be inhabiting too. Aware of this circularity, and also in awe of it, Derrida sees in Joyce's hypermnesic machine a powerful "program" that will also unleash a more terrifying danger.

One of the consequences of this program is that no reading can become "ideal" and thus will not contribute another ideality for the greater glory of culture as Husserl would have requested it. Reading cannot disentangle itself from either the materiality of an archive or from the living inheritance of actual families. We are aware of the curious fascination of Joyce scholars for manuscripts, drafts, first editions, autographs, holographs, letters, notebooks, all culled in the more than sixty volumes of the *James Joyce Archive*—with the constant addition of recently discovered proofs and unpublished manuscripts sold for a fortune at auctions. What may not be well-known is the no less curious fascination of Joyce's grandson for this scene: Stephen Joyce, heir and addressee of certain texts, still occupies today the position of moral guarantee in the Joyce industry, and intervenes regularly in the choice of translators, editors, and even texts that can be anthologized. This is why Derrida could not resist the pleasure of dedicating the first version of "Ulysses Gramophone" to Stephen Joyce. This spectral genealogy confirms that we are all "Joyce's grandsons"—we are all caught up in the technological apparatus already announced by Bloom in *Ulysses* when he imagined that all men and women's voices should be recorded so as to keep a trace after their death . . .

It is possible to generalize this principle: no critical discourse can free itself from its family history, no chosen affiliation could allow one to forget one's more or less direct filiation. This is why I have tried to situate Derrida in that French scene of phenomenology in the sixties, a scene dominated by the ghosts of Cavaillès and Kojève, and in which Gaston Bachelard, Tran Duc Thao, and Jean Hyppolite were the "masters," as much perhaps as Foucault, Althusser, and Blanchot. In the same fashion, when we talk of modernism in North American universities, it is impossible to forget the role of critics like Hugh Kenner or Harry Levin, who personally knew Joyce and Pound. Modernism took shape at the time of the European crisis in its own tradition, and most creators were keenly aware of their role in the dissemination of a tradition that they were partly creating. Joyce chose important relays like Valery Larbaud, Stuart Gilbert, Frank Budgen, Louis Gillet, Carlo Linati, Jacques Mercanton, Ernst Robert Curtius. These and others were to ensure his immortality, an immortality measured by the number of books and theses devoted to him. In that sense, as Nora Joyce herself expressed rather naïvely, there was only one other chap her husband had to get the better of, William Shakespeare. "Ulysses Gramophone" also echoes the unpleasant impression that nothing can be written on Joyce that would not have been manipulated or thought in advance by the writer.

This is also because, as Derrida explains, the entire work of Joyce thinks itself in the secondarity of a double filiation, caught up as it is between self-generation (the myth being the infinitely self-generating texts as one sees with *Finnegans Wake*) and the responsibility of the whole of a European tradition that open its ear to the other. In the *Wake*, the European should open itself to the other by turning into "earopen" (FW 419.14). Thus Derrida is right to gloss the process in these terms:

> *Finnegans Wake* is a little, a little what?, a little son, a very little grandson[16] of Western culture in its circular, encyclopedic, Ulyssean and more than Ulyssean totality. And then it is, simultaneously, much bigger than even this odyssey. *Finnegans Wake* comprehends it, and this prevents it, dragging it outside itself in an entirely singular adventure, from closing in on itself and on this event. What is called writing is the paradox of such a topology. (TW 26–27/26)

This paradox takes several figures in "Ulysses Gramophone"—some pointing to recurrent patterns like the signature, the postcards, the "yes yes" underpinning any performative, the disjuncture between competence and performance, while new traits are taken from the network of Joycean associations and signifiers: various communication machines, telephones, gramophones, the fragrance of perfumes and flowers, behind the "perfumative" the endless war of languages, the warring brothers, the name of Babel and He War . . .

With this, I would like to stress that the purely deconstructive moment does not and should not describe the whole intervention on Joyce. On the contrary, the general tone of "Ulysses Gramophone" is more assertive, ludic, and autobiographical than political, questioning, or debunking. This is the second "jou" of Joyce for Derrida. This reading of Joyce appears almost Nietzschean or, if one can risk this, Deleuzean, especially when it climaxes in a poetic rhapsody on Molly's Yesses. It looks as if Molly's final "Yes" had replaced the critique of philosophical foundation via self-presence. Similarly, by selecting only two words from *Finnegans Wake*, Derrida granted an allegorical and paradigmatic function to what might have been glossed as a simple bilingual pun—"He war" unites and splices "He was/Er war/War/He made war/wahr-heit"). The two words are in from II.1, in a passage dealing with children playing in the Chapelizod pub, but also replete with biblical overtones: "And shall not Babel be with Lebab? And he war. And he shall open his mouth and answer: I hear, O Ismael, how they laud is only as my loud is one" (FW 258.11–13).

All this, of course, has to be done without believing in any specialized Joycean "competence" or judging it from the height of a philosophical foundation. Following the example of Husserl and Joyce, Derrida refuses merely "telephoned" analyses, the mere completion of a reading program deducting effects from basic rules of composition and association. The noblest intentions can never save a programmatic approach, be they feminist, psychoanalytic, or even deconstructive. Partly thanks to Joyce, Derrida will have managed to launch a new practice of critical writing and to avoid its reduction to the production of mechanical effects. The material allegory that Derrida identifies in Joyce takes a number of striking and surprising figures in "Ulysses Gramophone," with all the new objects already mentioned, telephones, gramophones, secret signals, and even the television invented by Joyce in *Finnegans Wake*. No need to parade this machinery as a war machine debunking the metaphysics of origins and originality. There is no quarrel with the "metaphysics of presence" that does not at the same time conceal a jealous lover's quarrel. Love is thus always to be reinvented in its very impossibility, its relentless otherness. This would be the barely hidden secret of Derrida's writing—the madness of a love for pure alterity, on the strength of which we should feel as if every day was the first and the last as well.

Notes

1. R. G. Cohn, *L'Œuvre de Mallarmé* (Paris: Les Lettres, 1951), 15 passim.
2. Walter Benjamin, *The Origin of the German Tragic Drama*, trans. John Osborne (London: Verso, 1985), 213–14.

3. Ibid., 214–15.
4. Ibid., 280.
5. Roland Barthes, *Writing Degree Zero*, trans. Annette Lavers and Colin Smith (New York: Hill and Wang, 1968), 84–88.
6. Jean Hyppolite, *Logique et existence* (Paris: Presses Universitaires de France, 1953), 39.
7. Maurice Blanchot, *La Part du feu* (Paris: Gallimard, 1949), 325.
8. Ibid., 295, translation mine.
9. Emmanuel Levinas, *Totalité et Infini, Essai sur l'extériorité*, second edition (The Hague: Martinus Nijhoff, 1965), xv, translation mine.
10. Blanchot, *Part*, 305.
11. Roland Barthes, *Roland Barthes*, trans. Richard Howard (Berkeley: University of California Press, 1994), 179.
12. T. S. Eliot, "*Ulysses*, Order, and Myth," *Selected Prose of T. S. Eliot*, ed. Frank Kermode (New York: Harcourt Brace and Company, 1975), 175–78. See also Jed Deppman's essay, chapter 1 in this volume, for a consideration of the rapport between Eliot's essay and Derrida's reading of Joyce in the Husserl introduction.
13. Jacques Derrida, "An Interview with Jacques Derrida," *Acts of Literature*, ed. Derek Attridge (New York: Routledge, 1992), 33–75, 74.
14. T. S. Eliot, *The Sacred Wood* (London: Methuen, 1950), 49.
15. Ibid., 50.
16. In the French, there is here an untranslatable pun on "petit-fils" (grandson or small son): "un petit, un tout petit-fils."

Selection of Photographs

Figure 1. Jacques Derrida, 1982 Pompidou Center. Paris, France. *Photo courtesy of Fritz Senn.*

Figure 2. Jacques Derrida, 1984 James Joyce Symposium. Frankfurt-am-Main, Germany. *Photo courtesy of Morris Beja.*

Figure 3. Jacques Derrida, 1984 James Joyce Symposium. Frankfurt-am-Main, Germany. *Photo courtesy of Fritz Senn.*

Figure 4. Jacques Derrida, 1984 James Joyce Symposium. Frankfurt-am-Main, Germany. *Photo courtesy of Fritz Senn.*

Contributors

Editors

Andrew J. Mitchell is Assistant Professor of Philosophy (affiliated faculty of German studies) at Emory University, where he teaches courses in Heidegger and the Continental tradition. He is the coeditor of *Community and Communication: The Obsessions of Georges Bataille*, cotranslator of *Martin Heidegger's Four Seminars* (2003), and author of essays on Heidegger, Fassbinder, and James Joyce. He recently completed a monograph, *Heidegger Among the Sculptors: Body, Space, and the Art of Dwelling*, and a book-length study of Heidegger's later thought, *The Fourfold: Thing and World in Late Heidegger*.

Sam Slote is Assistant Professor in James Joyce studies and Critical Theory at Trinity College Dublin. He is the author of *The Silence in Progress of Dante, Mallarmé, and Joyce* (1999) and *"Ulysses" in the Plural: The Variable Editions of Joyce's Novel* (2004), and he is the coeditor of *How Joyce Wrote "Finnegans Wake": A Chapter-by-Chapter Genetic Guide* (2007), *Genitricksling Joyce* (1999), and *Probes: Genetic Studies in Joyce* (1995). A monograph on Joyce's Nietzschean Ethics will be published shortly.

Contributors

Louis Armand (Director of the Centre for Critical & Cultural Theory, Charles University, Prague) is author of *Technē: James Joyce, Hypertext and Technology* (2003) and *Event States: Discourse, Time, Mediality* (2007). He is the editor of *Joycemedia: James Joyce, Hypermedia and Textual Genetics* (2004), coeditor, with Clare Wallace, of *Giacomo Joyce: Envoys of the Other* (2002), and founding editor (1994) of the online journal *Hypermedia Joyce Studies*.

Derek Attridge (English, University of York) is the coeditor of *Post-Structuralist Joyce* (1984), a volume that introduced French readings of Joyce to English-speaking audiences, and the editor of Derrida's *Acts of Literature* (1992), a collection that brought Derrida's work to the attention of a generation of literary scholars. Professor Attridge is also author of numerous books on Joyce, literary language, and deconstruction, including *Peculiar Language* (1988), *Joyce Effects: On Language, Theory, and History* (2000), *The Singularity of Literature* (2004), and *Reading and Responsibility: Deconstruction's Traces* (2010). He is also editor of *The Cambridge Companion to James Joyce* (1990, revised 2004) and the coeditor of *Theory after "Theory"* (2011).

Geoffrey Bennington is Asa Griggs Candler Professor of Modern French Thought at Emory University. He has published fifteen books and many articles and chapters in English and French on philosophical and literary-theoretical topics, and has translated work by Derrida and Lyotard. He is a member of the French editorial team preparing Jacques Derrida's seminars for publication, and, with Peggy Kamuf, general editor of the English-language version of the seminars, for which he translated the two volumes of *The Beast and the Sovereign*. His most recent books are *Not Half No End* (2010) and *Géographie et autres lectures* (2011).

Christine van Boheemen-Saaf (Professor Emeritus, English, University of Amsterdam) is author of *Joyce, Derrida, Lacan, and the Trauma of History: Reading, Narrative, and Postcolonialism* (1999) and *The Novel as Family Romance: Language, Gender, and Authority from Fielding to Joyce* (1987). In addition to having written numerous articles on Joyce, she is the editor of *Joyce, Modernity, and Its Mediation* (1989) and coeditor of *Masculinities in Joyce* (2001). She serves as associate editor for *European Joyce Studies*.

Pascale-Anne Brault is Professor of French at DePaul University. Her articles on contemporary literature and thought have appeared in *The French Review*, *Romance Notes*, *Francographies*, *Critique*, *Cahiers de l'Herne*, and *Theatre Research International*, among others. She is the cotranslator with Michael Naas of Jacques Derrida's *The Other Heading*, *Memoirs of the Blind*, *Resistances of Psychoanalysis*, *Adieu*, *Rogues*, *Learning to Live Finally*, and *Athens Still Remains*. She is also the cotranslator of Jean-François Lyotard's *The Hyphen—Between Judaism and Christianity*, and Jean-Luc Nancy's *Noli Me Tangere: On the Raising of the Body* and *The Truth of Democracy*.

Simon Critchley was born in Hertfordshire in 1960, and currently lives and works in New York as Professor of Philosophy at the New School for Social Research. He failed dramatically at school before failing in a large number of punk bands in the late seventies and failing as a poet some time later. This was followed by failure as a radical political activist. By complete accident, he ended up at university when he was twenty-two and decided to stay. He found a vocation in teaching philosophy, although his passions still lie in music, poetry, and politics.

Jed Deppman (English and Comparative Literature, Oberlin College) is Irvin E. Houck Associate Professor in the Humanities at Oberlin College. He translated and, with Daniel Ferrer and Michael Groden, coedited *Genetic Criticism: Texts and Avant-Textes* (2004). He is the author of *Trying to Think with Emily Dickinson* (2008) and has written widely on Joyce, Flaubert, Valéry, and literary theory.

Tom McCarthy is a writer and artist. His novel *Remainder*, which won the 2007 Believer Book Award, is currently being adapted for cinema by Film4/Cowboy Films. His art projects have been shown internationally at galleries and museums including the Institute of Contemporary Arts London and the Moderna Museet Stockholm. His critical study *Tintin and the Secret of Literature* was published by Granta Books in 2006.

Laurent Milesi (English, Cardiff University) is editor of *James Joyce and the Difference of Language* (2003). He is the cotranslator of Derrida's 2002 book on Cixous, *H. C. for Life, That Is to Say* (2006). He has written numerous essays on Derrida, Joyce, and literary theory. He has also published several translations of Cixous' works, including an annotated translation of her study of Samuel Beckett, *Zero's Neighbour*, and *Philippines* (both 2010). He is also currently editing a collection of Cixous' short essays on Jacques Derrida and completing a monograph titled *Derrida On Dis/Location*. When all the aforementioned gives him some rest (hardly), he plays video games, on which a deconstructive study is in the works.

Michael Naas (Philosophy, DePaul University, Chicago) has written a number of studies bringing a deconstructive approach to literary texts. He is the author of *Miracle & Machine: Jacques Derrida and the Two Sources of Religion, Science, and the Media* (2011), *Derrida From Now On* (2008), *Taking on the Tradition: Jacques Derrida and the Legacies of Deconstruction* (2002) and *Turning: From Persuasion to Philosophy: A Reading of Homer's "Iliad"* (1995). He is the cotranslator with Pascale-Anne Brault of a number of works by Derrida, including *Learning to Live Finally* (2007), *Rogues: Two Essays on Reason* (2005), and *The Work of Mourning* (2001). He also c-edits the *Oxford Literary Review*.

Jean-Michel Rabaté is the Vartan Gregorian Professor in the Humanities at the University of Pennsylvania. Cofounder and curator of Slought Foundation (Philadelphia), he is also one of the managing editors of the *Journal of Modern Literature*. A fellow of the American Academy of Arts and Sciences, he has authored or edited thirty books on modernism, psychoanalysis, contemporary art, philosophy, Beckett, Pound, and Joyce. Recent books include *Lacan Literario* (2007), *1913: The Cradle of Modernism* (2007), *The Ethic of* the Lie (2008), and *Etant donnes: 1) l'art, 2) le crime* (2010). He is currently editing a collection of essays on modernism and theory.

François Raffoul is Professor of Philosophy at Louisiana State University. He is the author of *Heidegger and the Subject* (1999), *A Chaque fois Mien* (2004), and *The Origins of Responsibility* (2010). He is the coeditor of several volumes, *Disseminating Lacan* (1996), *Heidegger and Practical Philosophy* (2002), *Rethinking Facticity* (2008), and *French Interpretations of Heidegger* (2008). He has cotranslated several French philosophers, in particular Jean-Luc Nancy (*The Title of the Letter: A Reading of Lacan* [1992], *The Gravity of Thought* [1998], *The Creation of the World* or *Globalization* [2007] and *Identity* (forthcoming). He is the coeditor of the SUNY Press book series Contemporary French Thought.

Alan Roughley is a writer and musician who lives and works on Salt Spring Island, Canada. He worked with Lilliana Burgess, the widow of Anthony Burgess, and Patrick McDonagh from Concordia University, to establish the International Anthony Burgess Foundation in Manchester, England. Until 2010 he was the Chief Executive of the foundation and part-time Associate Professor of English at Liverpool Hope University. His books include *James Joyce and Critical Theory* (1991) and *Reading Derrida Reading Joyce* (1999), one of the first full-length studies of Derrida and Joyce. He is a coeditor of *Mapping Liminalities: Thresholds in Cultural and Literary Texts* (2007) and the editor of *Anthony Burgess and Modernism* (2008). His recent publications include a study of "the book of Esther" and literature and investigations of liminality. He is currently editing the diaries of Anthony Burgess and working on a collection of short stories.

Index

Abraham, 191–92
Adorno, Theodor, 121, 248
affect, 3, 11, 23, 38, 130n22, 250
  see also mood
affirmation ("yes," "oui"), 2, 3, 8–11,
  13, 15, 16n6, 19, 37, 38, 39,
  40n16, 41–86 passim, 93, 129n16,
  135, 151, 179–80, 184, 189–90,
  201–6, 210n2, 211n18, 238–39,
  267, 270–72, 274–79, 282, 293,
  296, 297
allegory, 283–4, 292, 297
ALP (Anna Livia Plurabelle), 37, 180,
  202–3, 227, 232–33, 236
Althusser, Louis, 296
Anderson, Laurie, 239
Aristotle, 125, 224n21, 252, 292
Armand, Louis, 8
Attridge, Derek, 10, 156, 159n6, 162n21,
  162n23, 218, 229, 237, 294
Aufhebung, 6, 135–42, 143n20
Austin, J.L., 74–75, 279n7

Babel, 3, 6–7, 10, 15n4, 16n8, 19,
  22–40 passim, 42, 44, 49, 50, 59,
  61, 62, 78, 141, 233, 236, 243,
  250, 291, 296–97
Bachelard, Gaston, 291, 296
Baird, John Logie, 221, 223
Bakhtin, Mikhail, 282
Barthes, Roland, 287, 291
Bataille, Georges, 6, 133
Bateson, Gregory, 214–15, 217
Baudelaire, Charles, 1, 91, 104n9185
Baudrillard, Jean, 247

Beckett, Samuel, 201
Benjamin, Walter, 1, 213, 245, 283–84
Bennington, Geoffrey, 207, 215, 280n7
Benveniste, Émile, 169
Bergson, Henri, 258
Berkeley, George, 292
Blanchot, Maurice, 65, 66, 266, 269,
  280n14, 287, 289–91, 296
Bloom, Leopold, 42–54 passim, 57,
  63, 75, 76, 77, 81, 179, 181n9,
  181n10, 181n11, 190–91, 202,
  204, 227, 272–74, 295
Bloom, Milly, 77, 170, 272–73
Bloom, Molly, 3, 9, 19, 37, 41, 44,
  49, 52, 54, 57, 58, 59, 65, 70–79
  passim, 84n43, 170, 180, 184–85,
  202–3, 271, 273, 276, 293, 297
Boheemen, Christine van, 14, 269
Borges, Jorge Luis, 120, 206
Bruno, Giordano, 204
Budgen, Frank, 71, 83n25, 84n43–44,
  254, 296
Burroughs, William S., 234

Campbell, Joseph, 250
Cavaillès, Jean, 296
Cavender, Anne L., 210n6
Celan, Paul, 1, 16n9, 266
de Certeau, Michel, 16n6, 202, 204
Chiesa, Lorenzo, 260n7
circumnavigation, 15, 20, 42, 46, 47,
  49, 50, 63, 65, 293
Cixous, Hélène, 9, 21, 22, 89, 201,
  206–10, 210n1, 210n8, 211n14,
  211n22, 281–82

Cohn, Robert Greer, 283
computers, 3, 8–10, 11, 12, 25, 59,
    63–65, 68, 79–80, 119, 213, 215,
    229, 238, 268, 278
Conrad, Joseph, 89, 92
copyright, 71, 240, 295
Critchley, Simon, 11
Curtius, Ernst Robert, 296
cybernetics, 213

Dante, 59, 291
Darwin, Charles, 221
Dastur, Françoise, 115
Davoust, J., 222
Debord, Guy, 214
Dedalus, Stephen, 42, 45, 49, 57, 63,
    67, 78, 90–91, 120, 124, 135, 164,
    168–72, 180, 181n9, 184, 186,
    190, 246, 273–74, 290, 292, 295
Deleuze, Gilles, 297
Deppman, Jed, 4, 298n12
Derrida, Jacques
    Acts of Literature, 126–27, 270
    Archive Fever, 172–74
    "Before the Law," 266
    "Circonfession," 206
    "Des Tours de Babel," 7, 42, 206, 218
    Dissemination, 6, 122, 139, 143n16,
        159n1, 163, 187, 210, 232–33,
        235, 239
    Echographies of Television, 219–20
    *Introduction to "Edmund Husserl's
        Origin of Geometry,"* 4–5, 15n5,
        27, 111, 113–21 passim, 127,
        141, 142, 163, 218, 228, 230–31,
        284–94
    The Ear of the Other, 205–6
    "Faith and Knowledge," 166, 168–69,
        172, 181n5
    "Force of Law," 265–68
    For What Tomorrow… A Dialogue,
        16n15, 180n2, 184, 190
    Given Time, 252, 254
    Glas, 6, 133–44 passim, 166, 169,
        172, 189, 201, 205, 211n13

Of Grammatology, 139, 155, 172,
    217, 283
H.C. for Life, That Is to Say, 166,
    180n2, 180n4, 181n13, 206–8
"I Have a Taste for the Secret," 272
"The Law of Genre," 266
"Living On: Border Lines," 206
Margins of Philosophy, 143n20,
    144n26, 223, 280n7
Memoirs of the Blind, 102, 107n48,
    179, 196, 226n36
Monolingualism of the Other, 16n9,
    166
"The Night Watch," 2, 13–14,
    16n15, 164–66, 173–79, 181n14,
    183–97
Parages, 84n33, 139, 279n2
"Passions," 270–71
Points… Interviews, 16, 112, 129n14,
    130n20, 134, 211n16
The Post Card, 6–7, 29, 31, 145–48,
    154–61 passim, 163, 187, 189,
    211n12, 218, 229–30, 233,
    235–36, 239–43, 269
Psyché, 7, 16, 81, 181n15, 210n2,
    210n4, 225n24
"Psychoanalysis Searches the States
    of Its Soul," 102, 187
"Scribble (writing-power)," 39n5
"Shibboleth: For Paul Celan," 16n9,
    279n3
Signésponge/Signsponge, 84n33, 280n7
Specters of Marx, 185, 196
Speech and Phenomenon, 129n13,
    130n21, 166–67
Spurs, 184–85, 189
The Sydney Seminars, 218
"This Strange Institution Called
    Literature," 267
"Two Words for Joyce," 2–3, 6, 7–8,
    10, 11, 13, 16n8, 21, 70, 119,
    129n15–17, 135, 141–42, 163–64,
    180, 180n1, 194, 201, 217–18,
    229–31, 233–35, 240, 242, 282,
    290–91, 293, 296

INDEX 309

"Ulysses Gramophone," 2, 3, 7–13
  passim, 21, 81n1, 112, 120, 121,
  129n16, 130n22, 164, 184, 189,
  201–2, 211n9, 211n11, 211n18,
  217–19, 229, 237–39, 268–72,
  275–79, 279n3, 280n10, 282, 293,
  295–97
Veils, 209, 212n24
"The Villanova Roundtable," 1, 13,
  16n9, 114, 127
Writing and Difference, 5, 15n2, 137,
  191, 193, 290
Descartes, René, 42, 81n1
desire, 14, 16n15, 56, 58, 61, 84n46,
  88, 91–94, 101, 152, 154, 159n3,
  214, 227, 230–31, 233–36, 252
différance, 35, 50, 52, 217, 253–54,
  256
Dostoyevsky, Fyodor, 282
double-bind, 7, 10, 30, 34, 36, 61, 139
Dublin, 43, 56, 124, 207, 227, 236,
  246–47, 250, 293
Dulac, C., 222
Dusailly, Jean, 214–16

Eco, Umberto, 228–29
Einstein, Albert, 258, 293
Elijah, 11, 55, 57, 62–65, 66, 70, 79,
  239, 277
Eliot, T.S., 128n4, 293–94
Ellmann, Maud, 269
Ellmann, Richard, 25, 106n34, 113,
  261n22
equivocation, 2–7, 12–15, 27, 61, 114,
  116–20 passim, 123, 128n8, 139,
  141–42, 217, 223, 231, 290–93
Eribon, Didier, 112–13
Euclid, 286–88

Faraday, Michael, 222
Farnsworth, Philo, 222
Fenton, Roger, 221
Ferrer, Daniel, 21, 159n6, 198n12, 269
Fordham, Finn, 261n21
Foucault, Michel, 6, 296

Frankfurt Joyce Symposium (1984), 7,
  21, 159n5, 217, 237–38, 268–71,
  276, 278
Freud, Sigmund, 40n11, 66, 81, 84n40,
  89, 90, 93, 94, 95–97, 98–99,
  104n11, 105n25, 107n43–44, 148,
  159n4172, 174, 180n4, 181n12,
  183, 187–88, 190–94, 218, 234,
  236, 241–42, 248–49
Frye, Northrop, 228

Gasché, Rodolphe, 16n7, 276, 280n13
Gell-Mann, Murray, 216, 224n18
Genet, Jean, 1, 66, 134–35, 142,
  142n4, 201
ghost, 2–3, 27, 32, 76, 78, 83n20, 91,
  93, 94, 161, 164–66, 169–70, 185,
  187, 188, 190, 193, 196, 217, 231,
  235, 242, 296
  see also specter
Gilbert, Stuart, 65, 296
Gillet, Louis, 296
Goethe, Johann Wolfgang von, 57,
  83n25, 203, 291

Hamlet, 76, 84n47, 87, 94, 187–88,
  193
Hardt, Michael, 248
Hartman, Geoffrey, 135
Hayman, David, 201, 210n1
HCE, 38, 149, 153, 191, 232–33,
  253–55, 260
Hegel, G.W.F., 4, 5, 6, 13, 46, 59,
  105n28, 117, 128n8, 133–44 passim, 201, 282, 288–90, 292
Heidegger, Martin, 1, 13, 16n8, 53–54,
  56, 116, 129n14, 159n2, 229,
  232–33, 241–43, 243n10, 254,
  256, 282, 286–87, 293
Heraclitus, 35
Hillis Miller, J., 6, 15n4
history, 8, 9, 26, 27, 61, 68, 120, 124,
  126, 128n4, 129n12, 141, 229,
  237, 255–56, 285, 288–90, 293–94
Hölderlin, Friedrich, 1

Homer, 10, 59, 61, 68, 89, 90, 95, 97, 98, 99, 102, 107n48, 125, 178–79, 187, 191–93, 196, 213, 256, 282, 294
Horkheimer, Max, 121
Husserl, Edmund, 4–5, 13, 15n5, 27, 111–31 passim, 141–42, 196, 218, 225n23, 228, 230–31, 281–82, 284–95, 297
hypermnesia, 8, 11, 12, 19, 24–25, 56, 60, 61, 62, 68, 70, 78, 119, 219, 223, 229, 230, 237, 239, 293, 295 *see also* memory
Hyppolite, Jean, 140, 288, 290, 296

Imai, Maasaki, 47
Ireland, 36, 45, 120, 208

Jacob and Esau, 161n13, 257
Jewish, 5, 16n9, 62, 96, 103n1, 136–38, 183, 185, 190–92, 246, 258, 290, 293
Job, 39n9, 91, 101, 104n18–19, 178, 187, 193
Johnson, Barbara, 244n23
Jones, Ellen Carol, 269
jouissance, 22, 40n10, 137, 249–50
Joyce, Giorgio, 250
Joyce, James
  Chamber Music, 3, 113
  "The Dead," 202
  Dubliners, 113, 202, 232, 286
  Finnegans Wake, 1, 3, 6–8, 15n4, 19, 22, 25–29, 35–40, 44, 48, 50, 59, 60, 69, 70, 79, 113, 114, 124, 125, 128n8, 129n12, 134, 135, 137, 139, 140, 142, 141, 145, 148–58, 159n6, 160n11, 161n12–14, 161n19, 162n21–22, 163, 180, 183, 194, 196, 201–2, 204–10, 210n7, 213–18, 220–23, 227–29, 232–37, 240–42, 245, 249–60, 281–82, 290, 292–93, 296–97
  Giacomo Joyce, 29, 242
  A Portrait of the Artist as a Young Man, 113, 125, 257

Ulysses, 3, 5, 8, 11, 19, 25, 37, 41–86 passim, 103n2, 125, 126, 128n4, 128n8, 129n16, 130n22, 135, 137, 159n5, 162n21, 165, 168–72, 175, 178–80, 180n2, 181n9, 181n10, 181n11, 184–86, 190–92, 202–3, 211n10, 216, 218, 229, 234, 237, 246–47, 265–66, 269–79, 281–82, 290, 292–95
James Joyce Foundation
  American, 62
  International, 237–39
Joyce, John Stanislaus, 254
Joyce, Lucia, 249
Joyce, Stephen James, 83n24, 295
Joyce, Nora, 69, 296
Judaism, *see* Jewish
Jung, Carl, 96–97, 106n34, 191–92
justice, 252–53, 256, 265–68, 270, 275, 277–79

Kafka, Franz, 266
Kamuf, Peggy, 280n7, 280n8
Kant, Immanuel, 37, 130n21
Kenner, Hugh, 296
Kojève, Alexandre, 140, 143n21, 289, 296
Kristeva, Julia, 234, 282

Lacan, Jacques, 99, 107, 174, 234, 236, 249–50
Lamb, Charles, 181n10
Larbaud, Valery, 296
laughter, 3, 11–12, 15n4, 19, 22–23, 25, 32, 38–39, 40n15, 45, 66–71, 77, 78–81, 83n20, 84n35, 204, 277–78
Lavergne, Philippe, 39n6, 39n7, 40n15
Leibniz, G.W., 15n5
Levin, Harry, 296
Levinas, Emmanuel, 5, 137, 143n12, 252–53, 275, 289–91
Lewis, Wyndham, 293
Liddell, Alice, 241
Linati, Carlo, 124, 125, 296

literary, 1, 2, 5, 10, 12, 26, 90, 95, 111, 112, 113, 120, 124, 125, 130n17, 131n25, 148, 157, 158, 195, 223, 250, 255, 257, 265–68, 270, 274–75, 278, 280n13, 291
Locke, John, 248
love, 3, 6, 8, 11–12, 23–24, 39, 30–31, 33, 36, 38, 46, 55, 77, 91, 102, 103n1, 106n29, 106n36, 129n15, 135, 136, 143n8, 151, 160n11, 209, 234, 242, 269, 297

MacArthur, Ian, 210n5
Mahoney, Peter, 280n7
Mallarmé, Stéphane, 1, 52, 84n47, 87, 129n12, 133, 142n3, 143n16, 185, 283, 288, 291
Marion, Jean-Luc, 116, 131n24
Marx, Karl, 246, 248–49, 252–53
maternity, 13–14, 16n9, 16n15, 88–103 passim, 107n44, 164–65, 167, 170–79, 181n10, 183–90, 192, 196
matricide, 13–14, 88–95, 98–103, 104n18–19, 165, 173, 175, 177–78, 183, 187–89, 192–94, 196–97
McCarthy, Tom, 11
McHugh, Roland, 236
McLuhan, Marshall, 215–16, 222–23, 226n37
memory, 4, 8, 9, 13, 19, 24, 26, 27, 37, 44, 56, 58, 59, 60, 64, 65, 69, 76, 78–80, 97, 98, 117, 119, 128n8, 129n15, 141, 143n20, 205, 208, 211n18, 219, 227, 230, 236–37, 239
 see also hypermnesia
Mercanton, Jacques, 5, 296
Milesi, Laurent, 9, 211n12
mimesis, 11, 56, 217–18, 225n25, 237
 see also representation
Mitchell, Andrew J., 6, 159n2
money, 11, 152–53, 245–49, 252–53, 255–57, 260
mood, 11–12, 68, 130n22, 289
 see also affect
Morris, Jan, 246

motherhood, *see* maternity
Mumford, Lewis, 214, 216

Naas, Michael, 14
Nash, John, 228
nationalism, 142, 145, 150–51, 157–58
Negri, Antonio, 248
New Criticism, 268
New Historicism, 268
Nietzsche, Friedrich, 11, 13, 64–65, 69, 111, 122–23, 130n19, 184, 189–90, 203–6, 210n3, 218, 297

Odysseus (Ulysses), 15n2, 20, 44, 46, 47, 61, 69, 80, 83n20, 88, 89, 95, 102–3, 108n50, 178–79, 185, 187, 191–93, 195–97, 227, 289, 296
Ogden, Charles, 216, 224n17
Orestes, 185, 190, 193
Osborne, Peter, 260n2
oui, *see* affirmation

Paris, 21, 49, 82n13, 215, 246, 274, 282
Paris, Jean, 87, 143n10, 206
Paris, Matthew, 240
paternity, 6, 13, 16n9, 78, 90, 99, 100, 107n43–44, 164, 168, 170–71, 173–75, 179, 181n10, 184
pathos, *see* mood
phantasm, 14, 69, 70, 77, 78, 88, 92–95, 98–100, 101, 105n25, 163–69, 171–80, 180n3, 180n4, 181n12, 185, 188
pharmakon, 28, 71, 75, 129n12, 210
phenomenology, 46, 112, 115, 120–21, 124, 129n13, 137, 218, 282, 284–85, 288–90, 292–93, 296
philosophy, 1–2, 4–5, 14–15, 19, 81n1, 114–18, 121, 135, 139, 141, 183, 185, 192, 195, 202, 229, 241, 252, 270, 280n13, 283–85, 289–90, 292–94
Plato, 4, 6, 7, 8, 9, 28, 59, 89, 115, 129n12, 147–48, 159n3, 183, 187, 195, 218, 240–41, 247, 283

pleasure principle, 102, 235
Ponge, Francis, 33, 66, 86n52, 266
portmanteau, 155–58, 161n18, 161n19, 161n20, 218
Pound, Ezra, 293, 296
presence, 3, 12–13, 55–56, 80, 94, 116, 120–21, 123, 125, 129, 130n21, 146, 149–50, 153, 157, 160n6, 160n9, 163, 185, 188–91, 193, 217, 221, 223, 249, 256, 272, 297
Proust, Marcel, 83n20, 99, 185, 258, 282
psychoanalysis, 27, 87, 96–97, 102, 104n11, 141–42, 183, 185, 187, 189, 191–94, 196, 249, 291

Rabaté, Jean-Michel, 4, 21, 22, 26, 48–50, 60, 68, 83n17, 113, 141, 160n9, 160n11278
Rabelais, François, 282
radio, 215, 217, 222
Reichert, Klaus, 50, 278
repetition, 5, 11, 19, 41, 53, 55–57, 65, 69, 75–76, 78, 88, 91, 117, 120, 130n21, 183, 185, 189–90, 193, 196, 202, 220, 228, 236–38, 256, 266, 271–72, 275, 287–90
representation, 34, 48, 61, 101, 105n25, 107n43, 123, 143n18, 217, 233, 236, 257, 267, 283, 288
 see also mimesis
responsibility (response), 3–4, 9, 12, 19, 24, 55, 64, 74–75, 77, 80, 93, 104n19, 112, 118–19, 127, 150, 163, 202, 231, 234, 265–67, 270, 275–79, 281, 294, 296
Ritter, Johann Wilhelm, 283
Rosenzweig, Franz, 71
Roudinesco, Elisabeth, 16n15, 184, 190, 198n10
Roughley, Alan, 8, 129n14, 154–55, 161n16, 243n8, 244n11
Rousseau, Jean-Jacques, 90

Saint Clare of Assisi, 222–23

Sartre, Jean-Paul, 1, 127n2, 134
Saussure, Ferdinand, 225n31
Schlossman, Beryl, 269
secret, 58, 89–90, 92, 101, 106n29, 118, 153, 160n11, 168, 185–86, 189–91, 193, 195, 248, 291, 297
Senn, Fritz, 113, 204, 211n10
Shakespeare, William, 59, 91, 187–88, 190, 250, 254, 274, 295–96
Shannon, Claude, 214, 216, 224n17, 225n31
Shaun, 28, 29, 30–31, 79, 145, 148–54, 157–58, 159n5, 160n8–9, 160n11, 161n12–13204, 241, 257–60
Shem, 28, 29, 30–31, 33, 79, 150, 152, 158, 161n13, 195–96, 241, 257, 259–60
Sheridan, Alan, 234
signature, 8–10, 12, 26, 37–39, 44, 56, 58–80 passim, 86n52, 95, 96, 98–99, 104n19, 123, 126, 131n25, 183–84, 186, 189, 194–95, 205–7, 211n18, 227, 238–39, 257, 271–78
Silesius, Angelus, 203
simulacrum, 9, 19, 26, 59, 73, 80, 247
Slote, Sam, 6, 16n8, 162n21
Socrates, 8, 122, 135, 147–48, 159n2, 183, 187, 236, 240–41
software, 3, 8–10, 25–26, 28, 121, 130n17
Sollers, Philippe, 218, 232–33, 237
specter, 28, 80, 88, 90–91, 93, 94, 164–66, 183, 185–89, 191, 193, 195, 197, 233–35, 240, 252–53, 295
 see also ghost
Spengler, Oswald, 213
Spinoza, Baruch, 38, 40n9
Stiegler, Bernard, 219
Stimmung, see mood
Sussman, Henry, 278
Szafraniec, Asja, 198n15

Tel Quel, 6, 281

telecommunication, 11, 19, 31, 48–57, 66, 84n26, 130, 164, 213–16, 218–19, 221–23, 229–30, 237–39, 271–72, 277, 282, 296–97
telecommunication, 15n4, 50, 55, 164, 213–16, 218–19, 221–23, 238, 272, 296
telephone, *see* telecommunication
Télévision Magazine, 216
television, 50, 213–16, 219–223, 229, 297
Tennyson, Alfred, 221
Theall, Donald, 215–17, 222, 225n25, 226n37
Tindall, William York, 38
Tintin, 254
totality, 2–3, 7–14 passim, 26, 27, 37, 59, 61, 68, 80, 114, 118, 128n8, 130n22, 137, 141, 189, 213, 219, 231, 238, 252–53, 277, 279, 289–96
Tran Duc Thao, 296
translation, 1–3, 7, 14, 22, 28, 33–35, 39n6, 40n9, 40n15, 42, 45, 47–49, 51, 57, 59, 61, 67, 72, 75, 77, 82n4, 82n13, 83n17, 85n50, 112, 115, 119, 133, 138, 140, 143n21, 145, 163, 186, 206, 224n17, 227, 268, 286–88
Trieste, 246–47, 250
Trilling, Jacques, 13–14, 87–108 passim, 165, 170, 173, 175–79, 183–87, 190–93, 195–96
Turing, Alan, 214

Ulysses, *see* Odysseus

Valéry, Paul, 83n20, 288, 291
Vico, Giambattista, 32, 59, 128n5, 202, 206, 259
Virilio, Paul, 219

Wall Street, 245, 251, 256
Weber, Samuel, 53, 160n10
Wiener, Norbert, 214
World War II, 213–14

Yates, Frances, 210n5
Yeats, William Butler, 255
Yerushalmi, Yosef Hayim, 198n10
yes, *see* affirmation

Zurich, 6, 15n4, 28, 97, 203, 233, 243

www.ingramcontent.com/pod-product-compliance
Ingram Content Group UK Ltd.
Pitfield, Milton Keynes, MK11 3LW, UK
UKHW041915140426
5217IPUK00013B/169